Major League Baseball Organizations

Major League Baseball Organizations

Team Performances and Financial Consequences

Frank P. Jozsa Jr.

LEXINGTON BOOKS
Lanham • Boulder • New York • London

Published by Lexington Books
An imprint of The Rowman & Littlefield Publishing Group, Inc.
4501 Forbes Boulevard, Suite 200, Lanham, Maryland 20706
www.rowman.com

Unit A, Whitacre Mews, 26-34 Stannary Street, London SE11 4AB

British Library Cataloguing in Publication Information Available

Library of Congress Cataloging-in-Publication Data Available

ISBN 978-1-4985-4278-4 (cloth : alk paper)
ISBN 978-1-4985-4280-7 (pbk : alk paper)
ISBN 978-1-4985-4279-1 (electronic)

∞™ The paper used in this publication meets the minimum requirements of American National Standard for Information Sciences—Permanence of Paper for Printed Library Materials, ANSI/NISO Z39.48-1992.

Printed in the United States of America

To my former baseball
coaches and teammates

Contents

Foreword ix

Preface xi

Acknowledgments xv

List of Abbreviations xvii

PART I AMERICAN LEAGUE

1 East Division 3

2 Central Division 41

3 West Division 79

PART II NATIONAL LEAGUE

4 East Division 119

5 Central Division 157

6 West Division 195

Conclusion 233

Appendix 237

Bibliography 249

Index 259

About the Author 265

Foreword

Widely understood by followers of the game, baseball achieved its distinction as our national pastime both through the calculated cultivation by entrepreneurs, sports officials, and the media, as well as its emulation by the country's youth in sandlots and the barnyards of America. In fact, baseball's development over the past century and a half mirrors those of broader society with respect to the challenges associated with institutional, regulatory, and economic change.

What Professor Frank P. Jozsa Jr.—a former athlete and the author of numerous books and articles on the sports industry—provides is twofold: first, a historical perspective of Major League Baseball's American League and National League highlighting the performances of teams as well as their owners and outstanding managers and players; and second, and unique in this book, a discussion of various factors associated with the operation of each team as a business enterprise including what elements contributed more than others to fan allegiance and what features are most important in determining the competitiveness, success, and uniqueness of a team as a profitable commercial organization.

In this regard, this book bridges the gap between those of us who enjoy baseball via team loyalties—the author identifies and compares rivalries between franchises in each division and league—and those who seek to better understand the "business" of baseball and the myriad of factors that contribute to it. Fans gain valuable insights and better understand the market value, revenue, operating income, gate receipts, and debt associated with various teams while the latter group gets a better appreciation of the evolution, challenges, and comparable elements that contribute to the financial success of any sports organization.

To put this in a broader but current, important, and realistic perspective, seldom does a year go by without a proposal for, or the building of, a new baseball ballpark somewhere in a midsize or large metropolitan area of the nation. All participants of such deliberations benefit from a serious reading of Dr. Jozsa's book.

Laddie Sula, Ph.D.
Professor Emeritus, Loras College

Tommy John
Former player, Major League Baseball

Preface

The most prominent and successful organizations in American professional team sports emerged, developed, and matured during different but distinct periods of time. When named, these different groups—from most to least experienced in each sport as of their 2015 season—include 140-year-old Major League Baseball (MLB)—officially the American League (AL) in 1901 and National League (NL) in 1876—and then the ninety-nine-year-old National Hockey League, ninety-four-year-old National Football League—American Professional Football Association in 1920–1921—sixty-seven-year-old National Basketball Association, and twenty-year-old Major League Soccer.

Despite *internal* problems as executives' conflicts and players' injuries, and also *external* issues such as economic recessions and government legislation, teams within MLB have performed in regular-season games, and then if qualified, they competed against each other in playoff series and types of postseason championships. Consequently, big-league baseball and their teams have become important, popular, and unique organizations in American culture, history, and society especially in years of the late-nineteenth, twentieth, and very early twenty-first centuries.

To organize and schedule games in each of its regular seasons and postseasons, MLB encouraged and promoted its teams to exist for years and even decades within their small, midsize, large, or very large metropolitan area and appeal to fans in local, regional, national, and even international sports markets. Essentially, professional baseball teams perform to provide entertainment for spectators and on television networks by competing in home and away games at new and/or renovated ballparks while also operating as franchises or commercial enterprises in order to earn maximum profits with sufficient amounts of cash inflows and revenues.

For various reasons, however, some teams previously located in metropolitan areas of America and also one in Canada ultimately folded because they had financial problems; inferior owners, coaches, managers and/or players; apathetic hometown fans; and/or simply underachieved for periods while playing rivals primarily in their division of the AL or NL.

PURPOSE

From researching such sport-specific sources as books, journals, newspapers, and websites on the Internet, and studying demographic, economic, and financial data and other information in the literature, *Major League Baseball Organizations* focuses on and analyzes thirty teams' historical regular-season and postseason performances, and also provides a recent financial profile of them while being competitive, profitable or unprofitable, and well-known enterprises. Certainly this is an important, newsworthy, and unique topic for different audiences because it includes existing big-league baseball franchises and reveals how effectively each of them competed and also operated, survived, and prospered or not prospered from a business perspective.

BOOK OVERVIEW

After the front matter, which consists of the foreword, acknowledgments, abbreviations, and preface, *Major League Baseball Organizations* includes six chapters followed by the conclusion and then the appendix, bibliography and index. As such, the following describes the organization of these chapters and also facts about their contents.

While the foreword, acknowledgments, and abbreviations are self-explanatory, each chapter discusses five MLB teams within a division. Assigned to one of two major sections—AL or NL—there are several subsections regarding each franchise. Sequentially, these focus on team performances, the current principal owner, home ballpark including its amenities and fan cost index, financial data with amounts of players' payrolls, and important business relations.

More specifically, the chapters denote when, where, and how effectively fifteen AL teams and then fifteen teams in the NL had performed and their financial status and significance as members of the world's most competitive and popular professional baseball organization. Readers learn, for example, which of them won division titles, pennants, and/or World Series while owned by an individual or group; construction cost, age, and rank of their ballpark; amounts fans spent for tickets and other items to attend their home games; teams' market value, revenue, operating income, gate receipts, and other financial information including their payrolls; and a few interesting topics and local activities, events, and projects that influence them as franchises. The contents also explain why some teams have succeeded more than others based on such things as attendances at games in their ballparks and also their win-loss records, market size, and estimated worth.

Within chapters, franchises are compared to current rivals in their division like the Boston Red Sox and New York Yankees in the AL East Division, Chicago White Sox and Detroit Tigers in the Central Division, and Oakland Athletics and Seattle Mariners in the West Division. Furthermore, their performances and financial results are ranked to others in their and the other league—AL or NL.

Teams whose nickname had most recently changed are included in the analysis but not those who formally existed at prior locations. For example, there is a chapter containing the AL Los Angeles Angels of Anaheim but not Philadelphia or Kansas City Athletics and another about the NL Atlanta Braves but not Milwaukee or Boston Braves. In other words the book answers questions regarding the history, productivity, and prosperity of baseball's least, average, and most prominent clubs as of their 2015 season.

Among its audiences, *Major League Baseball Organizations* was written and published for current and prospective owners and executives of MLB franchises and potential investors in these organizations; the MLB commissioner and his staff; practitioners and scholars who research the sports industry; college and university professors who teach undergraduate and graduate students majoring in sports administration, business, economics, history, management, and/or marketing; and also baseball fans of former but especially current AL and NL teams.

Acknowledgments

While organizing, writing, and editing the manuscript for this book during 2016, a few individuals provided information for it and thus helped me in different ways. Most important to my project, Pfeiffer University's library director and assistant professor of library science Lara Little found numerous readings about Major League Baseball franchises from such publications as *BusinessWeek*, *Forbes*, *Fortune*, *SportsBusiness Journal*, and the *Wall Street Journal*, and then promptly forwarded them to me. I appreciate Lara's professionalism and her dedication to spend time and obtain articles, reports, and studies for me regarding the business, economics, finance, and operations of teams in the sport. Certainly Lara is a superstar librarian for the university's administration, faculty and staff, and especially for the school's undergraduate and graduate students.

University of Michigan professor of sport management and codirector of the school's Center for Sport Management Rodney D. Fort explained how to apply economics and analyze the efficiency of teams and their historical performances and also success as franchises in big-league baseball. Besides such methods as frontier estimation, simple regression and multivariate approach, he suggested for me to research such important topics as these teams' attendances and ticket prices at home games and to include their markets, owners, managers, players, seasons, and postseasons. The coauthor of *Pay Dirt*, Professor Fort provides business and other historical data on professional sports teams at https://sites.google.com/site/rodswebpages/cod.

Former Loras College economics professor Laddie Sula, who coauthored this book's foreword, suggested I correlate team payrolls with World Series titles to determine the relationship between them. Besides Laddie, my high school and Babe Ruth League teammate and former big-league player Tommy John also agreed to coauthor the foreword of *Major League Baseball*

Organizations. Finally, *Forbes* magazine senior sports editor Kurt Badenhausen informed me that Major League Baseball teams' valuations and other new financial data about them will be released online. Special thanks to Laddie, Tommy, and Kurt.

My fiancée and best friend Maureen Fogle allowed me to use her computer to organize and write a manuscript for this book. Despite spreading books and files on the carpet in our office and also needing time to rewrite, edit, and print copies of chapters, she understood how important this project was for me to complete and then submit a professional copy of it to Lexington Books by the due date. Once again, thanks to Maureen for her cooperation and patience particularly since my retirement as a business/economics professor from Pfeiffer University in 2007.

While writing the manuscript of *Major League Baseball Organizations*, my lifelong friend and best buddy Dr. John A. Roshel Jr. died in Terre Haute, Indiana. Besides being a successful orthodontist for almost five decades, John loved his family and friends, and contributed to his community. I miss and will never forget him.

Frank P. Jozsa Jr.

Abbreviations

A's	Athletics
AA	American Association
AFCS	Atlanta-Fulton County Stadium
AL	American League
APSE	Associated Press Sports Editors
B2B	Business to Business Program
BOA	Bank of America
CBA	Collective Bargaining Agreement
CD	Central Division
CEO	Chief Executive Officer
CFL	Canadian Football League
CIBC	Canadian Imperial Bank of Commerce
CL	Continental League
CLP	Community Leaders Program
CMSU	Central Missouri State University
CNN	Cable News Network
CSN	Comcast SportsNet
CSNH	Comcast SportsNet Houston
CWL	Crane Worldwide Logistics
D.C.	District of Columbia
DHS	Department of Homeland Security
DOL	Department of Labor
DBPP	Diverse Business Partners Program
ECOT	Employee Community Outreach Team
ED	East Division
EEOC	Equal Employment Opportunity Commission
EGL	Eagle USA Airfreight

ERA	Earned Run Average
ESPN	Entertainment Sports Programming Network
EWS	Equifax Workforce Solutions
FCI	Fan Cost Index
FL	Federal League
FPs	Flex Packs
FS	Fox Sports
FSM	Fenway Sports Management
GBM	Guggenheim Baseball Management
GLP	Globe Life Park
HAG	Huntington Avenue Grounds
HSA	Houston Sports Association
ISFA	Illinois Sports Facility Association
IaaS	Infrastructure-as-a-Service
J.D.	Doctor of Law Degree
LED	Light-Emitting Diode
LHM	Legends Hospitality Management
LL.B	Bachelor of Laws
LLC	Limited Liability Corporation
LMC	Liberty Media Corporation
LP	Limited Partnership
LTD	Oscars Limited
MASN	Mid-Atlantic Sports Network
MBA	Master of Business Administration
MC	Magellan Corporation
ME	Major Energy
MIS	Michigan International Speedway
MLB	Major League Baseball
MVDBP	Most Valuable Diverse Business Partner
MVP	Most Valuable Player
NA	National Association
NABBP	National Association of Base Ball Players
NBA	National Basketball Association
NESN	New England Sports Network
NFL	National Football League
NHL	National Hockey League
NL	National League
NOA	Nintendo of America
OACS	Oakland-Alameda County Stadium
OPS+	On-Base Plus Slugging Percentages
OS	Outdoor Systems
PaaS	Platform-as-a-Service

PCL	Pacific Coast League
PL	Players League
RFID	Radio Frequency Identification
RKS	Robert F. Kennedy Stadium
RSN	Regional Sports Network
SEG	Sunburst Entertainment Group
SFLI	Sports Fan Loyalty Index
SMSA	Standard Metropolitan Statistical Area
TBS	Turner Broadcasting System
TMR	Team Marketing Report
TS	Turner South
UA	Union Association
VIP	Very Important Person
WD	West Division
WL	Western League
WNBA	Women's National Basketball Association
YES	Yankee Entertainment Sports
YGE	Yankee Global Enterprises

Part I

AMERICAN LEAGUE

Chapter One

East Division

Established in 1969 by Major League Baseball (MLB), the East Division (ED) of the American League (AL) included the Baltimore Orioles, Boston Red Sox, Cleveland Indians, Detroit Tigers, New York Yankees, and Washington Senators. The ED changed, however, when the Senators moved from Washington, DC, to the Dallas-Fort Worth area and the Milwaukee Brewers joined the division in 1972; Toronto Blue Jays entered the division in 1977; and Cleveland and Milwaukee shifted to the Central Division in 1994 and Detroit in 1998 as the Tampa Bay Devil Rays became a new member.

Given these changes, this chapter discusses the historical development and highlights the business and financial matters of AL teams based in Baltimore, Maryland; Boston, Massachusetts; New York City, New York; Tampa Bay, Florida; and Toronto, Canada. Which of them, for example, had the fewest division titles and most pennants? What were their market values, revenues, and gate receipts in 2015? Who is the least and most successful owner among the five clubs? How did their ballparks rank among fans? The answers to these and other questions are covered in the chapter.[1]

BALTIMORE ORIOLES

From 1902 to 1953, the AL's St. Louis Browns played 7,879 games and won 3,414 or approximately 43 percent of them. After winning their only pennant in 1944, the Browns were defeated in the World Series by the St. Louis Cardinals. In 1953, however, the club lost 100 games, finished eighth in the league, and attracted less than 300,000 fans to its games in St. Louis.

After beer magnate August A. Busch Jr. purchased the National League (NL) St. Louis Cardinals—who had a history of winning championships and shared Sportsman's Park with the rival Browns—the Browns' and ballpark owner Bill Veeck arranged to move his club from St. Louis to another city in 1953. First, he sold Sportsman's Park to Busch for $850,000 and second, signed a lease with the city of Baltimore to rent Memorial Stadium.

Eventually the league's team owners approved the Browns' move from eastern Missouri to the state of Maryland after Veeck sold his interest in the franchise for $2.4 million to a syndicate headed by Baltimore attorney Clarence Miles. Following the AL's 1953 season, the Browns relocated and then renamed Baltimore Orioles in 1954. The team's dismal performances, St. Louis' stagnant population base, and competition for local baseball fans with the popular and successful Cardinals caused the Browns to depart their home site after fifty-two years.

Team Performances

While in the AL from 1954 to 1968 and specifically a member of the ED from 1969 to 2015, the Orioles played 9,832 games and had victories in approximately 51 percent of them. During the period, they appeared in twelve playoffs and won nine division titles, six pennants, and three World Series. Among fifteen AL teams as of 2015, Baltimore tied for fourth with the Los Angeles Angels of Anaheim in number of titles and also with the Oakland Athletics in pennants, and tied for fifth in World Series championships with the Chicago White Sox. Based on these results, the Orioles have been above-average in their performances but not exceptional or spectacular while competing in the AL since 1954 (Table A1).[2]

When compared to twenty-nine other clubs in MLB as of 2015, the Orioles tied for ninth in both division titles and World Series titles, and also tied for tenth with the Athletics and NL San Francisco Giants in winning pennants. In short, Baltimore was in the top one-third of all teams in the sport during its sixty-two years and especially in their 1969–1971, 1973–1974, 1979, 1983, and 1996–1997 seasons. Alternatively, the club failed to make the playoffs consecutively in such periods as 1975–1978, 1984–1995, and 1998–2011 because of manager problems and not enough talented players at key on-the-field positions such as pitching.

Franchise Owner

Years after his parents immigrated to America from Greece, Peter Angelos graduated from the Eastern College of Commerce and Law and then University of Baltimore School of Law. He practiced criminal defense law following graduation and in 1961 founded his own firm and provided legal services for

Baltimore labor unions and their members. Angelos redirected his practice to civil class action suits during the 1980s and in 1982 successfully represented a large number of plaintiffs in asbestos litigation and later the state of Maryland in a suit against Philip Morris and Wyeth, who produced part of the diet pill combination fen-phen.[3]

During August 1993, a syndicate led by Angelos acquired the Baltimore Orioles franchise for $173 million in a bankruptcy court auction. This was $50 million more than any MLB franchise had previously sold for, and he owned 60 percent of it. Since that year, the club has won two ED titles but zero pennants and World Series. Compared to fourteen other AL team owners as of 2015, Angelos' Orioles tied for eighth in both winning titles and number of pennants but tied for twelfth and fourteenth respectively among twenty-nine other principal MLB owners. With respect to most team owners, Angelos has been mediocre and perhaps an inferior leader (Table A2).

According to various media reports, Angelos spends too much time and energy with his law practice and not enough money to improve the Orioles roster. He made wrong decisions, for example, by unnecessarily firing managers and refusing to invest in talented players. Others criticize him for being lackadaisical and not personally involved with his staff and players.

Despite Baltimore being in the playoffs in 2012 and 2014, many baseball fans and observers view Angelos's legacy as mixed. They cannot forget the Orioles' losing seasons, free agents left unsigned, and smart baseball executives who departed the organization in frustration. Although he has allowed his baseball managers to make more decisions, a few winning seasons out of many does not qualify him as a dynamic owner.

The ideal place for former player and current Hall of Famer Cal Ripken in the Orioles organization is being a minor or principal owner. Since retiring, Ripken has built himself a baseball empire in Aberdeen, Maryland, where his minor league team flourishes and plays its home games in a beautiful stadium. According to some experts in the sport, Ripken has the experience, knowledge, and support necessary for him to make the successful transition to becoming an MLB owner, but getting the opportunity to do it will be a challenge.

For starters, Ripken's net worth is approximately $75 million. Unfortunately for Cal, his career did not coincide with the massive explosion in the value of players' contracts thanks to television deals. The most income he earned in a season was $6.9 million in 1997. That is a considerable amount of 1997 dollars, but not enough to buy a minority share of a big-league team in 2016. Although Ripken earned about $71 million in twenty-one years, this sum is not sufficient compensation even for a mediocre starting pitcher in today's market. To try and own the Orioles, Ripken needs a very wealthy partner or money from several rich investors.

Oriole Park at Camden Yards

Located in northeast Baltimore, Memorial Stadium was not a typical multipurpose baseball facility with seats too distant from the field and structurally obsolete by the late 1980s. Therefore, the Orioles and city officials developed a plan to build a new ballpark in downtown Baltimore on land that once occupied the saloon of Babe Ruth's father. They hired architect Joseph Spear of HOK Sport to design a new stadium built similar to ballparks of the early 1900s with steel columns, beams, and trusses instead of concrete.[4]

Opened in April 1992 for the club's first home game that season, upper deck fans in Oriole Park at Camden Yards can see the city's skyline and eight-story high B&O Warehouse— constructed in 1899. The stadium consists of a three-tier grandstand that stretches from behind home plate, down the third base line to the left field pole and also down the first base line. The original 48,000 seats were replaced with larger green ones before the 2011 MLB season.

In a recent study by CSN Mid-Atlantic, Oriole Park at Camden Yards ranked third in MLB. According to an online report in *USA Today*:

> The original retro ballpark remains one of the very best. So many other parks built in the '90s and '00s tried to duplicate Camden Yards, but none truly could, for one good reason: the warehouse. It already existed, so the ballpark was built around it. You can't fabricate something like that. It has to be organic. It's remarkable to think it's been 22 [25] years since Camden Yards opened and completely changed the notion of the modern sports facility. It is starting to show its age just a bit, but it remains a gem, often imitated, never duplicated.[5]

Compared to fourteen other AL stadiums as of 2015, Oriole Park at Camden Yards was the eighth oldest facility and fourteenth most expensive to build at $107 million. Based on the team's estimated market value, it is worth $158 million and ranked tenth in the league. Among twenty-nine MLB venues, its age was tenth, construction cost twenty-seventh, and value twenty-second (Table A3).

For several years a Chicago-based company named Team Marketing Report (TMR) has prepared and published a Fan Cost Index (FCI) for the home games of teams in professional sports leagues. To attend a game for a typical family with two kids, an FCI includes the costs of four average-priced tickets, two cheapest-priced draft beers, four each cheapest-priced soft drinks and hot dogs, parking for one car, and two each game programs and least-expensive, adult-size adjustable caps. Costs are determined by telephone calls with team representatives, venues, and concessionaires and from questions asked during interviews.[6]

In the 2011–2015 MLB seasons, the FCIs for a family to attend a regular-season game at Oriole Park at Camden Yards ranged from a low of $163 in 2015 to a high of $176 in 2012. During this period among AL clubs, the Orioles ballpark's FCI ranked from ninth in 2011 ($174) to fourteenth in 2015. Compared to all MLB clubs, the ballpark's FCI was seventeenth in 2011 but only twenty-seventh in 2015 (Table A4).

To reveal specific costs for a recent year in MLB, the Orioles FCI in 2015 was approximately $163 and $10 or 6 percent more than in 2014. Listed from most to least in amount by item for one person, the team's nonpremium tickets averaged about $25, a cap $15, parking for one vehicle $8, one beer between $6 and $7, and a soft drink and hot dog each $1.50.

Among other teams in the league's ED, they had rankings and FCIs from most to least as follows in the 2015 MLB season: Red Sox first at $350; Yankees second at $337; Blue Jays sixteenth at $209; and Rays twenty-eighth at $157. These results indicate, in part, that Baltimore's fans paid less to be at a home game that season than those of the Red Sox in Boston, Yankees in New York, and Blue Jays in Toronto, but not at one of the Rays in Tampa Bay.

A premium ticket cost, on average, about $45 for a fan to attend an Orioles home game in 2015. This was $51 or 54 percent less than the league's average for a premium seat. Since the club's FCI was $48 below the amount of a typical MLB team, a family of four could buy nonpremium or premium tickets and enjoy a baseball game in Baltimore cheaper than in the majority of ballparks within the league. These costs and prices, in turn, were set by the Orioles organization to improve its home-game attendances and increase gate receipts and revenue.

Financial Data

Besides performing as teams in regular season and postseason games, MLB franchises are also commercial enterprises. To that end, their economic objective is to earn maximum revenue and obtain the greatest amount of profit on a fiscal basis from their operations. Although they share revenue with each other from such sources as national television contracts and other deals, it is important for them to efficiently allocate resources, determine and distribute payrolls, set nonpremium and premium ticket prices, and schedule investments in short- and long-term assets. To reveal and manage these activities, this section focuses on different parts of the Orioles franchise's business and how well its organization succeeds or does not succeed from a financial perspective.

According to data and other financial information published in *Forbes* for franchises in the AL as of their 2015 season, Baltimore ranked seventh in both its estimated market value at $1 billion and total revenue at $245 million, third in operating income at $31.4 million, eighth in gate receipts at $60 million, and tied for fourth with the Detroit Tigers each with a 15 percent debt-to-value ratio. Among only ED teams in the league, the Orioles had the third highest market value, revenue, gate receipts, and debt ratio, and also second most operating income to the Red Sox. Except for its relatively high operating income and debt, Baltimore was financially an average AL team in 2015 (Table A5).

Compared to twenty-nine other MLB clubs as of their 2015 season, the Orioles were fifteenth in both market value and revenue, tenth in operating income, seventeenth in gate receipts, and tied for twelfth with the Tigers in their debt percent. Based on most of this data, Baltimore was an average franchise among all MLB teams from a financial perspective although marginally above average in its operating income and debt. Overall, the team has been a stable enterprise and thus successful in operating at a profit.

Besides market size, salary inflation, and other factors, an MLB team's annual payroll partly reflects its commitment to players and their current and potential contribution individually and as a group to winning games in regular seasons and postseasons. From 2011 to 2015, for example, the Orioles payroll among fifteen AL teams ranged in rank from sixth in 2014 ($105 million) to ninth in 2011 ($85 million) and 2012 ($81 million). Among only ED teams, Baltimore was third in four of these years following the Yankees and Red Sox but also trailing the Blue Jays' $116 million in 2014 (Table A6).

Relative to the twenty-nine clubs in MLB, Baltimore's payroll tied for seventeenth with the Milwaukee Brewers in 2011, tied for eighteenth with the Washington Nationals in 2012, and also placed fifteenth in 2013, thirteenth in 2014, and fourteenth in 2015. Thus, for their 2011 to 2015 seasons, the Orioles payroll was relatively consistent and neither high nor low among its competitors in the AL and others in the NL.

Business Relations

Besides regular-season and postseason games, MLB franchises are involved in—and affected by—community events and business-related affairs and projects. The following are a few of them for Baltimore's big-league team.[7]

First, according to Brand Keys president Robert Passikoff, his Sports Fan Loyalty Index (SFLI) compares the intensity with which fans within a team's Standard Metropolitan Statistical Area (SMSA) support their home team versus corresponding values for fans of other teams in that market. The SFLI consists of variables that represent pure entertainment, authenticity, fan bonding, and history and tradition.

Based on interviews with hundreds of self-declared fans in each team's SMSA, the survey helps teams increase broadcast, ticket, and merchandise revenues by providing loyalty rankings and fan diagnostics in their home and national markets. These insights, in turn, enable the league and team management to identify areas, particularly emotional aspects that need strategic brand coaching. Among clubs in MLB, the Orioles ranked in the bottom five in 2011 and 2012, between sixth and twenty-fifth in 2013 and 2015, and tied for eleventh with the Reds in 2014.[8]

Second, as Oriole Park at Camden Yards ages, the team and ballpark's original architect—Kansas City-based Populous—planned more improvements to the facility as of late 2015. Future renovations may include constructing party decks in the left and right field corners of the upper deck similar to the 2012 center field retrofit, a new home plate club, and expansion of the group picnic area down the left field line. In addition the Orioles and Populous may create an open concourse on the first level by tearing out sections of seats, and the concessions and restrooms behind them, to create a large walk-through space with views to the ballfield.

Installing party decks in the ballpark's upper-deck corners is a good place to renovate. The center field rooftop deck has been popular for fans holding tickets to the fifty-one fixed seats and also for other spectators hanging out behind them at the bar and high-top tables and couches whose awnings protect them from the sun.

Third, according to data compiled by the *SportsBusiness Journal*, the Orioles averaged one of the highest television ratings in MLB despite a disappointing 2015 season. In fact, the team drew a 5.35 average household rating on the Mid-Atlantic Sports Network (MASN) through mid-September, unchanged compared with the same period during the previous season. The club ranked fifth in MLB that season, and slightly behind the 6.35 household rating posted by the Detroit Tigers. About 1.1 million households in the Baltimore market have a television, according to Nielsen, resulting in an average of 49,000 tuned into Orioles' games on any given night.

Fourth, a few years ago the Orioles' Information Technology Director Jim Kline adopted Microsoft Office 365. Success with the software led him to explore Microsoft Dynamics CRM Online to implement a customer affinity program. Kline thought about how the team could take advantage of Lync Online, which is included in its Office 365 subscription. Furthermore, he considered hosting some servers on Microsoft Azure as the team's Windows Server 2003 servers reached end-of-support.

Fifth, because of riots in the Baltimore area during the spring of 2015, calculations revealed that a forced shutdown of Camden Yards for six games could have cost the club approximately $6 million in gate receipts. Add in more than a $1 million in additional revenues from parking fees and concessions, and a price tag of close to $7.5 million for the team and its licensees were reasonable amounts. But this loss is relatively minor compared to those incurred by bars and restaurants near the stadium that closed for several days, and the foregone wages of ticket takers, ushers, and concession sellers who did not work for those games.

BOSTON RED SOX

In 1899, Western League (WL) president Ban Johnson declared his minor league group of baseball teams a major league and therefore renamed it American League (AL). One year later he announced the formation of a franchise in Chicago, which besides there, were other AL teams in Buffalo, Cleveland, Detroit, Indianapolis, Kansas City, Milwaukee, and Minneapolis. When the twenty-six-year-old NL refused to acknowledge his organization, Johnson decided to compete directly in more NL cities including Baltimore and Washington, DC, beginning in 1901.

Before the AL's 1901 season, the Buffalo Bisons were removed by Johnson and replaced by the Boston Americans. The owner of the new team, which played its home games at the Huntington Avenue Grounds, was millionaire Charles W. Somers. As a member of the AL from 1901 to 1907, the Americans won 528 or 51 percent of their games and finished first twice including a World Series in 1903, and also placed second, third, fourth, seventh, and eighth in other seasons.

In 1908, owner John I. Taylor dropped Americans and instead chose the nickname Red Sox, which referred to the red hose in the team's uniform. The word Sox, meanwhile, was previously adopted for the AL Chicago White Sox by newspapers needing a headline-friendly form of Stockings because "Stockings Win!" in large type would not fit on a page.

Team Performances

While a member of the AL from 1901 to 1968 and specifically the ED during MLB's 1969–2015 seasons, the Americans for seven years and Red Sox for another 108 played 17,862 games and won approximately 51 percent of them. Among other AL teams as of 2015, they tied for eighth with the Indians, Tigers, and Rangers each with seven division titles, and also ranked second in the league with both twelve pennants and eight World Series championships (Table A1).[9]

Within the ED as of 2015, Boston was fourth in number of division titles but second to the New York Yankees in winning pennants and World Series. Furthermore, compared to all teams in MLB, the Americans/Red Sox tied for fifteenth in division titles and finished third to the Yankees and NL Cardinals in both pennants and World Series titles. Based on these results, this Boston-based team has been superior in qualifying for postseasons especially during such consecutive years as 1915–1916, 1998–1999, 2003–2005, and 2007–2009. Alternatively, the club did not compete in the playoffs in such periods as 1969–1974, 1976–1984, 1991–1994, 2000–2002, and 2010–2012.

Since 1986, Red Sox teams have been more consistent at winning games than during the previous eighty-five seasons. Their performances improved for several reasons including better leadership from managers and coaches, more competent and talented players at key positions who could hit and score runs in games, and getting sufficient production from their pitching staffs.

Franchise Owner

During early 2002, MLB approved the sale of the Red Sox, Fenway Park, and 80 percent of the New England Sports Network (NESN) by the Jean R. Yawkey Trust and its trustee John L. Harrington to John Henry, Tom Werner, Larry Lucchino, and a group of investors for $380 million. Henry became the club's principal owner, Werner its chairman, and Lucchino its president and chief executive officer (CEO). Prior to acquiring the Red Sox, Henry was a minority owner of the Yankees and sole owner of the Florida Marlins while Werner and Lucchino were major or minor investors in other big-league franchises.

A lifelong baseball fan that grew up in the Midwest listening to Cardinals games on the radio, Henry has been an involved and passionate MLB owner who serves as chairman of a company in alternative-asset, financial-product innovation. When he purchased the club, Henry committed to field a team worthy of the fans' support; preserve what is good about Fenway Park and to take that experience to a higher level; market aggressively to a potentially broader region; actively participate in the community; end the curse of the Bambino; and win championships for Boston, New England, and the Red Sox nation.

Compared to teams' performances of other principal owners in the AL as of 2015, Henry's Red Sox since 2002 tied for eighth in winning two division titles and ranked first with three pennants and also World Series championships. Among owners of twenty-nine other clubs in MLB, Henry's Red Sox teams tied for twelfth in number of titles, ranked fourth in winning pennants, and tied for first with the NL San Francisco Giants in World Series victories.

Based on these results as of 2015, Henry has been a successful principal owner of Boston's big-league baseball franchise for fourteen years. Overall, his teams outperformed those of ED rivals and their owners including the Baltimore Orioles' Peter Angelos, New York Yankees' Hal Steinbrenner, Tampa Bay Rays' Stuart Sternberg, and the Toronto Blue Jays' Edward Rogers (Table A2).

A fan, struck by a foul ball that went behind home plate during a Red Sox game at Fenway Park in June 2014, sued Henry. Brookline, Massachusetts, resident Stephanie Taubin said in her lawsuit that she was above home plate in the EMC Club when a baseball came through an area usually protected by glass and hit her. Unfortunately, the glass had been removed for renovations. The suit claims Taubin suffered facial fractures and neurological damage. She seeks unspecified damages. The Red Sox told the *Boston Globe*, which is also owned by Henry, that the organization does not know the specifics of the suit and will not comment on pending litigation but that fan safety is a priority.[10]

Fenway Park

After becoming a charter member of the AL in 1901, the Red Sox, then known as the Americans, built Huntington Avenue Grounds (HAG) on site of a wasteland in Boston. A rickety wooden ballpark, HAG contained approximately 11,000 seats. While Americans and then Red Sox teams played there for a total of eleven MLB seasons, attendance averaged between a low of 4,100 per game in 1901 to a high of 8,900 in 1909.

Due to security problems, including potential fires and injuries to spectators at HAG, Red Sox owner and real estate magnate John Taylor decided to build a new ballpark near downtown Boston. After he sold himself a parcel of land in the 'Fens' as a site, the ballpark's construction began in September 1911 and ended before the team's 1912 season. Because of the new ballpark, the team's market value increased, causing Taylor to sell 50 percent of it in 1912 to Jim McAleer and Robert McRoy for $150,000.

Named based on its location, Fenway Park had 27,000 seats with the main steel and concrete grandstand extending from behind home plate down the base lines and connecting with wooden bleachers in the outfield. A fire occurred during May 1926 destroying the wooden bleachers along the left field foul line. Seven years later, Fenway Park was extensively renovated. After another fire destroyed most of the construction in January 1934, the ballpark was rebuilt and then reopened for the MLB season.

Since 2003, there have been several major improvements and upgrades completed at the ballpark. These involved such things as the Green Monster wall and additional club seats, the State Street Pavilion, and a new video scoreboard. To accommodate fans, seating capacity increased to more than 37,000 for day and night games.

In a recent study by CSN Mid-Atlantic, Fenway Park ranked tenth in MLB. According to the author of an online report in *USA Today*:

> Yeah, it wasn't built with the 21st century in mind. And to spend an evening there is to get way-too-acquainted with Red Sox Nation and Neil Diamond. But it's a wholly unique experience, and well worth it. The Green Monster hovers over everything. The Pesky Pole looks so out of place, you can't fathom how guys' actually hit home runs about 309 feet down the right-field line. You'll be cramped, you'll be sick of everything New England, but you'll be glad you went.[11]

Compared to fourteen other AL stadiums as of 2015, 105-year-old Fenway Park is the oldest facility, least expensive to initially build at less than $1 million, and based on the team's estimated market value, it is worth $403 million and ranked second in the league following Yankee Stadium. Among twenty-nine other MLB venues, the Red Sox's ballpark is the oldest with its construction cost tied for twenty-ninth with the Chicago Cubs' Wrigley Field, and fourth in value (Table A3).

As determined previously for Oriole Park at Camden Yards and later in the chapter for Yankee Stadium, Tropicana Field, and the Rogers Centre, the FCIs for a four-person family to attend a regular-season game at Fenway Park during the 2011–2015 MLB seasons ranged from a low of $336 each in 2012 and 2013 to a high of $350 in 2014 and also 2015. During the five-year period among AL clubs, the Red Sox ballpark's FCI at games was the highest for fans. Compared to all MLB clubs, Fenway Park's FCI was also the most expensive each year for several reasons (Table A4).

To reveal specific costs for a recent year in MLB, each home game at the Red Sox's ballpark in 2015 was approximately $350 for a family or about the same as in 2014. Listed from most to least in amount by item for one person, the average nonpremium ticket cost between $52 and $53, parking $35, a cap $25, one beer about $8, and a hot dog and soft drink each between $5 and $6.

Among ED teams besides the Red Sox, their ballparks' FCIs and ranks in 2015 were as follows: Yankees second at $337; Blue Jays sixteenth at $209; Orioles twenty-seventh at $163; and Rays twenty-eighth at $157. While MLB's average FCI equaled $211, the Red Sox, Yankees, and five other AL teams' games exceeded that amount.

With respect to premium tickets in the 2015 season, the Red Sox's averaged $180 each. This was considerably less than the Yankees' $305 but also more than the Orioles' $44, Blue Jays' $58, and Rays' $88. Compared to MLB's average ticket price of $96, Boston's premium seats cost $84 or 88 percent more for fans to attend its home games and sit in the best seats at Fenway Park.

With both nonpremium and premium tickets exceeding the league average by respectively $24 and $88, it is relatively expensive for a family to attend any Red Sox home games and purchase food items, beverages and caps, and also park near the facility. However, despite these costs and prices, the team is popular entertainment for local fans and frequently plays before capacity crowds even during losing seasons. This, in turn, suggests that the Red Sox organization maximizes its gate receipts, operating income, and revenue each season during April through September.

While average or per-game attendance ranged from 4,100 to 8,900 at HAG for the Americans, the Red Sox's varied at Fenway Park from a low of 2,300 in 1932 to a high of 37,800 in 2009. During the 2000s, however, the club's attendances were among leaders in the AL and also in the top one-third of MLB. Given these results, this Boston-based team has a legendary, optimum-sized, and unique ballpark for its fans.

Financial Data

As explained before for the Baltimore Orioles, MLB franchises are commercial enterprises. Their economic objective is to earn maximum revenue and obtain the greatest amount of profit on a fiscal basis from their operations. Although they share revenue with each other from such sources as national television contracts and other deals, it is important for them to efficiently allocate resources, determine and distribute payrolls, set nonpremium and premium ticket prices, and schedule investments in short- and long-term assets. To reveal and manage these activities, this section focuses on different parts of the Red Sox franchise's business and how well its organization succeeds or does not succeed from a financial perspective.

According to data and other financial information published in *Forbes* for franchises in the AL as of their 2015 season, Boston ranked second to New York in market value at $2.1 billion, revenue at $370 million, and gate receipts at $172 million. The team also had the highest operating income at $49.1 million but tied for eleventh with the Yankees, Blue Jays, Angels, and Mariners each with a zero percent debt-to-value ratio (Table A5).

Within the ED, the Red Sox had the most operating income, second highest market value, revenue, and gate receipts, and tied for third in its debt percent. Compared to twenty-nine other MLB clubs as of 2015, the team was third in market value, fourth in revenue and operating income, second in gate receipts, and tied for twenty-fifth in its debt-to-value ratio. Given this data, the Red Sox are a rich and valuable enterprise and also a lucrative business that historically rewards its owners, field managers, coaches, and players. In fact, only amounts of the AL's New York Yankees exceed—and NL's Los Angeles Dodgers and San Francisco Giants compare—to financials of the Red Sox.

Besides such things as history and tradition, size and wealth of the local sports market, success, and other factors, an MLB team's annual payroll partly reflects its commitment to players and their current and potential contribution individually and as a group to winning games in regular seasons and postseasons. From 2011 to 2015, for example, the Red Sox's payroll among all AL teams ranked from second in both 2011 and 2012 (each $161 million) and also 2013 ($149 million) to third in 2014 ($149 million) and 2015 ($168 million) (Table A6).

Among only the league's ED teams, Boston's payrolls ranked below those of the Yankees during the five-year period but exceeded the amounts of the Orioles, Rays, and Blue Jays each season. Compared to twenty-nine other clubs in MLB, the Red Sox's payments for players ranked third for the first two seasons of the period and then fourth in 2013 and fifth in both 2014 and 2015. Because of its success, tradition, and wealth as a franchise, the Red Sox have the ability and willingness to compensate players more than the majority of teams in the AL and NL. Except when it won a World Series in 2013, the club did not qualify for the playoffs in other years and thus paid too much in salaries to a number of its underperforming players.

Business Relations

Besides the above information, following are a few interesting but important and relevant topics about the business and commercial activities involving this Boston-based MLB team as reported in various online editions of the *SportsBusiness Journal* and other publications. As investments, they are expected to generate cash and other benefits resulting in additional revenue and perhaps gate receipts to improve the Red Sox organization and its operations.[12]

First, after its 2013 World Series victory, the Red Sox began to consider the use of flexible pricing based on demand and supply. The years of constant sellouts at Fenway Park insulated the club from needing to experiment with ticketing structures such as variable and dynamic pricing, which have swept through much of professional and college sports. In fact, Boston is the only

MLB team with fully static pricing. The club became interested in placing higher values on marquee games such as those against the New York Yankees and Chicago Cubs and also others on peak calendar dates.

Second, the franchise signed a multiyear deal with a Rhode Island jeweler to be the presenting sponsor of a renovated banquet space at Fenway Park. The Champions Club, as presented by sponsor's Alex and Ani, is the new name of the old Players Club, which is situated behind the right field seats in an area known as the Big Concourse. It is one floor below the Royal Rooters Club, a members-only lounge that opened in 2012.

The revamped Champions Club was one of three hospitality spaces remodeled as part of the team's $3 million investment in stadium upgrades. The 3,624-square-foot banquet room has a much brighter look after the Red Sox returned the space to its original layout by adding windows for natural light. The space is reserved for pregame meals for groups of two hundred or more people with a new movable wall that splits the room in two. A comprehensive audiovisual system with new televisions, including a few eighty-inch screens, provides better technology for group presentations.

Third, during early 2012, a director of Fenway Sports Management (FSM) decided to bring the English Premier League club Liverpool FC to the ballpark for an exhibition game against Italian power AS Roma, and also looked to revive college football at Fenway after an extended absence. Like ice hockey, FSM hopes Liverpool exhibitions occur at the ballpark every other year. Furthermore, the company will expand its role with Liverpool's North American tour in summers from being just a venue operator to tour promoter as it takes the soccer [football] club to other cities.

Fourth, at its spring training park in Fort Myers, Florida, the Red Sox created an experience drawing heavily from Fenway Park in Boston. The team's president and CEO, Larry Lucchino, refers to the Green Monster wall in left field as the dominant feature. Thus, right field at JetBlue Park, for example, has its share of Fenway-related icons such as a duplicate "Pesky Pole" and the red "Ted Williams" seat commemorating the longest recorded home run hit at Fenway, and it also has the same uniform numbers of retired Red Sox managers and players on display as in Boston. JetBlue Park was more than an opportunity to clone a beloved ballpark. The key driver for the $78 million experience was to consolidate major league and minor league baseball operations into one location for spring training, and therefore, follow the same path taken by other MLB clubs. Previously, the minor league organization was split between two facilities located elsewhere in Fort Myers.

Fifth, franchise co-owners Henry, Werner, and Lucchino have been replicated to a degree in Los Angeles, where Guggenheim Baseball Management (GBM) closed on a record-shattering $2.15 billion purchase of the Dodgers.

Like Henry and the Fenway Sports Group, GBM features a low-profile financial executive in Mark Walter atop the organizational chart. His partner Magic Johnson is comparable to Werner in being a more outgoing brand advocate with deep Los Angeles sports business relations, while Lucchino shares similarities with Stan Kasten, another hard-charging industry veteran who manages the Dodgers' day-to-day operations.

NEW YORK YANKEES

After finishing fifth in the 1901 MLB season and then eighth in 1902, Baltimore Orioles owners Frank Farrell and Bill Devery received permission from the AL to move their team from Baltimore to New York City before the 1903 season. They renamed it New York Highlanders, in part, because the team played its games at one of the highest points on Manhattan ("The Hilltop") and considerably uphill from the New York Giants' Polo Grounds. Highlanders were also short for "Gordon's Highlanders," the name of team president Joseph Gordon during 1903–1906 and also the famous British military unit called "The Gordon Highlanders."

As with other members of the AL, the media frequently referred to the Highlanders as New York Americans. However, *New York Press* sports editor Jim Price coined the unofficial nickname Yankees (or "Yanks") for the club in 1904, because it was easier to fit in the newspaper's headlines. In 1913, the Highlanders were officially renamed Yankees.

Team Performances

While performing in the AL as the Highlanders from 1903 to 1912 and then Yankees in the 1913–2015 MLB seasons, the club played 17,570 games and had victories in 56 percent of them. During 113 years, it won nineteen division titles, forty pennants, twenty-seven World Series, and appeared in fifty-two playoffs. Among AL teams as of 2015, the Yankees were first in winning championships. Other champions and New York's closest all-time competitors in the league have been the Red Sox and then such clubs as the Indians, Tigers, and White Sox (Table A1).[13]

Compared to others in MLB as of 2015, the Yankees rank first in numbers of division titles, pennants, and World Series titles. More specifically, the team has been consistent by appearing in at least two or more consecutive playoffs twice in the 1920s; once in the mid-to-late 1930s, early 1940s, and late 1940s/early 1950s; and also once in the mid-to-late 1950s, early 1960s, late 1970s, early 1980s, and 1995–2007 and 2009–2012. Alternatively, it did not qualify for postseasons in such consecutive years as 1903–1920, 1965–1975, and 1982–1994.

Because of the Yankees' great managers and ballplayers, playing home games in a legendary ballpark and within the largest and most lucrative sports market in America, this has been a dominant professional baseball franchise primarily since the early 1920s. Although other teams have challenged and defeated them in regular seasons and postseasons, they will likely be a good-to-very-good club in seasons after 2016 but not as overpowering as during earlier decades.

Franchise Owner

During late 2008, Hal Steinbrenner—the youngest and more reserved of the Steinbrenner sons—was given complete control of the Yankees organization in a unanimous vote by MLB owners. His late father George, the Yankees' former principal owner, asked Commissioner Bud Selig to approve the change in the fall of that year. While George's older son Hank represented the team in interviews with the media, Hal was more very involved in its daily operations and dealt with team executives while spending time in the club's offices in New York. When George died in 2010, Hal and Hank inherited the team with Hal becoming its principal owner, managing general partner, and cochairman of the franchise.

After attending Culver Military Academy, which is a college preparatory boarding school located in Culver, Indiana, Hal graduated from Williams College in 1991 with a Bachelor of Arts degree. Three years later, he earned a Master of Business Administration (MBA) degree at the University of Florida in Gainesville. In September 2007, Hal was elected chairman of the board of Yankee Global Enterprises, which owns the team along with 20 percent of Yankee Entertainment Sports (YES) and the New York City FC soccer team. In addition to those positions, he served as chairman and CEO of Steinbrenner Hotel Properties and on the board of directors of the Tampa Bay Boys and Girls Club.

Among AL teams and their principal owners as of 2015, Hal Steinbrenner's Yankees won three division titles and one each pennant and World Series. As such, he and three others owned clubs with three division titles including the Athletics' Lewis Wolff, Mariners' Nintendo of America, and Rangers' Ray Davis. While owned by Hal the Yankees tied for fifth with the Rays and White Sox each with one pennant, and also tied for second with the White Sox and Royals each with one World Series championship following Henry's Red Sox with three (Table A2).

During January 2016, Steinbrenner decided to approve a trade for embattled Cincinnati Reds pitcher Aroldis Chapman, and warned the public not to prejudge the player before MLB's investigation into the incident. Steinbrenner understood fans' concern and threats of protests against the Yankees for acquiring Chapman, who allegedly choked his girlfriend and mother of his child, and also fired eight bullets into his garage in an argument with her. The league's domestic violence policy stipulates it could discipline Chapman even in the absence of criminal charges. New York City Council Speaker Melissa Mark-Viverito publicly said she might boycott Yankee games after the deal because of the domestic violence charge. "I understand it is a very sensitive subject, as rightfully so," Steinbrenner said at the quarterly owners' meetings, "but we just have to wait and see. It's a touchy subject, but again, a man is innocent until proven guilty."[14]

Yankee Stadium

After playing ten seasons at 16,000-seat Hilltop Park, the New York Highlanders—renamed Yankees in 1913—moved to the 34,000-seat Polo Grounds and shared the ballpark with the NL New York Giants. Then from 1923 to 1973, the club played its home games at the 58,000-seat Yankee Stadium I—nicknamed "The House That Ruth Built" and "The Big Ballpark in the Bronx," and in the 1974–1975 seasons at 57,300-seat Shea Stadium and then at Yankee Stadium II from 1976 to 2008.

Due to Yankee Stadium II's deteriorating condition by the early 2000s, the team wanted a new ballpark for its home games to generate more attendances and revenue by providing fans with additional amenities and luxuries. As a result, groundbreaking began in August 2006 on a new venue adjacent to the original Yankee Stadium. While the team financed the $1 billion plus project, the city of New York spent more than $200 million for infrastructure and other improvements.[15]

During mid-April 2009, the new 52,000-seat Yankee Stadium opened for the team's first home game of the MLB season. The ballpark has the appearance and tradition of the original stadium with a grandstand that consists of four levels. While the lower two levels include 30,000 seats, the third level contains more than fifty luxury suites and the fourth a split-level upper deck.

Among its features, historic Monument Park is located beyond the outfield fence in center field; a high-definition video scoreboard is in the outfield; hand-operated auxiliary scoreboards are part of the right-center and left-center fences; and other amenities include luxury, outdoor and party suites, club seats, a martini bar and steakhouse, and picnic areas. In addition, a Yankees Museum displays memorabilia of their former great teams and players, while a Hard Rock Café exists in the Grand Hall. Despite these things, the club's average attendances declined from the low 50,000s per game during the 2005–2008 MLB seasons and then to the low-to-mid 40,000s. Undoubtedly other factors such as the team's performances and problems in the local economy influenced its home attendances.

Among those of all big-league teams as of 2015, Yankee Stadium was the most expensive to build, tied for twenty-seventh in age with the Mets' Citi Field, and ranked first with an estimated value of $593 million. Being one of five privately financed ballparks in the AL and also ten in MLB, it has contributed more gate receipts, operating income, and revenue to the Steinbrenner's baseball franchise since opening in 2009 (Table A3).

As published and previously analyzed for the ED's Orioles and Red Sox, FCIs were determined for the Yankees at their ballpark for their 2011 to 2015 seasons. During this period, these ranged from a low of $324 each in 2012 and 2013 to a high of $338 in 2011. Among AL clubs, the Yankees ballpark's FCI ranked second in these years but behind the Red Sox's Fenway Park. Compared to all MLB clubs, Yankee Stadium placed second throughout the period (Table A4).

To reveal specific costs for a recent year in MLB, Yankee Stadium's FCI in 2015 was approximately $337 or the same as in 2014. Listed from most to least in amount by item for one person at a home game, the team's nonpremium tickets averaged between $51 and $52, parking a vehicle $35, one cap $25, a beer $6, and a hot dog and soft drink each $5. For the FCIs and ranks of other AL's ED clubs in 2015, the Red Sox were first at $350; Blue Jays sixteenth at $209; Orioles twenty-seventh at $163, and the Rays twenty-eighth at $157. While MLB's average FCI in 2015 was $211, it cost fans 60 percent more to watch the Yankees compete at home against any other team.

With respect to premium tickets at home games in the 2015 season, the Yankees' averaged between $305 and $306 each. This was considerably greater than the Orioles' $44, Blue Jays' $58, Rays' $88, and Red Sox's $180. Compared to MLB's average premium ticket price of $96, these special seats cost $209 or 217 percent above average for spectators to attend home games and sit in the best seats at Yankee Stadium.

In a recent study by CSN Mid-Atlantic, Yankee Stadium ranked twentieth. According to an online report in *USA Today*:

> How do you replace the most famous ballpark in baseball history, one that played host to so many iconic moments in the sport's history over eight decades? Well, the Yankees decided to build a near-replica of the old place, right across the street. Except they made it bigger, more lavish and way more expensive (you'll notice how many of the overpriced field club seats always are empty). Which leaves the new Yankee Stadium feeling like something of a fraud? It looks like Yankee Stadium. It's called Yankee Stadium. But it's just not Yankee Stadium.[16]

With both nonpremium and premium tickets exceeding the league average by respectively $23 and $209 in 2015, it was and continues to be relatively expensive for a family to attend any Yankees home games and purchase food items, beverages, and caps, and also park near the facility. Although the team is popular and entertaining, it has not played before capacity crowds recently even during winning seasons. This indicates that the Yankees organization is not maximizing attendance at the ballpark and thus does not receive the most gate receipts, operating income, and revenue each season during its April through September home games.

Financial Data

As explained before for the Orioles and Red Sox, MLB franchises are commercial enterprises whose economic objective is to earn maximum revenue and obtain the greatest amount of profit on a fiscal basis from their operations. To manage daily activities and achieve their mission, this section focuses on different parts of the Yankees' business and how well the organization succeeds or does not succeed from a financial perspective.

According to data and other financial information published in *Forbes* for fifteen franchises in the AL as of their 2015 season, New York ranked first in market value at $3.2 billion and both revenue at $508 million and gate receipts at $269 million, and also eleventh in operating income at $8.1 million and tied for eleventh with the Red Sox, Blue Jays, Angels, and Mariners each with a zero percent debt-to-value ratio. Except for operating income, these are truly impressive amounts for the club (Table A5).

Among all MLB teams, the Yankees had the highest market value, revenue and gate receipts, but the twenty-second most operating income and tied for twenty-fifth in its debt percent. Financially, this club was a valuable and profitable enterprise in 2015 because of its ballpark, history and tradition, location in America's largest city, and such other factors as promotion in the media, memorabilia and merchandise sales, partnerships and sponsorships, and television broadcasts.

Besides such things as income and wealth of consumers in the local sports market, business activity in its region, and number of years in the sport, an MLB team's annual payroll partly reflects its commitment to players and their current and potential contribution individually and as a group to winning games in regular seasons and postseasons. From 2011 to 2015, for example, the Yankees payroll among fourteen other AL teams ranked first each year (Table A6).

Compared, however, to the payrolls of twenty-nine other clubs in the big-leagues during this period, the Yankees were first in 2011–2013 but second to the NL Los Angeles Dodgers in both 2014 and 2015. Because they signed or re-signed some free agents and/or veteran players including pitchers to multiyear contracts, the Dodgers payrolls were respectively $241 million and $230 million in 2014–2015, while the Yankees' equaled $208 million and $213 million. The Dodgers, meanwhile, were in two playoffs these seasons but lost too many games in the divisional series, while the Yankees qualified for the 2015 playoffs but were defeated in a wild card game. Despite their high payrolls, however, neither franchise was good enough to win a pennant and compete in a World Series.

Business Relations

Besides the above data and other information, following are a few interesting but important and relevant topics about the business and commercial activities involving the Yankees as reported in online editions of various publications. As short- and long-term investments, these activities were implemented, in part, to generate additional revenue and profit to improve this baseball organization's operations in the New York area and elsewhere.[17]

First, in November 2014, Bank of America (BOA) renewed one of its largest sports sponsorships in a deal with the Yankees franchise. The renewal added six years to a longtime Yankees-BOA business relationship and—as was the case across the sports industry—adjustments were made in the new deal to add more talent and also digital and social media inventory. Just before the new Yankee Stadium opened in 2009, however, BOA almost pulled the trigger on a "Premier Partnership" package that would make the financial institution the largest sponsor of the team's new ballpark. But because of the U.S. recession, BOA received bailout money from the federal government and changed its strategy to conclude a more traditional deal with the club.

Second, the Yankees—who broke away from MLB Advanced Media's renewal with StubHub to form their own secondary ticketing exchange with Ticketmaster—branded the initial year with their own resale platforms to be a success as of October 2013. The club apparently had significant boosts in walkup and group ticket sales business even as their total home attendance fell 7 percent in the season.

Perhaps more important to them, the creation of a Yankees Ticket Exchange curbed speculative resale listings by sellers without possession of the tickets that the club viewed as corrosive to the overall value of their tickets. The team, in fact, had some involvement with StubHub near their respective ballparks. Nevertheless, they sued to prevent StubHub from opening a pickup location near Yankee Stadium, and obtained a settlement that motivated StubHub instead to open a storefront much farther from the ballpark.

Third, MLB's on-field headwear rights-holder New Era signed an eight-year marketing agreement with the Yankees in 2013. One source pegged the deal's value at $20 million and said it includes a host of marketing rights, enhancement of its two company-branded stores in Yankee Stadium, and an extension of New Era's sponsorship of the Pinstripe Bowl—which is a non-Bowl Championship Series game that the company sponsors since it began in 2010.

The value of the deal is attributable to a various reasons. The Yankees are regularly—and historically—a top-selling team. The New York logo's perpetual dominance among MLB licensed-product sales is eclipsed only by its absolute dominance in overseas sales. Some estimates have Yankees-logoed products accounting for more than half of MLB licensed sales overseas. According to different sources, the Yankees' dominance in MLB licensing is even greater in headwear.

Fourth, Yankee Stadium became the first sports venue to be covered with a federal Safety Act designation and certification from the U.S. Department of Homeland Security (DHS) during 2013, marking what many in the security field believe will be a new era for how threats of terrorism are handled in sports. The federal recognition gives the team, as an award recipient, protection from having to pay claims that might be filed by victims against it in the event of a terrorist attack at the ballpark. Also, the standing could serve to lower the club's future insurance premiums as well—a path others in sports may follow by working to receive the DHS-backed recognition.

Fifth, several years ago the Yankees and their affiliates carried nearly $2 billion of debt according to sources who reviewed loan documents for the team's parent company, Yankee Global Enterprises (YGE) and the club's concessionaire, Legends Hospitality Management (LHM). In addition, the team was responsible for $1.2 billion of tax-exempt stadium bonds that were sold through a public entity. Combined, about $3.2 billion of debt obligations flow through YGE, though about one-third of that total burden falls on the equity partners in YES and LHM.

What also stands out about the debt is that only $97 million of it actually resides at the team. Baseball's debt regulations are applicable to the league's clubs, but not to the clubs' affiliates. It also underscores how the Yankees have shifted revenue to affiliates like YES and LHM, limiting the already steep revenue-sharing and luxury-fee payments, or about $100 million the club pays to MLB. The team also deducts about one-third of its $64 million annual stadium interest payment from its revenue-sharing commitment.

Sixth, Major Energy (ME) announced in early 2015 its new multiyear marketing partnership with the Yankees. The deal names ME as the team's official energy supply company. The partnership also provides ME with premier brand integration at Yankee Stadium and expands its presence in New York sports, complementing its already-in-progress partnership with the National Basketball Association (NBA) New York Knicks and Madison Square Garden. "We are very excited to begin a relationship with Major Energy and hope that its in-stadium signage and marketplace activation expands its brand awareness" said the Yankees senior vice president of corporate sales and sponsorships, Michael J. Tusiani.[18]

Seventh, Delta Airlines locked up home field advantage in late 2015 at Yankee Stadium as part of an extension on a sponsorship agreement with the Yankees that continues through 2023. The airline also extended its partnership with the NL Mets, which puts Delta in a position to be the official airline of both New York baseball teams. As such, Delta received the "Official Airline" and "Official Private Jet Carrier" titles for the Yankees and Mets.

TAMPA BAY RAYS

For decades, Tampa Bay, Florida, was used by several MLB teams to shake down their cities for renovations or a new ballpark. Indeed the AL Minnesota Twins, Oakland Athletics, Chicago White Sox, Texas Rangers, Seattle Mariners, and NL San Francisco Giants each threatened to move to the west coast of Florida. But after getting financing and other benefits from their cities, they decided not to relocate, which left Tampa Bay without a big-league team. After the White Sox began construction on a new ballpark in the mid-to late 1980s, Tampa Bay officials decided to build a ballpark that could be used to attract an existing or new team.

In 1991, MLB's hierarchy thought baseball teams in Miami and Denver were more feasible than expansion in Tampa. But after flirting with the Mariners and Rangers, Tampa officials were not deterred and seemed almost certain the city would be home to the Giants in 1993. Florida businessman Vincent J. Naimoli, in fact, made an agreement to purchase and then move the Giants that year from San Francisco to Tampa.

Most MLB officials, however, did not approve of the move and arranged for someone else to purchase and keep the Giants on the west coast. Naimoli was prepared to sue baseball. But after being promised an expansion team by MLB, he backed off and waited patiently. During an unfortunate player's strike in 1995, baseball's franchise owners unanimously approved Tampa Bay and Phoenix for expansion teams to begin play in 1998.

During April 1995, the newly-named Tampa Bay Devil Rays and city of St. Petersburg agreed on a thirty-year lease for the team to play its home games at the 45,400-seat Thunderdome. And then two years later, MLB owners assigned the Devil Rays to the AL's ED and join the Blue Jays, Orioles, Red Sox, and Yankees.

Team Performances

As a member of the league's ED from the 1998 to 2015 MLB seasons, the Devil Rays—renamed Rays in 2008—played 2,914 total games and had victories in approximately 46 percent of them. During the period, the club won two division titles and one pennant but zero World Series in four playoff appearances. Among fifteen teams in the AL as of 2015, the Rays ranked fourteenth in division titles and also tied for twelfth with the Angels in number of pennants and with the Astros, Mariners, and Rangers in World Series championships. Within the league's ED, Tampa Bay had fewer championships than each of the other four clubs (Table A1).

Compared to all MLB teams as of baseball's 2015 season, the Rays were tied for twenty-fifth with the NL Nationals in winning division titles, tied for twenty-third and with the AL Angels and also NL Diamondbacks and Rockies in pennants, and also tied for twenty-third with seven other teams each with zero World Series victories. More specifically, Tampa Bay's worst seasons consecutively were 1998–2007 while it's most successful besides 2008 included 2010–2011 and 2013. Except for when they appeared in AL playoffs, Rays' teams have been below-average in performances despite competing in a World Series.

During its eighteen years in the ED, some of the club's best players were traded, left after becoming free agents, or simply retired. These included outfielder Carl Crawford, pitcher David Price, and infielders' Carlos Pena, Ben Zobrist, and Aubrey Huff. The failure to keep these and other top performers on the roster for more than a few seasons caused problems for the franchise.

Franchise Owner

After spending years as a successful equity options trader at Goldman Sachs, Stuart Sternberg resigned from the company in 2002 and reportedly received a payment of $400 million. His passion for baseball developed as a child while playing the game in the streets and playgrounds of his neighborhood in New York's Brooklyn borough. One of Sternberg's most cherished memories was watching the Dodgers' Sandy Koufax pitch while attending his first MLB game with his father at Shea Stadium in 1965. Besides playing in various organized baseball leagues during his lifetime, Sternberg also coached his two sons' Little League teams for several years.

During May 2004, Sternberg purchased a 48 percent plurality-share in the previously named Devil Rays from principal owner Vince Naimoli for $200 million and then became their managing general partner in October 2005. He arranged his bid for a controlling interest in the team with fellow Goldman Sachs partner Matthew Silverman whom he later hired as the team's president. As the club's leading investor, Sternberg has been a low-key owner whose primary goal is getting its finances organized and budgeted including operating expenses and the players' payroll.

Before Sternberg the Devil Rays had the worst record in MLB, losing ninety-two or more games each season from 1998 to 2003. But since he became principal owner, the team has posted six winning seasons. While appearing in four postseasons, the club won two division titles and one pennant. Among AL teams as of 2015, the club tied for eighth in division titles and ranked fifth in winning one pennant but no World Series. Compared to twenty-nine other MLB teams, Tampa Bay was between eighth and twelfth in championships. In short, the Rays have significantly improved performance-wise since 2008 (Table A2).

In 2014, Bloomberg Business named the Rays fifth in ranking the "smartest spenders" among 122 major sports franchises after being first in 2009 and 2012. Also in 2014, Entertainment Sports Programming Network's The Magazine rated the Rays first in affordability among MLB teams, the fourth time they earned the top spot in the previous eight years. Although the franchise has been frugal but smart, Sternberg plans to improve the team's roster over time.[19]

Tropicana Field

Finished in 1990, the publicly financed Florida Suncoast Dome—renamed Thunderdome in 1992—was originally built for baseball, although the team renovated the stadium to make it even more like an MLB ballpark. The $85 million renovation included, in part, wider concourses and installation of Astroturf, clubhouses, dugouts, additional luxury suites, restrooms, elevators, escalators, administrative offices, and a reduction in capacity from 48,000 to 45,000. After Tropicana Juice purchased naming rights, the stadium's name changed to Tropicana Field in 1996.

People enter the ballpark's main entrance through a giant rotunda reminiscent of Brooklyn's Ebbets Field. Inside it, visitors are in the Centerfield Street area which includes a brewhouse, the team's store, the Capitan Morgan Deck, and Hitters Hall of Fame. Another feature at Tropicana Field is the thirty-five-foot, 10,000-gallon Rays Touch Tank where spectators can touch an actual ray fish in water.

Among teams' stadiums as of 2015, Tropicana Field is the sixth oldest in the AL. At $203 million, the ballpark's cost ranked eighth, but its value was only fifteenth at $98 million. Compared to twenty-nine other stadiums in MLB, Tropicana Field was eighth in age, twenty-first in cost, and twenty-ninth in value. Besides the Devil Rays/Rays' performances since 1998, this data reflects the ballpark's amenities, architecture, location, and size (Table A3).

As previously analyzed for the league's ED Orioles, Red Sox, and Yankees, FCIs were published for the Rays' ballpark in MLB's 2011 to 2015 seasons. During the period, these amounts ranged from a low of $139 in 2011 to a high of $170 in 2014. Compared to those of other AL teams, Tropicana Field ranked between thirteenth and fifteenth in cost for families and among all MLB teams, the stadium was twenty-fifth in 2011 and 2014, twenty-seventh in 2012, and twenty-eighth in 2013 and 2015 (Table A4).

To reveal specific costs for a recent year in MLB, Tropicana Field's FCI in 2015 was approximately $157 or $54 less than average and thus ranked twenty-eighth highest in baseball. Listed from most to least in amount by item for one person at a home game, the team's nonpremium tickets averaged between $21 and $22, a cap $10, and one beer, soft drink, and hot dog each $5. As reported by TMR, parking a vehicle for a game was free.

For other AL's ED teams, their stadium's FCIs and rankings in 2015 were respectively $350 and first for the Red Sox's Fenway Park, $337 and second for the Yankees' Yankee Stadium, $209 and sixteenth for the Blue Jays' Rogers Centre, and $163 and twenty-seventh for the Orioles' Oriole Park at Camden Yards. Based on this data, it was relatively inexpensive for a family to attend a Rays home game against their rivals in the division and league.

Regarding a premium ticket at Tropicana Field in 2015, its price was between $88 and $89 or 8 percent below the average in MLB. The tickets for premium seats at games of other teams in the ED included the Yankees' $305, Red Sox's $180, Blue Jays' $58, and Orioles' $44. Being a small-market team, the Rays charged low prices for their nonpremium and premium tickets to increase attendances at their home games and maximize revenue with more gate receipts.

In a recent study by CSN Mid-Atlantic, Tropicana Field ranked twenty-ninth. According to the author of an online report in *USA Today*:

> Built eight years before the region even had its own major-league team, the Trop has provided one of the worst environments in baseball history for 16 years now. It's the only permanent dome still being used in the majors. The lack of crowds leaves everything echoing throughout the park. And then there are the catwalks that hover over the field of play, with special ground rules written in case a batted ball strikes one of the four different rings. The Rays desperately want a new park, and they've been trying for years, but for now they remain stuck in this awful facility.[20]

For nearly a decade, the team has explored the possibility of building a new ballpark somewhere in Tampa or the St. Petersburgh area. Despite obstacles blocking potential construction such as funding and location issues, the Rays will continue seeking opportunities to replace Tropicana Field and build a new ballpark somewhere in the future. This will depend, in part, on owner Sternberg and his ability and determination to persuade city and county officials to build and finance all or part of the facility.

Financial Data

As explained before for the Orioles, Red Sox, and Yankees, MLB franchises are commercial enterprises whose economic objective is to earn maximum revenue and obtain the greatest amount of profit on a fiscal basis from their operations. To manage daily activities and achieve their mission, this section focuses on different parts of the Rays' business and how well its organization succeeds or does not succeed from a financial perspective.

According to data and other financial information published in *Forbes* for fifteen franchises in the AL as of their 2015 season, Tampa Bay ranked fifteenth in market value at $625 million, fourteenth in both revenue at $188 million and gate receipts at $33 million, and also twelfth in operating income at $7.9 million and third with a debt-to-value ratio of 22 percent. Among the league's ED teams, the Rays had the smallest market value, revenue and gate receipts, more operating income than the Blue Jays, and the highest debt percent (Table A5).

Compared to all MLB clubs as of their 2015 season, the team ranked between twenty-third and thirtieth except for its debt-to-value ratio which tied for seventh with the NL Padres. Given these results, Tampa Bay is the lowest-valued franchise in MLB and lacks enough revenue and gate receipts from its operations to be very valuable from a financial perspective.

Because of these matters, the club struggles to consistently win regular season games and thus division titles, pennants, and World Series. Nevertheless, the Rays improved to recently qualify for four playoffs in eight years while being managed by Joe Maddon and led by such players as slugger Evan Longoria and pitchers David Price and James Shields. As of 2016, Maddon coached the Cabs while Price and Shields pitched for other teams.

Besides such things as jobs and disposable income of consumers in the local sports market, business activities in its region, and number of years in the sport, an MLB team's annual payroll partly reflects its commitment to players and their current and potential contribution individually and as a group to winning games in regular seasons and postseasons. From 2011 to 2015, for example, the Rays payroll among fourteen other AL teams ranked from tenth

(2014) to fourteenth (2015). Within the ED, the Yankees and Red Sox had, respectively, the two highest amounts every season followed by the Blue Jays or Orioles (Table A6).

Compared to twenty-nine other clubs in MLB, the Rays' payroll ranged in rank from seventeenth in 2014 ($82 million) to twenty-ninth in 2011 ($41 million). Besides Tampa Bay, the AL's Indians, Astros, and Athletics and six NL teams each had payrolls less than $100 million in 2015. Even so, the Astros qualified for the playoffs but were defeated in the league's divisional series by the Kansas City Royals. Although the Rays appeared in four playoffs from 2007 to 2015, the club needs to significantly increase payroll and re-sign its best players to win another pennant as in 2008.

Business Relations

Besides the above information, following are a few interesting but important topics about the business and commercial activities directly or indirectly involving this Florida-based MLB team as reported in online editions of various publications. Other than revenue from their home games, the Rays generate cash and other financial benefits from advertising, marketing agreements, television broadcasts, and other projects, in part, to increase the payroll of the team's manager and players, and also to upgrade the organization's operations in the Tampa Bay area and elsewhere.[21]

First, the Rays' paperless entry system Flex Packs (FPs) card is offered initially at two price points and available in three-, six-, and nine-game options. The program takes the traditional concept of a flex plan and gives it a modern twist with some technological innovation. Designed to presell tickets in multiples of three, FPs provides such benefits for purchasers as being able to select any games and make those selections up until six hours before the first pitch; up to 50 percent discounts in certain locations for games; an RFID chip to track fans' purchases and spending patterns that enable the club to create targeted follow-up offers where the incentive is linked to the demonstrated preferences of the FPs cardholder; express lanes at concession stands; and access to in-game contests and pregame promotions.

Three objectives of the plan are to presell tickets and encourage single-game buyers to commit to three or more of them through value and convenience incentives; offer early seat selection, which returns some of the decision-making power to the consumer and greater customization; and give consumers the choice of high-demand opponents regardless of day of the week. The one planning element that clearly benefits the team requires that the pass is intended and designed for the purchaser to buy and attend three games.

Second, Rays' subsidiary Sunburst Entertainment Group (SEG) and the University of South Florida had discussions in 2011 to decide whether Sunburst should help the school to sell its season tickets for football and basketball games. As a firm, SEG is similar to the Red Sox's Fenway Sports Group and the White Sox's Silver Chalice who each develop new business ventures outside of their respective MLB operations. In central Florida, Sunburst sold group tickets and became involved in facility operations at Tropicana Field for the Beef 'O' Brady's Bowl in 2009 and 2010. Sunburst took on a greater role in its first year with the Under Armour All-America football game at the ballpark by selling tickets and producing the halftime show with hip-hop artist Fabolous.

Third, during his tenure with the franchise, team president Brian Auld managed various aspects of the team's business operations, including the departments of human resources, information technology, marketing, ticket sales, fan experience, and stadium operations. Building an employee friendly organization, his specific accomplishments include the addition of maternity and paternity benefits for all full-time staff, creation of a staff wellness program, and the establishment of a culture of community service through the Employee Community Outreach Team (ECOT). In addition, the team's staff volunteers one paid workday each month in the community, and ECOT assists by finding new opportunities.

Fourth, under a plan pending before Tampa's City Council as of early 2016, the club would play at least two more seasons at Tropicana Field. The proposed "memorandum of understanding" allows the Rays to look for new stadium sites in Pinellas and Hillsborough counties, but precludes the team from leaving St. Petersburg before 2018. It also creates financial incentives for them to stay in Tampa and requires the club to pay the city as much as $24 million if they leave before their lease at their ballpark expires in 2027.

Fifth, principal owner Stuart Sternberg continues to make investments in the organization both on and off the field. In January 2014, for example, the Rays awarded players two of the three largest free-agent contracts given by Sternberg's ownership group. They re-signed first baseman James Loney to a three-year, $21 million contract and brought back pitcher Grant Balfour with a two-year, $12 million pact. One year earlier the team signed Evan Longoria to a $100 million contract extension that could keep the all-star third baseman in a Rays uniform until 2023. That, in turn, was the team's largest ever financial commitment to a player—one who happened to be the first drafted under Sternberg.

Sixth, during May 2012, the franchise's Baseball Foundation and the Helios Education Foundation partnered to provide $1 million in college scholarships over five years for students participating in the Take Stock in Children program within Florida's Hillsborough, Pinellas, Sarasota, Manatee, and

Pasco counties. Each year, owner Sternberg and his family sponsor a playground construction project for kids in partnership with KaBoom! In fact, he and his family, and Rays' staff build the playgrounds.

Seventh, the Poynter Institute arranged for Sternberg, hockey's Tampa Bay Lightning owner Jeffrey Vinik, and football's Tampa Bay Buccaneers' cochairman Bryan Glazer to speak in late February 2016 with the Associated Press Sports Editors (APSE) and members of the general public about business trends and issues in pro sports. According to Poynter's president Tim Franklin, "This is a time of great change in both the media business and professional sports, so this is an opportune time for the owners, sports editors and the public to discuss the issues of the day, and the future. We're thrilled that these owners and the sports editors have chosen Poynter as the place for that conversation."[22]

TORONTO BLUE JAYS

During January 1976, the NL San Francisco Giants' owner Horace Stoneham agreed to sell his team for $13.25 million to a Toronto group led by Don McDougall and also including Labatt Breweries of Canada Ltd., Vulcan Assets Ltd.—owned by Howard Webster—and the Canadian Imperial Bank of Commerce (CIBC). Named the Toronto Giants, the team would play its home games in MLB's 1976 season at Exhibition Stadium. But after a U.S. court blocked the plan, American businessman Bob Lurie's syndicate purchased the Giants and kept them in San Francisco.

The city of Toronto, meanwhile, renovated Exhibition Stadium to accommodate MLB in anticipation of the San Francisco Giants relocating there and thus continued to pursue a big-league team. Then in mid-1976, MLB awarded the city of Toronto an expansion franchise along with Seattle, Washington. A consortium composed of Labatt Breweries and Webster (each 45 percent) and CIBC (10 percent) successfully purchased the rights for the franchise from MLB for a fee of $7 million.

Even after MLB awarded these franchises, however, the future of baseball in Toronto appeared uncertain because U.S. President Gerald Ford pressured MLB to give, Washington D.C., an expansion franchise instead of Toronto. The nation's capital city had been without a big-league team since the Senators moved to Arlington, Texas, following their 1971 season and became the Texas Rangers.

After this development there was speculation by Metro Toronto Chairman Paul Godfrey, among others, that Washington would be awarded Toronto's AL franchise and instead, Toronto would receive a NL expansion franchise. Nevertheless, Ford's attempts failed, and Toronto kept its new franchise.

When Toronto's franchise held a "name the team" contest in 1976, which involved more than 4,000 suggestions, "Blue Jays" was chosen by majority owner Labatt Breweries as an apparent tie-in with its feature brand, Labatt Blue. Yet, the team would have likely adopted blue as one of its colors since it had been the primary color for the city's top-level sports teams including the Toronto Argonauts in 1873.

Team Performances

While a member of the AL's ED from 1977 to 2015, the Blue Jays played 6,193 games and scored enough runs for victories in 49 percent of them. During the period, they won nine division titles and two each pennants and World Series championships and appeared in six playoffs. Among fifteen AL teams as of their 2015 MLB season, Toronto tied for fourth with the Angels in winning division titles, tied for tenth with the Rangers in number of pennants, and tied for seventh in World Series wins with the Indians, Royals, and Twins (Table A1).

Compared to twenty-nine other MLB teams as of 2015, the Blue Jays were tied for ninth with the Angels and Giants in number of division titles, tied for nineteenth with the Rangers, Marlins, and Padres in pennants, and tied for twelfth with several other teams in winning World Series. Based on these results, Toronto has been mediocre although average in its performances during thirty-nine seasons in the league.

Besides 1985, 1989, and 2015, the Blue Jays' most successful years were 1991–1993 when they won three ED titles and two World Series. During these MLB seasons, the club's total attendance exceeded four million each year at the SkyDome. Coached by AL Manager of the Year Cito Gaston, their productive players included slugger John Olerud, infielder Roberto Alomar, and outfielder Devon White. Alternatively, Toronto's two longest periods without appearing in a playoff were 1977–1984 and 1994–2014.

Although the Blue Jays outperformed Tampa Bay in the majority of regular seasons, the Red Sox and Yankees were competitive and dominated the ED. To consistently challenge others in its division after 2015, Toronto needs a more talented roster of players, including pitchers, and also another manager like Gaston.

Franchise Owner

Businessman Ted Rogers, who created Canada's largest cable-television and mobile-phone company and also founded Rogers Communications Inc., purchased the Blue Jays franchise from Labatts Breweries in 2000 for $160 million. Known as a visionary but also a workaholic and demanding boss, Ted died in late 2008 from an existing heart condition. As a result, his son Edward Rogers III inherited the team from his father.[23]

After graduating from the University of Western Ontario, Edward worked in the Philadelphia area for the Comcast Corporation from 1993 to 1996 before returning to Canada and joining the family business. For three years, he was vice president and general manager of paging, data, and emerging technologies for Rogers Wireless. Then from November 1998 until September 2000, Rogers III was vice president and general manager of the Toronto region for Rogers Cable Inc. and responsible for its financial and sales performances and customer satisfaction. After serving as president and chief executive officer of Rogers Cable from January 2003 to September 2009, Edward became deputy chairman of Rogers Communication and chair of the Rogers Control Trust.

During his tenure as owner of the Blue Jays since 2008, his teams won one division title but zero pennants and World Series. Compared to performances of other current AL owners' teams, Edward's ranked between fifth and thirteenth in performances. Among twenty-nine owners in MLB, his Toronto teams tied for twenty-first in division titles and also for fourteenth in pennants and ninth in World Series. Except for 2015, Edward has been below-average as an owner compared to his peers (Table A2).

Rogers Centre

After playing their home games in 30,900-seat Exhibition Stadium for twelve years, the Blue Jays moved into the new retractable roof SkyDome in 1989. Sixteen years later, Rogers Communication purchased the ballpark for $25 million and renamed it Rogers Centre. Located in downtown Toronto next to the CN Tower, it has five levels of seats that extend from right centerfield to home plate and then to left centerfield. All lower-level seats are movable and can form a football gridiron to host games of the Canadian Football League (CFL) Toronto Argonauts. Interestingly, the pitcher's mound rises and lowers hydraulically when not needed for baseball.

During late 2015, the team announced the installation of a dirt infield at Rogers Centre. This eliminated the dirt cut-outs around the bases. In addition, there is a possibility of installing a grass field at the ballpark in 2018. That depends on several factors including the Argonauts moving to another site in Toronto. Other than the ballpark's retractable roof, field turf, and large video scoreboard, the area includes the 350-room Rogers Centre Renaissance Hotel with seventy, or one-fifth, of its rooms overlooking the playing field.

Among big-league teams' stadiums as of 2015, Rogers Centre is the fifth oldest in the AL. At $370 million, the ballpark's cost ranked fourth of fifteen but its estimated value only ninth at $162 million. Compared to twenty-nine other stadiums in MLB, Rogers Centre was seventh in both age and cost, and twentieth in value. Besides the Blue Jays' performances since 1989, this data reflects the ballpark's amenities, architecture, location, and size (Table A3).

As previously analyzed for the ED's Orioles, Red Sox, Yankees, and Rays, FCIs were published for the Blue Jays' ballpark in MLB's 2011 to 2015 seasons. During the period, these amounts ranged from a low of $212 in 2011 to a high of $254 in 2013. Compared to those of other AL teams, the Rogers Centre's FCIs ranked between third and eighth, and among all MLB teams, they were between fifth and sixteenth (Table A4).

To reveal specific costs in U.S. dollars for a recent year, the Rogers Centre's FCI in 2015 was approximately $209 or 3 percent less than in 2014. Listed from most to least in amount by item for one person at a home game, the team's nonpremium tickets averaged between $25 and $26, parking a vehicle about $22, a cap $16, one beer $7, and a hot dog and soft drink each between $4 and $5. While the Blue Jays' FCI was $2 below MLB's average and ranked sixteenth, those of other ED clubs included the Red Sox's $350 (first), Yankees' $337 (second), Orioles' $163 (twenty-seventh), and Rays' $157 (twenty-eighth). Compared to all MLB teams' ballparks, it was neither expensive nor cheap for a family to attend Toronto's homes games.

Regarding a premium ticket at the Rogers Centre in 2015, its price was between $58 and $59 or 61 percent less than MLB's average of $97. Those of other teams in the ED included the Yankees' $305, Red Sox's $180, Rays' $88, and Orioles' $44. A midmarket team, the Blue Jays charged relatively low prices for their nonpremium and premium tickets in order to increase attendances at their home games and maximize the franchise's revenue including gate receipts.

In a recent study of MLB ballparks by CSN Mid-Atlantic, the Rogers Centre ranked twenty-seventh. According to the author of an online report in *USA Today*:

> I distinctly remember thinking the then-Skydome was the coolest stadium in the world when it opened 25 years ago. And at the time, it was a true marvel. It had a retractable dome. It had the biggest scoreboard anyone had ever seen. It had a hotel INSIDE the stadium, for crying out loud! These days, it just feels off. Like Epcot Center, you realize this place once felt futuristic but now feels like a bad example of what we thought the future would look like back in the '80s.[24]

During early 2015, the Blue Jays acknowledged that Rogers Centre needed improvement, but instead of pursuing a new stadium elsewhere, the club considered extensively retrofitting it to modernize the in-game experience for fans. An upgrade would cost approximately $200 million to $400 million in U.S. dollars. The team, which has looked at designs for stadium renovations and that a retrofit is feasible, has worked with the University of Guelph in Ontario to find ways of adding natural grass to Rogers Centre by 2018.

Financial Data

Big-league franchises are commercial enterprises whose economic objective is earning maximum revenue and obtaining the greatest amount of profit on a fiscal basis from their operations. To manage daily activities and achieve their mission, this section focuses on different parts of the Blue Jays' business and how well its organization succeeds or does not succeed from a financial perspective.

According to data and other financial information published in *Forbes* for fifteen AL franchises as of their 2015 season, Toronto ranked tenth in market value at $870 million, tied for ninth with the White Sox in revenue at $227 million, fourteenth in operating income at –$17.9 million, tied for tenth in gate receipts with the Astros at $48 million, and tied for eleventh with four other clubs in its debt-to-value ratio at zero percent. Within the league's ED, the Blue Jays had the smallest while negative operating income but also a larger market value and more revenue and gate receipts than the Rays (Table A5).

Among twenty-nine other MLB teams as of 2015, the Blue Jays' amounts were ranked between eighteenth and twenty-eighth including their debt ratio. Simply put, this Toronto-based franchise is below average as a sports business enterprise and financially inferior to many teams in the AL and NL. In fact these results occurred for Toronto because of several factors including its relatively low attendances at home games, obsolete ballpark, and dismal performances in many regular seasons.

An MLB team's annual payroll partly reflects its commitment to players and their current and potential contribution individually and as a group to winning games in regular seasons and postseasons. From 2011 to 2015, for example, the Blue Jays' payroll among fourteen other AL teams ranked in rank between fifth in 2014 at $116 million to twelfth in 2012 at $62 million (Table A6).

Compared, however, to the payrolls and ranks among twenty-nine other clubs in the big-leagues during this period, Toronto's was as low as $62 million in 2011 (twenty-third) and 2012 (twenty-fifth) to a high of $116 million in 2014 (ninth) and also in 2015 (sixteenth). Since the Blue Jays appeared in only one playoff series from 1994 to 2015 after winning consecutive World

Series in 1992–1993, the team's principal owner Edward Rogers and/or general manager Ross Atkins need to offer competitive contracts to talented veteran players and/or sign others when they become free agents. Otherwise the Red Sox and Yankees, and occasionally the Orioles, will continue to dominate the league's ED in future MLB seasons.

Business Relations

Besides the above information, following are a few interesting but important and newsworthy topics about the business and commercial activities directly or indirectly involving this Toronto-based MLB team as reported in online editions of various publications. The purpose is to highlight the Blue Jays and their development, opportunities, and success as an organization.[25]

First, the team's vice president of special projects Howard Starkman retired in 2014. An original employee of the club and a former publicist with the NHL Toronto Maple Leafs, he joined the Blue Jays in 1976, just weeks after it was awarded an AL franchise and even before getting a nickname. During Howard's tenure, he helped them transform the stadium landscape with opening of the SkyDome, winning two World Series, and slowly rebuilding their fan base after a devastating 234-day work stoppage in 1994. In addition, Sparkman served years as a key aide and confidante to the team's president and chief executive officer Paul Beeston. In an interview published by the *SportsBusiness Journal* in June 2014, he described his role and experiences with the team and how it adapted to various problems.

Second, after twenty-five years and advances in technology and use of common parts at newer stadiums, the Rogers Centre's majestic retractable roof had a fading and much older operations system that led to an overhaul for that portion of the roof structure. From 2011 to 2014, a structural engineering firm—that worked on sports facilities—determined the extent of roof upgrades. The total cost, including a newly designed mechanization system, was estimated at $9 million. The investment covered the tracks on which the roof runs, rubber underpadding, motors and wheels, and a new software system that controlled the operation. In other words everything that moved, or that the roof travelled on, needed to be replaced, upgraded, or repaired.

Third, when the Blue Jays competed well enough to make the playoffs in September 2015, a telecom analyst prepared a rough estimate of their financial gain because of the increased excitement of fans about the team and its postseason. He estimated the club could earn an additional $20 million at the gate and a boost of about $40 million from higher merchandise sales and advertising revenue while higher costs, including player salaries, might increase expenses by about $20 million. That would be a net increase of

$40 million or a profit of $20 million for the year, which represented about 50 cents per share of Rogers' then current stock price of $43.96 per share. Estimated in Canadian rather than U.S. dollars, the revenue impact would be a profit of almost $27 million. Rogers Communication, who owned the team and broadcast network Sportsnet, also expected a 10 percent increase in advertising revenue.

Fourth, Canada's largest processor of debit and credit card payments, Moneris Solutions Corporation, was confident that local pubs would reap the rewards of Blue Jays fever by estimating a boost of between 30 to 40 percent in business when the MLB playoffs started in late 2015—much like what the restaurant sector enjoyed in 2013 during the NHL Maple Leafs home playoff games. It was warm enough to sit outside on restaurant patios to enjoy the games with nibblies and a pint. While Toronto's sports bars near the Rogers Centre planned on prime-time crowds, the games' early start times did not change expectations for a pickup in sales. Besides television sets at bars, the games were also broadcast on speakers of the streets.

Fifth, according to CIBC World Markets' chief economist Avery Shenfeld, when it comes to excitement about a winning professional sports team like the Toronto Blue Jays, the economics are a zero-sum game. For example, what sports bars make in added revenue, other venues lose. High ratings for broadcast games bring in cash for broadcasters, but ratings suffer at competing channels. He also suggested that the team might actually be hurting the economy when people skip work to attend games at the Rogers Centre. Finally, Shenfeld argued that since no one gets a raise in salary because the Blue Jays win games, spending on the team actually reduces people's savings. They, in turn, have less to spend on other things.

Sixth, after employed for twelve years with the franchise and building a team that made its first playoff appearance in twenty-two years and came within two wins of a World Series appearance, general manager Alex Anthopoulos declined a contract offer to return to the Blue Jays in October 2015. He felt returning to the team would not be a good fit and thus was eventually replaced by Ross Atkins. Toronto posted average results during most of Anthopoulos's tenure until a series of trade-deadline moves in the summer of 2015 helped the club surge in the season's second half. They beat Texas in the AL division series before falling to Kansas City in the league's championship series.

To conclude this chapter about the all-time performances and recent business success of five AL ED teams as of their 2015 season, the Yankees won the most championships and played their home games in a big and expensive ballpark. They also ranked first in market value, revenue, operating income and gate receipts, and had the highest payroll. In addition, Red Sox games were more costly for fans than those of other teams in the division. Consequently, the Orioles and then Blue Jays and Rays followed the Yankees and Red Sox in performances and financial results.

NOTES

1. Two books about MLB franchises and their history are Frank P. Jozsa Jr., *Baseball, Inc.: The National Pastime as Big Business* (Jefferson, NC: McFarland, 2006), and James Quirk and Rodney D. Fort, *Pay Dirt: The Business of Professional Team Sports* (Princeton, NJ: Princeton University Press, 1992).

2. For performances of the Orioles and other teams in the AL's ED, see their website at http://www.mlb.com and historical information about them at "MLB Links," http://www.sportsecyclopedia.com, cited January 19, 2016, and the *Official Major League Baseball Fact Book 2005 Edition* (St. Louis, MO: Sporting News, 2005).

3. References about MLB franchise owners include "List of Major League Baseball Principal Owners," http://www.baseball-reference.com, cited January 22, 2016, and Frank P. Jozsa Jr., *American League Franchises: Team Performances and Business Success* (New York: Springer, 2015).

4. For specific details about MLB ballparks, including those of teams in the AL's ED, see their website and also http://www.ballparksofbaseball.com and http://www.ballparks.com.

5. The primary reading is "Ranking All 30 MLB Ballparks," http://www.csnmidatlantic.com/, cited January 26, 2016.

6. The 2011–2015 fan cost indexes of MLB and other professional sports teams at their home games in arenas, ballparks, or stadiums are available at http://www.teammarketing.com.

7. Regarding the Orioles' business relations, see Ryan Sharrow, "Orioles' TV Ratings on MASN among the Highest in MLB," http://www.bizjournals.com, cited October 5, 2015; "Baltimore Orioles Score Homerun With Office 365," http://www.microsoft.com, cited March 1, 2016; Edward Wyatt and Megan Specia, "The Cost of Closing the Baltimore Orioles Game during the Riots: $7.5 Million," http://www.mashable.com, cited May 5, 2015; Jeff Barker, "Orioles Begin to Look at Updating Camden Yards," http://www.baltimoresun.com, cited August 24, 2015.

8. "Pure Entertainment" reflects how well a team does, but more importantly, how exciting is its play. "Authenticity" denotes how well they play as a team defensively and offensively, which can be driven by such factors as a new stadium or a new manager. "Fan Bonding" indicates their respect and admiration for players. "History and Tradition" are about the game and team's part of a fan's and a community's rituals, institutions, and beliefs. For more about these variables, see "Fan Cost Index," http://www.teammarketing.com, cited January 25, 2016.

9. Besides the team's website, similar sources were used to research Red Sox history as the Orioles', including http//www.baseball-reference.com, http://www.sportsencyclopedia.com, http://www.mlb.com, and http://www.sportsalmanac.com.

10. One article is Marissa Payne, "Woman Suing Red Sox Owner After Being Hit by Foul Ball in Stadium," http://www.washingtonpost.com, cited February 9, 2016.

11. CSN Mid-Atlantic, "Ranking All 30 MLB Ballparks."

12. For business highlights of the Red Sox, topics were selected among others from various editions of the *SportsBusiness Journal* and other publications. See, for example, "Red Sox Introduce Variable Pricing for 2014 Season," http//www.m.mlb.com, cited February 1, 2016; Don Muret, "Red Sox Sign Jeweler Alex and Ani as Presenting Sponsor for Redesigned Banquet Space," http://www.sportsbusinessdaily.com, cited February 1, 2016; "Fenway Sports Management Announces Liverpool Club North America Summer Tour," http://www.reuters.com, cited February 2, 2016; Don Muret, "JetBlue Park: Fenway Takes Flight in Florida," http://www.sportsbusinessdaily.com, cited February 3, 2016; Zachary Rymer, "Boston Red Sox: Like It or Not, Timing Is Right for John Henry to Sell Team," http://www.bleacherreport.com, cited February 5, 2016.

13. Similar to the Orioles and Red Sox and later the Rays and Blue Jays, the performances and other information about the Yankees appear in articles on various websites.

14. Read "Yankees Owner Hal Steinbrenner Defends Trade for Aroldis Chapman," http://www.foxsports.com, cited February 9, 2016.

15. The source for the ballpark is "Yankee Stadium," http://www.ballparksofbaseball.com, cited February 1, 2016.

16. CSN Mid-Atlantic, "Ranking All 30 MLB Ballparks."

17. Yankees' business relations are in Terry Lefton, "Bank of America Renews Its Big Sponsorship with the Yankees," *SportsBusiness Journal* (November 10, 2014): 11; Ken Belson, "Yankees Resale Market Will Compete with StubHub," http://www.bats.blogs.nytimes.com, cited March 5, 2016; Terry Lefton, "Yankees Sign Eight-Year Marketing Agreement with New Era," *SportsBusiness Journal* (July 15, 2013): 4; David Broughton, "Yankee Stadium Secures Safety Act," *SportsBusiness Journal* (June 25, 2012): 16; Daniel Kaplan, "Yankees Group Carries Nearly $2 Billion in Debt," *SportsBusiness Journal* (September 20, 2010): 1; "Boston Red Sox: Like It or Not, Timing Is Right for John Henry to Sell Team," http://www.bleacherreport.com, cited February 5, 2016; Elizabeth Wolf, "Delta Extends Deals With Mets, Yankees," http://www.news.delta.com, cited May 15, 2016.

18. Eliott Wolbrum and Barry Smith, "Major Energy Inks Deal with New York Yankees on New Multi-Year Marketing Partnership," http://www.majorenergy.com, cited February 1, 2016.

19. See Ira Boudway, Evan Applegate, and Ritchie S. King, "Smartest Spenders in Sports 2014," http://www.bloomberg.com, cited February 1, 2016.

20. Besides "Ranking All 30 MLB Ballparks," another source is "Ranking MLB's Ballparks," http://www.athlonsports.com, cited January 26, 2016.

21. Such topics as Flex Packs cards and other business news are reported in articles on various online websites, including the Rays' at http://www.mlb.com. Also, see Don Muret, "Rays' Group among Those Seeking South Florida Ticket Sales Job," *SportsBusiness Journal* (May 2, 2011): 12; "Brian Auld," http://www.tampabay.rays.mlb.com, cited March 15, 2016; Alcides Segui, "St. Pete City Council Approves Rays

Stadium Deal," http://www.fox13news.com, cited April 1, 2016; "Helios Education Foundation and Rays Baseball Foundation Announce 2015 Scholars," http://www.helios.org, cited April 15, 2016.

22. "Business of Professional Sports: An Evening with the Owners of the Lightening, Rays and Buccaneers," http://www.poynter.org, cited February 5, 2016.

23. For the Blue Jays ownership, see "List of Major League Baseball Principal Owners" and the team's website at http://www.mlb.com.

24. The status of the Rogers Centre and other current big-league ballparks is in "Ranking All 30 MLB Ballparks."

25. Print and online editions of such magazines as the *SportsBusiness Journal*, *Business Week*, *Forbes*, and the *Wall Street Journal*, and website http://www.bizjournals.com have information about sports business topics and news, including financial data, regarding the Toronto Blue Jays franchise. For example, see Don Muret, "Original Retractable Roof in Toronto Getting $9M Modernization," http://www.sportsbusinessdaily.com, cited April 12, 2016; "Thinking Back with Howard Starkman," *SportsBusiness Journal* (June 30, 2014): 38; Shi Davidi, "Blue Jays to Part Ways with Stephen Brooks, Hire Indians' Andrew Miller," http://www.sportsnet.ca, cited April 12, 2016; James Fink, "Buffalo Bisons, Toronto Blue Jays Extend Affiliation Pact through 2018," http://www.bizjournals.com, cited April 13, 2016.

Chapter Two

Central Division

As described in the previous chapter, prior to 1969 there were no individual divisions in the American League (AL) or National League (NL) of Major League Baseball (MLB). However, because of expansion between 1969 and 1993, the AL and NL consisted of either six or seven teams each in the East Division (ED) and West Division (WD). Then in 1994 these two leagues realigned again and besides their ED and WD, they added a Central Division (CD). As a result, the AL's and NL's ED and CD each had five teams while their WD included four. After 1997, other differences occurred in divisions until 2013 when five each played in the ED, CD, and WD.

Given these changes in the structure of big-league baseball, this chapter discusses the historical development—and highlights the business and financial matters—of AL teams based in Chicago, Illinois; Cleveland, Ohio; Detroit, Michigan; Kansas City, Missouri; and Minneapolis, Minnesota as of MLB's 2015 season. Which of them, for example, had the most division titles and least pennants? What were their gate receipts, operating incomes, and debt ratios in 2015? Among the five clubs, which had the least and most successful owner in winning championships? How did these teams' current ballparks compare to others in MLB? The answers to these and other questions are topics covered in the chapter.[1]

CHICAGO WHITE SOX

From 1888 to 1891, the Sioux City Cornhuskers played in the Western Association and then in the Western League (WL) in 1894. That year, former major league star and manager Charles Comiskey purchased the Cornhuskers and transferred the team from Sioux City to Saint Paul, Minnesota, where it enjoyed some success during the next five seasons while named Saint Paul Apostles.

In 1900, the WL changed its name to American Baseball League, or simply American League (AL). Officially a minor league organization but subject to the governing National Agreement, the NL gave permission to AL president Ban Johnson to put a team in Chicago, Illinois, provided it did not use the city name as the team's brand.

With an opportunity to play its games before more baseball fans in a larger city, Apostles' owner Comiskey moved his team from St. Paul to Chicago's south side and nicknamed it White Stockings. After the White Stockings won an AL pennant in 1900, the league declined to renew its membership in the National Agreement and organized itself as a "major league" in 1901 with eight teams, including one each in Baltimore, Boston, Chicago, Cleveland, Detroit, Milwaukee, Philadelphia, and Washington, D.C.[2]

Team Performances

As a member of the AL for 115 MLB seasons and specifically the CD from 1994 to 2015, the White Sox—originally White Stockings—played a total of 17,851 games and had victories in approximately 50 percent of them. During the period they won six division titles, five pennants, three World Series, and appeared in nine playoffs. Compared to fourteen other teams in the league as of 2015, the club ranked thirteenth in winning division titles, tied for sixth with the Cleveland Indians in pennants, and tied for fifth with the Baltimore Orioles in World Series wins. Among clubs only in the league's CD, Chicago had the least number of division titles, more pennants than the Kansas City Royals and Minnesota Twins but also fewer World Series championships than the Detroit Tigers (Table A1).

Of all big-league teams as of their 2015 season, the White Sox tied for nineteenth with the NL New York Mets in division titles, tied for thirteenth with the Indians and also Mets and NL Atlanta Braves in pennants, and tied for ninth with the Orioles and NL San Francisco Giants in number of World Series victories. Based on these results, this Chicago-based franchise has been competitive and performed above average especially in MLB's postseasons of 1906, 1917 and 1919, 1959 and 1983, 1993 and 2000, and 2004 and 2008. Alternatively the White Sox failed to win enough games and qualify for playoffs in such consecutive seasons as 1907–1916, 1920–1958, and 1960–1982. This occurred, in part, because its managers were not effective leaders or smart decision makers and thus unable—or otherwise unprepared—to motivate their players.

Franchise Owner

Born into a Jewish family in Brooklyn, New York, as the son of a sewing machine salesman, Jerry Reinsdorf was a lifelong baseball fan who grew up near the city's Ebbets Field and attended the ballgame when African American Jackie Robinson debuted for the Brooklyn Dodgers in 1947. After finishing high school, Jerry earned a bachelor's degree from George Washington University and subsequently moved to Chicago in 1957.

Upon graduating from Northwestern University School of Law, Reinsdorf's first job was a tax delinquency case of White Sox owner Bill Veeck. In 1964, Jerry organized a law practice and developed a specialty in real estate partnership tax shelters. He sold his interests in the real estate partnership in 1973 and formed Balcor, which raised $650 million to invest in buildings under construction. Although Reinsdorf sold Balcor in 1982 for $102 million to Shearson Lehman Brothers—the investment banking and brokerage arm of American Express—he continued as president of the company for several years.

Brokered by American National Bank after arranging a limited partnership, Reinsdorf headed a syndicate that purchased the White Sox franchise from Veeck in 1981 for approximately $20 million. During his thirty-five-year tenure with the franchise, the White Sox reached the postseason five times including 2008 when they captured the league's CD title in a one-game playoff. The team also claimed four other division titles and in 2005 won the AL pennant and its third World Series.

Being the principal but longest owner of an MLB franchise as of 2015, Reinsdorf's teams have won more than 2,800 or 51 percent of their games. Compared to current owners of AL teams, his clubs ranked second in division titles, tied for fifth with the New York Yankees' Hal Steinbrenner and Tampa Bay Rays' Stuart Sternberg in winning pennants, and tied for second with Steinbrenner and the Kansas City Royals' David Glass in World Series victories. Among twenty-nine other MLB franchise owners, Jerry's teams were fifth in division titles, tied for eighth in number of pennants, and tied for fourth in World Series wins (Table A2).

Besides those accomplishments as an owner, Jerry has served on MLB's executive council and the ownership, player relations, relocation, legislative, and long-range labor planning committees. Also, he was instrumental in forming baseball's Diverse Business Partners Program in 1998. His long history of donating time led to being a board member of the Baseball Hall of Fame.

When he dies, control of the White Sox will pass to the executors of his will. During the summer of 2013, he strongly suggested they sell the team.

Because Reinsdorf holds a majority stake in the corporation that operates the team, that gives him—and the executors of his will—authority to sell it without approval of other investors. Several baseball experts believe that if sold in mid-2013, the team could have easily surpassed the $800 million paid in 2011 for the San Diego Padres. While other investors in the franchise agree that Reinsdorf has absolute control of any sales, they seem confused about what would ultimately happen to it. In fact, some of them indicated a desire to own the team well into the future.[3]

U.S. Cellular Field

From 1901 to 1909, the White Stockings/White Sox clubs played their home games at Chicago's 15,000-seat South Side Park. In 1910, the 28,000-seat White Sox Park—renamed Comiskey Park in 1913—opened, and the team competed in games there until 1990. When that facility became outdated, a new publicly financed, 44,300-seat ballpark was built for the White Sox across 35th Street and south of its predecessor. Opened in 1991, it was also called Comiskey Park but then renamed U.S. Cellular Field in 2003.

Since the early 1990s, the team's ballpark has been renovated several times involving its seats, decks, concourses, and sight lines. Its amenities include a multilevel interactive fundamentals skills deck in left field and also a two-level fan deck in center field, which provides a panoramic view of the playing field. Good locations exist throughout the outfield concourse for fans to mingle or view statues of former great White Sox players such as Frank Thomas and Nellie Fox. During summers, a popular area is the Rain Room where a cool mist relieves the heat.

In comparison to other ballparks in the AL as of 2015, U.S. Cellular Field ranked twelfth in construction cost at $137 million and eleventh in value at $152 million. Among all those in MLB, the ballpark was respectively twenty-fifth and twenty-fourth. Thus, the White Sox play their home games in a mediocre and less expensive facility than do other clubs in the league's CD but not the ED and WD (Table A3).

For several years a Chicago-based company named Team Marketing Report (TMR) has prepared and published a Fan Cost Index (FCI) for the home games of teams in professional sports leagues. To attend a game for a typical family with two kids, an FCI includes the costs of four average-priced tickets, two cheapest-priced draft beers, four each cheapest-priced soft drinks and hot dogs, parking for one car, and two each game programs and least-expensive, adult-size adjustable caps. Costs are determined by telephone calls with team representatives, venues, and concessionaires, and from questions asked during interviews.[4]

In the 2011–2015 MLB seasons, the FCIs for a family to attend a regular-season game at U.S. Cellular Field ranged in cost from a low of $208 in 2015 to a high of $258 in 2011. During this period among ballparks of fourteen AL clubs, its FCI ranked between third in 2011 to ninth in 2015. Compared to the venues of only ED teams, fans at White Sox home games had to spend more money at games in most seasons than did spectators at the Indians' Progressive Field and Royals' Kauffman Stadium but not the Tigers' Comerica Park or Twins' Target Field (Table A4).

To reveal specific costs for a recent year in MLB, this Chicago ballpark's FCI in 2015 was approximately $208 and almost the same total as in 2014. Listed from most to least in amount by item for one person, the team's nonpremium tickets averaged $26 each, parking one vehicle $20, a cap $18, a beer between $6 and $7, and a soft drink about $5 and hot dog $4. That year MLB's FCI was $211 and $3 or 2 percent more than the White Sox's.

Among other teams in the league's ED, they had rankings and FCIs from most to least as follows in the 2015 MLB season: Twins eighth at $229; Tigers thirteenth at $214; Royals fourteenth at $213; and Indians twenty-sixth at $166. Given these amounts, the White Sox do not charge fans and/or families either very high or low prices to attend and/or buy things at their home games. In other words, the franchise earns enough revenue and, in part, it's operating income from gate receipts.

The White Sox's average premium ticket was $88 at its home games in the 2015 regular season. Among other CD teams, this was less than the Royals' $105 but more than the Tigers' $73, Twins' $74, and Indians' $59. With the league's premium ticket price at $96, the White Sox offered their fans a bargain, comparatively, for the best seats in the ballpark. By setting reasonable but not cheap or expensive prices for premium and nonpremium tickets, this increased attendances at U.S. Cellular Field and thus generated more cash for the club than trying to gouge its customers.

In a recent study by CSN Mid-Atlantic, U.S. Cellular Field ranked twenty-eighth in MLB. According to an online report in *USA Today*, the author commented:

> Talk about bad timing. The White Sox opened their new stadium one year before Camden Yards opened in Baltimore. The difference is staggering. There's nothing retro about the new Comiskey Park. It's a monstrous stadium with symmetrical dimensions, a huge, steep upper deck and a view not of downtown Chicago but of the housing projects next to the Dan Ryan Expressway. They've done a few renovations to try to make the place look better, but there really is little than can be done with an eyesore like this.[5]

Financial Data

Besides performing as teams in regular-season and perhaps postseason games, MLB franchises are also commercial enterprises. To that end, their economic objective is to earn maximum revenue and obtain the greatest amount of profit on a fiscal basis from their operations. Although they share revenue with each other from such sources as national television contracts and other deals, it is important for them to efficiently allocate resources, determine and distribute payrolls, set nonpremium and premium ticket prices, and schedule investments in short- and long-term assets. To reveal and manage these activities, this section focuses on different parts of the White Sox as a business and how well its organization succeeds or does not succeed from a financial perspective.[6]

According to data and other financial information published in *Forbes* for franchises in the AL as of their 2015 season, Chicago ranked eighth in market value at $975 million, tied for ninth with the Blue Jays in revenue at $227 million, second in operating income at $31.9 million, twelfth in gate receipts at $43 million, and tenth in its debt-to-value ratio at 5 percent. Among the league's CD teams, the White Sox had the most operating income and second highest market value, third in revenue and fourth in gate receipts, and the smallest debt ratio. Although the club was very profitable in 2015, its other financials placed average in the league (Table A5).

Compared to all MLB teams as of 2015, the White Sox were sixteenth in market value, tied for eighteenth with the Blue Jays and NL Reds in revenue, ninth in operating income, tied for twenty-fourth with the NL San Diego Padres in gate receipts, and twenty-third in percent of debt-to-value. Based on these results, this Chicago-based team is average to below average as a sports business enterprise despite its above-average income.

Besides market size, salary inflation, and other factors, an MLB team's annual payroll partly reflects its commitment to players and their current and potential contribution individually and as a group to winning games in regular seasons and postseasons. From 2011 to 2015, for example, the White Sox payroll among fifteen AL teams ranged in rank from fourth in 2011 ($127 million) to tenth in 2015 ($110 million). Other than 2011, it had the second or third highest payroll in the league's CD.

Regarding amounts for all MLB teams, the White Sox payroll was above average in two of its seasons (2011 and 2013) but also twelfth in 2012, sixteenth in 2014, and then eighteenth in 2015. Thus, owner Jerry Reinsdorf paid his players roughly based on their performances as the team finished third and then second, fifth, and fourth twice in the CD.

Business Relations

Besides regular-season and postseason games, MLB franchises are involved in—and affected by—community events and business-related affairs and new projects. The following are a few of them for Chicago's AL team as of 2015.[7]

First, the White Sox signed a three-year partnership in 2013 with Magellan Corporation (MC) in which the Illinois-based steel distributor became the title sponsor of U.S. Cellular Field's Scout Seats, Scout Lounge, and use of premium-seating areas to promote local charitable and cultural institutions. Although financial terms were not disclosed, a key person in developing the deal was White Sox director of corporate partnerships activation, Gail Tucker.

Since MC was already an existing sponsor and suite holder of the club, the company quickly seized upon the opportunity for the Scout Seats—322 of them situated directly behind home plate—when United Airlines sought to shift its in-ballpark exposure to a large outfield sign. According to the team's chief marketing officer Brooks Boyer, "This is very valuable inventory we have with these seats, and we think it's going to send a very powerful message. With a b-to-b kind of relationship, the most important thing is relationships, and this will create a great deal of awareness."[8]

Second, for more details about renovations at U.S. Cellular Field in 2016, the new video board in center field dramatically altered the ballpark's backdrop. It replaced the existing video board installed in 2003 and the smallest among main video boards at all MLB stadiums. The new board is one of the ten largest in the league, according to the Illinois Sports Facility Association (ISFA). It has a ten-millimeter-pixel resolution—among the clearest available for stadiums and the same as the new boards at Chicago's Soldier Field—and takes up the majority of the scoreboard structure in center field that features various advertising signs. Also, new digital versions of the colorful pinwheels atop the center field board will be installed. Under the team's management agreement with the publicly owned stadium owner, ISFA must replace any obsolete components with modern ones if at least 75 percent of MLB's thirty stadiums have them.

Third, the White Sox had baseball's third-lowest average local television rating in 2014 at 1.15. The team's record was 73–89 following a 63–99 mark in 2013. The low ratings financially hurt owner Jerry Reinsdorf because he owned a piece of Comcast SportsNet Chicago, the regional sports network (RSN) that televises the club's games—meaning he directly benefits from the RSN's advertising revenue and dividends. The White Sox also had the third-worst attendance in MLB, and 5.5 percent lower in 2014. The team had hoped to improve in 2015 after signing three free agents including outfielder Melky Cabrera at $42 million, pitcher David Robertson at $46 million, and designated hitter Adam Laroche at $25 million. Despite these changes, the team finished 76–86 and fourth in the league's CD.

Fourth, a natural transition in personnel occurred in the White Sox front office in the summer of 2015. While Kenny Williams handed his general manager duties to Rick Hahn, Marco Paddy was hired to revamp the international scouting department. In addition, the club promoted Nick Hostetler to director of amateur scouting, with Doug Laumann moving into a senior advisor position. Laumann left his job in better shape than he found it by picking a more ambitious direction than Duane Shaffer did in his last days of 2006. Therefore, it is Hostetler's turn to put his spin on amateur scouting, and in an interview with writers on FutureSox, he referred to his days with the Atlanta Braves as an inspiration.

Fifth, since riding the World Series title to a franchise-record attendance in 2006, the White Sox's attendance at their home games dropped in each of the next eight years. They drew 1.65 million fans in 2014, which was just 56 percent of the 2.96 million they drew during the championship afterglow season.

Entertainment Sports Programming Networks' Jon Greenberg says White Sox chief marketing officer Brooks Boyer committed to reverse the attendance trend in 2015 with several internal initiatives to capitalize on the offseason excitement that helped increase season ticket packages. Besides expanding the sales staff with full-time employees chanting "one more ticket" and targeting the Cubs' territory in Northwest Indiana, the White Sox also made a big data push. Boyer says the goal is to make the game-going experience more personal for top customers and build a true incentive program to reward loyal fans.[9]

CLEVELAND INDIANS

After playing one year in the National Association, the Cleveland Forest Citys disbanded in 1872 but returned to professional baseball by joining the NL in 1879. Renamed Blues, the club played six seasons but dropped out of the league and entered the American Association (AA) in 1887 replacing Pittsburgh's team that transferred to the NL. Following two seasons in the AA, the Blues were renamed Spiders, and returned to the NL in 1889. One year later, Cleveland had a NL team and another in the new Players League (PL). However, the PL folded after its 1890 season and so did the AA in 1891. As a result, the NL was a baseball monopoly.[10]

From 1891 to 1899, the NL's Cleveland Spiders were successful most seasons. Although they never led the league in wins, the Spiders played in three postseasons but lost a championship series to Boston in 1892, defeated

Baltimore to win the Temple Cup championship in 1895, and lost a Temple Cup rematch with Baltimore the following year.[11]

By the late 1890s, Cleveland was an established big-league city and perfect for businessman Ban Johnson who turned his minor WL into major competition for the NL. Aided by financial support from Clevelander Charles Somers, Johnson's WL became known as the American League and, after a year of minor league play in 1900, went head-to-head with the NL starting in 1901. A member of the AL in 1900, one year later Cleveland joined seven other teams in MLB.

Team Performances

Nicknamed the Blues (1901), Broncos (1902), Naps (1903–1914), and finally Indians (1915–2015), Cleveland played 17,867 total games and had victories in approximately 51 percent of them. During 115 MLB seasons, they won seven division titles, five pennants, and two World Series in eleven postseasons. As of 2015, the CD Indians had fewer total championships than the Tigers and Twins but the same number as the White Sox and Royals (Table A1).

Among AL teams as of their 2015 season, Cleveland tied for eighth with the Red Sox, Tigers, and Rangers in number of division titles, tied for sixth with the White Sox in winning pennants, and tied for seventh with three other clubs in World Series titles. Compared to all big-league clubs, the Indians were respectively tied for fifteenth, tied for thirteenth, and tied for twelfth. Based on these results, this has been an average performing team within its division and league, and throughout MLB.

Besides winning World Series in 1920 and 1948, the Indians' most successful seasons consecutively were 1995 to 1999. They won five CD titles and two pennants led by such sluggers as Albert Belle, Jim Thome, and Manny Ramirez. Alternatively, the club did not qualify for the AL playoffs during the 1901–1919, 1921–1947, and 1955–1994 periods of MLB seasons. These underachieving Cleveland teams had inferior pitching staffs and also failed to score enough runs in home and away games to consistently win them. As of 2015, the club's most recent impressive performance was in 2013 when it finished second in the CD but then lost a wild card game and failed to continue in the playoffs.

Franchise Owner

Born in Cleveland Heights, Ohio, in 1931, Larry Dolan attended St. Ignatius High School. Later, he received an LLB degree from the University of Notre Dame in 1956 and then an honorary Doctor of Laws degree from Cleveland

State University. After leaving Notre Dame, Dolan served in the U.S. Marine Corps for two years where he attained the rank of first lieutenant. Discharged from the Marine Corps in 1958, Dolan worked as an assistant prosecutor in Geauga County, Ohio, before entering into private practice. He eventually became president and managing partner of Thrasher, Dinsmore & Dolan, a law group located in Chardon, Ohio.[12]

Through a family trust, Dolan acquired MLB's Cleveland Indians in 2000 for $323 million from Richard Jacobs, who along with his late brother David had paid $35 million for the club in 1986 and then eleven years later, took the Indians public. As part of the deal, however, Larry bought all the team's stock at just over $12 per share, making the franchise privately held once again in 2000.

During Larry's time as owner, the Indians were competitive in some years because of playoff appearances in 2001, 2007, and 2013, but also had periods without success including four seasons each with at least 91 losses. While Indians players' salaries were among the highest in MLB during Jacobs' last years as owner, they also have been among the lowest under Dolan. This led Cleveland fans to regard him as miserly, although others dispute his reputation.

Compared to the performances of other current owners of AL teams, Dolan's Indians (2000–2015) tied for eighth in winning division titles and pennants, and tied for fifth in World Series. Among all clubs in MLB and their respective owners, Cleveland tied for twelfth, tied for fourteenth, and tied for ninth. Therefore, for various reasons, Dolan has been a relatively unsuccessful owner based on his club's achievements at not winning championships despite appearing in four postseasons (Table A2).

In 2015, the Indians' minority owner Paul Dolan—named the organization's operating control representative in early 2013—hoped to sell his stake in the club for a rich price. Paul, who was under fire from fans for one of the smallest payrolls in the big leagues, hired privately held, boutique investment bank Allen & Company to shop roughly 30 percent of the team. The NL Padres, although not a winning club, sold for $800 million in 2012. Nevertheless, they attracted investors thanks to their $1.2 billion television deal. Without a big television contract, sports industry sources say, the Indians are worth about $600 million. Paul Dolan does not have deep enough pockets and needs a new investor to ramp up spending on salaries. The club's $76 million payroll in 2014 tied for twenty-first among MLB's thirty teams.[13]

Progressive Field

The Indians played their home games, historically, at League Park (1901–1915), Dunn Field (1916–1927), League Park and/or Cleveland Stadium (1928–1946), and then Cleveland Stadium (1947–1993). In 1985, David and Richard Jacobs purchased the Indians and hoped to build a new ballpark and improve the team's value. A few years after voters approved a bond issue in 1990, a 43,000-seat ballpark was built as part of an urban renewal project along with the Quickens Loan Arena for the National Basketball Association (NBA) Cleveland Cavaliers. Named Jacobs Park from 1994 to 2007, Progressive Insurance purchased naming rights in 2008 for $3.6 million per year for sixteen years and then renamed the Indians' ballpark, Progressive Field.[14]

Although fans may enter Progressive Field from several gates, many come through Gate C in center field. Revamped following the club's 2014 season, Gate C's area connects the ballpark to downtown Cleveland and contains Heritage Park, which is the Indians' Hall of Fame that features statues of such former great players as Bob Feller and Jim Thome.

After MLB's 2015 season, the Indians began phase two of their renovations to Progressive Field and then completed them by the spring of 2016. These included building a new enclosed club behind home plate on the main level of the ballpark that features a glass front for viewing games. Another amenity, the main concourse was scheduled to be opened from home plate to left field so fans never lose sight of the game. Additionally, the existing videoboard was replaced with a new, larger HD video/scoreboard.

Progressive Field—originally named Jacobs Field—has provided the city with many great memories including being host of the 1997 all-star game and those of the 1995 and 1997 World Series. The Indians success during the mid–1990s to early 2000s led to home attendances between 2.6 million and 3.4 million per year. Since 2003, however, the club's annual attendances have not exceeded 2.1 million.

In comparison to other AL ballparks as of 2015, Progressive Field ranked eleventh in construction cost at $175 million and fourteenth in value at $107 million. Among all those in MLB, the ballpark was respectively twenty-fourth and twenty-eighth. Thus, the Indians play their home games in an inferior and less expensive facility that do the majority of other clubs in the league's CD and at least three of the teams in the ED and WD (Table A3).

As previously provided in detail for the White Sox's U.S. Cellular Field, FCIs for the Indians' Progressive Field includes the costs of four average-priced tickets, two cheapest-priced draft beers, four each cheapest-priced soft drinks and hot dogs, parking for one vehicle, and two each game programs and least-expensive, adult-size adjustable caps.

In the 2011 to 2015 MLB seasons, for example, the FCIs for a family to attend a regular-season game at Progressive Field ranged from a low of $157 in 2013 to a high of $173 in 2012. During this period among those of fourteeen other AL clubs, Cleveland ballpark's FCIs ranked between tenth in 2011 ($171) to fifteenth in 2014 ($162). Compared to venues of only CD teams, it was less expensive for fans in most seasons to attend home games of the Indians at Progressive Field than the Tigers' at Comerica Park, Royals' at Kauffman Stadium, Twins' at Target Field, and White Sox's at U.S. Cellular Field (Table A4).

To reveal specific costs for a recent year in MLB, Progressive Field's FCI in 2015 was approximately $166 or about 3 percent more than in 2014. Listed from most to least in amount by item for one person, the team's nonpremium tickets averaged $22, a cap almost $17, parking a vehicle $12, one beer $4, and a hot dog and soft drink each $3. Thus, it was relatively cheaper and a bargain for fans to attend Indians home games in 2015 given the league's FCI of $211 and based on the amounts of the division's Twins ($229), Tigers ($214), Royals ($213), and White Sox ($208).

A typical premium ticket cost approximately $59 for a home game at Progressive Field in 2015. While the league's averaged $96 or 63 percent more than in Cleveland, best seats were more expensive for fans at home games of the Royals ($105), White Sox ($88), Twins ($74), and Tigers ($73). Such things as market size, number of jobs, fans' per capita income, historical performances, and pricing strategies caused differences in FCIs and also premium and nonpremium tickets of CD teams. Each of them, including the Indians, seeks to maximize revenue from their home games and generate more gate receipts and operating income for the franchise.

In a recent study by CSN Mid-Atlantic, Progressive Field ranked eighteenth in MLB. According to an article published online in *USA Today*:

> When it first opened, the then-Jacobs Field was hailed as one of the finest ballparks in the majors, the next Camden Yards. Unfortunately, it just simply has been overtaken by many others in the two decades since. Again, there's nothing particularly wrong with it. But neither is it particularly interesting or distinctive. There are too many suites along the third-base line, pushing the upper deck higher than it needs to be. The view of downtown Cleveland is perfectly fine, though hardly jaw-dropping.[15]

Financial Data

Besides performing as teams in regular-season and postseason games, MLB franchises are also commercial enterprises. To reveal and manage these activities, this section focuses on different parts of the Indians' business and how effectively its organization succeeds or does not succeed from a financial perspective.

According to data and other financial information published in *Forbes* for franchises in the AL as of their 2015 season, Cleveland ranked eleventh in market value at $825 million, twelfth in revenue at $207 million, tenth in operating income at $8.9 million, fifteenth in gate receipts at $30 million, and seventh with a debt-to-value ratio of 9 percent. Among the league's CD teams, the Indians had the second lowest market value and operating income, smallest revenue and gate receipts, but a higher debt ratio than the White Sox and Royals (Table A5).

Compared to twenty-nine other clubs as of MLB's 2015 season, Cleveland ranked twenty-fifth in market value, twenty-sixth in revenue, twenty-first in operating income, thirtieth in gate receipts, and sixteenth in its debt percent. Based on these results, the Indians are a struggling and below-average franchise from a financial perspective and not impressive or significantly competitive while operating in their division and league as a business enterprise.

Besides market size, salary inflation, and other factors, an MLB team's annual payroll partly reflects its commitment to players and their current and potential contribution individually and as a group to winning games in regular seasons and postseasons. From 2011 to 2015, for example, the Indians payroll among fifteen AL teams ranged in rank from tenth in 2012 ($78 million) and 2013 ($76 million) to twelfth in 2011 ($49 million), 2014 ($76 million), and 2015 ($87 million). For each season, Cleveland's payroll was lower than amounts of the White Sox and Tigers but not the Royals in 2011 and 2012 or the Twins in 2013 and 2014 (Table A6).

Among payrolls of all MLB teams in 2015, the Indians ranked from twentieth in 2012 and 2013 to twenty-sixth in 2011. Even if Cleveland's players are fairly or alternatively unjustly compensated, owners Larry and Paul Dolan get criticized by the media and fans for being stingy and not committed to winning championships. Since 2009, the team's annual attendances at home have been less than 23,000 per game and at or near the bottom of the league. Thus, the club's fan base may continue to dwindle and cause more financial problems for the franchise.

Business Relations

Besides regular-season and postseason games, MLB franchises are involved in—and also affected by—community events and internal and external business-related affairs, deals, and projects. The following are a few of them for Cleveland's AL team.[16]

First, after finishing 68–94 in MLB's 2012 season and fourth in the CD, the Indians reshaped their organization while headed by president Mark Shapiro. For example, they hired former Red Sox manager Terry Francona as manager; signed popular outfielder Nick Swisher to a $56 million contract, which was the largest free agent pact in franchise history; sold the SportsTime Ohio regional sports network (RSN) to Fox Sports in a deal estimated at more than $235 million; established a new ten-year television rights deal valued at more than $400 million; and changed the club's designated control executive from owner Larry Dolan to his son, team chairman Paul Dolan.

Second, the Indians faced an uncertain future with their 2012 Snow Days winter carnival at Progressive Field after the second edition of this offseason attraction ended with another financial loss. The club had expanded Snow Days—which featured ice skating, tobogganing, and other winter activities at the ballpark—by nearly two weeks and added an outdoor college ice hockey game between the University of Michigan and Ohio State University and named it the Frozen Diamond Faceoff. While that game drew 25,864 and by itself was profitable, attendance for Snow Days fell to an undisclosed number below the previous year's 50,000 and also did not generate a profit. The Indians were hampered by an unusually mild winter that brought warm, rainy weather to much of the nation's Northeast and Midwest. The franchise's financial losses were mitigated somewhat by the value of marketing exposure for the team during the winter events, where it continually promoted the availability of tickets for the next MLB season.[17]

Third, during early 2016, Cleveland reorganized its Latin American Operations department following the departure of director Ramon Pena. After a meeting, Koby Perez was promoted to director of Latin American scouting and reports to director of baseball operations Matt Forman. The team, including Perez, has eleven full-time scouts and two part-time scouts in Latin America. John Mirabelli, senior director of scouting operations, will be involved in all aspects internationally and domestically of the Tribe's scouting department. Chris Antonetti, president of baseball operations, said that Julio Rangel—the organization's assistant field coordinator— will participate more in the team's Latin American interests in the 2016 season. In addition, the club is moving soon into a new baseball academy in the Dominican Republic with Rangel involved in that operation.

Fourth, there is a perception that the Indians, who annually have one of the lowest payrolls in MLB, make millions in profits—thanks to eight-figure checks they receive from television networks and revenue sharing. The reality, according to team president Mark Shapiro, is that the Tribe's much-maligned ownership has suffered plenty of losses over the years, and any profits the Dolans earn go back into the team.

According to Shapiro, most of the club's revenue is dependent on local revenue, which is largely determined by size and wealth of the population. A number that Shapiro cites in reference to the Indians' attendance decline is Cleveland's downtown population, though increasing to a record level—it now exceeds 13,000 and is projected to rise to 23,000 by 2020 according to the Downtown Cleveland Alliance—still pales in comparison to most major league cities. Two other factors are the drop in Fortune 500 companies in Northeast Ohio, and how Greater Cleveland's population compares with other cities that have at least three major professional sports teams.

Fifth, from 2015 to 2017, the Indians will implement a major overhaul of the company's disaster recovery and business continuity services, which are currently based at the team's player-development complex in Arizona. The complex is limited in its bandwidth infrastructure, so accessibility by fans has become a major challenge. The move to hybrid cloud and mobile are the latest steps in the Indians' ten-year partnership with VMware. The two companies are working to improve scalability and implement consolidation even as the team's infrastructure expands.[18]

The Indians will use VMware's vCloud Air in order to move to a hybrid cloud environment, which includes migrating their disaster recovery/business continuity services out of the player development complex into a facility that provides infrastructure-as-a-service (IaaS) or platform-as-a-service (PaaS) solutions. The vCloud Air system will help the Indians extend their data to the cloud—a ready-to-run cloud that can run any app, any place. With hybrid cloud and mobility, the franchise has a doubleheader of technologies to enhance their organization in the coming years.

Sixth, Tiffin University's School of Business partnered with the team in a mentoring program designed to improve students' sales skills, gain real world experience, and increase their networking opportunities. Two students competed both individually, and as a group, to sell tickets for Indians' home games during early spring of 2016. While the top salesperson received game tickets, shadow experiences, an interview with the Indians human resource department, and scoreboard recognition, the group champion got similar perks in addition to an opportunity to present its marketing project in front of the club's top executive personnel.

DETROIT TIGERS

In 1894, the Detroit Tigers played at Boulevard Park as a charter member of the WL. One year later, franchise owner George Vanderbeck decided to build his team a new 5,000-seat ballpark, named it Bennett Park, and located the building at the corner of Michigan and Trumbull Avenues. During late April 1896, they played their first game at Bennett Park and defeated the Columbus Senators. Often referred to as the Tigers, they originally got their name from a military unit called the Detroit Light Guard, which was nicknamed, "Tigers." While in the eight-team league from 1894 to 1899, Detroit finished third and fifth each twice, and also sixth and seventh.

The WL was renamed American League in 1900. Managed by George Stallings, the Tigers were fourth in the league's regular season but finished more than twelve games behind the champion Chicago White Stockings. After the season, the AL declared itself to be a "major" baseball league. On April 25, 1901, the Tigers played their first MLB game at home in Detroit's Bennett Park before 10,000 fans, and defeated the Milwaukee Brewers in a remarkable ninth-inning comeback.[19]

Team Performances

As a member of the AL from 1901 to 2015, which included twenty-nine years in the ED plus another eighteen in the CD, Detroit played 17,891 games and had victories in approximately 51 percent of them. During the period, they won seven division titles, eleven pennants, and four World Series while appearing in sixteen postseasons. Among other teams in the AL as of their 2015 season, the Tigers tied for eighth with the Red Sox, Indians, and Rangers in winning division titles and also ranked third in number of pennants and tied for seventh with the Athletics in World Series wins. In the league's CD, Detroit had more total championships than those of the White Sox, Indians, Royals, and Twins (Table A1).

Compared to twenty-nine other teams in MLB as of 2015, Detroit tied for fifteenth in division titles, ranked fourth in pennants, and tied for seventh in World Series victories. Besides winning championships in 1945, 1968, and 1983, the Tigers most successful periods consecutively included 1907–1909, when they appeared in but lost three World Series; 1934–1935, when they lost and then won a World Series; and 2011–2014, when they lost an AL divisional series and two championship series, and also a World Series.

Alternatively the Tigers did not make the playoffs during such periods as 1910–1933, 1946–1967, 1973–1983, and 1988–2005. Because of their different but mediocre managers, lack of talented players (including pitchers), and other problems, these clubs failed to win enough games to qualify for any postseasons. Despite finishing only fifth in the CD in MLB's 2015 season, Detroit should be competitive at least temporarily because of such players as slugger Miguel Cabrera, pitcher Justin Verlander, and infielder Ian Kinsler.

Franchise Owner

Born to Macedonian immigrants, Mike Illitch graduated from Detroit's Cooley High School and then spent four years in the U.S. Marine Corps. After returning home, he signed a baseball contract with the Detroit Tigers and played second base for a few years on a team in the minor leagues. However, his career as a player ended due to a knee injury.

After leaving baseball, Ilitch started a pizza business in 1959. With the help of his wife Marian, the Ilitches opened Little Caesars Pizza Treat in Garden City, Michigan. This business became the first of what would be thousands of pizza restaurants through franchising. Eventually the family expanded from that into other types of restaurants, sports teams, and various enterprises.

Ten years after purchasing the National Hockey League (NHL) Detroit Red Wings, Mike acquired the Detroit Tigers for $82 million from the founder of Domino's Pizza, Tom Monaghan. Because of disputes within his baseball organization and high players' salaries, he operated the Tigers at a loss and later even regretted buying the team. Nevertheless, Illitch became determined to be a successful MLB owner. He gradually withdrew from many of his duties at Little Caesars during the 1990s to concentrate on his sports teams, especially the Tigers. After failing to make the playoffs from 1992 to 2005, his Tigers teams were in five postseasons through 2015 and appeared in two World Series but lost both of them.

Compared to other owners of AL franchises as of 2015, Illitch's teams ranked third in number of division titles, tied for second with the Royals' David Glass and Ranger's Nolan Ryan in winning pennants, and tied for fifth with ten owners each with zero World Series victories. Among all MLB franchise owners, Illitch's Tigers were respectively sixth, tied for fifth, and tied for ninth. Consequently Mike's teams have performed above average particularly since 2006, in part, because of his competitiveness to win games, make savvy investments, implement efficient leadership strategies, and determination to succeed in the professional sports industry (Table A2).

Comerica Park

Prior to MLB's 2000 season, the Tigers played their home games in two ballparks. Chronologically these were Bennett Park (1901–1911) and then Navin Field (1912–1937)—renamed Briggs Stadium in 1938—and twenty-three years later, renamed again to Tiger Stadium. At each facility, the club's annual attendances ranged from a low of 2,200 to a high of 6,300 at Bennett Park; 203,000 to 1.1 million at Navin Field; 580,000 to 1.9 million at Briggs Stadium; and 816,000 to 2.7 million at Tiger Stadium.

In 1992, new owner Mike Illitch initiated many cosmetic improvements to the ballpark, primarily adding the Tiger Den and Tiger Plaza. While the former was an area in the lower deck between first and third base that had padded seats and waiters, Tiger Plaza was constructed in the old players' parking lot and consisted of many concessionaires and a gift shop.

After the 1994 MLB players' strike, plans were made by officials to construct a new ballpark in Detroit, although many fans in the community preferred and campaigned to save the old stadium. When the campaign failed after a few years, ground was broken and construction began during mid-to late 1997 to build a new ballpark and replace historic but outdated Tiger Stadium.

Completed for opening day in early April 2000, more than 40,000 fans attended the Tigers first game at Comerica Park. Consisting of three levels, almost every seat in the main grandstand has a view of downtown Detroit. Fans can walk along the main concourse without losing sight of the playing field. In center field, there are several fountains that produce liquid fireworks after a home run. Along the left-center field wall are statues of such Hall of Fame players as Ty Cobb, Al Kaline, and Hank Greenberg. Besides a large HD video scoreboard, the ballpark includes a Ferris wheel and merry-go-round.

In comparison to other ballparks in the AL as of 2015, Comerica Park ranked fifth in construction cost at $300 million and fourth in value at $247 million. Among all those in MLB, the ballpark was respectively thirteenth and ninth. Thus, the Tigers play their home games in an above-average and more expensive facility that do the majority of other clubs in the league's CD and also of at least three in the ED and four in the WD (Table A3).

As previously discussed for the White Sox's U.S. Cellular Field and Indians' Progressive Field, FCIs were calculated for Comerica Park from the Tigers' 2011 to 2015 seasons. For a family to attend a regular-season home game in Detroit, the costs ranged from a low of $207 in 2011 and also 2013 to a high of $233 in 2012. During this period among ballparks of fourteen AL clubs, its FCI ranked between third in 2012 ($233) and 2014 ($219) to seventh in 2013 ($207). In the league's CD, the Tigers' Comerica Park had the highest FCI during two seasons but less than the Twins' Target Field in other years (Table A4).

To reveal specific costs for a recent year in MLB, Comerica Field's FCI in 2015 (ranked thirteenth) was approximately $214 or about 2 percent less than in 2014. Listed from most to least in amount by item for one person, the team's nonpremium tickets averaged about $29, parking one vehicle $20, a cap $16, single beer $5, and a hot dog and soft drink each between $4 and $5. For other clubs in the CD, their ballpark's FCIs and ranks were respectively the Twins' $229 and eighth, Royals' $213 and fourteenth, White Sox's $208 and seventeenth, and Indians' $166 and twenty-sixth.

The average premium ticket cost approximately $73 at Comerica Park in 2015. Although that price was 24 percent or $23 less than the league's amount, it was higher than premium seats at Twins and Indians home games but less than those of the Royals and White Sox. Thus, the Tigers organization sets prices for nonpremium and premium seats based on demand and other factors in order to earn the most revenue and also to collect more gate receipts and income from their operations in a season.

In a recent study by CSN Mid-Atlantic, Comerica Park ranked twelfth in MLB. According to the author of an article published online in *USA Today*:

> You wouldn't think downtown Detroit would make for much of a backdrop, but you'd be surprised. Comerica Park is another hidden gem, a well-thought-out, well-executed ballpark that makes Detroit look good. It's the little things that complete it: The stone tigers that encompass the park, the home plate-shaped dirt, the retired numbers and names above the outfield wall. It may not be enough to revitalize a devastated downtown area, but it is most definitely reason to visit the Motor City.[20]

Financial Data

Besides competing as big-league teams in regular-season and postseason games, MLB franchises are also commercial enterprises. To reveal and manage these activities, this section focuses on different parts of the Tigers as a business enterprise and how effectively its organization succeeds or does not succeeds from a financial perspective.

According to data and other financial information published in *Forbes* for franchises in the AL as of their 2015 season, Detroit ranked fifth both in market value at $1.125 billion and revenue at $254 million, and also fifteenth in operating income at –$20.7 million, fourth in gate receipts at $84 million, and tied for fourth with the Orioles each with a debt-to-value ratio of 15 percent. Among four other CD teams, the Tigers had the most market value, revenue and gate receipts, but also the largest operating loss and second highest debt percent (Table A5).

Compared to twenty-nine other MLB franchises in 2015, Detroit was thirteenth in market value and revenue, twenty-ninth in operating income, tenth in gate receipts, and tied for twelfth in its debt-to-value ratio. Based on these results, the Tigers are a valuable team that continues to generate above-average amounts of revenue and gate receipts. However, the club had too much debt and not enough cash flows from its operations in 2015 to earn any profits. From a financial perspective, owner Mike Illitch's staff needs to better control the team's expenses and limit its proportion of debt.

Besides market size, salary inflation, and other factors, an MLB team's annual payroll partly reflects its commitment to players and their current and potential contribution individually and as a group to winning games in regular seasons and postseasons. From 2011 to 2015, for example, the Tigers payroll among fifteen AL teams ranged in rank from second in 2014 ($163 million) and 2015 ($172 million) to sixth in 2011 ($105 million). Compared to other CD clubs, Detroit's payrolls increased from third in 2011 to first during 2012–2015. This data, in part, explains why the Tigers qualified for four consecutive playoffs and won one AL pennant in five recent MLB seasons (Table A6).

With respect to amounts for twenty-nine other teams during the period, the Tigers' payrolls were fourth and fifth each twice and also tied for tenth in 2011. Along with high payrolls of the AL Yankees and Red Sox, and NL Dodgers and Giants, the Tigers were successful in their performances after negotiating salaries and compensating such outstanding players as Miguel Cabrera, Justin Verlander, Victor Martinez, and former, but now Washington Nationals pitcher, Max Scherzer.

Business Relations

Besides regular-season and postseason games, MLB franchises are involved in—and also affected by—community events and internal and external business-related affairs, deals, and projects. The following are a few of these activities for Detroit's AL team.[21]

First, although eighty-plus-years-old, Mike Ilitch is emotionally and financially vested in his team but nevertheless has decided to maintain a lower profile. He rarely gives interviews to the media, and some of his children have assumed part of the leadership responsibilities of the family's sports teams. On a recent morning in Boca Raton, Florida, Mike and his wife Marian welcomed a reporter into their winter home. For ninety minutes, Mike shared his memories of building the family pizza business, realizing a dream by owning the Red Wings and then Tigers, and keeping a civic commitment to his beloved city. It was evident that they enjoyed a true partnership as a family and also with their businesses for decades.[22]

Second, buoyed by a tight race in the league's CD during the 2012 season plus Miguel Cabrera's effort to compete for baseball's first Triple Crown since 1967, the Tigers were poised to win MLB's local television ratings crown. With about two weeks left in the regular season, the team's games on Fox Sports (FS) Detroit were on pace to be the highest in Tigers history. These averaged a 9.13 rating, which was a huge 42 percent increase from 2011. The 168,000 average homes that tuned into Tigers games became the third-highest audience in MLB. "A lot of great story lines have captured the attention of the team's fans and that was reflected in the ratings" said Greg Hammaren, senior vice president and general manager of FS Detroit.[23]

Third, in 2010 the Tigers refinanced $130 million of their debt, signaling that sports finance continued to rebound from the depths of the national recession. This was also the first such deal since the resolution of the Texas Rangers' contentious bankruptcy and franchise sale, though the Tigers' refinancing had been negotiated for some time. There were worries that MLB's adversarial position against lenders in the Rangers' saga would prove problematic for future baseball financing. Indeed, there was a great deal of negotiation between MLB and the Tigers' main lender, Sumitomo Mitsui, about rights the league had in the event of default by the team.

These rights, outlined in what was known as a "consent letter," took up thirteen more pages than they did in the Tigers' original loan twelve years earlier. It could not be determined what information was in the extra pages, but MLB in the Rangers' case asserted its rights to push through the sale of the club to its preferred buyer despite any objections from lenders. Ultimately, a bankruptcy court ordered an auction, which resulted in a sale to the MLB-preferred ownership group led by Chuck Greenberg and Nolan Ryan.

The Tigers' deal, however, was an operating company loan, which meant that all of it is lent directly to the club. In the Rangers' deal, most of the debt was lent above the team, and MLB and the team argued that lenders were entitled only to the amount directly lent to the club. In Detroit's case, if the team were to bankrupt, the matter would be more straightforward because the lien held against the team equals the amount of the loan.

Fourth, the decision by owner Mike Ilitch to fire president, CEO, and general manager Dave Dombrowski in early August 2015 was a surprise and caused negative reactions in the baseball community but also altered the team's front-office organizational chart. Getting all the attention was Ilitch's decision to replace Dombrowski after fourteen seasons with longtime assistant general manager Al Avila, who became the full-time general manager and an executive vice president.

But in the announcement about Dombrowski and Avila was a sentence noting that Duane McLean, the team's executive vice president of business operations, would report directly to Ilitch. That gave McLean—who declined to comment about it to the press—an increased profile as the organization decided how to plot its financial future. With Illitch's support, he will be the top Tigers front-office executive when the team negotiates perhaps its most important contract. That is the franchise's local television broadcast rights deal.

Fifth, as of late 2015, the state's Pure Michigan travel and tourism campaign continued during Tigers games at Comerica Park and at Michigan International Speedway (MIS) during the annual NASCAR event in August 2016. The Michigan Strategic Fund board, which controls the marketing effort's purse strings, approved extensions for the Pure Michigan branding deals at both venues. Pure Michigan will spend $325,000 annually over three years under a marketing relationship originally established in 2012 with the Tigers. The company will also spend $700,000 in 2016 and $750,000 in 2017 to remain the title sponsor of the Pure Michigan 400 race at MIS.

At Comerica Park, the Pure Michigan logo is on bench backs and railings in both teams' dugouts, and behind home plate during the Tigers' home games as part of an ad rotation aimed at television viewers. It was on a light tower in right field through 2014. The deal also includes ten thirty-second Pure Michigan ads on the team's in-house TigerVision that appears on the 300-plus television monitors throughout the ballpark during games, and also on thirty fifteen-second digital banner ads according to the campaign's memo to the Michigan Strategic Fund.

Sixth, owner Mike Illitch is determined to bring a World Series championship to Detroit, and to do so, he opened his checkbook. ESPN's Buster Olney believes that while Justin Upton improves the Tigers, his $132.75 million, five-year contract is bad business. Besides Upton, Detroit also has major contractual obligations with Miguel Cabrera ($240 million through 2023); Jordan Zimmerman ($110 million over five years); Justin Verlander (four years each at $28 million); Anibal Sanchez ($16.8 million in 2016 and 2017 with a $16 million option or $5 million buyout in 2018); and Victor Martinez ($18 million in each of three seasons). Although Illitch seems to have little concern about payroll, these massive contracts could pay off in future seasons. The team, however, may find itself in a gigantic hole financially when its players cannot produce at a high level.

KANSAS CITY ROYALS

The AL's Athletics (A's) moved from Philadelphia, Pennsylvania, to Kansas City, Missouri, in 1955. But after thirteen dismal seasons, the club relocated from there to Oakland, California. Thus, the Midwestern city was left without a professional minor or major league baseball team for the first time since 1883, which was a year before the Kansas City Cowboys played in the twelve-team Union Association.

As a result of the A's decision to relocate, Missouri Senator Stuart Symington threatened to introduce legislation removing baseball's antitrust exemption unless Kansas City was granted a team in MLB's next expansion. At its winter meetings in 1967, MLB responded to the Senator's threat by awarding both Kansas City and Seattle, Washington expansion teams to open in the league's 1971 season.

Not satisfied with having Kansas City wait three years for professional baseball to return, Symington pressured MLB to allow the new teams to start playing in 1969. This shortcut, in turn, may have contributed to the financial collapse of the AL's Seattle Pilots, who had to play before they were ready to be competitive.

For a fee of $5.5 million, pharmaceutical executive Ewing Kauffman won the bidding rights for the new Kansas City franchise. He nicknamed his team the "Royals" after the American Royal—a livestock show, horse show, and rodeo held annually in Kansas City since 1899. The team's logo, a crown atop a shield with the letters "KC" inside the shield, was created by Hallmark Cards' artist Shannon Manning, who lived in the city. Initially the club played its home games in 17,500-seat Municipal Stadium and later in 37,900-seat Royals Stadium, which in 1993, was renamed Kauffman Stadium.[24]

Team Performances

As a member of the AL from 1969 to 2015 and specifically in the league's CD for twenty-two years, the Royals played 7,475 games and achieved victories in approximately 48 percent of them. In forty-seven total MLB seasons, they won eight division titles, four pennants, and two World Series in nine postseasons. Among fourteen other AL teams as of their 2015 season, Kansas City ranked seventh in number of division titles, eighth in winning pennants, and tied for seventh with the Blue Jays, Indians, and Twins in World Series victories. Compared to only the league's CD teams, the Royals had fewer total championships than the Tigers and Twins but an equal number as the White Sox and Indians (Table A1).

Regarding all MLB clubs as of 2015, Kansas City tied for thirteenth with the NL Pirates in winning division titles, ranked seventeenth in number of pennants, and tied for twelfth with several other teams in World Series titles. The Royals, therefore, have been average in their performances while playing clubs in the league's CD and also others in the AL and throughout MLB.

Kansas City's teams were in consecutive postseasons and most successful during periods 1976–1978, 1980–1981, 1984–1985, and 2014–2015. Indeed, they won World Series in 1985 and 2015 but lost them in 1980 and 2014. Besides Hall of Famer George Brett, a few of their top players were Amos Otis, Willie Wilson, Bud Black, Alex Gordon, and Lorenzo Cain. Alternatively, the club failed to make playoffs in such back-to-back seasons as 1969–1975, 1982–1983, and 1986–2013. In fact, the Royals were frequently in third, fourth, or fifth place of their division. To become competitive and win more championships, the club needs smarter managers, productive players, and improvements at various positions on the ballfield.

Franchise Owner

The son of Marvin Glass and Myrtle Van Winkle, David Glass was born on a farm in Oregon County, Missouri, and grew up in Mountain View, Missouri.

Years later, he graduated from Missouri State University in Springfield. The school's Glass Hall, which contains business and management classes for undergraduate and graduate students, was named after him.

Before buying the Royals franchise in 2000 for $96 million, David was a longtime executive at Walmart. His career there lasted twenty-five years after serving in several different high-ranking positions. The first half of it at Walmart was spent in the accounting and finance departments—primarily as vice chairman, chief financial officer, and executive vice president of finance.

In 1988, Glass was promoted to president and CEO—a position he held for twelve years until stepping down to purchase the Royals. He was a key figure in Walmart's ascension to the top of the retail world and as a top executive, focused on increasing the company's shareholder value while maximizing its profit. After being named Retailer of the Year by members of the retail industry in 1986 and 1991, he was inducted into the Retail Hall of Fame in 2000. A member of the Board of Walmart Stores since 1977, his fortune came primarily from stock options and bonuses.

Among principal owners of AL franchises as of 2015, Glass's teams tied for thirteenth in division titles with those of the Blue Jays' Edward Rogers, tied for second in pennants with those of the Tigers' Mike Illitch and Rangers' Nolan Ryan, and tied for second in World Series with those of the Yankees' Hal Steinbrenner and White Sox's Jerry Reinsdorf. Compared to twenty-nine other owners in MLB, Glass's Royals were respectively tied for twenty-first in division titles, tied for fifth in winning pennants, and tied for fourth in total championships (Table A2).

As of 2013, some baseball experts considered Glass to be one of the worst owners in MLB because the Royals' payroll had consistently shrunk; he did not spend enough money on quality free agents that the team needed to compete despite having a good core of young and talented hitters; and because he took one of the most successful teams of the early to mid-1980s and fifteen years later operated it inefficiently. Rather than invest money from revenue-sharing into the franchise, he may have simply kept and/or squandered a major part of it. Recently, however, his status among owners significantly improved because his Royals teams appeared in two World Series and won one of them in 2015 after losing the other in 2014.

Kauffman Stadium

Municipal Stadium was the home site of baseball's Kansas City Athletics (1955–1967) and the Royals (1969–1972), Negro League's Monarchs during 1923–1931 and 1937–1954, and the NFL Kansas City Chiefs from 1963 to 1971. While the gridiron at Municipal Stadium extended over the baseball diamond into right-centerfield, portable bleachers were placed in left field. In 1976, the building was demolished and the area containing it redeveloped to become a single-family housing neighborhood.

Construction on the Truman Sports Complex, which included the Royals' ballpark and also Kansas City Chiefs' Arrowhead Stadium, began during mid-July 1968. Originally known as Royals Stadium—then Kauffman Stadium from 1993 to 2015—the team played its first game there in April 1973. The ballpark is very colorful with approximately 40,793 seats, all facing second base and arranged in three tiers in such colors as maroon, gold, and orange. It was the AL's first ballpark with Astroturf as the playing surface. The most unique feature of the stadium is the water fountains beyond the outfield fence since people know Kansas City as the "City of Fountains." The fountains stretch more than three-hundred feet horizontally and have a ten-foot-high waterfall that descends from an upper cascade pool that serves as a background for two water pools. A twelve-story scoreboard, in the shape of the Royals' crest, is located beyond the center field fence.

From 2007 to 2009, the Royals sponsored a two-year, $256 million renovation of Kauffman Stadium. Phase I of it included new bullpens, expansion of seats in the Crown Club and Dugout Suites, and an LED auxiliary scoreboard in the left field wall. The crown scoreboard in centerfield was replaced by a new high definition video scoreboard. Renovations continued on to the dugout level concourse and exterior work to widen concourses at all levels and also on the outfield plaza to connect the entire ballpark. Other attractions for fans at Kauffman Stadium include a kids' area known as the "Little K," a right field sports-bar themed restaurant named Taste of KC, and the Royals' Hall of Fame in left field. Because of these renovations, the ballpark's capacity has increased to 38,200.

Compared to ballparks of fourteen other AL teams as of 2015, Kauffman Stadium ranked fourth at forty-four-years-old, sixth in construction cost at $272 million, and twelfth in value at $134 million. Among those of all MLB clubs, the Royals' home was sixth in age, sixteenth in cost, and twenty-sixth in value. According to these results, Kansas City's stadium is attractive and colorful, but likely an outdated facility for spectators (Table A3).

Similar to the ballparks of the CD's White Sox, Indians, Tigers, and later Twins, FCIs were calculated for Kauffman Stadium from the Royals' 2011 to 2015 seasons. For a family to attend a regular-season home game there, the costs ranged from a low of $160 in 2011 to $213 in 2015. During this five-year period in the AL, its FCIs ranked between sixth in 2015 to twelfth in 2012 and 2013. Among only CD teams, baseball games at Kauffman Stadium and the Indians' Progressive Field were least expensive of the group in 2011 through 2015 (Table A4).

To reveal specific costs for a recent year in MLB, Kauffman Stadium's FCI in 2015 (ranked fourteenth) was approximately $22 or about 11 percent more than in 2014. Listed from most to least in amount by item for one person, the team's nonpremium tickets averaged between $29 and $30, a cap $15, parking one vehicle $10, beer $6–$7, and a hot dog and soft drink each $5. That year it cost relatively more, therefore, for fans to attend Tigers' and Twins' home games but not those of the White Sox and Indians.

With their average premium tickets priced at $105 each in 2015, the Royals had the eighth highest cost in MLB and greater than the White Sox's $88, Twins' $74, Tigers' $73, and Indians' $59. Based on these and other amounts, Kansas City maximizes its revenue and earns enough from gate receipts to continue its business operations in regular seasons at Kauffman Stadium.

In a recent study by CSN Mid-Atlantic, Kauffman Stadium ranked ninth in MLB. According to an article published online in *USA Today*:

> Perhaps the most under-appreciated ballpark in the majors, Kauffman Stadium is an anomaly. Built in the early '70s when so many cookie-cutter, multi-purpose stadiums opened, it is a baseball-only ballpark that has stood the test of time quite well. The Royals did some renovations a few years ago, including the removal of some of the famed fountains beyond the outfield fence (I wish they kept them all), but the place didn't need a whole lot of work. It may be 41 years old, but it's still a great place to watch a ballgame, and testament to some smart design from a couple generations ago.[25]

Financial Data

Besides competing as teams in regular-season and postseason games, MLB franchises are also commercial enterprises. To reveal and manage these activities, this section focuses on different parts of the Royals' business model and how efficiently it succeeds or does not succeed from a financial perspective.

According to data and other financial information published in *Forbes* for franchises in the AL as of their 2015 season, Kansas City ranked fourteenth in market value, eighth in revenue, fourth in operating income, seventh in gate receipts, and tied for eighth with the Athletics both with debt-to-value ratios of 8 percent. Although the Royals had the second-lowest estimated net worth as an enterprise in the league, their other amounts were above average and even impressive for a small-market team (Table A5).

Among twenty-nine other MLB franchises in 2015, Kansas City was twenty-eighth in market value but also sixteenth in revenue, eleventh in operating income, fourteenth in gate receipts, and tied for seventeenth with the Athletics and NL Phillies in percent of debt-to-value. Except for their relatively low market value, the Royals ranked second in revenue and operating income, and also third in gate receipts among CD teams. Despite not being a highly valued franchise, Kansas City is at least average in other financial results and more successful as a business than several midsized teams. These results reflect owner David Glass and his experience, knowledge, leadership, and success as a former chief executive of Walmart Stores.

Besides population size, salary inflation, and other factors, an MLB team's annual payroll partly reflects its commitment to players and their current and potential contribution individually and as a group to winning games in regular seasons and postseasons. From 2011 to 2015, for example, the Royals' payrolls among AL teams ranged in rank from ninth in 2013 ($78 million) and 2015 ($112 million) to fourteenth in 2011 ($36 million). Compared to four other CD clubs, Kansas City's payrolls grew from fifth in 2011 to second in 2015. This increase, in part, explains why the Royals had a winning record during three consecutive seasons (2013–2015) and appeared in two World Series after finishing only fourth and then third in the CD during respectively 2011 and 2012 (Table A6).

Relative to amounts for twenty-nine other teams during the five-year period, the Royals' payrolls were as high as seventeenth in 2013 and 2015 and lowest as thirtieth in 2011. In other words, owner David Glass became increasingly more generous and awarded his players based on their ability to contribute runs and win additional games in regular seasons and series in postseasons. This was a successful and profitable strategy for the franchise after finishing only fourth or fifth in the CD during 2004–2011. Regarding the 2016, 2017, and 2018 MLB seasons, it will be interesting to compare how competitive the Royals are in their division and league given changes in their players' payrolls.

Business Relations

Besides performances in their regular-season and postseason games, MLB franchises are involved in—and also affected by—different community events and also internal and external business-related affairs, deals, and projects. The following are a few of these topics for Kansas City's AL team.[26]

First, after extracting themselves from a massive sea of blue at the championship parade following baseball's 2015 season, the Royals' vice president of marketing and business development Mike Bucek and his colleagues were back in their offices facing a simple, almost overwhelming question: How do we top 2015? In ways beyond the club's first World Series title in thirty years, the team was one of baseball's top business stories throughout the year. For example, it set a franchise attendance record of 2.71 million; posted the largest attendance increase of any team; led all MLB clubs in local-market television ratings; and sent the most starters to the all-star game in Cincinnati. Indeed, the local-market television results—a sixty rating and an eighty share for the Royals' clinching of Game 5—were a powerful story.

Second, following their first World Series appearance in twenty-nine years in 2014, the Royals organization anticipated positive effects on attendance and sponsorships traditionally enjoyed by upstart playoff clubs. But some of that expected growth will not come from the Kansas City area. Rather, club executives began to target such cities as Omaha, Nebraska; Wichita and Topeka, Kansas; Des Moines, Iowa; and even Little Rock, Arkansas, as potentially new revenue sources. Taken together, those outer markets historically have represented a mid-single-digit percentage of the team's attendance base. But with the surprise postseason run in 2014—only the Royals' third winning season since 1995—these outer markets could eventually grow into more than 10 percent of the team's total revenue.

Third, the Royals had an opportunity for another big honor in 2015 if they won *Sports Illustrated's* Sportsman of the Year Award. Unable to choose only one player, *Sports Illustrated* nominated the entire team as one of twelve contenders for the award that included Ronda Rousey, Serena Williams, Jordan Spieth, American Pharoah, Lionel Messi, Novak Djokovic, Carli Lloyd, Steph Curry, Usain Bolt, Simone Biles, and Thomas Davis.

The sport magazine's Richard Ditch wrote about the Royals' World Series victory as follows: "Fueled by a heartbreaking loss to the [San Francisco] Giants in the 2014 World Series, the Royals played a thrilling brand of aggressive baseball on their way to winning their first World Series since 1985. They came-from-behind against the [Houston] Astros in the AL Division Series, knocked off the [Toronto] Blue Jays in six games in the AL championship series, and finally rolled over the NL [New York] Mets in five games." However, because she won three Grand Slam titles, finished with a 53–3 record and ranked number one in the world for the fifth time in her career, Serena Williams won Sportsman of the Year award.[27]

Fourth, at the beginning of the offseason in late 2015, the Royals' general manager Dayton Moore and owner David Glass promised to re-sign free-agent leftfielder Alex Gordon. Coming off a World Series victory, everyone was riding a wave of emotion, and these promises might have occurred in the heat of the moment. However, as the offseason continued, speculation indicated that Gordon would sign a five-year, $100 million contract, at a minimum. Then a report denoted that the team had no chance after offering him a four-year deal worth from $48 to $52 million. During early 2016, the Royals kept their promise. With a new four-year, $72 million contract, Gordon will remain with the Royals until he is thirty-five-years-old.

Fifth, during 2010 Royals general manager Dayton Moore hired Ned Yost to manage a rebuilding project that was treading water and losing public approval. In the seasons since then, the two forged a symbiotic relationship that served as a backbone for two World Series appearances and the franchise's first world championship in three decades. Then during mid-February 2016, Moore and Yost shared the same decision again. As pitchers and catchers reported to spring training, the club announced contract extensions that could keep them together with the Royals for at least three seasons. The sixty-one-year-old Yost, whose contract was set to expire after the 2016 season, agreed to an extension through 2018. Although Moore also agreed to an extension, the club did not reveal his deal's years.

MINNESOTA TWINS

Founded in 1900 by a syndicate headed by sports entrepreneur Ban Johnson, the Washington Senators played in the AL and won a World Series in 1924 but then lost others in 1925 and 1933. When principal owner Clark Griffith—who purchased the franchise during the 1910s—died in 1955, he left his 50 percent share of it to his nephew Calvin.

After Calvin sold Griffith Stadium to the city of Washington and then leased it back, some fans speculated that the team was planning to move as did the Boston Braves, St. Louis Browns, and Philadelphia Athletics in the early 1950s. Following an early flirtation with San Francisco—where the New York Giants moved after their 1957 season—Griffith began courting Minneapolis-St. Paul. This was a prolonged process that resulted in his rejecting the Twin Cities' first offer before agreeing to relocate there. Although the league initially opposed it, a deal was made in October 1960 whereby the Senators would move from Washington to the Minneapolis-St. Paul area and then be replaced by a new Senators team in 1961.

The NBA Minneapolis Lakers relocated to Los Angeles in 1960 due to poor attendance which was caused, in part, by the reluctance of fans in St. Paul to support the team. Griffith was determined not to alienate fans in either city so he refused to name his team after one city or the other, so he chose "Twin Cities Twins."

When MLB objected to that title, Griffith renamed it Minnesota Twins However, the team was allowed to keep its original insignia—TC for Twin Cities—on its baseball caps. Eagerly greeted in Minnesota after arriving in 1961, the club brought a nucleus of talented players from Washington such as sluggers Harmon Killebrew and Bob Allison; infielders Zoilo Versalles and Hal Naragon; and pitchers Camilio Pascual and Jim Kaat.[28]

Team Performances

A member of the AL (1961–1968) and then the league's West Division (1969–1993) and finally the CD (1994–2015), the Twins played 8,771 games and had victories in approximately 49 percent of them. In eleven playoff appearances, they won ten division titles, three pennants, and two World Series. Compared to performances of other AL teams as of their 2015 season, Minnesota ranked respectively third, ninth, and tied for seventh with the Blue Jays, Indians, and Royals. Among only CD teams, it had fewer total championships than the Tigers but more than the White Sox, Indians, and Royals (Table A1).

In contrast to all MLB clubs as of 2015, the Twins were eighth in division titles and also were eighteenth in winning pennants and tied for twelfth with several other teams in number of World Series championships. Except for division titles, Minnesota's performances have been average during its fifty-five seasons in the big-leagues.

Besides winning World Series in 1987 and 1991, the club's most successful years consecutively were 1969–1970, 2002–2004, and 2009–2010. During these periods, such players as Tony Oliva, Kirby Puckett, and Joe Mauer had outstanding seasons as hitters while pitchers Jim Perry, Frank Viola, and Johan Santana led in number of wins. Alternatively, Minnesota was least successful in such back-to-back years as 1961–1964, 1971–1986, 1992–2001, and 2011–2015. These Twins teams were not consistent and failed to make the playoffs because of management problems, poor player performances, and competition in their division from the White Sox, Indians, Tigers, and Royals, and also from clubs in the league's ED and WD.

Franchise Owner

In 1984, Minnesota billionaire-banker Carl Pohlad purchased the Twins franchise from Calvin Griffith and other minority owners for approximately $38–$44 million. After Carl died in 2009, his son Jim inherited the team. To prepare for a career, he earned a business administration degree at the University of California and later became a certified public accountant.

Besides serving as president of Starquest Securities LLC and as vice president and director of the Pohlad's various businesses, Jim was an owner and chairman of the board and also executive vice president of Marquette Financial Companies. While there, he led the acquisition of several fast-growing specialty finance organizations to expand Marquette's products into such areas as automobiles, equipment, construction, land development, and commercial real estate financing. His civic activities have included work on behalf of organizations and programs that support the well-being and interests of children and families in the Twin Cities and surrounding communities.

When his dad Carl acquired the Twins, Jim was an analyst who did financial planning and projections for the baseball organization. For example, he estimated the team's revenue stream and remembers when its payroll and revenue amounts were about equal. To Jim, this meant financial break-even for the club especially from the mid- to late 1980s into the 1990s. During the early 2000s, he was active in helping the city build a new ballpark and later committed an additional $55 million to providing Target Field with such amenities as Kasota Stone siding, a full roof canopy, and construction of Target Plaza outside the stadium.

Compared to the results of other AL franchise owners as of 2015, Jim Pohlad's Twins tied for second with two division titles, and also tied for eighth in the league with zero pennants and for fifth with zero World Series. Among all MLB owners, his Minnesota clubs since 2009 had respectively tied for twelfth, tied for fourteenth, and tied for ninth. In the CD, Pohlad's Twins had won fewer total championships than did owner Reinsdorf's White Sox, Illitch's Tigers, and Glass's Royals but the same number as Dolan's Indians. Based on his club's performances since 2009, Jim has been a mediocre but not an above-average or superior owner (Table A2).

Target Field

From 1961 to 1981, the Twins played their home games at 48,000-seat Metropolitan Stadium and then another twenty-eight seasons at the 46,500-seat Hubert H. Humphrey Metrodome. After experiencing problems with the latter ballpark including its deterioration and inability to generate enough revenue for the franchise, the state's legislature approved financing for the construction of a new ballpark in May 2006. According to the legislation, the county's share was about two-thirds of the cost while the Twins paid for the other portion of it. In September 2008, the Target Corporation acquired naming rights for twenty-five years at Target Field in downtown Minneapolis.

The 40,000-seat ballpark, which reflects Minnesota's urban sophistication and outdoor vitality, has a facade that consists of limestone while a canopy covers much of the upper deck seats. Most fans enter the building through Target Plaza—a parklike space located outside the right field entrance gate. This landscaped area features a 1,500-pound bronze glove, statues of famous Twins players, and a wall tribute to Minnesota ballparks and Metropolitan Stadium.

Besides heated concessions, restrooms, a restaurant, and also lounge areas on each level of the ballpark, fans can gather for food and beverages inside the Legends Club Lounge, the Met Club, and the Town Ball Tavern, which celebrates Minnesota's amateur baseball history. Themed concessions are also located throughout Target Field including Taste of Twins territory, Hennepin Grille, Senior Smokes, and Frankie V's Italian.

Before MLB's 2016 season, the Twins reconfigured the center field seating area into a multilevel fan space. Located directly below the Minnie and Paul figures in center field, the area features a Twins-themed pub with Minnesota-branded food options on the upper level. Named "CATCH," the lower level area is premium space for season ticket members.

Compared to fourteen other AL ballparks as of 2015, Target Field ranked third in construction cost at $435 million and seventh in value at $183 million. Among all MLB stadiums, the Twins' ballpark was sixth in cost and seventeenth in value. Thus, this is a more expensive facility than those of clubs in the CD and a majority of them in the league, but only average in value as an asset relative to twenty-nine other teams' ballparks (Table A3).

As previously discussed for ballparks of four other CD teams, FCIs were calculated for Target Field from the Twins' 2011 to 2015 seasons. For a family to attend a regular-season home game in Minneapolis, the costs ranged for them from a low of $213 in 2011 to a high of $229 in 2015. During the period in the AL, the ballpark's FCIs ranked between third in 2015 to sixth in 2013 and 2014. Among only CD teams, baseball games at Target Field were more expensive than those at Cleveland's Progressive Field and Kansas City's Kauffman Stadium but comparable in cost to games at Chicago's U.S. Cellular Field and Detroit's Comerica Park (Table A4).

To reveal specific costs for a recent year in MLB, Target Field's FCI in 2015 (ranked tenth) was approximately $229 or about 7 percent more than in 2014. Listed from most to least in amount by item for one person, the team's nonpremium tickets averaged between $32 and $33, a single cap $20, beer $8, parking one vehicle $6, and a hot dog and soft drink each about $5. In comparison, the Twins' FCI exceeded MLB's by $18 or 8 percent.

The average premium ticket cost approximately $74 at Target Field in 2015. Although that price was 23 percent or $22 less than MLB's average amount, it was higher than premium seats at Tigers and Indians home games but less than those of the Royals and White Sox. Thus, the Twins set prices of their nonpremium and premium seats at their home games to increase attendance, maximize revenue, and earn greater gate receipts from their operations. Otherwise, Minnesota sports fans might prefer to see local games of the NFL Vikings and/or NBA Timberwolves.

In a recent study by CSN Mid-Atlantic, Target Field ranked seventh in MLB. According to an article published online in *USA Today*:

> I had heard great things about the Twins' new park before seeing it for myself last week, and it didn't disappoint. This is a really, really nice ballpark in a very nice city. The best touches, in my opinion: The limestone backstop and wall

next to the left-field foul pole, the overhanging upper decks in the outfield that make the place feel like something of a caldron and, of course, the great Twins logo high above center field, with Mr. Minneapolis and Mr. Saint Paul shaking hands across the Mississippi River.[29]

Financial Data

Besides competing as teams in regular-season and postseason games, MLB franchises are also commercial enterprises. To reveal and manage these activities, this section focuses on different parts of the Twins' business model and how efficient the organization succeeds or does not succeed from a financial perspective.

According to data and other financial information published in *Forbes* for franchises in the AL as of their 2015 season, Minnesota ranked ninth in market value at $895 million, eleventh in revenue at $223 million, seventh in operating income at $21.3 million, sixth in gate receipts at $71 million, and also second with a debt-to-value ratio of 25 percent. Among CD clubs the Twins, for example, had a lower market value and less revenue than the White Sox and Tigers with different amounts of operating income and gate receipts, but also the highest debt percent of the group (Table A5).

Compared to all MLB teams as of 2015, the Twins' amounts were respectively eighteenth, twenty-third, fifteenth, twenty-third, and fifth. Except for its debt ratio, Minnesota is an average franchise from a financial perspective and as a business enterprise. To improve financially among other clubs in their division and league, the Twins need to reduce debt and/or increase their market value by successfully competing in regular-season games and qualify for more postseasons in order to win another championship.

Besides population growth, salary inflation, and other factors, an MLB team's annual payroll partly reflects its commitment to players and their current and potential contribution individually and as a group to winning games in regular seasons and postseasons. From 2011 to 2015, for example, the Twins' payroll among AL teams ranged in rank from fifth in 2011 ($112 million) and 2012 ($112 million) to thirteenth in 2014 ($72 million). Compared to four other CD clubs, Minnesota's payrolls were second and third each twice and fourth once. For one or more reasons including their disappointing performances and more improvements in financial accounts and statements, Twins owner Jim Pohlad decided to significantly reduce his team's payroll after the 2012 season (Table A6).

Given amounts for twenty-nine other teams during the period, the Twins' payrolls were ninth twice and then twenty-second in 2013, twenty-fourth in 2014, and nineteenth in 2015. After ranking in the top third of all MLB clubs for two years, Minnesota changed its strategy regarding the compensation of players and therefore ended in or near the bottom one-third of all teams from 2013 to 2015. During the five-year period of performances, the Twins had four consecutive losing seasons but then finished second in the CD when their players' payroll increased by $36 million or 50 percent in 2015.

Business Relations

In addition to regular-season and postseason games, MLB franchises are involved in—and also affected by—different community events and also recent internal and external business-related affairs, deals, and projects. The following are a few of these news items for Minnesota's AL team.[30]

First, the Twins operate out of baseball's coastal limelight and entered 2015 with four straight losing seasons. Yet, the club was widely respected thanks in part to a highly regarded ballpark experience at Target Field, successful staging of the 2014 MLB All Star game, and an organizational philosophy of being early adopters in many league efforts including MLB Advanced Media's push toward mobile ticketing and iBeacon technology. Laura Day, the club's executive vice president of business development, is an organization superstar. She joined the club during its 1991 championship season and is well into her second stint after brief periods with the neighboring Women's National Basketball Association's Minnesota Lynx and former Victory Sports. Working closely with team president Dave St. Peter, Day oversees a broad portfolio that includes ticketing, marketing, sales, corporate partnerships, and stadium operations. As a business leader, she is fair, open-minded, and collaborative.[31]

Second, the Twins suffered a revenue loss of at least seven figures in 2013 because of snow and rain plaguing their home schedule at Target Field. Besides postponing three games, they played several others despite subfreezing wind chills that required round-the-clock snow removal efforts. More specifically, the weather-induced revenue losses affected nearly every facet of their in-stadium business including fewer walk-up sales, increased no-shows, and lower per-capita concession and merchandise sales among fans who braved the elements.[32]

Third, after signing Korean superstar baseball player Byung Ho Park to a four-year, $12 million contract in late 2015, the Twins hoped this deal would create new cross-cultural marketing opportunities during 2016–2019. Team executives believe that if Park is successful and popular in games, this may reveal a new audience and also expand marketing activities not just with Koreans, but with others outside of the team's traditional fan base.[33]

In fact, several Twins' sponsors that do business with South Korean companies immediately reached out to the club to talk about promotional ideas.

Two of the largest and best-known Korean businesses, Samsung and LG, phoned the team to set up discussions. Two other MLB teams with similar regional appeal—Pittsburgh Pirates and Texas Rangers—each received interest and exposure after the arrival and success of their Korean players. The gains occurred not just in South Korea, but also among Koreans in the United States and Asian-Americans who connect with Korea because of its pop music, television dramas, and movies. The Twin Cities contain about 20,000 Koreans, many who are or were students at the University of Minnesota, and also are home to tens of thousands more Korean Americans.

Fourth, for people without cable television or who want to watch baseball games online even if they do have cable, few rules were as frustrating as MLB's blackout of local teams. Fans could spend $120 for MLB's streaming package, but if they tried to watch the Twins anywhere near the Twin Cities, their games were blacked out. During late 2015, MLB dropped its blackout restriction. In order to watch any of them, people may have to subscribe—in the case of Twins fans to Fox Sports North—a restriction that allowed MLB to strong-arm consumers into buying the appropriate cable television package. Even if cable television customers, they will not be able to watch the games on smartphones through the MLB At Bat app. Games will only be available via the Fox Sports Go app. However, it is not clear whether the games will be available on smartphones even with the app.

Fifth, some tips to help a field-service business get started by replicating the Twins are a change in leadership; hire young but potentially good talent; look to the organization's veterans; and do not forfeit the future for short-term success. These occurred, for example, when the team hired former player and current Hall of Famer Paul Molitor to replace manager Ron Gardenhire after its 2014 season; added such talented players as Miguel Sano, Aaron Hicks, and Byron Buxton; re-signed Tori Hunter who is a leader and great mentor by instilling a winning attitude in young players; and instead of bold and risky decisions, the Twins made only minor changes involving their roster of players. As a result of these and other tips, the club won thirteen more games in 2015 than 2014 and finished second in the CD.

NOTES

1. Two books about MLB franchises and their history are Frank P. Jozsa Jr., *Major League Baseball Expansions and Team Relocations: A History, 1876–2008* (Jefferson, NC: McFarland, 2010); and James Quirk and Rodney D. Fort, *Pay Dirt: The Business of Professional Team Sports* (Princeton, NJ: Princeton University Press, 1992).

2. For specific information regarding how, when, and where expansion teams organized and then joined MLB, see such sources as "MLB Links," http://www.

sportsecyclopedia.com, cited January 19, 2016, and the *Official Major League Baseball Fact Book 2005 Edition* (St. Louis, MO: Sporting News, 2005).

3. Jared S. Hopkins and Melissa Harris, "Reinsdorf Recommends Selling Sox after He Dies," http://www.articles.chicagotribune.com, cited February 9, 2016.

4. This data is available online at "Fan Cost Index," http://www.teammarketingreport.com, cited January 25, 2016.

5. For this and other comments concerning the quality of current MLB stadiums, see "Ranking All 30 MLB Ballparks," http://www.csnmidatlantic.com, cited January 26, 2016.

6. For 2015 MLB teams' financial data, read the article by Kurt Badenhausen, Michael Ozanian, and Christina Settimi, "MLB Worth $36B As Team Values Hit Record $1.2B Average," http://www.forbes.com, cited January 18, 2016.

7. Business activities, events, and other commercial news and topics about the White Sox and its managers, players, owners, and seasons are reported online. For example, see Danny Ecker, "Cubs, Sox TV Ratings Are a Tale of Two Cities," http://www.chicagobusiness.com, cited March 15, 2016, and Doug Padilla, "White Sox GM Denies Conflict with Boss Kenny Williams," http://www.espn.go.com, cited April 1, 2016.

8. For the club's relationship with Magellan, see Eric Fisher, "White Sox Sponsor Links Deal to Charities," http://www.sportsbusinessdaily.com, cited January 28, 2016.

9. Jon Greenberg, "Sox Pulling Out Stops to Bump Attendance," http://www.espn.go.com, cited April 15, 2016.

10. The Cleveland Indians and other CD teams' histories are discussed partly in Frank P. Jozsa Jr., *American League Franchises: Team Performances and Business Success* (New York: Springer, 2015).

11. The brainchild of Pittsburgh Pirates president William Temple, the Temple Cup was the name of a best-of-seven postseason series and trophy awarded to the winner of the first and second place NL teams from 1894 to 1897. However, players' lack of enthusiasm doomed the series. While second place teams won three of the four series, attendance at games was abysmal. This caused its cancellation after the league's 1897 season.

12. Besides reviewing owners' profiles on their team's website, see "List of Major League Baseball Principal Owners," http://www.baseball-reference.com, cited January 22, 2016.

13. Paul Hoynes, "Paul Dolan Has No Interest in Selling Majority Share of Cleveland Indians," http://www.cleveland.com, cited February 12, 2016.

14. For an overview of MLB ballparks including their amenities, capacities, costs, dimensions, renovations, and other specifications, see http://www.ballparksofbaseball.com.

15. Other than the article in note 5 and teams' websites at http://www.mlb.com, another reading is "Ranking MLB's Ballparks," http://www.athlonsports.com, cited January 26, 2016.

16. The sources for business topics of the Cleveland Indians, in no specific order, include "TU School of Business Partnering with Cleveland Indians for Real World

Experience," http://www.tiffin.edu, cited February 1, 2016; Mike McIntyre, "Cleveland Indians Cancel Snow Days at Progressive Field Because Crowds Were Too Small," http://www.cleveland.com, cited June 1, 2012; Paul Hoynes, "Cleveland Indians Reorganize Latin American Baseball Operations," http://www.cleveland.com, cited February 15, 2016; Kevin Kelps, "Losing Proposition? Shapiro Says Dolans Haven't Turned a Profit during 'a few' Indians Seasons," http://www.crainscleveland.com, cited September 1, 2015.

17. Eric Fisher, "Snow Go? Indians to Evaluate Winter Carnival After It Doesn't Spin Profit for Second Year," http://www.sportsbusinessdaily.com, cited January 23, 2016.

18. "Cleveland in the Cloud: Overhauling the Indians' Infrastructure," http://www.vmware.com, cited February 17, 2016.

19. Notes 1 and 10 contain information about the history of the Detroit Tigers and later the Kansas City Royals and Minnesota Twins.

20. CSN Mid-Atlantic, "Ranking All 30 MLB Ballparks," http://www.csnmidatlantic.com, cited January 26, 2016.

21. Examples of Tigers' business news include: Daniel Kaplan, "Tigers Refinancing $130M a Good Sign," http://www.sportsbusinessdaily.com, cited September 13, 2010; Michael Rosenberg, "For Impatient Tigers Owner Illitch, Firing Dombrowki Was a Personal Move," http://www.si.com, cited September 1, 2015; Bill Shea, "Pure Michigan Extends Relationship with Tigers, MIS," http://www.crainsdetroit.com, cited December 16, 2015.

22. See Christopher Botta, "Detroit's Delivery Man," http://www.sportsbusinessdaily.com, cited February 19, 2016.

23. John Ourand and David Broughton, "Multiple Story Lines Help Lift Tigers to Top of Local TV Ratings List," http://www.sportsbusinessdaily.com, cited February 21, 2016.

24. For the history, team performances, franchise owner, Kauffman Stadium, business highlights, and other information about the Kansas City Royals, see readings in Notes of this chapter.

25. CSN Mid-Atlantic, "Ranking All 30 MLB Ballparks."

26. Kansas City Royals' business relations were published in "Royals Continue 'Forever Royal' into the 2016 Season," http://www.ksn.com, cited February 1, 2016; Eric Fisher, "World Series: Outer Markets Will Drive Royals' 2015 Ticket Growth," http://www.bizjournals.com, cited October 31, 2014; Max Rieper, "Alex Gordon Signs 4-Year Deal with Royals," http://www.royalsreview.com, cited January 6, 2016; John Sleezer, "Royals Extend Contracts of Manager Ned Yost, GM Dayton Moore," http://www.kansascity.com, cited February 18, 2016.

27. Read Pete Grathoff, "The Royals Are up for Sports Illustrated's Sportsman of the Year Award," http://www.kansascity.com, cited February 22, 2016.

28. Beside its website at http://www.mlb.com, see sources in Notes 2 and 4–7 for the Twins' seasons, performances, ballpark, fan cost index, and business highlights.

29. CSN Mid-Atlantic, "Ranking All 30 MLB Ballparks."

30. The business relations and specific topics about the Twins are in articles within magazines, newspapers, and on the team's website at http://www.mlb.com. For

example, see Nick Halter, "Fans Will Finally Be Able to Stream Minnesota Twins Games in Minnesota," http://www.bizjournals.com, cited November 19, 2015; and Ken Powtak, "Hall of Famer Rod Carew Touched by Twins' Tribute on 1st," http://www.businessinsider.com, cited February 27, 2016.

31. Eric Fisher, "Laura Day, Minnesota Twins," *SportsBusiness Journal* (September 14, 2015): 12A.

32. See Eric Fisher, "Weather Cost Twins 'Deep into Seven Figures,'" *SportsBusiness Journal* (April 29, 2013): 35.

33. Evan Ramstad, "Twins See Lots of On-Field and Off-Field Possibilities with New Player from South Korea," http://www.startribune.com, cited December 5, 2015.

Chapter Three

West Division

As discussed in chapter 2, prior to 1969 there were no individual divisions in the American League (AL) or National League (NL) of Major League Baseball (MLB). However, because of expansion between 1969 and 1993, the AL and NL consisted of either six or seven teams each in the East Division (ED) and West Division (WD). Then in 1994 the two leagues realigned again and besides their ED and WD, they added a Central Division (CD). As a result, the AL's and NL's ED and CD each had five teams while their WD included four. After 1997, other differences occurred in divisions until 2013 when five each played in the ED, CD, and WD.

Given these changes in the structure of big-league baseball, this chapter discusses the historical development—and highlights business and financial topics—of AL teams based in Houston, Texas; Anaheim, California; Oakland, California; Seattle, Washington; and Arlington, Texas, as of MLB's 2015 season. Which of them, for example, won the least number of division titles but most pennants? What were their estimated market values, revenues, and debt-to-value ratios in 2015? Among the five clubs' owners, which of them had the greatest and worst success at winning World Series? How did these teams' current ballparks compare to others in their amenities, attendances, and costs? The answers to these and other questions are subjects covered in the chapter.[1]

HOUSTON ASTROS

From 1888 to 1961, the minor league Buffaloes were Houston's only professional baseball club despite local officials' efforts to attract a big-league team. Given MLB's refusal to consider expansion, businessmen George Kirksey and Craig Cullinan, oilman and real estate magnate R.E. Smith, and county judge and former Houston mayor Roy Hofhienz organized the Houston Sports Association (HSA) in 1960 as a way to seek a big-league franchise.[2]

To compete with the established AL and NL, the group joined with would-be owners from other cities and announced the formation of a Continental League (CL). As a result, the AL and NL each decided to expand from eight to ten teams to protect the sport's current and future markets. Nevertheless, plans eventually fell through for Houston's potential franchise after the Buffaloes' owner Marty Marion could not agree with the HSA to sell his team. In addition, the CL folded in August 1960.

A few months later, the NL granted an expansion franchise for $1.8 million to the HSA in which its team could begin playing in the league's 1962 season. According to MLB's Constitution, the HSA had to obtain territorial rights from the Buffaloes in order to exist in the metropolitan area. Thus, negotiations started again to acquire the minor league team. During early 1961, the HSA succeeded in purchasing the Buffaloes after they played their final season and were then replaced by the city's new NL club.

In a name-the-team contest, the new Houston club was nicknamed Colt .45s because the Colt .45 pistol had been known as "the gun that won the west." With navy blue and orange uniform colors, the first Colt .45s was a group of scrubs formed mostly through an expansion draft following MLB's 1961 season. One year later, it joined nine other NL clubs including the expansion New York Mets and also World Series runner-up Cincinnati Reds.

Team Performances

As a member of the NL from 1962 to 1968 and then the league's WD (1969–1993) and finally CD (1994–2012), the Colt .45s—renamed Astros in 1965—had 3,999 victories and were competitive enough to win seven division titles and one pennant in nine playoff appearances. Their most successful years consecutively were 1980–1981, 1997–1999, and 2004–2005 when they competed in playoffs that included a pennant but then a loss in the 2005 World Series to the AL Chicago White Sox. Alternatively, the club's worst string of seasons was 1962–1979, 1982–1985, 1987–1996, and 2006–2012.

From 1998 to 2009, the Astros' attendances at home averaged between 30,000 and 37,700 per game but then declined during their 2010–2012 seasons to respectively 28,700, 25,500, and 19,800. Except for 2006 and 2008, the club lost a majority of its total games, including over one hundred of them in 2011 and 2012. Because of its poor performances in the NL's WD and other factors, Houston sports fans gradually lost interest in—and failed to support—their hometown MLB team.

Following a transfer of the franchise's ownership from Drayton McLane to Jim Crane in 2011, the Astros' shift from the NL to AL WD became official and also effective for MLB's 2013 season. Initially, McLane and Crane both resisted a switch to the AL. In the end, however, Crane relented. All it took, according to the *Houston Chronicle*, was a $70 million discount on Crane's $680 million purchase price with McLane and MLB splitting the cost of the inducement in half.[3]

The ratification of baseball's new collective bargaining agreement (CBA) completed the sale. However, some factors caused delays in the deal such as due diligence on Crane and also MLB's preoccupation with the Los Angeles Dodgers' ownership mess for much of the year. Furthermore, there were complaints from female and minority employees about hiring practices at a company operated by Crane.

The CBA negotiations had a perpetual and concurrent effect on the sale of the club. At the behest of the baseball players union, MLB officials agreed to realign and thus divide the sport's competitive structure into two, fifteen-team leagues. As a result, the Astros were the most logical candidate to move elsewhere—apart from the sale—given the existence of ready-made, in-state division rival Texas Rangers. Although the process was lengthy and imperfect, with repeated interruptions and the uncomfortable history of Crane's settlement with the Equal Employment Opportunity Commission (EEOC), the outcome benefitted big-league baseball. That the Astros franchise effectively sold its NL identity for the sum of $70 million denotes how much it mattered in the first place.

After joining the AL in 2013, Houston finished fifth, fourth, and second in its division. In 2015, the Astros had an 86–76 record and qualified as a wild card team, defeated the New York Yankees in the playoffs, but then lost in five games to the Kansas City Royals in the league's divisional series. Such Astros players as infielder Jose Altuve, designated hitter Evan Gattis, and pitcher Dallas Keuchel were outstanding during the club's regular-season (Table A1).

Franchise Owner

Born in St. Louis, Missouri, Jim Crane became a loyal fan of the hometown NL Cardinals. As a young man, he put his passion for baseball into action at Central Missouri State University (CMSU)—later renamed University of Central Missouri—where he was a standout pitcher for the Mules' baseball team from 1973 to 1976. After earning his bachelor of science degree in industrial safety from CMSU, Jim worked in a loss-control job evaluating commercial risks for an insurance company but then moved to Houston, Texas, in 1982 and entered the freight forwarding business.[4]

During March 1984—when he was thirty years old and with $10,000 borrowed from his sister—Crane founded Eagle USA Airfreight (EGL). In his first office in Houston with one employee, Jim handled loading and trucking tasks. After his business became profitable in its first year, Jim gradually but ultimately built EGL into an organization that included more than 10,000 employees with 400-plus facilities in 139 countries.

In August 2008, Jim formed Crane Worldwide Logistics (CWL), which is a premier global provider of customized transportation and logistics services. Besides being the chief executive officer (CEO) and president of the Crane Capital Group, he also became owner of Champion Energy Services, which ranks in the top five of nonutility-affiliated retail electric providers in America and among the top twenty retail electricity companies in the nation.

Since acquiring the Astros in late 2011, Jim's goal was and continues to be developing a ball club that has sustained success at the major league level. While building a top-notch farm system, he wants fans to have a memorable experience attending the club's home games. Following years of neglect of the Astros' system, former general manager and scouting director Ed Wade and Bobby Heck began the process of filling the Astros organization with athletic, talented, and young minor leaguers.

To replace Wade and Heck, Crane hired Jeff Luhnow from the St. Louis Cardinals organization and let him restock the system, develop talented and young athletes into prime-time baseball players, and utilize the best forward-thinking analytics to maximize their strengths. Thus, Crane helped accomplish great results for the team in 2015 by staying out of the way of those entrusted with operating his franchise.

From 2011 to 2015, Jim Crane's teams did not win a championship. Compared to performances of other AL owners, the Astros ranked fifteenth with zero division titles, tied for eighth with several others in winning zero pennants, and tied for fifth in number of World Series. Among all current owners of MLB clubs as of 2015, Crane's Astros were respectively tied for twelfth, fourteenth, and ninth. Despite these results, Jim has the leadership skills to improve his team and motivate players to win more regular-season games and eventually a championship (Table A2).

Minute Maid Park

Following the Colt .45s' seasons at Colt Stadium (1962–1964), the NL Astros played their home games at the Astrodome (1965–1999). By the early to mid-1990s, however, the stadium lacked amenities of new retro ballparks and had an Astroturf field with numerous seats distant from the ballfield.[5]

When franchise owner Drayton McLane threatened to move his club elsewhere, voters approved a referendum in late 1996 to fund the construction of a new ballpark on a twenty-five-acre site in downtown Houston. Built with steel and concrete in addition to a brick and limestone exterior, the 41,574-seat ballpark features a retractable roof plus a 50,000-square-foot sliding glass door that provides a view of the city's skyline with or without an open roof.

Originally known as Enron Field before the Enron Corporation went bankrupt during 2000–2001, the facility received its current name, Minute Maid Park, in 2002. Besides a huge HD video scoreboard, a wild-west steam locomotive and twenty-degree-angled Tal's Hill, the ballpark includes such attractions as Phillips 66 Homerun Alley, the team store named The Shed, and a FiveSeven Grille in honor of former players, Jeff Bagwell and Craig Biggio.

Among ballparks of AL teams as of 2015, Minute Maid Park tied for twelfth with the Tigers' Comerica Park in age and also ranked seventh in construction cost and eighth in value. But compared to ballparks of all MLB teams, the Astros' home tied for seventeenth in age in addition to being seventeenth in cost and nineteenth in value. According to this data, Houston's ball club plays its games in an average but not inferior or superior stadium (Table A3).

For several years a Chicago-based company named Team Marketing Report (TMR) has prepared and published a Fan Cost Index (FCI) for the home games of teams in professional sports leagues. To attend a game for a typical family with two kids, an FCI includes the costs of four average-priced tickets, two cheapest-priced draft beers, four each cheapest-priced soft drinks and hot dogs, parking for one vehicle, and two each game programs and also least-expensive, adult-size adjustable caps. These costs are determined by telephone calls with team representatives, venues, and concessionaires, and from questions asked during interviews.

In the 2013–2015 MLB seasons, the FCIs for a family to attend a regular-season Astros game at Minute Maid Park were respectively $224, $216, and $220. During this period among those of fourteen other AL clubs, Houston ballpark's FCI ranked fifth in both 2013 and 2014, and also fourth in 2015. Compared to the venues of only the league's WD teams, Astros fans paid more to attend regular-season games in Houston each year than did those of the other four teams at their ballparks in Anaheim, Oakland, Seattle, and Arlington (Table A4).

To reveal specific costs for a recent year in MLB, Houston's ballpark's FCI in 2015 was approximately $220 or almost 2 percent more than in 2014. Listed from most to least in amount by item for one person, the team's non-premium tickets averaged between $31 and $32, parking one vehicle $15, a cap $14, a beer $5, and a hot dog and soft drink each between $4 and $5. The league's FCI, meanwhile, was $211 or 6 percent less in 2015 than the amount paid at games in Minute Maid Park.

Among other teams in the WD, they had rankings and FCIs from most to least as follows in the 2015 MLB season: Mariners fifteenth at $212; Athletics nineteenth at $195; Rangers twentieth at $191; and Angels twenty-first at $190. Given these amounts, Astros home games were expensive then because of various factors including the ballpark's location, population and growth of the local sports market, consumer's income, and recent improvement of the club.

Houston's average premium ticket was approximately $100 at its home games in the 2015 regular-season. Among other WD teams, this was less than the Mariners' $206 but greater than the Athletics' $52, Rangers' $62, and Angels' $76. With the league's premium ticket price at $96, Astros fans paid a small amount more for their seats at Minute Maid Park than did spectators at most other MLB ballparks. For both nonpremium and premium tickets, the Astros assigned prices for seats to maximize their revenue with more gate receipts.

In a recent study by CSN Mid-Atlantic, Minute Maid Park ranked fourteenth in MLB. According to an online report in *USA Today*, the author said:

> OK, it's quirky. Really quirky. Maybe too much so. There's Tal's Hill in center field, which is an accident waiting to happen. There's a way-too-short wall in left field, plus an odd angle back to the bullpens in deep left-center. There's a locomotive filled with fake giant oranges above the wall. But in spite of all that, it really is a nice park, especially when the roof is open.[6]

Financial Data

Besides performing as teams in regular-season and perhaps postseason games, MLB franchises are also commercial enterprises. To that end, their economic objective is to earn maximum revenue in order to obtain the greatest amount of profit on a fiscal basis from their operations. Although they share revenue with each other from such sources as national television contracts and other deals, it is important for them to efficiently allocate resources, determine and distribute payrolls, set nonpremium and premium ticket prices, and schedule investments in short- and long-term assets. To reveal and manage such activities, this section focuses on different parts of the Astros' business and how well its organization succeed or does not succeeds from a financial perspective.[7]

According to data and other financial information published in *Forbes* for franchises in the AL as of their 2015 season, Houston ranked twelfth in market value at $800 million, fifteenth in revenue at $175 million, sixth in operating income at $21.6 million, and also tied for tenth in gate receipts with the Blue Jays at $48 million, and first in the league with a truly high 34 percent debt-to-value ratio. Among WD clubs, the Astros were worth more the Athletics and had the least amount of revenue of the group, but earned less operating income than the Mariners and gate receipts of three other clubs (Table A5).

Compared to all MLB teams in 2015, Houston was twenty-sixth in market value, thirtieth in revenue and fourteenth in operating income, tied for twenty-second in gate receipts, and tied for first with the NL Marlins in their debt percent. Except for their income from operations, the Astros struggle as a business enterprise because of relatively low attendances at their home games, not enough gate receipts and revenue, and high debt. From a financial perspective, this is a below-average franchise in the league.

Besides market size, salary inflation, and other factors, an MLB team's annual payroll partly reflects its commitment to players and their current and potential contribution individually and as a group to winning games in regular seasons and postseasons. From 2013 to 2015, for example, the Astros payroll among AL teams was fifteenth in 2013 ($18 million) and also in 2014 ($44 million) and 2015 ($69 million). During the three-year period, these were the lowest payrolls in the league (Table A6).

Among payrolls of all MLB teams, Houston's ranked thirtieth in 2013 and twenty-ninth in both 2014 and 2015. In comparison the NL Marlins had baseball's lowest payroll in 2014 at $28 million and the NL Diamondbacks in 2015 at $65 million. For the Astros to improve and win one or more games in playoffs, the club needs to be competitive and continue increasing salaries of their players especially those with great potential as pitchers and powerful but consistent batters.

Business Relations

Besides regular-season and postseason games, MLB franchises are involved in—and affected by—internal affairs, community events, and business-related activities and projects. In no specific order, the following are a few of them for Houston's AL team as of 2015.[8]

First, after launching their own regional sports network (RSN) in 2014, the Astros' 0.35 rating on Comcast SportsNet Houston (CSNH) was the AL's lowest but also the lowest local number in the history of the franchise. The primary reason for the team's dismal rating was distribution. Only a fraction of pay television subscribers have access to CSNH, which did not have a deal with satellite providers DirecTV and the Dish Network, or with telecommunications companies like AT&T and Verizon. Astros games on its RSN averaged about eight thousand homes in the Houston market. That was baseball's lowest average local audience since those of the 2008 Washington Nationals.

Second, the Astros developed a $40 million signature sponsor initiative in 2012 called the Community Leaders Program (CLP) that blends some of the club's largest sponsors with a significant civic revitalization effort. Created by team owner Jim Crane with the aid of Houston mayor Annise Parker, CLP features several major corporate partners, each displayed on a new sign being constructed on Minute Maid Park's left field light tower. Of the $40 million in combined sponsor commitments over a five-year period, $18 million was earmarked to build and repair youth baseball and softball fields in the city's disadvantaged neighborhoods.

Third, the Astros created an online fan research forum aimed at quickly collecting fan sentiment on new team initiatives. The forum—developed in 2012 with the aid of MLB Advanced Media—includes people of various ticket-purchasing levels with the club. Fan sentiment played a major part in shaping club decisions. These included, for example, keeping pistols on the throwback Colt .45s players jerseys despite initial concerns from MLB; definitively retaining the Astros name for the long term; and adopting a more liberal policy on bringing food into games at Minute Maid Park.

Fourth, as part of MLB's Diverse Business Partners Program (DBPP), the Houston Astros Baseball Club committed to incorporate diversity into all aspects of their business operations. More specifically, the club's DBPP provides an equal opportunity for minority- and women-owned businesses to supply goods and services to the organization. The Astros' goal is to create mutually beneficial partnerships with suppliers that provide high-quality goods and services at a competitive price. By actively pursuing objectives of the DBPP, the team enhances its contribution to the economic growth and development of the local community.

Fifth, at the Astros first home game in April 2016, it was played under Musco's cutting-edge SportsCluster Green LED system. As part of continued upgrades to Minute Maid Park, the new lighting system provides unprecedented levels of energy efficiency and enhances the spectator experience at the ballpark. The new system—which replaced the original metal halide lighting equipment that was installed when the 40,000-seat stadium opened in 2000—consumes less energy, require less maintenance, and offers special effects to enhance the ballpark's entertainment experiences for fans. In fact, the ballpark became the second in MLB to install Musco's innovative LED product.

LOS ANGELES ANGELS OF ANHEIM

During 1957, Brooklyn Dodgers owner Walter O'Malley purchased the Pacific Coast League (PCL) Los Angeles Angels from Chicago Cubs owner

Phil Wrigley and also acquired the rights to an MLB team in Los Angeles—where he moved the Dodgers a year later. Ordinarily, that would preclude any subsequent AL team to exist in the Los Angeles area. However, to prevent the proposed CL from becoming a reality, in 1960 the NL and AL agreed to each expand by two new teams.[9]

Although expansion teams were supposed to be located only in cities without MLB, that agreement broke down. When the NL placed the Mets in New York City to become its tenth franchise, the AL announced plans to put an expansion team in Los Angeles to begin play in 1961. Former cowboy movie actor and owner of Golden West Broadcasters, Gene Autry, attended the MLB owners' meeting in St. Louis in 1960 to win broadcasting rights for the new team's games.

When O'Malley heard about maverick-promoter Bill Veeck's interest in owning a new MLB team, he invoked his exclusive right to operate one in southern California rather than compete with Veeck. After it became obvious that O'Malley would never sign off on a deal if Veeck was a co-owner, Veeck's partner Hank Greenberg withdrew from the negotiations.

After another bid by Chicago insurance executive and future Oakland Athletics owner Charlie Finley failed, Autry was persuaded to submit a bid. Autry—who had been a minority stockholder in the Angels' PCL rival, the Hollywood Stars—agreed, and as a result, he purchased the franchise from MLB for a fee of $2.1 million. In 1961, his Los Angeles Angels joined nine other AL teams.

Team Performances

As a member of the AL from 1961 to 1968 and then the league's WD since 1969, the Angels played 8,780 games and had victories in approximately 50 percent of them. During the period, they won nine division titles and one each pennant and World Series in ten playoff appearances. In comparison to the performances of fourteen other AL teams as of MLB's 2015 season, the club tied for fourth with the Orioles and Blue Jays in division titles, tied for twelfth with the Rays in winning pennants, and ranked eleventh in World Series titles. Among their WD competitors, the Angels won more total championships than the Astros, Mariners, and Rangers but not the Athletics (Table A1).

Based on the all-time results of current MLB teams as of 2015, the Anaheim-based Angels tied for ninth in division titles, tied for twenty-third in pennants, and tied for twentieth in World Series victories. Besides its world championship in 2002, the franchise's most productive years consecutively were 2004–2005 and 2007–2009 because of manager Mike Scioscia and such outstanding players as right fielder Vladimir Guerrero, pitchers John Lackey and Ervin Santana, and infielder/outfielder Chone Figgins. For various reasons, however, Angels' teams failed to make the AL playoffs during back-to-back seasons of 1961–1978, 1987–2001, and 2010–2013.

Since 2004, the Angels have appeared in seven playoffs but lost four of these games in the divisional series and others in the AL championship series. Led by manager Scioscia, outfielder Mike Trout was and continues to be their best player. From 2012 to 2015, Trout was a four-time all-star and silver slugger winner; selected Rookie of the Year in 2012; and finished first once and second three-times for the league's Most Valuable Player (MVP) award. For Los Angeles to compete for another championship, the team needs better and more consistent performances from sluggers Albert Pujols and Kole Calhoun and also pitchers Garrett Richards and Jared Weaver.

Franchise Owner

A native of Tucson, Arizona, and oldest of eleven children, Mexican-American Arte Moreno graduated from high school in 1965 and then was drafted into the U.S. Army. Following two years in the military he enrolled at the University of Arizona and earned a degree in marketing after which the Eller Outdoor advertising company hired him in the late 1970s.

Several years later, Moreno left his job with Eller and became an employee of Outdoor Systems (OS), where he was very successful as the company's president and chief executive officer (CEO). When Moreno and his partner William Levine took OS public in 1996, its stock soared, so they sold the company three years later for more than $8 billion to the Infinity Broadcasting Corporation

With baseball being his favorite pastime, Moreno and several other investors purchased the minor league Salt Lake Trappers in 1986. The team, which the group owned until 1992, was a successful venture at least from a business perspective. But in the early 2000s, Moreno sought to own an MLB franchise. First he attempted to buy controlling interest in his home state's Arizona Diamondbacks. After that effort failed, Moreno focused on acquiring the Anaheim Angels—officially renamed Los Angeles Angels of Anaheim in 2005.

During April 2003, Moreno agreed to purchase the Angels from the Walt Disney Company for approximately $180 million. One month later, Commissioner Bud Selig announced the sale was approved by MLB. In Anaheim, baseball fans were uncertain as to whether they were happy or not about the sale and change in the franchise's ownership. Although it was widely known that Disney executives wanted to sell their team, there were concerns about someone from outside southern California taking control of it. One thing everyone knew and understood was that Arturo Moreno loved sports and to win games and championships.

Since 2003, Moreno's teams have won six division titles but zero pennants and World Series while appearing in six playoffs. Compared to the owners of other AL clubs and their performances as of 2015, the Angels ranked respectively first, tied for eighth, and tied for fifth. Among all MLB owners, this Anaheim-based franchise tied for third in division titles, for fourteenth in winning pennants, and for ninth in World Series. Thus, Moreno has been a successful owner within the league's WD but not when competing for a pennant in games of the divisional and championship series (Table A2).

With his influence declining and status in the game low in 2015, some observers speculate that it might be time for Moreno to sell the Angels. According to estimates in *Forbes* magazine, his original investment is worth over $1 billion just twelve years later. As a veteran he understands why former president Gerald Ford declared victory for the United States and then abandoned the conflict in Vietnam. As such, it might be time for Moreno to congratulate himself for making the Angels a top-tier franchise in Anaheim and hop on a helicopter headed for Tempe, Arizona.[10]

In other words, Gene Autry founded the Angels, Disney won a ring, and Arte made them a winner. Undoubtedly Moreno has been a productive owner in the team's history, but the honeymoon may be over. Although he aspired to make the franchise a west coast version of the New York Yankees organization, recent events involving incidents with players occasionally make him a corporate crank instead of a lovable visionary.

Angel Stadium of Anaheim

During their history of MLB seasons, the Angels played home games at Wrigley Field (1961), Dodger Stadium (1962–1965), and Anaheim Stadium (1966–1997)—renamed Edison International Field in 1998—and then six years later, Angel Stadium of Anaheim. Since it opened in 1966, the facility has hosted many events other than baseball, including professional football.[11]

In the 1970s, the National Football League (NFL) Rams looked to move from the Los Angeles Coliseum to Anaheim Stadium. By the 1980 sports season, the ballpark became a multipurpose facility and thus home to both the Angels and Rams. It was enclosed and expanded by 23,000 seats increasing capacity to more than 65,000. Also, a new scoreboard was installed on the façade of the outfield roof when the "Big A" scoreboard moved to the parking lot. Additional upgrades included new executive and media boxes, and a sound system.

During January 1994, an earthquake damaged Anaheim Stadium when the Sony Jumbo Tron broke from the roof in left field, crashing into the upper deck, and destroying hundreds of seats. After their 1994 season, the Rams moved from Los Angeles to St. Louis, allowing the Angels to convert the facility back to exclusively baseball.

After renovations in the mid-1990s, the ballpark improved. As of 2015, there were many amenities in it including the Pepsi Perfect Game Pavilion, dugout-level seating, and three club restaurants. They are the Knothole Club—a sports bar located on the club level down the right field line; Diamond Club—an upscale restaurant with outdoor seating; and the Homeplate Club—which overlooks the main entrance to the ballpark.

Among ballparks of AL teams as of 2015, Angel Stadium of Anaheim ranked second in age and also thirteenth in construction cost and fifth in value. But in comparison to all MLB teams, it tied for being fourth-oldest in age, twenty-sixth highest in cost, and tied for tenth in value with the NL Phillies' Citizen Bank Park. According to this data, Anaheim's MLB club plays its home games in an outdated and inferior stadium (Table A3).

As previously denoted for the Astros, FCIs were also published for home games of the Angels. Regarding the 2011–2015 MLB seasons, it cost a family to attend a regular-season game at Angel Stadium from a low of $129 in 2011 to a high of $197 in 2013. During the five-year period among those of fourteen other AL clubs, the ballpark's FCI ranged in rank from ninth in 2013 to fourteenth in 2011. Compared to the venues of only the league's WD teams, Angels fans paid the lowest amounts except in 2013 when FCIs at the Rangers' Globe Life Park and Athletics' O.co Coliseum each amounted to less than $197 (Table A4).

To reveal specific costs for a recent year in MLB, the Angels ballpark's FCI in 2015 was ranked twenty-first at approximately $190 or almost 3 percent less than in 2014. Listed from most to least in amount by item for one person, the team's nonpremium (premium) tickets averaged $27 ($76), a cap $16, parking one vehicle $10, a hot dog and beer each between $4 and $5, and a soft drink about $3. In comparison, the typical ballpark's FCI exceeded the Angels' by $21 or 10 percent.

Among other teams in the league's WD, they had rankings and FCIs from most to least as follows in the 2015 MLB season: Houston tenth at $220; Mariners fifteenth at $212; Athletics nineteenth at $195; and Rangers twentieth at $191. Given these amounts, Angels home games were relatively inexpensive for families to attend because of various factors, including the ballpark's location and amenities, comparatively low ticket prices, and the team's performances plus its popularity in the local sports market.

In a recent study by CSN Mid-Atlantic, Angels Stadium ranked thirteenth in MLB. According to an online report in *USA Today*, the author wrote:

> Though the basic foundation of the stadium opened nearly 50 years ago, it was gutted and rebuilt in the '90s, so it doesn't feel at all like an old ballpark. This is just a pleasant place to watch a ballgame. The weather is usually fantastic. The home team is usually good. The stands are usually packed. And Disneyland is only five minutes away. What more do you need?[12]

During early 2014, team owner Arte Moreno met with officials from the city of Tustin in Orange County to discuss the possibility of building a new baseball stadium there. One potential site would be the decommissioned Marine Corps Air Station, which would be accessible via three freeways and located across the street from the Tustin Metrolink train station. In retrospect, Moreno was extremely frustrated by Anaheim mayor Tom Tait's reluctance to accept his proposal in which the Angels would spend $150 million to renovate their stadium in exchange for a sixty-six-year, $1-a-year lease to develop 155 acres of land in the parking lot.[13]

Financial Data

As commercial enterprises, it is important for MLB franchises to efficiently allocate resources, determine and distribute payrolls, establish nonpremium and premium ticket prices, and schedule investments in short- and long-term assets. This section focuses on different results of the Angels' business model and how well the organization succeeds or does not succeed from a financial perspective.

According to data and other financial information published in *Forbes* for franchises in the AL as of their 2015 season, the Angels ranked third in market value at $1.38 billion and also in revenue at $304 million and gate receipts at $93 million, ninth in operating income at $16.7 million, and tied for twelfth with four other teams each with a zero percent debt-to-value ratio. Among only those in the league's WD, the club was first except for its operating income and debt percent (Table A5).

Compared to twenty-nine other MLB teams in 2015, the Angels ranked seventh in both market value and gate receipts, fifth in revenue and seventeenth in operating income, and tied for twenty-fifth in their debt-to-value ratio. Based on these results, this is a lucrative, prosperous, and valuable business enterprise from a financial perspective because of its location, mid-to-large fan base, popularity, team performances in recent seasons, and owner Moreno's investments in the franchise.

Besides market size, salary inflation, and other factors, an MLB team's annual payroll partly reflects its commitment to players and their current and potential contribution individually and as a group to winning games in regular seasons and postseasons. From 2013 to 2015, for example, the Angels payroll among AL teams ranged from third in 2011 ($138 million) and 2012 ($153 million) to fourth in 2013–2015. During the five-year period, however, the club had the highest payrolls in the WD (Table A6).

In comparison to payrolls of twenty-nine other MLB teams, the Angels ranked fourth in 2011 and 2012, seventh in 2013 and 2015, and eighth in 2014. Only the AL's Yankees and Red Sox and also NL's Dodgers and Phillies had consistently higher rankings of amounts during the majority of these seasons. If their payroll steadily improves, the Angels will continue to be a competitive team and challenge others in the WD for titles and also the league for winning pennants.

Business Relations

Besides regular-season and postseason games, MLB franchises are involved in—and affected by—community events and business-related affairs and projects. In no specific sequence, the following are a few of them for Anaheim's AL team as of 2015.[14]

First, the Angels had neither a Hispanic marketing department or marketing agency nor a Hispanic marketing plan in 2013—even though they play in a city that is 53 percent Hispanic, a county that is 30 percent Hispanic, and a metro market that is 44 percent Hispanic. "When you're talking about the biggest markets in this country, people of Hispanic heritage have become, in essence, the mainstream in those marketplaces," said Angels' vice president Robert Alvarado, who was in his thirteenth season with the club after spending six years with Coors Brewing Company. "So we tend to look at a lot of the things we do already in our marketing scheme and strategy and say—hey, what's scalable?" By scalable, Alvarado means they ask whether a program or tactic will play across both the Hispanic and general markets because if it only plays in the general market, it probably will not be a broad success in today's Los Angeles market.

Second, as the new general manager of the Angels, Billy Eppler's first major decision in 2015 was acquire Andrelton Simmons—a defensive maestro for the Atlanta Braves the last four seasons—in exchange for the veteran shortstop Erick Aybar and two top pitching prospects. Simmons was a two-time Rawlings Gold Glove winner, and recently named MLB's defensive player of the year. But Eppler said the importance of shortstop, and the scarcity of elite, available players in their prime at that position, caused him to be aggressive and trade for Simmons.

Third, according to an article in the *Los Angeles Times*, the Angels ruthlessly squeezed its stadium workers in contract talks for the second time in four years. The newspaper first reported this issue during the last round of contract talks in 2011 when the team provoked discontent among workers with very little leverage. Although workers voted to authorize a strike, that event never occurred.

In 2015, however, things appeared to worsen when the team tried to strap hundreds of stadium workers—represented by the Service Employees International Union—into a six-year contract with minimal pay raises. Workers say the team's offer on wages and working conditions reflect the poor treatment they received in general. In fact, they linked the downturn in labor relations at Angel Stadium of Anaheim to the arrival of Moreno as the franchise's new owner in 2003.

Fourth, Angels' chairman Dennis Kuhl believes it takes a group effort to keep people in the stands at the club's home games—that is, from the front office to janitors, ushers, and parking attendants that interact with fans before, during, and after each game. In other words, it is no different from any other business: a respected brand plus great customer service leads to repeat customers. "Our brand itself is well-known, but we also wanted to demonstrate great customer service," says Kuhl, who served as the team's president until 2009. "But that is only part of it. You have to reach out to the community in which you live. We have to let our fans know they're a big part of us being here in Orange County and Los Angeles." Kuhl and the club's leadership team picked three items to serve as the outward identity of the organization: the color red, the name "Angels," and the club's capital "A" logo. The use and appearance of these things is carefully managed to promote brand association throughout the fan base.

Fifth, Angels' president John Carpino said in 2014 that releasing the value of Angel Stadium property to the media—as requested by local government officials—will lead to an unworkable situation in the team's ongoing lease negotiations with the city. City officials argued that taxpayers should know the entire property's worth in addition to value of land that could be developed either by the team or by the city should owner Moreno move his team elsewhere when he has the opt-out clause to do so in 2019. But those financial documents with amounts, if released without proper context as Carpino contended in a letter to the Anaheim City Council, could be misunderstood by people.

OAKLAND ATHLETICS

While in the AL from 1901 to 1954, the Philadelphia Athletics—also known as the Philadelphia White Elephants—played in eight World Series and won five of them. Following that success, however, things soured quickly. As the Depression and war years lingered on, money became tight and regular-season attendances lean. With little wealth beyond the club itself, the downturn in attendance financially hurt the Mack family more than other MLB owners.

In 1950, owner-manager Connie Mack was eighty-six-years-old, out of touch, and struggling to keep the Athletics solvent while the crosstown NL Phillies were popular, successful, and NL champions. The Mack family held on before finally selling the team in 1954 for $6.7 million, plus $1.2 million for Connie Mack Stadium, to Midwestern magnate Arnold Johnson who then moved the club to Kansas City and renamed it the Kansas City Athletics (A's). While there, the club finished no higher than sixth in the league during thirteen MLB seasons.

After Johnson died in 1960, his estate sold 52 percent of the team's stock to businessman Charlie Finley for approximately $1.9 million. Later, Finley acquired the other 48 percent for about $1.8 million. Despite making promises to Kansas City fans, Finley was constantly looking for a better home for his club. He even agreed to deals with officials in Dallas, Texas, and Louisville, Kentucky, before MLB eventually permitted him to move the A's to Oakland, California, after their 1967 season, in part, because the city had completed construction on the Oakland-Alameda County Coliseum. If not for the new ballpark, nobody knows where Finley and his A's team would find a home.

Team Performances

While playing one year in the AL and then from 1969 to 2015 in the league's WD, the A's had 3,975 victories in approximately 52 percent of their games. During the period, they won sixteen division titles, six pennants, and four World Series in eighteen playoff appearances. In comparison to fourteen other teams in the league as of 2015, Oakland ranked second to the Yankees in division titles, tied for fourth with the Orioles in winning pennants, and tied for third with the Tigers in number of World Series titles. Within only the WD, Oakland had the most total championships followed by the Angels, Rangers, Mariners, and Astros (Table A1).

Among all MLB clubs as of their 2015 season, the forty-eight-year-old Oakland A's ranked third in division titles, tied for tenth in pennants, and tied for seventh in winning World Series. The club's most successful seasons consecutively were 1971–1975, 1988–1990, 2000–2003, and 2012–2014. These championships occurred, respectively, because of such players as pitcher Catfish Hunter and slugger Reggie Jackson; infielder Rickie Henderson and outfielder Jose Canseco; pitcher Barry Zito and hitter Jason Giambi; and slugger Josh Donaldson and pitcher Bartolo Colon. In addition to them, their outstanding managers were Dick Williams, Tony La Russa, Art Howe, and Bob Melvin.

The team, however, did not qualify for the playoffs in several periods including 1976–1980, 1982–1987, 1993–1999, and 2007–2011. Nevertheless, based on its rankings in this section and other information, Oakland has been very competitive in its division and league, in part, because of its managers who motivated their players, athletes who had excellent performances in regular-season and postseason games, and different owners who contributed to the franchise's historical accomplishments.[15]

Franchise Owner

Born in 1935 into a Jewish family in St. Louis, Lewis Wolff was raised in the middle-class suburb of University City, Missouri. After graduating from the University of Wisconsin, where he and former MLB Commissioner Bud Selig were fraternity brothers, Wolff earned a Master of Business Administration (MBA) degree from Washington University in St. Louis.

After working as a real estate appraiser in St. Louis during the late 1950s, Wolff's company sent him to California where he opened a regional office and in 1963 also cofounded a real estate consulting firm. Later, he became successful developing the booming San Diego housing and commercial market, and in the 1970s, Wolff accepted a position with 20th Century Fox managing its worldwide real estate investments.

In 1994, Wolff and his partner Philip Maritz opened Maritz, Wolff & Company in St. Louis. The business firm owned hotel and resort properties worldwide. Several years later, they orchestrated the $800 million sale of five hotels. Meanwhile Wolff had been co-owner of the National Hockey League (NHL) St. Louis Blues and National Basketball Association (NBA) Golden State Warriors. During April 2005 he and an ownership group, which included The Gap heir John Fisher, purchased the Oakland Athletics franchise for $180 million from Stephen Schott and Ken Hofmann.

Compared to other owners of AL teams as of their 2015 season, Wolff's A's tied for fourth in winning three division titles and also tied for eighth with zero pennants and for fifth with zero World Series titles. Among all MLB owners, his Oakland teams ranked respectively tied for seventh, eighth, and ninth. Based on these results, Wolff has been mediocre but occasionally above average as a franchise owner since 2005 (Table A2).

In Entertainment Sports Programming Network's (ESPN) annual fan ranking survey of professional sports franchises, Oakland's ownership group led by Wolff—but also including majority owner John Fisher and executive vice president Billy Beane—ranked last among 122 teams. After three straight postseason appearances, the A's finished with the worst record in the AL in 2015. The voting public was critical of Wolff because the team never spent enough money on payroll and also had particular issues with a front office that dealt fan favorites Josh Donaldson in 2015 to the league's Blue Jays and one year later, outfielder Yoenis Cespedes to the NL's Mets.[16]

O.co Coliseum

From 1968 to 1997 the A's played their home games at the Oakland-Alameda County Stadium (OACS)—renamed Network Associates Coliseum during 1998–2004, McAfee Coliseum in 2005, OACS again in 2009, and finally O.co Coliseum in 2011. During these MLB seasons, the club's annual attendance exceeded two million only eleven times.

A three-tiered stadium, OACS was built in a circular shape with many seats stretching from the foul poles and bleachers beyond the outfield fence. Two Diamond Vision video scoreboards exist above both the left and right field bleachers. Few renovations occurred until the NFL Raiders returned from Los Angeles to Oakland in 1995. In fact, the stadium was expanded with outfield bleachers replaced by a four-tier section of 22,000 seats—all orange being changed to green—and video boards installed above the stadium rim down both left and right field base lines.

After renaming its ballpark four times, the team closed the third deck of O.co Coliseum beginning in 2006. This decision moved fans closer to the field and made games more intimate. Although it has 60,000 seats, the stadium's capacity is actually about 35,000. Some fans arrive for games on BART METRO, and before each game they may also tailgate, discuss baseball, and mingle with each other.

Among ballparks of AL teams as of 2015, O.co Coliseum was the third oldest following the Red Sox's Fenway Park and the Angels' Angel Stadium. In addition, the ballpark ranked ninth in construction cost and thirteenth in value. But compared to those of all MLB teams, the A's home facility was fifth in age and also twenty-second to build and twenty-seventh in value. According to this data, Oakland's ball club plays its home games in a relatively inferior stadium (Table A3).

As discussed before for ballparks of the Astros and Angels, the TMR Company published prices and other costs for the home games of the A's. In the 2011–2015 MLB seasons, the FCIs for a four-person family to attend a regular-season game at O.co Coliseum ranged from a low of $178 in 2011 to a high of $200 in 2014. During the five-year period among ballparks of fourteen other AL clubs, the O.co Coliseum's FCI ranked eighth in 2011 and 2012, eleventh in 2013, and tenth in 2014 and 2015. In comparison to venues of only the league's WD teams, Oakland's fans paid less each year than spectators at the Mariners' home games in Seattle and Astros' games in Houston but more in some seasons than those at Angels' games in Anaheim and Rangers' in Arlington (Table A4).

To reveal specific costs for a recent year in MLB, O.co Coliseum's FCI in 2015 was about $195 or approximately 3 percent less than in 2014. Listed from most to least in amount by item for one person, the team's nonpremium tickets averaged $24, parking one vehicle $20, a cap $15, a hot dog between $5 and $6, beer $5 each, and a soft drink from $4 to $5. In comparison, the typical MLB ballpark's FCI exceeded the A's by $16 or 8 percent.

Among other teams in the WD, they had rankings and FCIs from most to least as follows in the 2015 MLB season: Astros tenth at $220; Mariners fifteenth at $212; Rangers twentieth at $191; and Angels twenty-first at $190. Based on their ballpark's FCI, A's home games were less expensive in 2015 than the Astros' and Mariners' but only a few dollars more than the Rangers' and Angels'. In turn, this pricing strategy generated maximum revenue from gate receipts for the franchise from games at O.co Coliseum.

The A's average premium ticket was approximately $52 at its home games in MLB's 2015 regular season. Among other WD teams, this was less than the Mariners' $206, Astros' $99, Angels' $76, and Rangers' $62. With the league's premium ticket price at $96, Oakland's fans paid a relatively smaller amount for the best seats at O.co Coliseum than did spectators at the majority of other MLB ballparks. For their nonpremium and premium tickets, the A's assigned competitive but fair prices to attract more fans and collect additional money from them at home games.

In a recent study by CSN Mid-Atlantic, the O.co Coliseum ranked thirtieth in MLB. According to an online report in *USA Today*, the author stated:

> The shame is, this once was a nice stadium. Back before Al Davis built the monstrosity that has overtaken the center-field bleachers as an upper deck for his Raiders, the Coliseum offered up gorgeous views of the mountains in the distance. These days, there are no mountains to be seen, only a decrepit stadium that feels even older than it is. Have we mentioned the recurring raw sewage problem? The A's and their fans deserve so much better than this, but they remain stuck in limbo while MLB tries to find a way to let them [possibly] relocate to San Jose, encroaching on territory the Giants claim is solely theirs.[17]

Financial Data

As commercial enterprises, it is important for MLB franchises to efficiently allocate resources, determine and distribute payrolls, set nonpremium and premium ticket prices, and schedule investments in short- and long-term assets.

This section focuses on different results of the A's business model and how well the organization succeeds or does not succeed from a financial perspective.

According to data and other financial information published in *Forbes* for franchises in the AL as of their 2015 season, Oakland ranked thirteenth in market value at $725 million, revenue at $202 million and gate receipts at $42 million, and also eighth in operating income at $20.8 million, and tied for eighth with the Royals in their 8 percent debt-to-value ratio. Among only the league's WD clubs, the A's had the smallest market value and gate receipts of the group but larger amounts than others in some years except for the Mariners.

Compared to twenty-nine different MLB teams in 2015, the A's were twenty-seventh in both market value and revenue, sixteenth in operating income, tied for twenty-sixth with the NL Diamondbacks in gate receipts, and tied for seventeenth with the AL Royals and NL Phillies in their debt-to-value percent. Based on this data and other information, Oakland struggles from a financial perspective because of its outdated ballpark, relatively small market size, business and ownership issues, and attendance problems (Table A5).

Besides market size, salary inflation, and other factors, an MLB team's annual payroll partly reflects its commitment to players and their current and potential contribution as a group to winning games in regular seasons and postseasons. From 2011 to 2015, for example, the A's payroll among fifteen AL teams ranged from tenth in 2011 ($66 million) to fourteenth each in 2012 ($55 million), 2013 ($47 million), and 2014 ($47 million). Except for the Astros, the club had the lowest payrolls in the WD during the period (Table A6).

In comparison to payrolls of twenty-nine other MLB teams as of their 2015 season, the A's ranked from twenty-first in 2011 to twenty-ninth in 2012. Only the AL's Astros and Rays and also NL's Marlins and Padres had comparable amounts to Oakland's despite a significant increase in the 2015 season. This, in part, frustrates A's fans about owner Lewis Wolff and his decision to not sign free agents and veteran players to expensive, multiyear contracts.

Business Relations

Besides regular-season and postseason games, MLB franchises are involved in—and affected by—internal policies, community events, and business-related affairs and projects. In no specific order, the following are a few of them for Oakland's AL team as of 2015.[18]

First, the A's paid about $250,000 in 2014 to settle claims that they illegally underpaid their clubhouse workers and interns. Under an agreement with the U.S. Department of Labor (DOL), at least eighty current or former workers received a total of $266,358 according to a department spokesperson. The DOL's Wage & Hour Division continues its discussions with the A's and looks for future opportunities to provide meaningful compliance assistance. Interestingly, the investigations have not gone unnoticed by MLB officials.

Second, the A's offer a wide range of special event areas and outstanding food service to suit groups or company's needs. From small business meetings to large corporate events, O.co Coliseum has space for groups. For example, there is one conference room available for intimate board meetings. Located on the eastside of the stadium, this room accommodates up to thirty-five guests and is equipped with tables and chairs. In the Eastside Club, the North Alcove is available for pregame business meetings. This place accommodates up to eighty people. Located on the Club Concourse Level above the outfield area, the Club offers forty thousand square feet of space for business and social events. From sales meetings to receptions, it provides amenities for up to three thousand guests.

Third, a few days after Alameda County said it wanted to sell its stake in the Oakland Coliseum sports complex—a move that could smooth out negotiations for a planned $1 billion sports, housing, and retail complex on the site—A's owner Lew Wolff objected to the buyout proposal. At a meeting of local leaders in the summer of 2014, Wolff said it would not simplify matters if the county sold its stake in the complex to the city of Oakland.

To continue hosting the A's and perhaps NFL Raiders, Oakland and county leaders negotiated to build Coliseum City, a plan promoted by Floyd Kephart's New City Development. That deal would include a $900 million home for both professional teams. City and county officials declared that removing one public entity from the mix would streamline the process. But others believe that a buyout would add yet another level of potentially drawn-out deal-making to an already fraught and complex negotiating process between the two governments, sports teams, and private developers.[19]

Fourth, sticking to their positions against helping pay for new stadiums, Oakland's city leaders watched MLB keep the A's out of San Jose while the NFL denied the Raiders a site in Los Angeles in 2016. Even the NBA Warriors will play games in Oakland for another three seasons while they battle twin lawsuits against their proposed move to San Francisco.

For now, Oakland is the "Hotel California" of professional sports and better positioned to keep the A's and Raiders now that the teams' first choices for relocation appear off the table, according to Stanford University sports economist Roger Noll. But that does not solve the underlying issue: that the city lacks the financial and political will to help pay for new stadiums, and its teams have been unwilling to commit to a market that cannot match the wealth found on the other side of the Bay Area. The city is offering to essentially split the 120-acre Coliseum complex between the Raiders and A's, but both teams have said they want full control of the site. The A's, who say they do not need a stadium subsidy, are looking at other locations but haven't yet found anything to their liking.

From an economic standpoint, the A's have more incentive than the Raiders to stay in Oakland. While NFL teams share television revenue equally, local television rights are an increasingly big chunk of a baseball team's revenues. That would make the A's more valuable in a new Oakland stadium than they would be in a smaller city such as Charlotte, North Carolina; Portland, Oregon; or San Antonio, Texas. A sports business consultant and former A's executive said he expects the team to eventually build a new stadium in Oakland, which is still a viable big-league city.

Fifth, more than ten years after the publication of *Moneyball*, the baseball landscape changed in no small part because of the A's success and the massive publicity their methods occasioned. In fact, every team employs statistical analytics and advanced sabermetrics. Thus, the A's are back at square one: they still need to compete with big-market teams like the Yankees and Red Sox, but now all of them are aware of the A's long-held advantage. How, then, do the A's still manage to compete, in an enlightened day and age?

Author of *Baseball Prospectus*, Andrew Koo's theory is that the A's have found another undervalued statistic that correlates strongly to performance. That statistic, in a nutshell, is the fly-ball rate of hitters. Koo argues that a key to the A's fantastic 2012 and 2013 seasons was their acquisition and deployment of fly-ball hitters—as opposed to ground-ball hitters. For business leaders, here are two key points: finding market inefficiencies is an ongoing concern and also remember why you are hiring people in the first place.[20]

SEATTLE MARINERS

Minor league baseball was played in Seattle, Washington, in the 1890s and then continuously during 1898–1968. The Pacific Coast League (PCL) fielded a team from 1903 to 1906 and again beginning in 1919. The most popular local team was the Seattle Rainiers, named after nearby Mount Rainier.

Although referred to as the Indians in 1921, Rainier Brewing Company and team owner Emil Sick renamed them Rainiers. Sick also built the club a 15,000-seat ballpark, and labelled it Sick's Stadium. During the 1950s, Hall of Famer Rogers Hornsby and legend Fred Hutchinson each managed the Rainiers and led them to championships. But after Sick sold his team in 1960, eight years later it folded because of poor attendance at games and financial problems.[21]

After Seattle's first MLB team, the Pilots, finished last in the AL's WD and financially were unable to stay afloat in Sick's Stadium, they moved to Milwaukee after their 1969 season. Almost immediately, plans began to bring another big-league team to the city. The first step was to build a multipurpose, domed stadium for big-time professional sports. During its development, however, the city of Seattle filed a lawsuit against MLB. Because baseball's franchise owners feared the potential harm of a lawsuit, they decided to honor Seattle with a new team during the next expansion phase.

By the mid-1970s, an expansion team was a hollow promise in the city. As a result Seattle tried to attract an existing MLB team to move into the new 59,100-seat Kingdome, which was to be completed in 1976. Meanwhile, a group of investors were ready to buy the AL Chicago White Sox and move the club to the Emerald City (Seattle's nickname during the mid-1980s), but baseball officials refused to allow this charter franchise to leave the Windy City. Concerned about additional lawsuits and also relocation threats, MLB fulfilled its promise and awarded Seattle an expansion team to begin play in 1977. A syndicate, which included Hollywood movie star actor Danny Kaye, purchased the franchise for $6.25 million.

Team Performances

While a member of the league's WD from the 1977 to 2015 season, the Mariners played 6,193 games and had victories in 46 percent of them. During the period, they won three division titles but zero pennants and World Series in four playoff appearances. Compared to fourteen other AL clubs as of 2015, Seattle ranked respectively thirteenth, tied for fourteenth with the Astros, and tied for twelfth with the Rays, Astros, and Rangers. Among only teams in their division, Seattle had fewer total championships than those of the Angels, Athletics, and Rangers (Table A1).

With respect to all MLB teams as of 2015, the Mariners were twenty-fourth in winning division titles, tied for twenty-seventh in pennants, and tied for twenty-third in number of World Series victories. According to this data, Seattle has performed below average while competing against others in the AL because of such things as its managers' problems in making decisions, inferior player performances, and wrong or misguided ownership actions.

To 2015, the Mariners most productive seasons were in 1995, 1997, and from 2000 to 2001. Led by manager Lou Piniella, their best players included pitcher Randy Johnson and sluggers Ken Griffey Jr. and Alex Rodriguez, and infielder Bret Boone. Alternatively, the club failed to qualify for the playoffs during such consecutive periods as 1977 to 1994 and 2002 to 2015. In part, too much competition from the Angels, Athletics, and Rangers and lack of talented players at key positions were reasons for Seattle finishing regular seasons between second and seventh in its division.

The Mariners had high hopes for 2016 and also 2017. The same could be said about 2014, so there are reasons to be skeptical. While injuries took their toll, the bullpen was disastrous, and it seemed every important player had a slow start. Although the club provided depth across the board during the offseason, none of that matters if superstar Robinson Cano does not perform at least to expectations.

The team signed Cano to a ten-year, $240 million contract in 2014, and time to fulfill that contract is running out. While he has several years left on the deal, talks have already started about moving him from second to first base. Once Cano plays at first base, his contract significantly overpays him. Initially, team officials thought that Cano would exceed the value of his contract for the first few years while underperforming it during later years.

Franchise Owner

In 1989, radio station owner Jeff Smulyan paid approximately $80 million to purchase the Seattle Mariners franchise from George Argyros, a southern California land developer. Argyros had acquired the Mariners for $13.1 million in 1981 from a group headed by entertainer Danny Kaye who originally obtained them when MLB expanded in the late 1970s.

While owned by Smulyan and his syndicate, the Mariners improved in their performances by finishing fifth in the league's WD in 1990 and 1991. Unfortunately, he mortgaged his radio stations to buy the team and thus had to sell it after the Security Pacific Bank demanded he repay his loan of $40 million. Besides Seattle, syndicates from other cities tried to acquire the franchise. However, the Mariners' lease on the local stadium required Smulyan to offer his club to a local group at an independently appraised price.

Nintendo of America (NOA), a large and rich international company based in the Seattle suburb of Redmond, Washington, and led during the late 1980s/early 1990s by Minoru Arakawa and his son-in-law Hiroshi Yamauchi, offered to raise a majority of the $100 million selling price and $25 million in operating capital from their consortium—The Baseball Club of Seattle. With Arakawa voting the Yamauchi family's stock, NOA owned approximately 60 percent of the group, which also included investors from the area's high-technology companies. Investors and their share of the team were respectively John McCaw (9 percent), a director of McCaw Cellular; Christopher Larson (22 percent) of Microsoft Inc.; Frank Shrontz (undisclosed percent), the president and CEO of The Boeing Corporation; and John Ellis (undisclosed percent), the president and CEO of Puget Sound Power & Light Company.

During September 2013, the Mariners' eighty-five-year-old principal owner and retired chairman of NOA, Hiroshi Yamauchi, died at a hospital in central Japan. Under Yamauchi's ownership, the Mariners built a strong relationship with Japan and had several outstanding Japanese players sign with the club including ten-time, all-star right fielder Ichiro Suzuki.

Two years after he replaced Yamauchi, the fifty-five-year-old CEO and president of NOA, Satoru Iwata, had died of bile duct cancer. According to Howard Lincoln, the Mariners' CEO and member of the team's board of directors, Iwata's death would have no immediate impact on the franchise. As of early 2016, NOA owned 55 percent of the club and had no intention of selling it.[22]

In comparison to the principal owners of other AL teams as of their 2015 season, NOA tied for fourth in division titles with the Yankees' Hal Steinbrenner, Athletics' Lewis Wolff, and Rangers' Ray Davis. For winning zero pennants and World Series, respectively, NOA tied for eighth and fifth in the league. Among all MLB owners, the Seattle-based company tied for seventh in division titles, for fourteenth in pennants, and for ninth in World Series titles. Consequently, NOA has been neither outstanding nor inferior as an owner during its six-year history in MLB (Table A2).

Safeco Field

For more than two decades, sports fans watched the Mariners play their home games at the concrete and sterile Kingdome. Although it was revolutionary when opened in the late 1970s, by the early-to-mid-1990s a new wave of ballparks were being built in baseball, which made the Kingdome an outdated but semipopular facility.[23]

The Mariners, therefore, wanted a new state-of-the-art ballpark for their fans, and also the franchise needed it as a way to increase its revenue because of financial losses in 1993 and 1994. Since a new ballpark was seen as a way to solidify the city's sense of community and lead to economic development, the team would not sign a long-term lease to remain in Seattle if ground was not broken for a modern stadium by 1996.

In 1994, the King County Stadium Alternatives Task Force was established after tiles from the Kingdome's roof crashed onto several seating areas forcing the team to play on the road for the rest of the season. Then in 1995, Washington State's governor together with King County developed the Public Facilities District to oversee site selection, design, construction, and management of a new ballpark. Although voters rejected a proposal to increase the sales tax in September 1995, one month later the state's legislature authorized funding for a stadium.

After choosing a site directly south of the Kingdome, the Mariners unveiled plans for their ballpark in early 1997. Besides following the same neotraditional pattern as every new ballpark built in the 1990s, it featured a brick façade with natural grass and a retractable roof. The roof was necessary because of Seattle's rainy weather, and a major portion of the team's fans lived within an hour of the stadium. As a result, 47,500-seat Safeco Field opened in mid-July 1999.

Safeco Field has several amenities and attractions including the Bullpen Market and such things as the Fan Walk's personalized bricks, local food vendors, an open-pit barbecue, and one of the best views of the game from behind the center field fence. Located at the end of the left field line on the upper deck, Lookout Landing provides incredible views of inside and also outside the ballpark. In addition, there is an Outside Corner Picnic Patio, a Children's Hospital playfield, and the largest video board in baseball.

Among ballparks of AL teams as of 2015, Safeco Field was the fifth youngest, second most costly to build, and sixth highest in value. But compared to those of all MLB teams, the Mariners' home venue ranked sixteenth in age and also fourth in construction cost and fifteenth in value. According to this data, Seattle's baseball club plays its home games in an expensive but middle-aged and medium-valued stadium (Table A3).

As discussed before for ballparks of the Astros, Angels, and Athletics, the TMR company published costs for fans at Mariners home games. In the 2011–2015 MLB seasons, the FCIs for a four-person family to attend a regular-season game at Safeco Field ranged from a low of $183 in 2011 to a high of $212 in 2015 and also in rank from seventh in 2011, 2012, and 2015 to eighth in 2013 and 2014 among AL teams. Other than Astros games at Minute Maid Park in Houston during the 2013 to 2015 seasons, Seattle's cost more to be at than those for fans at games in Angel Stadium of Anaheim, O.co Coliseum, and Globe Life Park (Table A4).

To reveal specific costs for a recent year in MLB, the Mariners' ballpark's FCI in 2015 was $212 (ranked fifteenth) or 2 to 3 percent more than in 2014. Listed from most to least in amount by item for one person, the team's non-premium (premium) tickets averaged $31 ($206), parking for one vehicle $20, a cap $10, beer $6, and a hot dog and soft drink each between $4 and $5. In comparison, the typical ballpark's FCI was, on average, $211 in 2015.

Among other WD teams and their ballparks, they had rankings and FCIs from most to least as follows in the 2015 MLB season: Astros tenth at $220; Athletics nineteenth at $195; Rangers twentieth at $191; and Angels twenty-first at $190. Given these amounts, Seattle's home games were relatively expensive for families to attend because of various factors including the ballpark's location and its amenities, population and growth of the local sports market, and the city's cost-of-living and consumer's disposable income.

In a recent study by CSN Mid-Atlantic, Safeco Field ranked sixth in MLB. According to an online report in *USA Today*, the author said:

> It's the best of the domes, in large part because it's not actually a dome. The retractable roof at Safeco closes when it rains, but it doesn't completely enclose the ballpark. That makes it feel more like you're outdoors (even if it does require bringing a jacket to the game). The left-field bullpens and overhanging bleachers are among the best features of the Mariners' home of the last 15 years. The Nats [Washington Nationals] will be paying their first visit there since 2008 in September [2016].[24]

Financial Data

As commercial enterprises, it is important for MLB franchises to efficiently allocate resources, determine and distribute payrolls, set nonpremium and premium ticket prices, and schedule investments in short- and long-term assets. This section focuses on different results of the Mariners' business model and how well the organization succeeds or does not succeed from a financial perspective.

According to data and other financial information published in *Forbes* for AL franchises as of their 2015 season, Seattle ranked sixth in both market value at $1.1 billion and revenue at $250 million, and also fifth in operating income at $26.4 million, ninth in gate receipts at $56 million, and tied for eleventh with four other clubs in their zero percent debt-to-value ratio. Among only the league's WD teams, the Mariners had the most operating income but a smaller market value and less revenue and gate receipts than the Angels and Rangers (Table A5).

Compared to all MLB clubs as of 2015, Seattle was fourteenth in both market value and revenue, twelfth in operating income, twentieth in gate receipts, and tied for twenty-fifth in its debt-to-value. From a financial perspective, this team is an average business enterprise but also superior economically to such AL clubs as the Rays, Indians, and Athletics.

An MLB team's annual payroll partly reflects its commitment to players and their current and potential contribution as a group to winning games in regular seasons and postseasons. From 2011 to 2015, for example, the Mariners payroll among AL teams ranged in rank from sixth in 2015 ($123 million) to twelfth in 2013 ($60 million). For various reasons, the league's WD Angels and Rangers had higher payrolls than the Mariners during the period (Table A6).

In comparison to payrolls of twenty-nine other MLB teams as of their 2015 season, the Mariners ranged in rank from eleventh in 2015 to twenty-fifth in 2013. Since the club finished third once and fourth four-times in its division since 2011, franchise owner NOA needs more productivity from its roster of players in games especially after increasing their payroll by 38 percent or from $89 million in 2014 to $123 million in 2015.

Business Relations

Besides regular-season and postseason games, MLB franchises are involved in—and affected by—internal policies, community events, and local business-related affairs and projects. In no specific order, the following are a few of them for Seattle's AL team as of 2015.[25]

First, the Mariners' blockbuster television deal with Root Sports Northwest kicked off with the 2014 season. The club's rights fee will average $103 million over eighteen years with the total value of the deal, including the team's equity stake, worth an estimated $2.5 billion. The Mariners put the money to work with a ten-year, $240 million contract for superstar Robinson Cano before the 2014 season and a four-year, $58 million agreement with slugger Nelson Cruz. While the team posted its best record since 2007, attendance jumped 17 percent but ranked only twenty-third in baseball with Safeco Field filled to 53 percent of its capacity. Despite a significant increase in payroll, Seattle's attendance per game in 2015 fell from ninth to tenth in the league.

Second, during late 2013, the Mariners agreed to a new seventeen-year local television contract with DirecTV Sports Networks estimated in worth at $2 billion. With an average annual value of $118 million, that amounts to a $73 million increase over their previous deal, which paid the team $45 million per year. In addition, every big-league club will get a $25 million increase in revenue from MLB's new national television contracts which went into effect in 2014. In other words, the Mariners will realize a $98 million increase in revenue every year just from television contracts.

Third, in late 2015, Seattle's front office continued to fall into place with Tom Allison being promoted to oversee the organization's scouting operations. Allison had spent the previous three years as director of professional scouting, but in a revamped structure under new general manager Jerry Dipoto, he will also direct the club's efforts in amateur and international scouting.

The Mariners also promoted scout Lee MacPhail IV to fill Allison's former role as director of professional scouting. MacPhail reports to Allison under the new alignment as will amateur scouting director Tom McNamara and director of international operations Tim Kissner. Although officials did not confirm these personnel changes, the club also hired Andy McKay to replace Chris Gwynn as their director of player development. McKay had spent three years as the NL Rockies' peak performance coordinator—or mental-skills coach—after fourteen years as a coach at Sacramento City College.

Fourth, although former outfielder Ken Griffey Jr. came close to being a unanimous choice for the National Baseball Hall of Fame, three voters (.7 percent) failed to name him on their ballot. One of the greatest MLB players of all time, he received the highest percentage ever topping former New York Mets' pitcher Tom Seaver's 98.8 percent.[26]

During his twenty-two seasons (thirteen with the Mariners), Griffey hit .284 with 630 career home runs—sixth-most ever—and also had 2,781 hits, which ranked him fiftieth all time. A thirteen-time all-star, Griffey was the AL's MVP in 1997. Not only do his statistics place him among all-time leaders in the big-leagues and make him a dominating player for much of his career, he also earned respect for being one of the few sluggers of his era to avoid using steroids when performance-enhancing drugs were prevalent in the sport.

Fifth, according to a report published online by cbssports.com in early 2015, the Mariners' best team ever was in 2001 when they had a 116–46 record in the regular season but lost to the Yankees in the league's championship series. Besides winning the WD by fourteen games, Seattle outscored its opponents by 300 runs and never lost ten games in any month.

In contrast, the club's worst season was 2010. At 61–101 and fourth in the division, it was last in runs, hits, doubles, triples, homers, batting average, and on-base and slugging percentages. In fact, the Mariners were *much worse* than their rivals. While the league averaged 721 runs, Seattle scored only 513 or 100 fewer than the second-lowest team, Baltimore Orioles. The Mariners' offense was so bad that pitcher Felix Hernandez was good enough to win the Cy Young award despite having a mediocre 13–12 pitching record. The team, meanwhile, was 17–17 in Hernandez's starts but unfortunately 44–84 in other games.

TEXAS RANGERS

Following the Washington Senator's relocation to the upper Midwest in 1960 and being renamed Minnesota Twins, the AL preferred not to lose its presence in the nation's capital city. Consequently, the league expanded and replaced the former Washington team with another one. From 1961 to 1971, the new Senators played 1,772 games and won approximately 41 percent of them. During their first eight years, they finished between sixth and tenth in the AL and then fourth, sixth, and fifth in the league's ED.[27]

After several seasons, the Senators were on the verge of leaving Washington but MLB and the city had no immediate expansion options. In part, the problem preventing any success of baseball in Washington was the nearby

Baltimore Orioles who reduced the Senators' fan base in half and was one of the league's prominent teams.

Struggling with attendances at less than 10,000 per game, the Senators received an offer from officials in the Dallas-Fort Worth area to move there in 1972. For years, Dallas-Fort Worth tried to lure a big-league team including the Oakland Athletics, but MLB rejected that effort in 1962. Seven years later, the metropolitan area in northeastern Texas fell short in attempting to win one of baseball's four expansion slots. That, in turn, motivated Dallas-Fort Worth officials to attract an existing team.

As a result, the city expanded a minor league ballpark close to a turnpike in nearby Arlington, Texas. With the Senators struggling in Washington, their owner Robert E. Short began looking for another site for his team. When Dallas offered him a multimillion dollar, upfront payment for television and radio broadcast rights, Short asked other AL franchise owners for permission to move his club from Washington to Arlington. With the Orioles already entrenched in the D.C. area, the owners had no problem with Short's request and ten days before the end of the MLB's 1971 season, approved it. Renamed Texas Rangers and located in the Dallas-Fort Worth area, Short sold his investment in the team for $10 million to a syndicate headed by Texas businessman Brad Corbett.

Team Performances

While a member of the league's WD from 1972 to 2015, the Rangers played 6,992 games and had victories in approximately 49 percent of them. During the period, they won seven division titles, two pennants, and zero World Series in seven playoffs. Among fourteen other AL teams in 2015, Texas tied for eighth with the Red Sox, Indians, and Tigers in winning division titles, tied for tenth with the Blue Jays in number of pennants, and tied for twelfth with the Rays, Astros, and Mariners in World Series titles. With respect to only WD clubs, the Rangers had fewer championships than the Angels and Athletics (Table A1).

In comparison to twenty-nine other MLB teams as of their 2015 season, Texas tied for fifteenth in division titles, tied for nineteenth in pennants, and tied for twenty-third in World Series titles. According to these results and other information, the Rangers have been an average team in their division and league during forty-four years in MLB.

Besides its postseasons in 1996 and 2015, the club's successful years consecutively were 1998–1999 and also 2010–2012. Their most prominent players included pitcher Ken Hill, catcher Ivan Rodriguez, outfielder Josh Hamilton, infielder Ian Kinsler, and slugger Adrian Beltre. Alternatively, the team failed to qualify for the playoffs in back-to-back seasons of 1972–1995, 2000–2009, and 2013–2014. In those years, it had inferior performances because of managers' bad decisions and other mistakes, not enough talented players (especially pitchers), and other problems.

With a franchise-record 96 wins in 2011, the Rangers' best team won the AL's divisional and championship series in route to their second consecutive pennant and within one strike of winning a World Series. On offense, they ranked third in runs, second in hits, third in doubles, second in homers, fourth in steals, first in average, third in on-base percentage, and second in slugging. Also, five of their pitchers each had at least thirteen wins and three an outstanding earned run average (ERA). In contrast to 2011 and their other playoff appearances, Texas's clubs won fewer than sixty games in 1972–1973, 1981, and 1994.

Franchise Owner

After competing in four high school sports during the early 1960s, Ray Davis attended LeTourneau College in Longview, Texas, on a scholarship and played guard on the school's basketball team. Davis also played baseball at LeTourneau but had to move to first base and shortstop after starting out as a Little League catcher—until a ball hit him in the throat.

Ray worked in the energy industry for forty years and then retired as the CEO of Energy Transfer Partners and Energy Transfer Equity in 2007. He remained as a director of these companies while operating Avatar Investments LP, a Dallas-based investment firm. In 2008, Davis made his first appearance on the Forbes 400 list, ranking 367th with a net worth of $1 billion.

When the Rangers were offered for sale in 2010, Davis joined a group headed by Chuck Greenberg and Nolan Ryan to purchase the franchise. He and investor Bob Simpson provided most of the $593 million sale price, and as a result, they became cochairmen of the club. Nevertheless, both of them have remained behind-the-scenes as senior consultants while allowing Greenberg and Ryan to operate the team as CEO and president, respectively. This arrangement continued after Greenberg left the organization in 2011 and ceded his position to Ryan.

Following Ryan's resignation from the franchise in 2013, MLB approved the Rangers' request for Davis to replace him as the person in control. This, in turn, made Davis the primary official accountable to the commissioner's office for the team's operations. However, he and Simpson have largely kept in the background, leaving general manager Jon Daniels as the operating executive of the club.

For his effectiveness among principal owners of AL teams as of 2015, Davis's Rangers tied for fourth with three division titles, tied for second with two pennants, and tied for fifth with zero World Series championships. Compared to all owners of MLB franchises, his baseball clubs were respectively tied for seventh, tied for fifth, and tied for ninth. Thus, the Rangers have performed above average since Davis purchased them in 2010 (Table A2).

A thoughtful and dedicated owner and also a thorough, results-driven leader who has been an asset to the sport in recent years, Davis was appointed by MLB Commissioner Rob Manfred to baseball's eight-member executive council and to international and game-day media committees. Historically, Rangers executives have never served on any of these committees before Davis.

Globe Life Park

From 1972 to 1993, the Rangers played their home games in Arlington Stadium. However, because of Texas's summer heat and humidity, the ballpark was the hottest ballpark in MLB. Thus, almost all Rangers home games, even those on Sundays, were played at night. As a result, the team began lobbying for a new stadium in the late 1980s and then during October 1990, the Rangers and city of Arlington agreed to build it.

After construction began in April 1992 and then ended twenty-three months later, The Ballpark in Arlington—renamed Ameriquest Field in 2005, Rangers Ballpark in Arlington in 2008, and finally Globe Life Park (GLP) in 2014—opened for the team's 1994 season. Designed with ideas from bygone stadiums, the 49,000-seat ballpark resembles Brooklyn's Ebbets Field with its red brick façade and arches. Besides a brick Wall of Fame containing information about every Rangers team, it is the only retro ballpark with enclosed seats and a four-story office complex surrounding the playing field.

More specifically, GLP's amenities include such things as 120 luxury suites divided into two tiers; a large video scoreboard located above the home run porch in right field; a Rangers Baseball Hall of Fame that contains team artifacts and captures the franchise's history; the Kid's Zone, which provides interactive games for kids and all-you-can-eat seats in the upper home run porch; an expanded home plate club; the Capital One club; and a new merchandise store.

Among ballparks of AL teams as of 2015, GLP tied with the Indians' Progressive Field for the ninth youngest while being the tenth most expensive to build, and third highest in real estate value. But compared to those of all MLB teams, the Rangers' home site tied for eleventh in age and also ranked twenty-third in construction cost and eighth in value. According to the data, this Texas baseball club plays its home games in a relatively young but highly valued building with plenty of nice features (Table A3).

As discussed before for ballparks of the Astros, Angels, Athletics, and Mariners, the TMR company published costs for fans at Rangers home games. In the 2011–2015 MLB seasons, the FCIs for a four-person family to attend a regular-season game at GLP ranged from a low of $159 in 2011 to a high of $203 in 2014. Among those of fourteen other AL teams, the ballpark varied in rank from tenth in 2012 ($183) and 2013 ($196) to twelfth in 2011 ($159). During most years, it cost less for fans to attend Rangers' home games than any in Houston and occasionally for games played in Anaheim, Oakland, and Seattle (Table A4).[28]

To reveal specific costs for a recent year in MLB, GLP's FCI in 2015 was $191 (ranked twentieth) or approximately 6–7 percent less than in 2014. Listed from most to least in amount by item for one person, the team's nonpremium (premium) tickets averaged $23–$24 ($62–$63), a cap about $18, parking one vehicle $12, a beer and hot dog each $5, and a soft drink between $4 and $5. Interestingly, Texas's home games cost $20 or almost 10 percent less for families in 2015 than did those of the typical MLB team.

Among other WD teams and their ballparks, they had rankings and FCIs from most to least as follows in the 2015 MLB season: Astros tenth at $220; Mariners fifteenth at $212; Athletics nineteenth at $195; and Angels twenty-first at $190. Given these amounts, Rangers home games were relatively inexpensive for families to attend because of various factors including GLP's location and its amenities, population growth of the local sports market, people's disposable income, and the popularity of baseball as opposed to other major sports in the Dallas-Fort Worth Area.

In a recent study by CSN Mid-Atlantic, GLP ranked twenty-sixth in MLB. According to an online report published in *USA Today*, the author said:

> Why does the Rangers' ballpark rank so low? Let's count the ways: 1) It's too big, like so many other things in Texas, 2) It's too hot, like so many other things in Texas, because it has a southeasterly orientation for no good reason, 3) It's too contrived (the overhanging upper deck in right field feels completely out of the place with the rest of the park, and 4) It has had about 17 different names [actually 4] over the last two decades.

Financial Data

As commercial enterprises, it is important for MLB franchises to efficiently allocate resources, determine and distribute payrolls, set nonpremium and premium ticket prices, and schedule investments in short- and long-term assets. This section focuses on different results of the Rangers' business model and how well the organization succeeds or does not succeed from a financial perspective.

According to data and other financial information published in *Forbes* for franchises in the AL as of their 2015 season, Texas ranked fourth in both market value at $1.22 billion and revenue at $266 million, and also thirteenth in operating income at $3.5 million, fifth in gate receipts at $74 million, and sixth in its debt-to-value ratio at 13 percent. Compared to other teams in the league's WD, the Rangers had the lowest operating income but highest gate receipts. Consequently, this is a relatively valuable AL franchise with enough revenue from ticket sales to continue its operations at home games in GLP (Table A5).

Among twenty-nine other MLB clubs in 2015, the Rangers ranked eleventh in market value, tenth in revenue, twenty-fourth in operating income, tied for eleventh with the NL Mets in gate receipts, and fourteenth in its debt-to-value ratio. Except for its operating income, this Arlington-based big-league team is an above-average organization from a financial perspective and also competitive as a business enterprise within the professional sports industry.

An MLB team's annual payroll partly reflects its commitment to players and their current and potential contribution individually and as a group to winning games in regular seasons and postseasons. From 2011 to 2015, for example, the Rangers payroll among AL teams ranged in rank from fifth in 2015 ($144 million) to seventh in 2012 ($92 million), 2013 ($97 million) and 2014 ($101 million). For various reasons, the WD Angels had higher payrolls than Texas during the five-year period (Table A6).

In comparison to payrolls of twenty-nine other MLB teams as of their 2015 season, the Rangers ranged in rank from eighth in 2015 ($144 million) to fourteenth in 2014 ($101 million). Since the club finished second four times since 2011, its players have produced excellent results in regular-season and postseason games by winning a World Series in three playoff appearances.

Business Relations

Besides regular-season and postseason games, MLB franchises are involved in—and affected by—internal decisions, policies and rules, and also community events and local business-related achievements, affairs, and projects. In no specific order, the following are a few of them for Anaheim's AL team as of 2015.[29]

First, no MLB club as of 2014 has experienced more major organizational changes than the Rangers. Since the departure of president of business operations Rick George and chief executive Nolan Ryan, the team installed cochairman Ray Davis as its designated control executive; became responsible for approximately $300 million in future salary commitments by acquiring players Prince Fielder and Shin-Soo Choo; signed a ten-year ballpark naming-rights deal with Globe Life Insurance reportedly worth $50 million; and continued on a multiyear effort to upgrade Globe Life Park. In addition to these changes, the Rangers' former head of stadium operations Rob Matwick had his duties expand in the transition and become the senior day-to-day executive running the club's business operations.

Second, the heartbreaking case of a Rangers fan falling to his death during July 2011—while catching a foul ball tossed to him by the franchise's iconic star Josh Hamilton—required an urgent and elite crisis communications response from the franchise. Under exceptionally difficult circumstances, the Rangers delivered as an organization. After team president Nolan Ryan took command and answered questions in a postgame news conference, Hamilton followed to share his thoughts with reporters. A trust fund was established on the team's website, stadium officials were accessible and informed, and the response was accountable, sincere, and swift.

Third, Texas hired former Boston Red Sox executive Joe Januszewski in 2011 to be executive vice president for business partnerships and development, which completed a dramatic executive reshaping that co-owner Chuck Greenberg believed would help transform the club. Januszewski, whose eight-year run in Boston coincided with the growth of the Red Sox franchise, remaking of Fenway Park and acquisition of Liverpool FC [Football Club], followed recent team hires of Rick George from the PGA Tour, Todd Taylor from the Milwaukee Brewers, and Jay Miller from Ryan-Sanders Baseball. George was assigned to be CEO of the Rangers; Taylor as their executive vice president for ticket sales and marketing; and Miller a senior vice president.

Fourth, the Rangers unveiled some new aesthetic changes for Globe Life Park that take effect for the 2016 season. The biggest addition is a gigantic 34-by-94–foot LED video board that stands tall above the visitors' bullpen area in center field. In addition to the new video board, the club announced it will swap out the foul poles used since 1972 for new ones, which gives fans a special opportunity at the team's Fan Fest event.

According to executive vice president of ballpark entertainment and production Chuck Morgan: "The addition of a new Daktronics HD-quality video board in left field falls right in line with our ownership's commitment to having the best ballpark experience for our fans. Just as the Globe Life Park upgrades have done in previous years, the addition of this video board will add to the in-stadium experience and create a unique atmosphere that you cannot get at home."[30]

Fifth, an ambitious proposal for a $200 million development near Globe Life Park and the NFL Cowboys' 101,000-seat AT&T Stadium includes a grand hotel, restaurants, shops, and convention space. The project will cover 100,000 square feet to the southwest of the Rangers' ballpark but subject to city council approval. A birds-eye rendering of the project shows a big hotel with a rooftop pool attached to shops and restaurants. There also will be 35,000 feet of convention space. If approved, construction on the development would likely begin in 2016 or 2017. It is not yet known which restaurant, shop, or hotel brands would be in the area. The Rangers are floating a public-private partnership to make the concept work with the city contributing about $50 million to the project.

NOTES

1. Two books about the history of big-league teams are Frank P. Jozsa Jr., *American League Franchises: Team Performances and Business Success* (New York: Springer, 2015); and James Quirk and Rodney D. Fort, *Pay Dirt: The Business of Professional Team Sports* (Princeton, NJ: Princeton University Press, 1992).
2. For how the Houston Colt .45s and other clubs in the league's WD formed and then performed in MLB's regular-seasons and postseasons, see their website on http://www.mlb.com and results on http://www.baseball-reference.com.
3. Barry M. Bloom, "Astros Sale to Crane, Move to AL Approved," http://www.m.mlb.com, cited March 1, 2016.
4. See the careers of baseball's franchise owners such as Jim Crane and others at http://www.mlb.com and "List of Major League Baseball Principal Owners," http://www.baseball-reference.com, cited January 22, 2016.
5. A useful online reference of MLB teams' ballparks is http://www.ballparksofbaseball.com.
6. This is reported in "Ranking All 30 MLB Ballparks," http://www.csnmidatlantic.com, cited January 26, 2016, and also in "Ranking MLB's Ballparks," http://www.athlonsports.com, cited January 26, 2016.
7. Kurt Badenhausen, Michael Ozanian, and Christina Settimi, "MLB Worth $36B As Team Values Hit Record $1.2B Average," http://www.forbes.com, cited January 18, 2016.
8. For the Astros' business relations topics, see John Ourand and David Broughton, "Ratings for Dodgers, Astros Show Challenge of Starting RSN," http://www.sportsbusinessdaily.com, cited September 29, 2014; Eric Fisher, "Astros Eye $40M for Civic-Sponsored Program," http://www.sportsbusinessdaily.com, cited June 25, 2012; Eric Fisher, "Astros Enlist MLBAM to Create Online Fan Research Forum to Gain Feedback on Team Initiatives," *SportsBusiness Journal* (April 30, 2012): 7; "Astros Diversity Program," http://www.houston.astros.mlb.com, cited May 1, 2016; "Houston Astros Set to Install Musco's LED Lighting System," http://www.musco.com, cited February 25, 2015.

9. See websites in note 2 of this chapter.

10. For information about the Angels' owner and his goals, see, for example, "Is It Time for Arte Moreno to Sell the Angels?" http://www.halosheaven.com, cited March 2, 2016.

11. The history of MLB ballparks and specific data about them such as their construction costs, financing, and renovations is in note 5 of this chapter.

12. This quote was taken from sources in note 6 above.

13. The reference is Bill Shaikin, "Tustin Wants Angels, But Who Pays for the Ballpark?" http://www.latimes.com, cited March 3, 2016.

14. For the Angels' business highlights and other news about the franchise, there are online articles from sports magazines, Anaheim and Los Angeles newspapers, and the team's website. For business relations, see Bill King, "Angels Seek Messaging That Will Play across Both the Hispanic and General Markets," http://www.sportsbusinessdaily.com, cited June 24, 2013; Bill Shaikin, "Angels Acquire Andrelton Simmons from Braves for Erick Aybar, Prospects," http://www.latimes.com, cited November 12, 2015; Michael Hiltzik, "The Rich L.A. Angels Try to Nickle-and-Dime Their Stadium Workers—Again," http://www.latimes.com, cited February 9, 2015; Erick Cassano, "How Dennis Kuhl Develops Repeat Customers for the Los Angeles Angels of Anaheim," http://www.sbnonline.com, cited July 5, 2011.

15. Another relevant source for MLB clubs' performances and records is the *Official Major League Baseball Fact Book 2005 Edition* (St. Louis, MO: Sporting News, 2005).

16. "122 Pro Sports Franchises—Ranked!" http://www.espn.go.com, cited March 4, 2016.

17. See note 6 in this chapter.

18. Some Oakland Athletics' business relations topics, for example, include Josh Eidelson, "Oakland A's Will Pay Back Wages to Interns and Clubhouse Workers," *Business Week* (September 1, 2014): 1; Eric Fisher, "A's, Giants Take Public Their Longtime Territorial Dispute over San Jose," http://www.sportsbusinessdaily.com, cited March 12, 2016; Marlize Van Romburgh, "Why Oakland A's Owner Is Not a Fan of Proposed Oakland Coliseum Buyout," http://www.bizjournals.com, cited August 3, 2015.

19. Read "Oakland A's Scoping Out Sites for New Stadium," http://www.mercurynews.com, cited March 6, 2016.

20. Andrew Koo, "A Decade after *Moneyball*, Have the A's Found a New Market Inefficiency?" http://www.regressing.deadspin.com, cited March 1, 2016.

21. "Complete Baseball Team and Baseball Team Encyclopedias," http://www.baseball-reference.com, cited January 19, 2016.

22. Art Thiel, "Death of Nintendo CEO Won't Affect Mariners," http://www.sportspressnw.com, cited March 5, 2016.

23. In this book's bibliography and cited in note 5, see http://www.ballparksofbaseball.com.

24. Two significant readings are "Ranking All 30 MLB Ballparks" and "Ranking MLB's Ballparks."

25. Seattle Mariners' business relations include such readings, for example, as Bill King and John Ourand, "The RSN Conundrum," *SportsBusiness Journal* (March 17, 2014): 1; Maury Brown, "The Mariners New TV Deal Gives Added Flexibility, But Will They Use It?" http://www.lookoutstanding.com, cited April 19, 2016; Bob Dutton, "Seattle Mariners Promote Tom Allison to Oversee All Baseball Scouting Operations," http://www.thenewstribune.com, cited October 21, 2015; Ryan Divish, "Mariners Announce Title Changes, Additions to Baseball Operations Staff," http://www.seattletimes.com, cited October 29, 2015.

26. Ryan Divish, "Ken Griffey Jr. Elected to Baseball Hall of Fame, Sets Voting Record," http://www.seattletimes.com, cited March 4, 2016.

27. Similar sources were used for the history, team performances, franchise owner, Globe Life Park, financial data, and business highlights of the Rangers as for other WD teams.

28. See "Fan Cost Index," http://www.teammarketingreport.com, cited January 25, 2016.

29. For the Texas Rangers franchise's business relations, see Candace Carlisle, "Texas Rangers to Upgrade Part of Globe Life Park in Arlington," http://www.bizjournals.com, cited January 8, 2016; Richard Durrett, "Rangers Fan Dies after 20-Foot Fall," http://www.espn.go.com, cited May 15, 2016; T. R. Sullivan, "Ryan Announces Retirement from Rangers' CEO Post," http://www.m.mlb.com, cited May 16, 2016.

30. This information is in Tim Roberts, "New Video Board and Foul Poles Coming to Globe Life Park," http://www.cw33.com, cited March 1, 2016.

Part II

NATIONAL LEAGUE

Chapter Four

East Division

Prior to 1969 there were no individual divisions in the American League (AL) or National League (NL) of Major League Baseball (MLB). However, because of expansion between 1969 and 1993, the AL and NL consisted of either six or seven teams each in the East Division (ED) and West Division (WD). Then in 1994 the two leagues realigned again and besides their ED and WD, they added a Central Division (CD). As a result, the AL's and NL's ED and CD each had five teams while their WD included four. After 1997 other differences occurred in divisions until 2013, when five each played in the ED, CD, and WD.

Given these changes in the structure of big-league baseball, this chapter discusses the historical development—and highlights financial data and business relations—of NL teams based in Atlanta, Georgia; Miami, Florida; New York City, New York; Philadelphia, Pennsylvania; and Washington, D.C., as of MLB's 2015 season. Which of them, for example, won the most division titles but fewest pennants? What were their estimated values, operating incomes, and gate receipts in 2015? Among the five clubs' owners, which of them had qualified for the most playoffs and won or lost any World Series? How did these teams' current ballparks compare to others with respect to their amenities, attendances, and costs to fans at home games? The answers to these and other questions are elements covered in the chapter.[1]

ATLANTA BRAVES

After playing five seasons and winning four championships in the National Association of Professional Base Ball Players—or simply National Association (NA)—the Boston Red Stockings joined the NL in 1876. Renamed

Beaneaters in 1883, Doves in 1907, Rustlers in 1911, Bees in 1936, and then Braves from 1941 to 1952, the club won a World Series in 1892 and 1914 but also was defeated in one by the AL's Cleveland Indians in 1948.[2]

By 1952 the Braves had lost much of their fan base to the AL's Boston Red Sox. As a result, they were expected to move to Milwaukee, Wisconsin, which was home of their top minor-league affiliate although Braves owner Lou Perini promised to help Milwaukee attract an existing MLB team and most people thought it would be the struggling St. Louis Browns. But in early 1953, Perini cited declining support from local fans and announced his decision to move the Braves from Boston to Milwaukee.

From 1953 to 1965, the Milwaukee Braves played thirteen seasons above .500 and won two pennants besides a World Series in 1958. However, while playing their home games at 43,700-seat County Stadium, the club's attendances gradually declined from 28,400 per game in 1957 to 6,800 in 1965. Despite the Braves' attendance and financial problems, city of Milwaukee officials attempted to block the franchise from relocating elsewhere by filing lawsuits against them alleging antitrust violations, disregard of stadium lease agreements, and refusal to negotiate with prospective local buyers of the franchise. When Braves ownership countersued, the county board rejected a cash settlement of $500,000 that would have allowed the franchise to move immediately to Georgia, the south's Peach State.

Consequently the Braves played their 1965 MLB season in Milwaukee under extremely unfavorable circumstances as the team's management and local government officials engaged in vigorous public and courtroom disputes. Needing to make a final decision regarding the location of the franchise for baseball's 1966 season, owner Perini and his brothers opted to move it to Atlanta and its expanding population and potentially lucrative television market.

Team Performances

As a member of the NL for three seasons (1966–1968) and the league's WD from 1969 to 1993 and then the ED during 1994–2015, the Braves competed in 7,957 games and had victories in approximately 52 percent of them. During the period, they won seventeen division titles, five pennants, and one World Series in nineteen playoffs. Respectively in number of different championships, the club ranked first, tied for eighth with the New York Mets, and tied for tenth with the Arizona Diamondbacks. Among only the league's ED teams as of their 2015 season, Atlanta had the most total championships but fewer pennants than the Philadelphia Phillies (Table A7).

In comparison to twenty-nine other MLB teams as of 2015, the fifty-year-old Braves were second in division titles, tied for thirteenth with the Mets and AL White Sox and Indians in pennants, and tied for twentieth with the Diamondbacks and AL Angels in winning World Series. Based on these results, Atlanta has been above-average performance-wise especially against its rivals in the NL's ED but also while playing those in other divisions.

The Braves' most successful periods consecutively were 1991–1993, 1995–2005, and 2012–2013. Besides manager Bobby Cox and such Hall of Fame pitchers as Tom Glavine, Greg Maddux, and John Smoltz, the club featured sluggers Ron Gant, Terry Pendleton, and Andruw Jones. Because of strong competition from its rivals, mediocre players at key positions and other reasons, the club failed to qualify for NL playoffs in consecutive seasons including, for example, 1966–1968, 1970–1981, 1983–1990, and 2006–2009.

According to a study of big-league teams, Atlanta ranks fourth in performances among thirty MLB franchises since the mid- to late 1960s. After a few miserable years in the late 1980s, the Braves excelled from 1991 to 2005 by winning their division in every season played to completion. They performed in four of five World Series yet won only one of them. With a corps of young pitchers and the leadership of manager Cox, the Braves abruptly reversed their course in 1991 by going from last to first, which began a winning streak that lasted until 2005.[3]

Franchise Owner

During the early 2000s, Liberty Media Corporation (LMC) owned a broad range of electronic retailing, media, communications, and entertainment businesses and other investments. These diverse ownerships were attributed to two tracking stock groups—the Liberty Interactive group, which included Liberty's investments in QVC, Provide Commerce, IAC/InterActiveCorp, and Expedia—and the Liberty Capital group, which included Liberty's interests in Starz Entertainment, News Corporation, and Time Warner.[4]

After a year of negotiations, LMC acquired the Atlanta Braves franchise from Time Warner Incorporated during mid-2007 for approximately $450 million. Based on that deal, Terry McGuirk remained in charge of the team after the sale along with general manager John Schuerholz and manager Bobby Cox. Also, Hall of Famer and then-current MLB home run leader Hank Aaron's role increased in his position of senior vice president. Meanwhile, city-owned Turner Field remained under the Braves' control and its name did not change. According to McGuirk, the new ownership could not go below the team's payroll of $87.3 million for players but was certainly encouraged to invest more resources into the franchise.

In a *Wall Street Journal* article, which reported the finalization of the sales deal on the newspaper's website, Time Warner had transferred the Braves, a group of craft magazines, and $1 billion in cash to LMC in exchange for about sixty million shares of its common stock. Based on the stock's closing price, the market value of those shares was about $1.27 billion.[5]

Major League Baseball's approval of the sale ended an era of Braves ownership, which began when the franchise was purchased for $11 million in 1976 by Ted Turner, who also had taken control of the National Basketball Association (NBA) Atlanta Hawks. In fact, the cable television mogul used these sports teams as a national tool to bring attention to his burgeoning cable empire that eventually evolved into the Cable News Network (CNN), Turner South (TS), and the Turner Broadcasting System (TBS).

Compared to owners of other NL teams as of 2015, LMC tied for ninth with the Milwaukee Brewers' Mark Attanasio in number of division titles, tied for seventh in winning zero pennants, and tied for fifth with zero World Series victories. Among all MLB owners, the company was respectively tied for twenty-first, tied for fourteenth, and tied for ninth. Since 2007, LMC has been neither a superior nor inferior owner of the Braves franchise with respect to it winning championships (Table A8).

As an owner, LMC's plan to issue stock in the Braves organization during 2016 opened the window to some new details about the franchise's economic performance. In late 2015, for example, the company filed a lengthy document with the U.S. Securities and Exchange Commission about its decision to issue a "tracking stock" that allowed investors and baseball fans to buy and sell shares in the team. The document revealed that the Braves' revenue fell by $15 million in the first nine months of 2015 while their expenses declined by $25 million. Interestingly, the Braves had an operating loss for the season—through September 30—but otherwise a profit if not for its amounts of depreciation and amortization.[6]

Turner Field

From 1966 to 1996 the Braves played their home games at 51,500-seat Atlanta Stadium—renamed Atlanta-Fulton County Stadium (AFCS) in 1976. During the thirty-one-year period, the team's average attendances at its ballpark ranged from a low of 6,800 per game in 1975 to a high of 47,900 in 1993 and peaked in total during the latter season.

After the city of Atlanta was chosen to host the 1996 Olympic Games, city officials and the Braves agreed to join forces and build a new multipurpose stadium. Following the Games, it would be converted into a baseball-only facility. With a brick and limestone exterior, the stadium had temporary bleachers beyond the outfield fence for the Olympics and then later was retrofitted and converted for baseball games.

Opened in April 1997 and named Turner Field, the new ballpark has many entrances with most fans arriving there through the Grand Entry Plaza. That area contains entertainment and also concessions for food plus game-filled pavilions; Scouts Alley; Toomer Field; a large photograph of Hank Aaron's 715th home run; Braves Hall of Fame; and Monument Grove. Other attractions are Turner Beach, which features a cabana bar, picnic area, and lounge chairs, and statues of Aaron and other great, former players.[7]

Compared to the ballparks of fourteen other NL teams as of 2015, nineteen-year-old Turner Field tied as the fourth oldest and was twelfth most expensive to build and also eighth in value. Among those of all MLB clubs, the Braves' home field ranked in a tie for fourteenth in age and placed nineteenth in construction cost and thirteenth most valuable. These results indicate, in part, that Atlanta needs a modern ballpark with amenities in order to generate more revenue from gate receipts at the Braves' home games (Table A9).

After their lease expires in 2016, the Braves will move from Turner Field into a new stadium named Sun Trust Park. This is necessary, in part, because Turner Field requires at least $150 million in infrastructure improvements, new seats, and other renovations to be a viable facility for the team. Located in downtown Atlanta, Georgia State University will purchase the old ballpark and parking lots for the school's football team and its other intercollegiate sports programs.

For several years a Chicago-based company named Team Marketing Report (TMR) has prepared and published a Fan Cost Index (FCI) for the home games of teams in professional sports leagues. To attend a game for a typical family with two kids, an FCI includes the costs of four average-priced tickets, two cheapest-priced draft beers, four each cheapest-priced soft drinks and hot dogs, parking for one vehicle, and two each game programs and also least-expensive, adult-size adjustable caps. These costs are determined by telephone calls with team representatives, venues, and concessionaires, and from questions asked during interviews.[8]

In the 2011–2015 MLB seasons, the FCIs for a family to attend a regular-season Braves game at Turner Field ranged from $169 in 2011 to $174 in 2015. During this period among ballparks of fourteen other NL clubs, Atlanta's ballpark's FCI ranked ninth in 2011, eleventh in 2012–2014, and twelfth in 2015. For only the league's ED teams, it was cheaper for fans to attend Braves' home games than those of the other four clubs (Table A10).

To reveal specific costs for families at games during a recent year in MLB, Turner Field's FCI in 2015 was $3 or approximately 2 percent more than in 2014. Listed from most to least in amount by item for one person, the team's nonpremium (premium) tickets averaged between $19 and $20 ($51 and $52), parking one vehicle and a cap each $15, a beer $7, and a hot dog and soft drink each between $4 and $5. The league's FCI, meanwhile, was $211 or 21 percent more in 2015 than the amount typically spent by families at Braves games at Turner Field.

Among other teams in the ED, they had rankings and FCIs from most to least as follows in the 2015 MLB season: Phillies fourth at $252; Nationals seventh at $232; Marlins ninth at $224; and Mets eleventh at $219. These differences in FCIs occurred because of their team's popularity and competitiveness, and also the population, population growth, and income per capita of sports fans in the local market.

In a recent study by CSN Mid-Atlantic, Turner Field ranked twenty-fourth in MLB. According to an online report in *USA Today*, the author said:

> I often wondered what the lifespan of the modern ballpark would be. The multipurpose facilities of the '60s and '70s survived roughly 30-to-40 years before being torn down. Will the new parks become obsolete so soon as well? In Atlanta, the answer is yes. Despite being less than 20 years old, Turner Field already is being replaced, with the Braves building a brand-new stadium in the suburbs set to open in 2017. What's wrong with the current ballpark? Well, it was originally built for the Olympics, so it does feel too big and a little un-baseball-like. And as is the case in several middle-of-the-road ballparks listed above, it has no real defining characteristic. Unfortunately, the initial renderings of the new park don't blow you away, either, so the Braves' next home may be nothing more than a newer version of their current one.[9]

Financial Data

According to data and other financial information published in *Forbes* for franchises in the NL as of their 2015 season, Atlanta ranked eighth in market value at $1.15 billion, sixth in revenue at $267 million, seventh in operating income at $33.2 million, tied for tenth with the Colorado Rockies in gate receipts at $58 million, and fifteenth in its debt-to-value ratio of zero percent. Among only the league's ED teams, the Braves had the lowest debt percent and also were second, third, or fourth in revenue and other amounts (Table A11).

Compared to all MLB teams in 2015, Atlanta's market value ranked twelfth, revenue ninth, operating income eighth, gate receipts tied for eighteenth, and debt-to-value tied for twenty-fifth. According to these rankings, the Braves franchise is an average but also valuable and profitable business with enough cash and sufficient revenue to effectively operate in the professional sports industry.

Besides market size, salary inflation, and other factors, an MLB team's annual payroll partly reflects its commitment to players and their current and potential contribution individually and as a group to winning games in regular seasons and postseasons. From 2011 to 2015, for example, the Braves payroll among NL teams ranged in rank from a low of eighth in 2011 ($87 million) to a high of twelfth in 2015 ($89 million). During the period, Atlanta's payroll was more than the Marlins' each year but below amounts of the Phillies and in some seasons those of the Mets and Nationals (Table A12).

Among payrolls of all MLB teams, the Braves' ranked from fifteenth in 2011 to twenty-third in 2015. In comparison, the AL Royals had baseball's lowest payroll or thirtieth highest in 2011 at $36 million and so did the NL Diamondbacks in 2015 at $65 million. Thus, Atlanta's ballplayers were compensated based on their teams' performances that included losses in two NL playoffs out of five regular seasons.

Business Relations

Besides regular-season and postseason games, MLB franchises are involved in—and affected by—internal affairs, community events, and business-related activities and projects. In no specific order, the following are a few of them for Atlanta's NL team as of 2015.[10]

First, the Braves' naming rights deal for its new ballpark with Sun Trust Bank was speedy and also kept secret from the public. Worth more than $10 million a year over twenty-five years, it is the second biggest contract in MLB and required just three months to conduct formal negotiations. Rather than putting the naming-rights opportunity in the marketplace through a request-for-proposal process, the club made invitations to a small group of relatively large companies. Club officials declined to specify the number, but most of them were Braves sponsors. The private process was designed to more efficiently yield a partner willing to play a major role throughout the creation of the ballpark and mixed-use development project, which will cost more than $1 billion and projected to open in 2017 in Cobb County, Georgia.

Second, the Braves relocated their top minor league affiliate in 2009 from Richmond, Virginia, to Gwinnett County in Atlanta's northeast suburbs The initial concept was similar to the current Cobb County plan: that is, to take advantage of the market's north side population explosion and create a large mixed-use development surrounding the ballpark. However, in the case of the AAA Gwinnett Braves, the mixed-use development surrounding Coolray Field had not happened as of 2013 because the construction and opening of the ballpark occurred during the nation's recession and the club in its five seasons ranked no higher than twelfth in attendance in the multiteam International League.

Third, the Braves drew more than 20,000 fans during August 2011 to a wide-ranging social media effort dubbed #BravesBash. Besides interacting with players on digital platforms, the live streaming event on the club's Facebook page drew more than 13,000 fans while a crowd of more than 2,200 listened to a conference call with broadcaster Jim Powell and different players. More than one hundred Skype video calls between fans and players were made and received including one with the MLB Fan Cave, while more than three thousand individual tweets were sent out with the #BravesBash hashtag. For charity, the media effort was a fund-raiser for the team's Foundation.

Fourth, the Braves and their division rival Miami Marlins scheduled to play a regular-season game in July 2016 at a newly-constructed ballpark at Fort Bragg, North Carolina, to celebrate America's servicemen and servicewomen. That is the first regular-season game of an American professional sport ever played on an active U.S. military base. As a gift of the two clubs and their players, MLB and the MLB Players Association reported that the new 12,500-seat ballpark at the most populated military installation in the United States will be converted after the game to a permanent softball field and multipurpose facility for those who serve at Fort Bragg.

Fifth, although the Braves have one of baseball's longest local television rights deals, there is an upside when it eventually ends. In a conference call to security analysts in early 2016, LMC's chief executive officer (CEO) Greg Maffei said that while sports broadcasting star—the Entertainment Sports Programming Network (ESPN)—must deal with the potential losses from cable watchers cutting their relationship and also deliver thinner television bundles, the Braves hope for better revenue once their twenty-year local rights deal expires in 2027. In another business transaction, Braves' owner LMC closed in December 2015 on $207 million in financing for The Battery, a mixed-use project adjacent to Sun Trust Park.

MIAMI MARLINS

Four years after baseball's new collective bargaining agreement (CBA) permitted the NL to expand by two teams to match the AL's total of fourteen, businessman H. Wayne Huizenga began to pursue an expansion franchise. Following a presentation by three south Florida groups—including Huizenga's—and one from the Miami Beacon Council to the NL expansion committee, MLB eventually announced a list of six possible sites. Based on bids from the four groups, the league awarded a new team in 1991 to a syndicate headed by Huizenga for $95 million and another to a syndicate from Denver, Colorado.

As a result, Miami's Joe Robbie Stadium was renovated and converted into a baseball facility. During March 1991, more than 125,000 total people attended two exhibition games at the ballpark. A few months later, MLB owners unanimously approved the Florida Marlins and the Colorado Rockies as baseball's two newest NL franchises. Florida adopted the nickname "Marlins" from titles of previous minor league teams based in the state. These were the Miami Marlins of the International League from 1956 to 1960, and a Miami Marlins team that played in the Florida State League from 1962 to 1970 and during 1982–1988.

From July to December 1991, the following activities involved the Marlins organization: the club hired Pittsburgh Pirates executive Carl Barger as its first president and also Fredi Gonzalez as a minor league manager; the team unveiled its new logo before approximately 1,700 guests at Turnberry Isle & Country Club; and former Montreal Expos general manager Dave Dombrowski became executive vice president and general manager of the new Florida baseball franchise.

For other activities during the six-month period, the Marlins signed an agreement to enter a team in the minor Gulf Coast League's Central Division beginning in June 1992; endorsed a one-year agreement with the Erie Sailors of the New York-Penn League for the 1992 season; hired Rene Lachemann to be manager of their big-league club; and signed sixteen-year-old pitcher from the Dominican Republic, Clemente Nunez, to a minor league contract and assigned him to the Gulf Coast rookie league.

Team Performances

As a member of the NL's ED from 1993 to 2015, Florida—renamed Miami Marlins in 2012—played 3,658 games and had victories in approximately 46 percent of them. During the period, they won zero division titles but two each pennants and World Series in two playoff appearances. Among fourteen other NL teams as of their 2015 season, the Marlins tied for fourteenth with the Rockies in division titles, tied for tenth with the Padres in winning pennants, and tied for sixth with four other NL clubs in number of World Series titles. With respect to only those in the league's ED, Miami had fewer total championships than the Braves, Mets, and Phillies but not the Nationals (Table A7).

Compared to all MLB teams as of 2015, the Marlins tied for twenty-eighth with the Rockies and AL Astros in winning division titles, tied for nineteenth with the Padres and AL Blue Jays and Rangers in number of pennants, and tied for twelfth with eight others in World Series victories. Based on this data, Miami has been below average in all-time performances and except for the Astros, Rockies, and Rays, inferior to its rivals in both leagues.

The twenty-three-year-old Marlins' most successful seasons were 1997 and 2003. To win two World Series, their most productive players were starting pitchers Kevin Brown and Alex Fernandez, and also batters Moises Alou and Bobby Bonilla in 1997, and sixteen years later, pitchers Dontrelle Willis and Mark Redman, and hitters Juan Pierre and Luis Castillo. Because of wrong, misguided, and/or ill-timed manager decisions, poor player performances by rookies and veteran players, and/or too much competition from other ED clubs, Florida/Miami teams failed to appear in NL playoffs consecutively during 1993–1996, 1998–2002, and 2004–2015.

Because of their two each pennants and World Series championships since 1993, a baseball analyst surprisingly placed the Marlins fourth on the list of MLB franchises. This was primarily because of two factors: first, they averaged a championship about every eleven years, which is better than all but a few teams; and second, they never lost a playoff series, which earned them additional points for playoff efficiency. The ranking of each team's success was based on its number of years in existence and how many playoff appearances it took to win a World Series. Each of Miami's championships was improbable because of not winning a division title. Edgar Renteria's walk-off single in game seven of the 1997 series will live on in infamy while the club's 2003 Series victory against the Yankees was one of the biggest upsets in baseball history.[11]

If slugger Giancarlo Stanton stays healthy, the 2016 Marlins should perform better than most fans think regarding the season. Nearly everyone in the lineup is entering the prime of his career, and players Dee Gordon, Christian Yelich, Justin Bour, and Derek Dietrich all hit well in 2015. Furthermore, they have the great but forty-plus-year-old Ichiro Suzuki, who is super fun and will contribute runs to the team's offense and also compete as an outfielder.

Franchise Owner

Born into a Jewish family in Manhattan, New York, Jeffrey Loria became interested in baseball at an early age and watched his first Yankees game in the late 1940s. He attended New York City's Stuyvesant High School and then Yale University, where he initially took pre-med courses. With a requirement to take a history class, Loria instead chose art history as his major.

After college, he worked in a newly established art-buying program for Sears & Roebuck and in 1965 opened an art dealer business on Manhattan's Upper East Side specializing in twentieth-century masters. His collection included works by Pablo Picasso and Henry Moore, and in 1968 Loria graduated from Columbia Business School.

Four years after acquiring the minor league AAA Oklahoma City 89ers in 1989, Loria sold the team and decided to eventually buy one in MLB. During December 1999, he acquired a 24 percent share of the NL Montreal Expos for $18 million and became their managing general partner. When a series of cash calls over the next two years went unanswered, Loria ended with 94 percent of the Expos franchise.

During early 2002, Marlins owner John Henry formed a group to buy the AL Boston Red Sox. Loria's Expos, who were supposed to be eliminated from the league before contraction plans stalled, sold his failing Montreal franchise to MLB. That, in turn, enabled him to buy the Marlins from Henry for approximately $158 million in 2002.

In comparison to fourteen other NL franchise owners and the performances of their teams as of 2015, Loria's Marlins tied for eleventh in division titles, tied for fourth in winning pennants, and tied for third in number of World Series titles. Among all MLB owners in championships, his Miami-based team respectively tied for twenty-fifth, tied for eighth, and tied for fourth. Except for winning division titles, Loria's club was very successful in at least one postseason while competing against its rivals in both leagues (Table A8).

In a recent study of thirty MLB owners, Jeffrey Loria ranked twenty-fifth of the group. According to the study's author, he has occasionally spent a lot of money on players but also was at the helm of the Marlins' fire sale after the 2005 season in an attempt to shed payroll and trying to get Miami-Dade County to help finance a new stadium for his team. He pulled a similar stunt when owning the Expos in 2000. Moreover, Loria is known as one of the worst offenders at pocketing money from revenue-sharing and supposedly he attempted to hide profits while getting taxpayers to pick up more of the tab on the team's new stadium. If there was a poster boy for everything that fans disliked about ownership—greed, dishonesty, and profits—that person would likely be Loria.[12]

Marlins Park

From 1993 to 2011 the Marlins played their home games at a multipurpose facility in Miami Gardens, Florida. It was initially named Joe Robbie Stadium (1993–1996) and then renamed Pro Player Stadium (1997–2004), Dolphins Stadium (2005–2008), Land Shark Stadium (2009), and then Sun Life Stadium (2010–2011). During this nineteen-year period of MLB seasons, the club's attendance ranged from a high of 37,800 per game in 1993 to a low of 10,100 in 2002. Because of heat, humidity, and rain, and playing their games in a stadium partially built for football, the Marlins needed a modern ballpark with amenities to attract fans and generate more revenue from gate receipts.

Three years after city and county commissioners approved funds for a new ballpark, construction began on it but was temporarily delayed in 2011 by a lawsuit challenging the use of public money for the project. Eventually built for $515 million, Miami-Dade County paid the majority of the costs while the city of Miami contributed $13 million and the Marlins $155 million. Located in Little Havana on the site of the former Orange Bowl, 37,400-seat Marlins Park was completed in early 2012. Thus, the team moved from baseball's largest to smallest ballpark.

Besides a retractable roof and outside glass panels, Marlins Park has several unique features. These include, for example, a tall structure behind the outfield's left-center field fence that has moving waves along the bottom and spins marlins, seagulls, and flamingos anytime a Marlins player hits a home run; a pool and next to it a private seating area providing classic Clevelander food and entertainment for fans; and behind home plate on both sides of the backstop, twin 450-gallon saltwater aquariums containing up to fifty fish protected by bulletproof glass.

Compared to the ballparks of fourteen other NL teams as of 2015, four-year-old Marlins Park was the newest and third most expensive in the league but least in value. Among all those of MLB clubs, Miami's home venue ranked thirtieth in age and value and also fifth in construction cost. According to this data, the Marlins have a modern ballpark with enough amenities to generate more gate receipts and thus revenue and profit for the franchise (Table A9).

In the 2012–2015 MLB seasons, the FCIs for a family to attend a regular-season game at Marlins Park in Miami ranged from a low of $221 in 2014 to a high of $242 in 2012. During this period among ballparks of fourteen other NL clubs, its FCI ranked third in 2012, sixth in 2013 and 2015, and seventh in 2014. For only the league's ED teams, it was cheaper for fans to attend Braves' home games than those of the other four clubs including Miami's (Table A10).

To reveal specific costs for a recent year in MLB, the Marlins' ballpark's FCI in 2015 was $3 or almost 2 percent more than in 2014. Listed from most to least in amount by item for one person, the team's nonpremium (premium) tickets averaged between $28 and $29 ($167 and $168), a baseball cap $20, parking one vehicle $15, beer and a hot dog each $6, and a soft drink between $4 and $5. Thus, fans paid $13 or 6 percent more to attend games at Marlins Park than those of the typical MLB team.

Among other teams in the league's ED, they had rankings and FCIs from most to least as follows in the 2015 MLB season: Phillies fourth at $252; Nationals seventh at $232; Mets eleventh at $219; Braves twenty-fourth at $174. These FCIs occurred partly because of differences in teams' popularity and competitiveness, and also the population, population growth, and disposable income of sports fans in the local market.

In a recent study by CSN Mid-Atlantic, Marlins Park ranked twenty-third in MLB. According to an online report in *USA Today*, the author said:

> Give Jeff Loria this much: He built a ballpark that is uniquely Miami. It may not be your cup of tea, with the Clevelander Bar behind the left-field bullpen, the bright colors and the million-dollar thingamabob sculpture behind the center-field fence. But it doesn't look like any other ballpark in the world, and there's something to be said for that. On the other hand, this feels less like a ballpark than an amusement park. Plus there's the whole swindling local taxpayers to get the place built thing, which never looks good.[13]

Financial Data

According to data published in *Forbes* magazine for NL teams as of MLB's 2015 season, the Marlins ranked fifteenth in market value at $650 million, revenue at $188 million and gate receipts at $32 million, and also ninth in operating income at $15.4 million, and first in its debt-to-value ratio at 34 percent. Among only the league's ED clubs, the Marlins had the lowest amounts except for operating income but also the highest debt percent (Table A11).

In comparison to all MLB teams as of 2015, Miami was twenty-ninth in market value and gate receipts, tied for twenty-eighth with the AL Rays in revenue, eighteenth in operating income, and tied for first with the AL Astros in their debt-to-value. From a financial perspective, the Marlins are a below-average business enterprise and because of their relatively low revenue and gate receipts yet high debt percent, they struggle to become more valuable as an MLB franchise.

Besides market size, salary inflation and other factors, an MLB team's annual payroll partly reflects its commitment to players and their current and potential contribution individually and as a group to winning games in regular seasons and postseasons. From 2011 to 2015, for example, the Marlins payroll among NL teams ranged in rank from a low of thirteenth in 2011 ($56 million) to a high of fifteenth in 2012 ($56 million), 2013 ($28 million), and 2014 ($28 million). During the five-year period, Miami's payroll was the smallest in its division each season but not the league in 2011, 2013, and 2015 (Table A12).

Among payrolls of all MLB teams as of 2015, the Marlins ranked from twenty-fourth in 2011 to thirtieth in 2014. This explains, in part, why the team finished between third and fifth in the ED during these years. If owner Jeffrey Loria fails to increase the club's payroll in future seasons, there is less incentive for players to perform well enough to be in the playoffs and win a division title, pennant, or World Series.

In August 2015, Marlins fans were uncertain about the team's multiple moves—highlighted by salary-dumping, thirteen-player deals involving the NL Dodgers and Braves. After these trades, the Dodgers are subsidizing 25 percent of the Marlins' payroll. This suggests that Miami owner Jeffrey Loria is not just stingy with his money anymore, but now cheap even though he shops for players with a 25 percent coupon.[14]

Business Relations

Besides regular-season and postseason games, MLB franchises are involved in—and affected by—internal affairs, community events, and business-related activities and projects. In no specific order, the following are a few of them for Miami's NL team as of 2015.[15]

First, the Marlins received $142 million in revenue-sharing—highest in baseball—during the first four years (2012–2015) of MLB's CBA, which is 57 percent of what franchise owner Loria spent on his forty-man player roster. Is he and owners of such small-market teams as the AL Rays and Royals and NL Padres and Pirates doing right by their fans when it comes to spending money they get from richer rivals such as the AL Yankees and Red Sox and NL Cubs and Giants? Just how, exactly, is all their revenue-sharing money being used? Fans of teams that get the loot but also those that pay it deserve to know the facts about the distribution of these amounts.

Second, the Marlins implemented a Baseball to Business Program (B2B). It is a professional network of team partners, suite holders, local leaders and season ticket holders, and the various firms they operate in the Miami area. It was developed to "connect the dots" between members in the Marlins business community, and thus make them more knowledgeable, productive, and successful.

Members of B2B receive personal attention from the Marlins' executive membership group. A member profile is generated based on a needs assessment survey, review of annual goals, and a customer identification process. Introductions are made via signature programs available exclusively to B2B members. Membership is inclusive given an organization's level of participation with the team. The B2B has distinct but generous benefits for members at the platinum, gold, and silver levels.

Third, the Ricoh Company deepened its relationship with the Marlins in April 2015 by becoming the franchise's "Official Document Solutions Partner." The new partnership builds on a three-year relationship in which Ricoh helped the baseball organization improve its accounts payable workflows and ultimately achieve increasing levels of information mobility. Ricoh also became the title sponsor for the most exclusive seating, lounge, and business conference space in Marlins Park.

Recently named the Ricoh Diamond Club, the elegant setting located just behind the ballpark's home plate hosts season ticket owners and VIP guests for dining, hospitality, baseball, and business meetings. For its part of the agreement, Ricoh equips the Diamond Club's exclusive conference room—known as the Ricoh Business Center—with an ultrashort throw projector and other powerful business technology to improve collaboration and information sharing. In short, the Ricoh Business Center is a new feature offered to Ricoh Diamond Club season ticket holders and Marlins' partners.

Fourth, whenever the Marlins play at home, there is one key activity to every player's pregame ritual. They visit Hugo "Juice" Tandron, the team's in-house barber and perhaps the only one in professional baseball. The heavily-tattooed, forty-five-year-old has a steady stream of clients—including players and staff—and opens his service six hours prior to home games and also does house calls during the off-season. Even visiting players ask him for a haircut, and leave a signature on his wall to mark their time there. During MLB spring training, Hugo drives up the coast to cut hair for the Marlins and their neighbors in Jupiter, the St. Louis Cardinals and Washington Nationals.

Fifth, whenever a professional sports team introduces a new primary logo, the reaction from fans is immediate, virulent, and unmistakably negative. So when the Marlins' new logo was leaked during October 2011, much of the digital sport's logo-hoi-polloi pounded on the trademark like they would a mouse if it appeared in a children's nursery. Perhaps the hatred from bloggers was rooted in fans' passion for the original logo—which the team launched in 1993—because it featured a traditional mark other than its use of the popular color teal blue. Any new primary logo will jump-start apparel sales, but as always, on-field performances will be the ultimate judge of sales success. Even so, retailers and manufacturers known for being cautiously optimistic at best about anything new praise the Marlins' fresh mark.[16]

NEW YORK METS

The Brooklyn Dodgers and New York Giants abandoned the New York area for respectively Los Angeles and San Francisco, California, leaving the nation's largest city without a NL franchise in 1958. One year later, attorney William Shea announced the formation of a third major baseball league and named it the Continental League (CL). After a contentious 1960, Shea and other CL officials made an agreement with the established major leagues.[17]

In exchange for abandoning the CL by Shea and his group, MLB created four new expansion franchises—two in each league. New York City received one of the NL teams with Joan Whitney Payson and her husband Charles Shipman Payson, being former minority owners of the New York Giants, as its principal owners along with George Herbert Walker Jr.—uncle of former President George H. W. Bush—who served as vice president and treasurer until 1977. Previous Giants director M. Donald Grant, the only member of the board to oppose the Giants' move, became chairman of the franchise's new board of directors.

The New York team required a nickname. Among those suggested, the finalists were "Bees," "Skyscrapers," and "Jets" as well as the eventual runner-up, "Skyliners." Although the Paysons preferred "Meadowlarks," the ownership group ultimately selected "Mets" because it was closely related to the club's existing corporate name, New York Metropolitan Baseball Club, Inc.; harkened back to "Metropolitans," a historically significant name used by an earlier New York baseball team in the American Association (AA) from 1883 to 1887; and because its brevity naturally fit in newspaper headlines. Thus "Mets" were received with broad approval among fans and the media.

Team Performances

A member of the NL for seven years and specifically the league's ED from 1969 to 2015, the Mets played 8,608 games and had victories in approximately 48 percent of them. During the period they won six division titles, five pennants, and two World Series in eight playoffs. Among NL teams as of 2015, the fifty-four-year-old club ranked eighth in winning division titles, tied for eighth with the Braves in number of pennants, and tied for sixth with four others in World Series. Within the league's ED, the Mets had fewer total championships than the Braves and Phillies but not the Marlins and Nationals (Table A7).

In comparison to twenty-nine MLB clubs as of their 2015 season, the Mets tied for ninetieth in winning division titles, tied for thirteenth in pennants, and tied for twelfth in World Series titles. According to these results, the Mets' performances have been average based on the abilities and talents of their managers and players, competition from rivals, and the franchise owners' decisions about such things as the team's payroll and improving its roster by signing free agents and veterans.

Besides winning World Series in 1969 and 1986, the Mets had successful back-to-back seasons in 1999–2000. During these years, the club's top players included such pitchers as Tom Seaver, David Cone, and Dwight Gooden, and sluggers' Edgardo Alfonzo, Keith Hernandez, Robin Ventura, Carlos Beltran, and Curtis Granderson. Alternatively the team failed to qualify for postseasons consecutively, for example, in 1962–1968, 1974–1985, 1989–1998, and 2006–2014 because of problems with its managers and players and also superior performances by other NL clubs especially in the ED.

In a 2013 research study, the Mets ranked fifteenth historically among thirty MLB franchises. According to the author, few teams were as miserable as the Mets in the 1960s when only seven others had a lower, average winning percentage. During Davey Johnson's six-year tenure as their manager, the Mets averaged ninety-six wins each season and won two division titles and finished second four times. Prior to that period, the team had a string of seven years of finishing last or next-to-last in the ED. Interestingly, this is the only NL franchise in existence since 1962 without a player winning a Most Valuable Player (MVP) award.[18]

Franchise Owner

Born into a Jewish family in Bensonhurst, Brooklyn, Fred Wilpon attended the city's Lafayette High School. While there, he was a baseball fan and later a pitcher and freshman in college. After graduating with a bachelor of arts degree from the University of Michigan, he sold calculators while his wife worked as a secretary for the former Brooklyn Dodgers president Branch Rickey, whom Fred knew from their neighborhood.

In 1972, Wilpon and his brother-in-law Saul Katz co-founded Sterling Equities (SE), a commercial real estate development company. Using resources from SE, he and Katz built a development of townhouses in a suburb of Westchester County, which became very successful. Seeking to minimize their tax obligations, they purchased real estate throughout the United States that had favorable tax treatment. This strategy turned out to be a boon since they unknowingly acquired property at the bottom of the real estate market.

Wilpon bought a small stake in the Mets franchise when Charles Shipman Payson sold the team for $21 million in 1980, with publishing company Doubleday & Company owning the remaining share of it. Then six years later, Doubleday president Nelson Doubleday Jr. sold his company, including an investment in the Mets, to Germany's Bertelsmann AG. Even so, Wilpon had a right of first refusal in a sale and threatened to exercise it. In the resulting settlement, Nelson Doubleday Jr. and Wilpon agreed to purchase the Mets for $95 million and become equal partners in the team.

During 2002, the Wilpon family purchased the remaining portion of the Mets from Doubleday Jr. for $391 million. Fred had been president of the team from 1980 to 2002 and also served as its CEO since 1980 and chairman of the board since 2003. Besides being CEO and chairman of the board, Wilpon was also chairman of SE.

Compared to the performances of owners of fourteen other NL franchises as of 2015, Fred's Mets tied for fifth in winning two division titles, tied for fourth with one pennant, and tied for fifth with zero World Series victories. Among all MLB owners, his New York-based club respectively tied for twelfth, tied for eighth, and tied for ninth. According to these results, Wilpon has not been tremendously successful in baseball despite the Mets playing in a very large and wealthy sports market and being the owner of a valuable franchise with plenty of cash (Table A8).

Since 2014, co-owner Katz has been willing to sell his portion of the team. According to baseball analysts, he is tired of spending millions to prop up the franchise. Nevertheless, Katz has been hesitant to sell because that could jeopardize Wilpon's future role in the club. As a result, Katz remains locked into subsidizing part of the team's losses in an effort to support Wilpon, who considers the team a family heirloom and wants his son Jeff, a partner/director, to control it indefinitely.[19]

It is unknown whether Katz has diligently or seriously searched for potential buyers. Several bankers involved with pro sports organizations have been asked to help appraise Katz's stake in the team, which is the first step toward brokering a sale. However, to find a buyer willing to spend huge amounts of money for a share in the team—without having a major voice in operating it—is likely to be difficult.

In 2011, for example, the Mets tried to sell a $200 million share, but their deal with hedge fund titan David Einhorn fell apart because Einhorn, in part, requested a greater role in the team's decision-making, which normally is not given to minority stakeholders. In addition, he wanted a pathway to eventual majority control of the franchise.

Citi Field

After two seasons at the Polo Grounds, the Mets played their home games in Shea Stadium from 1964 to 2008. While at these ballparks, the team's attendances ranged from a low of 9,600 in 1979 to a high of 49,900 in 2008. Although Shea Stadium was a multipurpose stadium that fans both loved and hated, it lacked the modern amenities of new ballparks built since the early to mid-1990s.

In 2006, the club revealed plans for a new ballpark and received approval to issue bonds for its construction. After officially breaking ground, it was built in the parking lot beyond the outfield fence of Shea Stadium. Financial service company, Citigroup Incorporated, purchased naming rights to the new ballpark for $20 million annually over twenty years.

Named Citi Field, the 42,000-seat ballpark has 42 percent of its seats in the lower deck. The main three-tier grandstand extends from the right field pole to home plate and down to the left field pole into left centerfield. The stadium has at least fifty luxury suites and in right field, the Pepsi Porch seats more than one thousand fans. The seating area, modeled after Detroit's Tiger Stadium, overhangs the playing field and allows for easy home runs.

Citi Field has such amenities as an enhanced outfield picnic area adjacent to the batter's eye known as Taste of the City; an interactive Mets museum with club memorabilia and Hall of Fame displays; two HD video scoreboards; the famous Big Apple located behind the center field fence that rises each time a Mets player hits a home run; and a skyline atop a restaurant in center field.

Compared to other NL teams' ballparks as of 2015, Citi Field is the fourteenth oldest and senior to only five-year-old Marlins Park; the most expensive to build; and tied for sixth in value with Philadelphia's Citizens Bank Park. Among those of all MLB teams, the Mets' home venue is tied for twenty-seventh in age and also second in construction cost to Yankee Stadium, and tied for tenth in value. Thus, Citi Field is an upscale, modern, and deluxe facility that provides entertainment for fans while at the Mets' home games (Table A9).

In the 2011–2015 MLB seasons, the FCIs for a family to attend a regular-season Mets game at Citi Field ranged from $219 in 2015 to $241 in 2011. During this period among ballparks of fourteen other NL clubs, Citi Field's FCI ranked between second in 2011 to seventh in 2013 and 2015. For only the league's ED teams, it was cheaper for fans to attend Mets' home games in four seasons than those of at least one other club (Table A10).

To reveal specific costs for a recent year in MLB, the Mets' ballpark's FCI in 2015 was $10 or almost 5 percent less than in 2014. Listed from most to least in amount by item for one person, the team's nonpremium (premium) tickets averaged between $25 and $26 ($83 and $84), parking one vehicle $22, a baseball cap $20, a hot dog between $6 and $7, beer about $6, and a soft drink $5. In other words, it cost an additional $8 for a family to attend a game at Citi Field than one at the typical ballpark in MLB.

Among other teams in the league's ED, they had rankings and FCIs from most to least as follows in the 2015 MLB season: Phillies fourth at $252; Nationals seventh at $232; Marlins ninth at $224; and Braves twenty-fourth at $174. These FCIs occurred, in part, because of differences in these teams' popularity and competitiveness, and also the population, population growth, and income per capita of sports fans in the local market.

In a recent study by CSN Mid-Atlantic, Citi Field ranked twenty-fifth in MLB. According to an online report in *USA Today*, the author said:

> Let's make one thing clear: Citi Field is so much better than Shea Stadium, which was the single worst place on Earth. And I don't just say that because I once got food poisoning in the media dining room. The problems with Citi

> Field, however, are many. It's too big. It's too dark. It's too confusing (you can't walk all the way around the main concourse; you have to take stairs or escalators up and then back down). And the original outfield dimensions were so bad, the Mets wound up moving the fences in after only a couple of seasons of play. It's a completely contrived ballpark out in the middle of Flushing Meadows, where the crowds are drowned out by the planes taking off from nearby LaGuardia Airport every couple of minutes.[20]

Financial Data

According to data and other financial information published in *Forbes* for franchises in the NL as of their 2015 season, the New York Mets ranked fifth in market value at $1.35 billion, eighth in both revenue at $263 million and operating income at $25 million, seventh in gate receipts at $74 million, and third in the debt-to-value ratio at 26 percent. Among only the league's ED clubs, the Mets had the highest market value but not their amounts of revenue, operating income, and gate receipts (Table A11).[21]

Compared to all MLB teams as of 2015, this New York club was eighth in market value, twelfth in revenue, thirteenth in operating income, tied for eleventh with the AL Rangers in gate receipts, and fourth in debt percent. From a financial perspective, the Mets are a valuable franchise and profitable business but with large debts relative to their market value.

Besides market size, salary inflation, and other factors, an MLB team's annual payroll partly reflects its commitment to players and their current and potential contribution individually and as a group to winning games in regular seasons and postseasons. From 2011 to 2015, for example, the Mets payroll among NL teams ranged in rank from a low of fourth in both 2011 ($118 million) and 2012 ($118 million) to a high of twelfth in 2014 ($71 million). During the five-year period, New York's payroll among the league's ED teams was the second largest for two seasons but then below the Phillies and Nationals in 2013–2015 (Table A12).

Among payrolls of all MLB teams as of 2015, the Mets ranked from eighth in 2011 and 2012 to twenty-fifth in 2014. While franchise owners Wilpon and Katz significantly reduced amounts paid to their ballplayers after the 2012 season, the team finished third in its division in 2013, second in 2014, and first in 2015. Simply put, the Mets improved their performances despite players' lower total salaries.

Business Relations

Besides regular-season and postseason games, MLB franchises are involved in—and affected by—internal affairs, community events, and business-related activities and projects. In no specific order, the following are a few of them for New York's NL team as of 2015.[22]

First, a promotional calendar built around Friday, Saturday, and Sunday home games is one of the hallmarks of the new way that Mets' executive vice president and chief revenue officer Lou DePaoli markets the team Targeting 'tweens to younger, thirty-something singles, there are twelve T-shirt giveaways—"Free Shirt Fridays"—and four concerts on Saturdays including performers such as Boyz II Men and Huey Lewis.

The forty promotional dates during Fridays-Sundays are eight more than the team had during its 2013 season. Sundays are pegged as family days, with fun planned for families at the plaza outside the park and kids being allowed to run the bases during the "Mr. Met Dash" after every Sunday game. To that end, the club augmented its sales and marketing staff by adding three sales positions and two service positions plus ten additional ticket sales positions, and building an in-house group to generate analytics around ticket sales and their sponsors' return on investment.

Second, the franchise's AAA affiliate in Buffalo sought a new partner in 2012. The Buffalo Bisons-New York Mets alignment brought two losing seasons and a third all but assured, and sharply declining attendance at Coca-Cola Field, which at one time, was the top ballpark in minor league baseball. The Bisons' losses in games became unpopular in Buffalo, being one of only five minor league markets containing affiliates of two big-league teams.

The Bisons were rumored to be heading toward an alignment with the Toronto Blue Jays, which for four years have held an unwieldy affiliation with Las Vegas. Named the 51s, that minor league team is more than 2,200 miles from Toronto in one of the most outdated stadiums in Class AAA. The Mets, meanwhile, may be headed to the Pacific Coast League with their Class AAA club since Buffalo was the only International League franchise with an expiring affiliation deadline.

Third, the Mets are targeting as potential fans the estimated two million lesbian, gay, bisexual, and transgender (LGBT) residents and families in the greater New York City area. With an announcement of the team's planned "pride night" in the 2016 baseball season, the message was clear: the Mets want the LGBT community to know they want them as fans, clad in the club's signature orange and blue, and filing into Citi Field in the city's borough of Queens.

To denote their commitment, the Mets joined a few MLB franchises in celebrating the LGBT community with an official event and became the first professional team in New York—the U.S. metro area with the highest total LGBT population of any city—to host a pride night. Amid shifting national sentiment and growing acceptance of these people, sports franchises have lagged in embracing them. While the Mets directly seek to include the LGBT community, an increasing number of teams in sports leagues could soon do the same and thus boost their bottom line while embracing a potential fan base largely ignored by pro sports organizations.

Fourth, franchise owner Jeff Wilpon thinks slugger Yoenis Cespedes' decision to stay with the Mets signals a change in how athletes view his often-struggling team. Rather than sign a long-term offer elsewhere, Cespedes agreed to a contract that allows him to opt out after one year, after which he could join what appears to be a free-agent market without as much top talent. He received a $10 million signing bonus, payable within thirty days of the deal's approval by MLB, and salaries of $17.5 million in 2016 and $23.75 million in each of the final two seasons. Also, Cespedes gets a full no-trade provision and after the 2016 season, may decide to become a free agent. The Mets, however, have the right to make a qualifying offer, which would entitle them to a high draft pick as compensation if Yoenis signed with another team.

Fifth, the Mets are building a fan engagement hub that uses analytics to generate a 360-degree view of fans. The data will help the club to personalize communications and promotions. By analyzing information from social media, mobile and email, the team will accurately gauge fan sentiment relating to different players and games. Also, it will be able to interact with fans on league and team sites, social media channels, and public forums. The Mets plan to analyze all data including when and where fans buy tickets to seats they select, what drinks they enjoy with their hotdogs, and the merchandise they buy—to improve game-day experiences.

PHILADELPHIA PHILLIES

While in the NL from 1880 to 1882, the Worcester Brown Stockings had a 90–159 record overall and finished fifth once and then eighth twice among eight teams. After they folded in late 1882, the league replaced them with a team from Philadelphia owned by sporting goods manufacturer Al Reach and attorney John Rogers. Although some sources contend that Reach and Rogers bought the Brown Stockings and moved them to Philadelphia, it was false. In fact, no players from Worcester played for Philadelphia in 1883. Thus, it was an expansion team.

During its early years in the NL, the new team changed its name from "Quakers" to "Philadelphias," which was common for sports teams in that era to be named after their home city. However, because the word "Philadelphias" was difficult to fit in newspaper headlines, some writers continued to call them the "Quakers" while others shortened the team's name to "Phillies." In 1890, baseball fans and the media accepted "Phillies" as its official nickname. As such, this is one of the longest continually-used nicknames in professional sports by a team in the same city.

Team Performances

As a member of the NL from 1883 to 1968 and then the league's ED for another forty-seven years, the Quakers/Phillies played 20,177 games and had victories in approximately 47 percent of them. More specifically, they won twelve division titles, seven pennants, two World Series, and appeared in fourteen playoffs. Among fourteen other NL teams as of their 2015 season, the club ranked fourth in winning division titles, tied for fifth with the Pirates in number of pennants, and tied for sixth with four different clubs in World Series titles. With respect to all-time performances of four other teams in the league's ED, Philadelphia won more total championships than the Marlins, Mets, and Nationals, but not the Braves (Table A7).[23]

Compared to twenty-nine other clubs in MLB as of 2015, the Phillies were sixth in number of division titles, tied for eighth in pennants, and tied for twelfth in World Series titles. According to these results, this 133-year-old franchise has been competitive and performed above average against rivals in its division and league, and also when ranked with those in the AL.

Besides losing five World Series and winning others in 1980 and 2008, Philadelphia was in consecutive playoffs during 1976–1978, 1980–1981, and 2007–2011. During some of these seasons the club's top players included sluggers Mike Schmidt, Chase Utley, and Ryan Howard, and pitchers Steve Carlton, Roy Halladay, and Cliff Lee. Because of poor manager decisions, inferior player performances, and other reasons, the Phillies failed to qualify for consecutive playoffs during such periods as 1969–1975, 1984–1992, and 1994–2006.

Since 1883, the 1980 Phillies have been one of the franchise's best all-time teams. Led by MVP Mike Schmidt, Cy Young winner Steve Carlton, and such other players as Pete Rose, Bob Boone, Greg Luzinski, Bake McBride, and Tug McGraw, that group brought the club its first World Series victory. Among those in the NL, they were in the top three in runs, hits, doubles, triples, homers, batting average, on-base percentage (OBP), slugging, earned run average (ERA), and strikeouts.[24]

In contrast, Philadelphia's 1940 team was the worst. They scored just 394 runs while allowing 706, and finished last in the league in runs, hits, homers, steals, OBP, and slugging. In addition, the pitching staff had the highest ERA and allowed the most walks among teams in the NL. Defensively, the

Phillies also committed the most errors and had the league's worst fielding percentage.

Franchise Owner

Born in 1946, Dave Montgomery attended Phillies home games at Connie Mack Stadium as a kid. Before attending college, he worked delivering newspapers and also coached a high school baseball team. While enrolled as an undergraduate student in liberal arts and then a history major at the University of Pennsylvania, Dave continued to attend Phillies games with future governor Ed Rendell. Following college, Montgomery graduated from the Wharton Business School in 1970.

After interviewing for positions with the Scott Paper Company and Quaker Oats, and despite being encouraged by Rendell to apply for a job with the NBA Philadelphia 76ers, Montgomery contacted former Phillies pitcher Robin Roberts about a job with the baseball club. Hired as a member of the team's sales department in 1971, he became director of sales and marketing in the mid-1970s and head of its business department by 1980.

Along with baseball executive Bill Giles, Montgomery purchased the Phillies in 1981 for approximately $31 million and became their executive vice president. When Giles left the team presidency to become its chairman in 1997 and also focus on getting a new stadium, he recommended Montgomery to replace him as team president. As such, Montgomery became the first Philadelphia native to operate the club in over sixty years.

In August 2014, Montgomery took a leave of absence from the Phillies to get treatment for jawbone cancer. After returning to the team in January 2015, he became chairman while Giles became chairman emeritus. Pat Gillick, who served as interim president during Montgomery's absence, assumed the role permanently.

In comparison to the performances of other NL teams based on the tenure of their owner in 2015, Montgomery's Phillies ranked second with eight division titles, tied for first with the Cardinals' William DeWitt Jr. in winning four pennants, and tied for third in World Series with the Marlins' Jeffrey Loria. Among all MLB clubs, Philadelphia was respectively second, tied for first, and tied for fourth in performances. Since 1981, Montgomery's teams won thirteen championships partly because of his thirty-five years of experience as an owner and also being a prominent leader of the franchise (Table A8).

According to a 2012 study of all MLB owners, Montgomery ranked ninth best among them. Since 2000, his decisions made the Phillies one of the most organized and successful teams in MLB. With a quality front-office and executive staff, the Phillies won five consecutive division crowns during

2007–2011 including a World Series in 2008. He spent enough money to sign some key players to lucrative, long-term deals. In the study, the NL's other ED team owners were ranked as follows as of 2012: Nationals' Ted Lerner seventeenth; Braves' Liberty Media Corporation twenty-second; Marlins' Jeffrey Loria twenty-fifth; and Mets' Fred Wilpon thirtieth.[25]

Citizens Bank Park

Before MLB's 2004 season, various Quakers and then Phillies teams played their home games chronologically at Recreation Park (1883–1886), Philadelphia Baseball Grounds (1887–1894), Baker Bowl (1895–1937), Shibe Park (1938–1952), Connie Mack Stadium (1953–1970), and Veterans Stadium (1971–2003). During this period, the club's attendance ranged from a low of 1,600 per game in 1902 to a high of 38,700 in 1993.

Because of Veteran Stadium's bad turf and problems sharing the facility with the National Football League (NFL) Philadelphia Eagles, the Phillies needed and wanted a new ballpark by the late 1990s. After considering three different sites including Chinatown, Liberty Yards, and property adjacent to Veterans Stadium, a site in the Philadelphia Sports Complex was chosen as the location for the club's new ballpark and also for a new football stadium for the Eagles. Philadelphia's city council approved the construction of these venues, financed in part by a 2 percent rental car tax, largely paid by visitors to the metropolitan area. According to that deal, the Phillies agreed to pay for any construction overruns and also maintenance of the ballpark. Similar to most other teams in MLB, the Phillies sold naming rights to their ballpark to Citizens Bank for $95 million over twenty-five years.

Opened during mid-April 2004, 43,600-seat Citizens Bank Park consists of a lower deck, suite level, and upper deck. The main grandstand extends from the left field foul pole to home plate down to the right field foul pole and then into right center field. There is a break in the upper deck along the first base side, allowing the seating area to be closer to the ballfield. Additional seating is available behind the left field fence.

Besides the seating bowl and main HD video scoreboard, the ballpark has several amenities. These include a gigantic Liberty Bell to celebrate home runs and a festive outdoor entertainment area named Ashburn Alley. It features a street-fair—type atmosphere complete with picnic areas; family-fun activities; treasured Philadelphia moments in baseball; enhanced concessions with plenty of Philadelphia flavor; clear views to the playing field; and a special viewing area overlooking the pitchers' bullpens.

Compared to the ballparks of fourteen other NL teams as of 2015, twelve-year-old Citizens Bank Park was the seventh most expensive and tied for sixth with the Mets' Citi Field in value. Among all those of MLB clubs, Philadelphia's home ballpark tied for twenty-third in age and ranked eleventh in construction cost and tied for tenth in value. According to these results, the Phillies have a modern ballpark with enough amenities to generate more revenue from gate receipts for the franchise (Table A9).

In the 2011–2015 MLB seasons, the FCIs for a family to attend a regular-season game at Citizens Bank Park ranged from $240 in 2011 to $258 in 2014. During this period among ballparks of fourteen other NL clubs, Philadelphia's FCI ranked third in 2011 and second from 2012 ($257) to 2015 ($252). For only the league's ED teams, it was more expensive for fans to attend Phillies home games in four seasons than those of the other four clubs (Table A10).

To reveal specific costs for a recent year in MLB, the Phillies' ballpark's FCI in 2015 was $6 or almost 3 percent less than in 2014. Listed from most to least in amount by item for one person, the team's nonpremium (premium) tickets averaged between $37 and $38 ($83 and $84), a baseball cap $20, parking one vehicle $16, beer approximately $8 each, a soft drink $4, and a hot dog between $3 and $4. Based on the league's average FCI of $211 in 2015, the games at Citizens Bank Park had cost above-average for families.

Among other teams in the league's ED, they had rankings and FCIs from most to least as follows in the 2015 MLB season: Nationals seventh at $232; Marlins ninth at $224; Mets eleventh at $219; and Braves twenty-fourth at $174. These FCIs occurred, in part, because of differences in teams' popularity and competitiveness, and also the population, population growth, and income per capita of sports fans in the local market.

In a recent study by CSN Mid-Atlantic, Citizens Bank Park ranked fifteenth in MLB. According to an online report in *USA Today*, the author said:

> We're now entering the indistinguishable middle of the pack. All of these ballparks have some similarities, none of them especially exciting. Call them the modern-day cookie cutters. Philadelphia has probably the best of this group, notable for the dark red brick and two-tiered bullpen behind the center-field fence. But there's not a whole lot else that defines Citizens Bank Park aside from the Phanatic (who is great) and the local fan base (which is not).[26]

Financial Data

According to data and other financial information published in *Forbes* for franchises in the NL as of their 2015 season, Philadelphia ranked seventh in both market value at $1.25 billion and revenue at $265 million, fifteenth or last in operating income at –$39 million, sixth in gate receipts at $89 million, and tenth in its debt-to-value ratio at 8 percent. Among only the league's ED clubs, the Phillies had the third highest market value and most gate receipts but also the worst operating income (Table A11).

Compared to all MLB teams as of 2015, Philadelphia was tenth in market value, eleventh in revenue, thirtieth or last in operating income, ninth in gate receipts, and tied for seventeenth with the AL Royals and Athletics in their debt ratio. Except for the club's negative operating income, it is an average to above-average business enterprise in MLB from a financial perspective.

Besides market size, salary inflation, and other factors, an MLB team's annual payroll partly reflects its commitment to players and their current and potential contribution individually and as a group to winning games in regular seasons and postseasons. From 2011 to 2015, for example, the Phillies payroll compared to fourteen other NL teams' ranged in rank from first in 2011 ($172 million) and 2012 ($174 million) to fourth in 2015 ($133 million). During the five-year period, Philadelphia's payroll among only the league's ED teams was the highest during four seasons but declined to second in 2015 because of the Nationals' $174 million payment (Table A12).

With respect to payrolls of all MLB teams as of 2015, the Phillies ranked from second in 2011 and 2012 to ninth in 2015. For various reasons, these results indicate that owner Dave Montgomery overpaid his players during MLB's 2012–2015 seasons because, in part, the club finished only third, fourth, and then fifth twice in the ED. But it also was first in 2011 despite losing in the NL divisional series to the Cardinals.

Business Relations

Besides regular-season and postseason games, MLB franchises are involved in—and affected by—internal affairs, community events, and business-related activities and projects. In no specific order, the following are a few of them for Philadelphia's NL team as of 2015.[27]

First, the Phillies feature several themes to entertain fans at their regular-season games in Citizens Bank Park. For example, these include Scouts Night, Mystery Item Giveaway Night, and Jackie Robinson Salute in April; Youth Softball Celebration, Deaf Awareness Night, and First Responders Night in May; Greek Heritage Celebration, Runners Day, and Fellowship Night in June; In the Biz Night, Christmas Night, and Star Wars Night in July; Summer Camp Day, Goya Latino Family Celebration, and Pride Night in August; Grandparents Day in September; and Octoberfest in October.

Besides these events and exclusive giveaway items, the club schedules discount dates for nurses, military, tour and travel and also senior citizens, and provides a mentoring program appreciation night. In short, Philadelphia has a number of diverse, successful, and unique ways to attract individuals and groups to increase attendances to games at its ballpark.

Second, during early March 2016, former Phillies general manager Ruben Amaro Jr.—now the Red Sox first base coach—discussed the perception that his regime in Philadelphia was well behind the curve in terms of analytics in an interview with Fangraphs' David Laurila. Amaro claimed that while his club may not have been as progressive as some of the most aggressive adopters of statistical analysis, the Phillies were more up to speed than they let on.

In the interview, Amaro said: "You can't ever deny the numbers. That's true for every general manager and every baseball person, regardless of whether you're 'old school' or 'new school.' I've always believed in analytics. I just didn't make it all public (in Philadelphia). I thought it was more of a competitive advantage for me to keep our thought-process about analytics closer to the vest. I didn't think it was anybody's business but our own as to how we evaluated."[28]

These were, of course, bold claims to make, especially in the face of years of stories to the contrary, which highlighted the Phillies' belief in more traditional means of evaluation. Amaro discussed the balance between data and scouting, new data from Statcast, and evaluating players at different age levels. Regardless of whether one believes his initial claims or not, the issue these comments raise is interesting because there certainly could be value to keeping operational methodology close to the vest for a big-league organization.

Third, although the Phillies turned into losers on the diamond in 2014 and 2015, they won on the balance sheet thanks to a twenty-five-year television agreement with Comcast SportsNet Philadelphia that started with the 2016 season and worth more than $5 billion. While the team owns 25 percent of the regional sports network (RSN), Comcast makes the deal work because of high subscriber fees. According to the contract, SportsNet Philadelphia charges carriers $4.20 per month, per subscriber, which is the fourth-highest of any RSN in the league.

Although it has not appeared in the standings, the team's owners invest much of the revenue from television deals on the field. In 2014, for example, the Phillies had a payroll of $179 million or third highest in baseball. But with $73 million going to just three players—Cole Hamels, Ryan Howard, and Cliff Lee—general manager Ruben Amaro had little flexibility under MLB's $189 million, payroll luxury-tax limit.

Fourth, the Phillies farm system ranked sixth among MLB teams in 2015. Being the most improved system overall, they rose from the bottom third in baseball from 2014 thanks in large part to adding four top-100 prospects including pitcher Jake Thompson (number fifty-nine), outfielder Nick Williams (number sixty-three), and catcher Jorge Alfaro (number sixty-eight) from the Texas Rangers in the Cole Hamels trade, plus outfielder Cornelius Randolph (number ninety-seven) in the first round of the players draft. In addition, their past two first-rounders—shortstop J. P. Crawford (number 6) and pitcher Aaron Nola (number twenty-two)—continue to get better and better at their respective positions on the field. In comparison to the Phillies, other teams' farm systems in the division were first (Braves), fourth (Mets), fifteenth (Nationals), and twenty-second (Marlins).

Fifth, the Phillies starting rotation ranked twenty-ninth and like the Atlanta Braves, they collected some intriguing young arms during their rebuilding phase. But also like the Braves, the Phillies need an opportunity and some luck to have a halfway decent rotation in 2016. Young starters Aaron Nola and Jerad Eickhoff look like the best of the bunch in Philadelphia, and Jeremy Hellickson may likely return to his excellent 2011–2012 form before he hits free agency following the 2017 season. For rotations of other ED teams, they ranked second (Mets), third (Nationals), eighteenth (Marlins), and thirtieth (Braves).

WASHINGTON NATIONALS

From 1969 to 2004, the Montreal Expos were a member of the league's ED. They played 5,698 games and won approximately 48 percent of them. To qualify for the 1981 playoffs, the club finished second in its division but lost in the NL championship series to the Dodgers. Thirteen years later, the Expos were three games ahead of the Braves until MLB players initiated a general strike. Shortly thereafter, team owners cancelled each league's regular season and postseason.[29]

For eight years the Expos played their home games at Montreal's 28,500-seat Jarry Park Stadium and then during 1997–2004, at the city's 66,300-seat Olympic Stadium. Their attendances while there ranged from a low of 9,547 per game in 1999 to a high of 28,600 in 1983. With a history of numerous structural and financial problems, Olympic Stadium was viewed by baseball fans as a white elephant. This, in turn, caused the team to operate inefficiently, lose money as a business enterprise, and play its games with an inferior roster of players and several unsuccessful managers.

In November 2001, franchise owners voted unanimously to downsize MLB by two teams. Supposedly these were the NL Expos and AL Minnesota Twins, who reportedly voted against contraction. Subsequently, the Red Sox were sold to a partnership led by John W. Henry, owner of the Florida Marlins. However, for Henry's group to assume ownership of the Red Sox, Henry sold the Marlins to Jeffrey Loria while MLB purchased the Expos from Loria.

When Minnesota's Metropolitan Sports Facilities Commission—which operated the Metrodome—won an injunction requiring the Twins to play there in 2002, MLB was unable to revoke the Twins franchise. Thus, the Twins and Expos remained in their league. In the CBA signed with the MLB Players Association in August 2002, contraction was prohibited until the end of the contract in 2006.

With contraction no longer an option for a few years, MLB began looking for a relocation site for the Expos. Some of choices included Oklahoma City, Oklahoma; Washington, D.C.; San Juan, Puerto Rico; Monterrey, Mexico; Portland, Oregon; somewhere in northern Virginia such as Arlington or Dulles—part of Washington, D.C.'s metropolitan area; Norfolk, Virginia; Las Vegas, Nevada; and Charlotte, North Carolina.

After evaluating bids from these and other cities in 2004, MLB selected Washington, D.C., because of its location, population and population growth, workers' relatively mid-to-high income including government employees, and the city's plan to eventually replace Robert F. Kennedy Stadium with a new ballpark. Derived from the former Washington baseball team with the same name and used interchangeably with Senators or simply "Nats," the new club was nicknamed "Nationals."

Team Performances

From 2005 to 2015 in the league's ED, the Nationals played 1,780 games and had victories in approximately 48 percent of them. During the period, they won two division titles but zero pennants and World Series in two playoff appearances. Among fourteen other NL clubs, Washington ranked twelfth in winning division titles, tied for fourteenth with the Brewers in pennants, and tied for twelfth with the Brewers, Rockies, and Padres in number of World Series titles. Furthermore, the club had fewer total championships than any in the league's ED (Table A7).

Compared to the performances of all MLB teams as of 2015, the Nationals tied for twenty-fifth in division titles, tied for twenty-seventh in pennants, and tied for twenty-third in World Series victories. Based on these results, this eleven-year-old team has been below-average performance-wise when playing rivals in the league including the Braves, Marlins, Mets, and Phillies.

Thus far, the club's most successful seasons were 2012 and 2014. During these years, its prominent players included such sluggers as Adam LaRoche and Ryan Zimmerman and pitchers Gio Gonzalez and Jordan Zimmerman in 2012, and then two years later, hitters Ian Desmond and Anthony Rendon, and pitchers Stephen Strasburg and Doug Fister. Because of inferior performances by players and other reasons, the club failed to make the playoffs from 2005 to 2011 and in 2013 and 2015.

Regarding the franchise's future performances, besides signing slugger Bryce Harper to a multiyear contract, pitcher Zimmermann received a qualifying offer and signed a five-year, $110 million contract with the Detroit Tigers in November 2015. He turned down a deal that would have been "team friendly" for the Nationals, and with the addition of pitcher Max Scherzer's $210 million contract, the Nationals did not have the budget to match the money offered to Zimmerman in free agency, regardless of how Scherzer's payout was structured.

The bigger question mark, however, was Stephen Strasburg. After MLB's 2016 season, the former number one draft pick and most enigmatic player on Washington's roster had been free to sign with whatever team offered him the most money. With the support of his agent, Scott Boras, Strasburg negotiated and signed a seven-year, $175 million contract during the spring of 2016.

Franchise Owner

Born into an Orthodox Jewish family in northwest Washington, D.C., Ted Lerner graduated from Roosevelt High School in 1944 and then served with the U.S. Army as a typist at the end of World War II. Five years later, he earned an associate of arts degree from George Washington University and also an LLB from its Law School.

While in school, Lerner sold homes on the weekends which piqued his interest in real estate. In 1952, he borrowed $250 from his wife and founded real estate company Lerner Enterprises in Rockville, Maryland—which operates primarily throughout the Washington, D.C., metropolis. Eventually, Lerner Enterprises became the largest private landowner in the region containing the nation's capital with a portfolio of commercial, retail, residential, and hotel properties and also owning Chelsea Piers in New York.

After MLB bought the Montreal Expos from Jeffrey Loria in 2002 for $120 million, several prominent groups entered the bidding process to acquire the franchise. A few years later, Ted Lerner's group—which included former Atlanta Braves executive Stan Kasten—was selected over those headed by former Seattle Mariners owner Jeffrey Smulyan and also by Washington Baseball Club's Fred Malek and Jeffrey Zients who worked for years to bring a big-league club to the capital.

At an evening news conference in a downtown hotel following the sale, Kasten said the Nationals would involve minorities in the initial hiring process for permanent full-time jobs. In addition to front-office positions for some of the black and Hispanic ownership partners, another priority of new owners Lerner and Kasten was to improve customer experiences at the ballpark.

Regarding the performances of NL teams with respect to their current principal owners as of 2015, Lerner's Nationals tied for fifth with the Mets, Reds, and Diamondbacks in winning division titles, tied for seventh with six clubs in pennants, and also tied for fifth with zero World Series titles. Among all MLB teams and their respective owners, Washington was respectively tied for twelfth, tied for fourteenth, and tied for ninth. Based on this data, Ted has been a mediocre owner and not very successful based on the accomplishments of his team (Table A8).

In 2015, Lerner received a lifetime achievement award from the Urban Land Institute. Columnist George Will praised him for opening the Nationals' Baseball Academy in Southeast D.C. The franchise and its charitable arm paid $3 million or 20 percent of the project's cost—or about what they pay pitcher Max Scherzer for a third of a season. D.C. taxpayers, meanwhile, contributed $10.2 million and MLB $1 million.

Nationals Park

From the 2005 to 2007 MLB seasons, the Nationals played their home games at multipurpose Robert F. Kennedy Stadium (RKS). While there, the team's attendances steadily declined from 33,700 per game in 2005 to 23,900 in 2007. Built in 1961, RKS lacked many amenities of newer ballparks. Before the Expos had moved to D.C. following their 2004 season, Washington city agreed to build a new ballpark for the team. After disputes among members of the D.C. Council on how to finance the facility, the Council and MLB negotiated a deal in 2006 that authorized public financing to construct the stadium.

Without naming rights as of 2016, 43,700-seat Nationals Park opened for big-league games in 2008. The ballpark, unlike traditional stadiums, has a sleek but modern design that features mostly glass and a steel façade. Similar to the Braves' Turner Field in Atlanta, many fans enter it through outfield areas that lead from the Navy Yard Metro Station. Open concourses exist throughout the ballpark with escalators and ramps delivering fans to their seats.

Nationals Park has many amenities. These include such things as 1,800 padded luxury seats; 2,500 club seats, more than 1,000 suite seats, and a 500-seat founder's club; a baseball-inspired restaurant named PNC Diamond Club; Homestead's Grey Bar, which honors the Negro Leagues; a kid's play area with various games; the Red Porch where fans watch games from a different perspective; and several Kwanzan Japanese cherry trees in the center field plaza and left field concourse. In 2018, the ballpark will host MLB's All Star game.

Compared to the ballparks of fourteen other NL teams as of 2015, nine-year-old Nationals Park was the second most expensive built at $611 million and fifth highest in value at $282 million. Among those of all MLB clubs, Washington's home ballpark tied for twenty-sixth in age and ranked nineteenth in construction cost and thirteenth in value. According to these results, the Nationals play their home games in a modern ballpark with enough amenities to generate more gate receipts and thus revenue and profit for the franchise (Table A9).

In the 2011–2015 MLB seasons, the FCIs for a family to attend a regular-season game at Nationals Park ranged from a low of $196 in 2011 to a high of $236 in 2013. During this period among stadiums of other NL clubs, Washington's ballpark's FCI ranked between fourth in 2013 to ninth in 2012. For only the league's ED teams, it was more expensive for fans to attend home games of the Phillies—except in 2015—compared to the Nationals and those of the Braves, Marlins, and Mets (Table A10).

To reveal specific costs for a recent year in MLB, the Nationals' ballpark's FCI in 2015 was $5 or approximately 2 percent more than in 2014. Listed from most to least in amount by item for one person, the team's nonpremium (premium) tickets averaged between $36 and $37 ($111 and $112), a baseball cap $12, parking one vehicle $10, beer between $6 and $7, a hot dog almost $6, and a soft drink $5. Based on the league's FCI of $211 in 2015, games at Nationals Park were above average in cost for families.

Among other clubs in the league's ED, they had rankings and FCIs from most to least as follows in the 2015 MLB season: Phillies fourth at $252; Marlins ninth at $224; Mets eleventh at $219; and Braves twenty-fourth at $174. These FCIs occurred, in part, because of such factors as differences in these teams' popularity and competitiveness, and also the population, population growth, and disposable income of sports fans in the local market.

In a recent study by CSN Mid-Atlantic, Nationals Park ranked sixteenth in MLB. According to an online report in *USA Today*, the author said:

> Look, you may not like or agree with this. Nationals Park, to its credit, is a very fan-friendly ballpark, with wide concourses and good field views from just about any seat. But it simply has no defining characteristic, no distinct charm. Think about it this way: What's the first thing you think of when you think of Nationals Park? It's tough to come up with something. The big video board? The Red Porch area? The cherry blossoms that bloom for only a week or so in early-April? The distant view of the Capitol dome from a handful of sections in the upper deck? I just wish there was something that stood out about this place. A quirk in the outfield fence. A view of the Anacostia River. A view of more of the city. A unique bullpen. Something. Anything. Instead, we're left with a very nice—but wholly indistinguishable—ballpark in the nation's capital.[30]

Financial Data

According to data and other financial information published in *Forbes* for franchises in the NL as of their 2015 season, Washington ranked sixth in market value at $1.28 billion and also fifth in revenue at $287 million, operating income at $41.4 million and gate receipts at $92 million, and second in its debt-to-value ratio at 27 percent. Among only the league's ED clubs, the Nationals had the second highest market value and debt ratio in addition to the most revenue, operating income, and gate receipts (Table A11).

Compared to all MLB teams as of 2015, Washington was ninth in market value, eighth in both revenue and gate receipts, sixth in operating income, and third in debt percent. From a financial perspective, the Nationals are a valuable franchise and prosperous business that generates sufficient cash flows and revenue from operations despite its relatively large debt-to-value ratio.

Besides market size, salary inflation, and other factors, an MLB team's annual payroll partly reflects its commitment to players and their current and potential contribution individually and as a group to winning games in regular seasons and postseasons. From 2011 to 2015, for example, the Nationals payroll compared to fourteen other NL teams' ranged in rank from a high of second in 2015 ($174 million) to a low of twelfth in 2011 ($63 million). During the five-year period, Washington's payroll among the league's ED teams was the second lowest in 2011–2012 and then increased each year by significant amounts because the team signed some talented free agents and veteran players to expensive, multiyear contracts. These included bonuses and incentives for it to become more competitive and win additional regular-season games and perhaps a pennant and World Series (Table A12).

With respect to payrolls of all MLB teams as of 2015, the Nationals ranked from third in 2015 ($174 million) to twenty-second in 2011. For various reasons, these results indicate that owner Ted Lerner fairly and efficiently compensated his players during MLB's 2011–2015 seasons which, in part, caused the club to improve and finish third once and first and second each twice in the ED. Moreover, Lerner increased players' payrolls because of the team's surplus revenue from lucrative local, regional, and national television deals.

Business Relations

Besides regular-season and postseason games, MLB franchises are involved in—and affected by—internal affairs, community events, and business-related activities and projects. In no specific order, the following are a few of them for Washington's NL team as of 2015.[31]

First, the Nationals created a second version of the team's ultra-exclusive Club 24 in 2015 at their ballpark after the first edition quickly sold out. Named K Street Boxes, they mimic the newly constructed Club 24 by combining amenities of an indoor club and a private suite. The Boxes feature permanently assigned indoor tables, outdoor opera-box–style seating, and membership in the club's business networking group—Partner Alliance. K Street Boxes have twenty-four total seats, sold in six separate four-seat blocks. Pricing starts at $95,000 with a minimum three-year commitment and includes premium parking, waiter service, access to all home games and concerts at Nationals Park, and all food and beverages with the exception of hard liquor. The pricing for K Street Boxes begins at the high end of the Club 24 rates, in part because of their proximity to home plate along the stadium's first-base side.

Second, the Nationals signed several sponsorship deals in 2013, which created an aggregate annual revenue increase of more than 20 percent in the category. Although exact figures were not available, the boost from the new and renewed deals put the club among MLB's top tier in sponsorship sales, and also in accord with Washington's status as one of the most affluent and educated U.S. markets. Beyond many of the typical sign- and media-driven activations, some deals involved more unusual elements. The HBO alignment, for example, was a short-term deal driven by the network's show *Veep* that featured a mascot likeness of lead character Selina Meyer—portrayed by actress Julia Louis-Dreyfus—participating in the club's famed Racing Presidents Dash.

Third, the team struck a multiyear deal in 2012 with Comcast Business, a unit of Comcast Cable, to develop an improved high-speed data network at Nationals Park. The new, Ethernet-based network supports the club's internal data needs—including the content on its main video board and the ballpark's press box—and significantly boosts the existing Wi-Fi network accessible by fans.

Although financial terms were not disclosed, the deal included a marketing component in addition to development of the data network. The Nationals-Comcast alignment came as MLB Advanced Media led an effort to boost venue connectivity at all thirty MLB ballparks. Data demand continues to mushroom, fueled by social media, video streaming, mobile food ordering, and many other activities.

Fourth, the Nationals admitted more than five hundred fans each minute through the turnstiles for their 2012 opening home series—or more than triple their previous peak entry rates—thanks to the new radio frequency identification system (RFIS) at their ballpark. Developed in partnership with the U.S. division of London-based customer management firm Fortress GB,

RFIS expanded the team's Red Carpet Rewards online fan loyalty program by connecting ticketing, concessions, merchandising, parking, and the loyalty program into one computerized system.

Fifth, each year Washington's business community welcomes the Nationals for their new season. Besides players, the team's coaches and manager, ownership group, and some executives attend the event. Held at the Grand Hyatt Washington Hotel during April 2016, there was a VIP reception and luncheon.

The starting lineup and premium tables, which consisted of eight seats plus one player/coach and a team representative, each cost respectively $4,600 and $3,750. Priced at $2,350 each, a standard table included eight seats plus two team representatives but without guarantee of a player. At $500 per ticket, the VIP reception featured interesting comments from Nationals players. The business community's Board of Trade donates money from the event to the team's Dream Foundation whose mission is to improve the lives of children and teenagers in the region by focusing on their academics and the arts, nutrition, and sports.

NOTES

1. Two books about the history and success of MLB franchises are Frank P. Jozsa Jr., *National League Franchises: Team Performances and Business Success* (New York: Springer, 2015) and James Quirk and Rodney D. Fort, *Pay Dirt: The Business of Professional Team Sports* (Princeton, NJ: Princeton University Press, 1992).

2. For performances of the Atlanta Braves and other MLB teams in this chapter, see information about them at http://www.mlb.com, http://www.baseball-reference.com, and http://www.sportsalmanac.com.

3. Read, for example, Charles Miller, "Ranking All 30 MLB Franchises over the Past 50 Years," http://www.athlonsports.com, cited March 7, 2016.

4. Besides profiles on their teams' websites, other sources to research franchise owners' careers and their personal businesses include articles in various journals, magazines and newspapers, and also in editions of *BusinessWeek*, *Forbes*, *SportsBusiness Journal*, and *Wall Street Journal*.

5. See Barry M. Bloom, "Braves Sale is Approved," http://www.m.mlb.com, cited April 1, 2016.

6. Tim Tucker, "Liberty Media, Pitching Braves Stock Plan, Discloses Finances," http://www.ajc.com, cited March 1, 2016.

7. For details including amenities about Turner Field and other MLB ballparks of NL and AL teams, one of the best and most reliable online references is http://www.ballparksofbaseball.com.

8. "Fan Cost Index," http://www.teammarketingreport.com, cited January 25, 2016.

9. See “Ranking All 30 MLB Ballparks,” http://www.csnmidatlantic.com, cited January 26, 2016.

10. Business highlights of the Braves were reported online in different articles of magazines, newspapers, and other sources. For example, see Eric Fisher, “Braves, Sun Trust Move Quickly, Quietly on Ballpark,” *SportsBusiness Journal* (September 22, 2014): 8; “Braves Digital ‘Bash’ Draws More Than 20K,” http://www.sportsbusinessdaily.com, cited May 18, 2016; “Braves Say AAA Team Will Remain in Gwinnett Co.,” http://www.entertainmentmanagementonline.com, cited May 18, 2016; “Braves, Marlins to Play at Fort Bragg Military Base July 3,” http://www.si.com, cited May 18, 2016.

11. For the Marlins’ rank as an MLB franchise, see note 3 in this chapter and also “122 Pro Sports Franchises—Ranked!” http://www.espn.go.com, cited March 4, 2016.

12. Among various readings, there is Rick Weiner, “Power Ranking Every MLB Owner From Worst to First,” http://www.bleacherreport.com, cited March 3, 2016.

13. Other than note 9, also review “Ranking MLB’s Ballparks,” http://www.athlonsports.com, cited January 26, 2016.

14. See Ryan Yousefi, “The Dodgers Are Now Paying 25 Percent of the Marlins’ Payroll,” http://www.miaminewtimes.com, cited March 11, 2016.

15. The Marlins’ business relations appear in such articles as “Baseball to Business,” http://www.miami.marlins.mlb.com, cited May 15, 2016; “Ricoh and Miami Marlins Partner for Baseball and Business,” http://www.ricoh-usa.com, cited May 16, 2016; “Miami Marlins Official Barber Hugo ‘Juice’ Tandron Becomes Cult Hero,” http://www.miamiherald.com, cited May 17, 2016; John Heyman, “Inside Baseball: Rival Executives Upset by Marlins’ Tiny Revenue,” http://www.cbssports.com, cited May 18, 2016.

16. Terry Lefton, “Loria’s Eye for Art Key to Logo,” http://www.sportsbusinessnews.com, cited March 13, 2016.

17. Frank P. Jozsa Jr., *Major League Baseball Expansions and Team Relocations: A History, 1876–2008* (Jefferson, NC: McFarland, 2010).

18. Charles Miller, “Ranking All 30 MLB Franchises over the Past 50 Years.”

19. Michael S. Schmidt, “Co-Owner of the Mets Is Said to Be Interested in Selling,” http://www.nytimes.com, cited March 10, 2016.

20. See notes 9 and 13 in this chapter for the history and status of the Mets’ Citi Field.

21. Kurt Badenhausen, Michael Ozanian, and Christina Settimi, “MLB Worth $36B As Team Values Hit Record $1.2B Average,” http://www.forbes.com, cited January 18, 2016.

22. The New York Mets’ business relations topics appear in different articles on websites and various editions of city newspapers and sports magazines. A few, for example, are Robert Boland, “Wilpon’s Financial Morass Offers Lessons for Franchise Owners,” http://www.sportsbusinessdaily.com, cited May 18, 2016; Terry Lefton, “DePaoli, Mets Working for the Weekend,” http://www.sportsbusinessdaily.com, cited May 18, 2016; Tim Marcin, “How New York Mets’ LGBT Pride Night Can Increase Fans and Profit for MLB Franchises,” http://www.ibtimes.com, cited February 23, 2016.

23. Besides data in http://www.baseball-reference.com, http://www.sportsalmanac.com, and http://www.sportsencyclopedia.com, see the *Official Major League Baseball Fact Book 2005 Edition* (St. Louis, MO: Sporting News, 2005).

24. Matt Snyder, "Franchise Best/Worsts: Philadelphia Phillies," http://www.cbssports.com, cited March 13, 2016.

25. Rich Weiner, "Power Ranking Every MLB Owner from Worst to First."

26. The reference for this quote is "Ranking All 30 MLB Ballparks."

27. The Phillies' business relations include John George, "Phillies CEO Breaks Down TV Deal," http://www.sportsbusinessdaily.com, cited May 18, 2016; Bob Ford, "Phillies Changing the Way They Do Business," http://www.articles.philly.com, cited May 18, 2016; Scott Butler, "Phillies Must Develop an Organizational Business Model," http://www.philsbaseball.com, cited May 18, 2016.

28. David Laurita, "Ruben Amaro on Analytics (and Evaluation)," http://www.fangraphs.com, cited March 11, 2016.

29. For team performances, franchise owner, ballpark, financial data, and business relations of the Nationals, see various notes above with respect to similar data and readings concerning the Braves, Marlins, Mets, and Phillies.

30. "Ranking All 30 MLB Ballparks" and "Ranking MLB's Ballparks" contain information about the history and other aspects of Nationals Park.

31. For the National's business relations, see Matthew Kaminski, "Cross Country: The Money Feud Spicing up the Nationals-Orioles Rivalry," *Wall Street Journal* (October 4, 2014): A11; Eric Fisher, "Nationals Re-Create Successful Club 24 with K Street Boxes," *Sports Business Journal* (March 2, 2015): 6; "Play Ball: Nats Deploy Software, Social Media to Boost Game Experience," http://www.bizjournals.com, cited May 18, 2016; "SAIC Continues Sponsorship of the Washington Nationals Patriotic Series," http://www.businesswire.com, cited April 4, 2016.

Chapter Five

Central Division

As described in chapter 4, prior to 1969 there were no individual or geographic divisions within the American League (AL) or National League (NL) of Major League Baseball (MLB). However, because of expansion between 1969 and 1993, the AL and NL consisted of either six or seven teams each in the East Division (ED) and West Division (WD). Then in 1994 the two leagues realigned again and besides their ED and WD, they added a Central Division (CD). As a result, the AL's and NL's ED and CD each had five teams while their WD included four. After 1997, other differences occurred in divisions until 2013 when five each played in the ED, CD, and WD.

Given these changes in the structure of big-league baseball, this chapter discusses the historical development—and highlights financial data and business relations—of NL teams based in Chicago, Illinois; Cincinnati, Ohio; Milwaukee, Wisconsin; Pittsburgh, Pennsylvania; and St. Louis, Missouri as of MLB's 2015 season. Which of them, for example, won the fewest division titles but most pennants? What were their estimated values, revenues, and gate receipts in 2015? Among the five clubs' owners, which of them had qualified for the least number of playoffs and won or lost any World Series? How did these teams' current ballparks compare to others with respect to their ages, attendances, and costs to families at home games? The answers to these and other questions are elements covered in the chapter.[1]

CHICAGO CUBS

After playing as an independent professional team for one year, the Chicago White Stockings joined the wild and wooly National Association of Base Ball Players (NABBP) in 1871. While a member of the association for three seasons, they finished second to the Philadelphia Athletics in 1871, withdrew from it the next two years because of devastation and recovery from a Chicago fire, but then reentered and finished fifth in 1874 and seventh in 1875.[2]

During the NABBP's existence, businessman and White Stockings president William Ambrose Hulbert was disgusted by the organization's failure to enforce players' contracts, dominance of the Boston Red Stockings—who won four consecutive championships, and its inability to adopt a mandatory schedule. In addition, gambling and alcohol were also serious problems with games often suspected of being 'thrown.' As a result, Hulbert spearheaded the formation of a new, stronger, and more ethical professional baseball organization.

In the NABBP's last year, Hulbert secretly but successfully convinced owners of the Red Stockings, New York Mutuals, St. Louis Browns, Hartford Dark Blues, Philadelphia Athletics, and also the Louisville Greys and Cincinnati Reds to join the White Stockings in his new group which he established as the National League of Professional Baseball Clubs or simply National League. This transformation, in turn, caused the NABBP to fold since its remaining members shut down operations or reverted to amateur or minor status. The following sections discuss performances and other information for MLB seasons of the Chicago White Stockings (1876–1889)/Colts (1890–1897)/Orphans (1898–1902)/Cubs (1902–2015) and then four other NL clubs.

Team Performances

As a member of the league for 140 years and specifically the CD from 1994 to 2015, Chicago's NL team—simply nicknamed "Cubs"—played 20,738 games and had victories in approximately 51 percent of them. During the period they won five division titles, ten pennants, two World Series, and appeared in nineteen playoffs. Among the league's teams as of their 2015 season, the Cubs tied for ninth with the Diamondbacks and Padres in winning division titles and also second in number of pennants and tied for sixth with four other clubs in World Series titles. Chicago, however, had fewer total championships than the CD's Reds, Pirates, and Cardinals (Table A7).

In comparison to all those in MLB as of 2015, the Cubs tied for twenty-first in division titles, ranked fifth in winning pennants, and tied for twelfth in World Series victories. Based on these results, this team has not been outstanding while performing against others in its division and league although it has been memorable and very popular among baseball fans within the Chicago metropolitan area and those in such Midwest states as Indiana and Iowa.

Besides losing seven World Series from 1910 to 1945 and competing in various playoffs since 1969, the club's most successful periods consecutively were 1885–1886, 1906–1908, and 2007–2008. Throughout these seasons Chicago had many talented players including John Clarkson, Mordecai Brown, Rogers Hornsby, Billy Herman, Ryne Sandberg, Sammy Sosa, Ernie Banks, Derrek Lee, and Ryan Dempster. Alternatively the club failed to be in back-to-back postseasons of 1876–1884, 1887–1905, 1919–1928, 1946–1983, 1989–1997, and 2009–2014. These dismal performances occurred, in part, because of managers' wrong decisions, inferior players at key positions, too much competition from its division rivals, and other historical problems.

According to a recent study, the Cubs surprisingly placed fifth all-time as an MLB franchise. Despite the lack of World Series titles since 1907–1908, they have one of the sport's most loyal fan bases and routinely post a high operating income. In 2012, for example, Chicago had MLB's largest operating income—and more than $2 million greater than the second-place Baltimore Orioles. In addition, their revenue was fourth because the club somehow found a way to fill seats—even for mid-week games in the afternoons against opposing teams from more than one thousand miles away.

Their fourteen players in the Hall of Fame rank third all-time as does the farm system. If the Cubs make the playoffs more regularly and perhaps win a World Series every twenty-five years or so, they would be in second place as a franchise following the New York Yankees but ahead of the San Francisco Giants (second), St. Louis Cardinals (third), and Boston Red Sox (fourth).

Franchise Owner

Born and raised as a Roman Catholic in Omaha, Nebraska, Tom Ricketts was eight years old when his father Joe founded Ameritrade. Joe wanted his children to establish themselves and succeed through hard work and therefore did not allow them to join Ameritrade until they were at least thirty-years-old. In 1984, Tom moved from Omaha to Chicago in order to attend the University of Chicago where he received a bachelor's degree in 1988 and five years later, a Master of Business Administration (MBA).[3]

Tom's success in business was obvious in the late 1980s when he joined the Chicago Board Options Exchange as a market maker and held that position until the early 1990s. From 1995 to 1996, he served as vice president of Mesirow Financial until moving to ABN AMRO as a vice president in their brokerage division. While there, Ricketts pioneered the idea of using the Internet and other technologies to help companies sell their investment-grade bonds directly to retail investors, as opposed to selling only to institutions. In 1999, Tom left ABN AMRO and founded Incapital LLC, which then was a technologically oriented investment bank focused exclusively on underwriting, marketing, and distributing fixed income securities to individual investors.

In April 2007, wealthy entrepreneur Sam Zell publicized his intention to purchase the Chicago-based Tribune Company. After acquiring it, Zell announced the sale of the Cubs and related entities including Wrigley Field and also his 25 percent share of SportsNet Chicago, which was money he needed to support the ailing Tribune.

Led by Tom, the Ricketts family's proposal for the Cubs was selected by MLB owners as the winning bid during late January 2009. Although the family had sold thirty-four million Ameritrade shares to raise $403 million for the Cubs deal, they still controlled about 16 percent of the company's stock and two board seats. As of early to mid-2016, Tom was chairman of the Cubs' board of directors while his siblings Pete, Laura, and Todd Ricketts served as members.

Compared to performances of NL teams under their current owners as of 2015, Ricketts' Cubs tied for eleventh in winning division titles, tied for seventh with zero pennants, and tied for fifth in number of World Series victories. Among twenty-nine other owners of MLB clubs, his Chicago teams respectively tied for twenty-fifth, tied for fourteenth, and tied for ninth. Since 2009, Tom Ricketts has not been a successful owner among the group because of the Cubs' zero championships (Table A8).

Wrigley Field

Before 1916, this team played its home games at various ballparks in Chicago including the 23rd Street Park (1876–1877), Lakefront Park (1878–1884), West Side Park (1885–1890), South Side Park (1891–1893), and West Side Grounds (1894–1915). During this forty-year period, attendances ranged from a low of 1,300 per game in 1890 to a high of 8,500 in 1908 even though the club had appeared in five World Series against AL clubs and won two of them.[4]

When businessman Charles Weeghman bought the Federal League (FL) Chicago Whales, he built his team a new 14,000-seat ballpark in the largely undeveloped north side of Chicago. Initially known as North Side Park until Charles renamed it Weeghman Field, the $250,000 ballpark originally had only one deck of a V-shaped grandstand with wooden bleachers in the outfield. The Whales played there for two seasons and finished second in 1914 and first in 1915.

After the FL went bankrupt following its 1915 season, a syndicate led by Weeghman and mogul William Wrigley acquired the Cubs franchise for $500,000 with the NL contributing $50,000 of the price. One year later, they moved their team from West Side Grounds to Weeghman Field, which was renamed Cubs Park in 1920 and then six years later, Wrigley Field.

During the 1920s, the ballpark was renovated including its grandstands and bleachers plus ivy being planted along the base of the outfield wall. Since the opening of new bleachers in 1937, the facility's next biggest transformation began with a $575 million project in 2014. It will overhaul the entire ballpark within five years. Besides demolishing the bleachers and adding a new video board, for example, the exterior wall will be pushed back in order to expand the bleachers, widen the concourses, and add more concessions. The project's other components include upgrading the steel infrastructure, installing a new roof to replace the existing wooden one, and returning the façade to its original 1930s appearance.

Compared to the ballparks of fourteen other NL teams as of 2015, 102-year-old Wrigley Field—originally Weegham Field—is the oldest but also least expensive to build and third highest in value. Among those of all MLB clubs, the Cubs' home venue ranked second in age to the Red Sox's Fenway Park and tied for twenty-ninth in construction cost and fifth most valuable. These results indicate, in part, that Chicago plays in an old but unique and legendary ballpark with enough amenities to generate sufficient gate receipts from the team's home games (Table A9).

For several years a Chicago-based company named Team Marketing Report (TMR) has prepared and published a Fan Cost Index (FCI) for the home games of teams in professional sports leagues. To attend a game for a typical family with two kids, an FCI includes the costs of four average-priced tickets, two cheapest-priced draft beers, four each cheapest-priced soft drinks and hot dogs, parking for one vehicle, two each game programs, and also least-expensive, adult-size adjustable caps. These costs are determined by telephone calls with team representatives, venues, and concessionaires, and from questions asked during interviews.[5]

In the 2011–2015 MLB seasons, the FCIs for a family to attend a regular-season Cubs' game at Wrigley Field ranged from $298 in 2013 to $305 in 2011. During this five-year period among ballparks of fourteen other NL clubs, Chicago's FCI ranked first each season. Among all big-league teams' ballparks, Wrigley Field was third in cost for families following Boston's Fenway Park and New York's Yankee Stadium (Table A10).

To reveal specific costs during a recent year in MLB, the Cubs' ballpark's FCI in 2015 was $4 or 1 percent less than in 2014. Listed from most to least in amount by item for one person, the team's nonpremium (premium) tickets averaged between $44 and $45 ($113 and $114), parking one vehicle $25, a baseball cap $20, beer almost $8, a hot dog approximately $6, and a soft drink between $4 and $5. Thus, families paid $89 or 30 percent more to attend Cubs games at Wrigley Field in 2015 than those at the typical teams' ballpark.

Among other clubs in the league's CD, they had rankings and FCIs from most to least as follows in the 2015 MLB season: Cardinals sixth at $236; Brewers twenty-second at $182; Pirates twenty-third at $175; and Reds twenty-fifth at $166. These differences in FCIs occurred because of these teams' popularity and competitiveness, population and population growth of their metropolitan area, and disposable income and wealth of sports fans in the local marketplace.

In a recent study by CSN Mid-Atlantic, Wrigley Field ranked fourth in MLB. According to an online report in USA Today, the author said:

> It's so hard to try to compare a ballpark built 100 years ago with one built in the last decade, but Wrigley Field is one of the 30 current MLB ballparks, so we'll try our best. To step into the Friendly Confines is to step back in time. That can be bad in some cases (try sitting way under the overhang and directly behind a pole, or try navigating your way through the rustic concourse) but the good far outweighs the bad. There simply is nothing like a Chicago summer afternoon spent in the bleachers at the corner of Clark and Addison. The ivy. The manual scoreboard. The rooftops. The rest of Wrigleyville outside the stadium. If you've never been, you need to put this one on your list.[6]

Financial Data

According to data and other financial information published in Forbes for franchises in the NL as of their 2015 season, Chicago ranked third in both market value at $1.8 billion and revenue at $302 million, second in operating income at $73.3 million, and fourth in gate receipts at $113 million and also in its debt-to-value at 24 percent. Among only the league's CD teams, the Cubs had the highest market value and debt percent, most revenue, but second-highest operating income and gate receipts (Table A11).

In comparison to twenty-nine other MLB teams as of 2015, Chicago's market value was fifth, operating income second, and revenue, gate receipts and debt ratio each sixth. According to these rankings, the Cubs are a very valuable and profitable team, and also a successful business organization from a financial perspective.

Besides market size, wage inflation and other factors, an MLB team's annual payroll partly reflects its commitment to players and their current and potential contribution individually and as a group to winning games in regular seasons and postseasons. From 2011 to 2015, for example, the Cubs payroll—compared to those of fourteen other NL teams—ranged in rank from second in 2011 ($125 million) to eleventh in 2014 ($73 million). During the five-year period, Chicago's payroll among the league's CD teams was the highest in 2011, declined to third during 2012–2013 and in 2015, but also placed fifth in 2014. These changes, in part, reflect the team's poor performances and owner Tom Ricketts' decision to reduce fixed costs and increase its profits (Table A12).

With respect to payrolls of all MLB teams as of 2015, the Cubs ranged in rank from sixth in 2011 to twenty-third in 2014. For various reasons, the team's payroll significantly decreased from 2011 to 2012 but then increased by 60 percent in 2015. These fluctuations in players' payments contributed, in some way, to the club's morale and losing records during four consecutive seasons but also to its improvement by competing for a pennant in 2015.

Business Relations

Besides regular-season and postseason games, MLB franchises are involved in—and affected by—internal affairs, community events, and business-related activities, decisions, and projects. In no specific order, the following are a few of them for Chicago's NL team as of 2015.[7]

First, according to chairman Tom Ricketts, the Cubs look forward to launching their own regional sports network (RSN). Although tempting, there are many variables for the Cubs to consider in 2020 when they control television rights for their games. Because of such things as distribution fees and perhaps sharing broadcast time with the National Football League (NFL) Chicago Bears and/or National Hockey League (NHL) Chicago Blackhawks and also the RSN's startup costs, hiring the best talent in an era of innovation and technology, and selecting the best partner or partners are each challenges and potential problems for the Cubs franchise to resolve.

Second, Cubs manager Joe Maddon's meeting with his so-called "lead bulls"—eleven players—during March 2016 went smoothly regarding the team's policies. The timing, however, seemed strange in the wake of the AL White Sox's debacle involving the decision to ban the fourteen-year-old son of Adam LaRoche from the clubhouse and LaRoche's subsequent retirement. The biggest topic for the Cubs, according to Maddon, was not about allowing kids in the clubhouse but whether players should wear shorts while traveling to away games. Maddon said kids would be allowed in the team's clubhouse until three hours before a game with exceptions for family emergencies. He also frowned on rules from decades ago forbidding players to wear non-collared shirts.

Third, Cubs' owners control more than half of the rooftop business of buildings across the street from Wrigley Field after buying three more properties in early January 2016. Greystone Sheffield Holdings, a Chicago-based venture firm owned by the Ricketts family, purchased Beyond the Ivy rooftop buildings at 1010 and 1038 W. Waveland Avenue and also the Sky Lounge

Wrigley Rooftop at 1048 W. Waveland beyond the left field bleachers. Costs of the buildings were not immediately available through the Cook County records website. Anyway, this is the latest strategic move in a long–running effort by Cubs' owners to take over the rooftop market after fighting with rooftop owners regarding the team's right to put up outfield signs that block some of their views into the ballpark.

A few years ago, the Cubs signed a twenty-year revenue-sharing agreement with rooftop property owners and took out a $6 million loan against the property in 2006. The revenue-sharing contracts allow rooftop owners to sell tickets to fans to watch games from their buildings in exchange for paying the team 17 percent of their pretax revenue. The rooftops were collectively generating about $2.5 million in ticket revenue annually for the team. But in recent MLB seasons, the Cubs and rooftop owners disagreed about pricing discounts especially when the team struggled in games and at the gate.

Fourth, since the end of the 2014 MLB season, several companies and the Cubs signed long-term "legacy partner" sponsorship agreements, the largest of which are worth $8 million to $9 million per year. Ten of these companies are now in the team's top-tier partner category including Anheuser-Busch, Toyota, and American Airlines, up from three before 2014.

Many of the deals stretch nearly a decade. But these contracts are just the tip of the iceberg when it comes to revenue potential from sponsorships and new things to be sold at a renovated Wrigley Field. Video boards, naming rights to entrance gates, and more than 18,000 square feet of new signage at the stadium are waiting to be populated by brands hopping on the Cubs bandwagon. When the stadium renovation and redevelopment of its surrounding area are finished, these sponsorships may generate more than $30 million in new annual revenue.

Fifth, as of early 2016, the Cubs will budget for only twenty-week offseason work schedules rather than twenty-six-weeks due to the team's expectations in the postseason. The new clubhouse, ticket office, Plaza, office development, and structural work in Wrigley Field's seating bowl and main concourse are being worked on in the offseason. When finished, the Cubs will have one of the largest clubhouses in baseball and cost to build than any of them. Approximately 28,000 square feet of it are on the Plaza side while the other 2,000 exists on the ballpark side and houses the batting cages and other spaces.

CINCINNATI REDS

Founded in 1866, the original Cincinnati Red Stockings became baseball's first fully professional team in 1869. Through 1870, they had won 130 consecutive games before being defeated by the Brooklyn Atlantics. After the Red Stockings lost many players and dissolved, its name went to Boston where, in 1871, a new team featuring some of Cincinnati's former stars began to play for the Boston Red Stockings.[8]

In 1876, a new Cincinnati Red Stockings team became a charter member of the NL. During five seasons, the club played 342 games and won only 36 percent of them while finishing above .500 twice. Because it violated such rules as serving beer at games and allowing alcohol at its ballpark on Sundays, the team was expelled from the league following its 1880 season.

A third Cincinnati team with the same name was founded in 1881 and became a founding member of the American Association (AA), which opened in 1882. The Red Stockings club played eight seasons in the AA, won a pennant in 1882, and had one of the highest all-time average winning percentages of any Reds club at .589.

In late 1889, the Red Stockings and Brooklyn Dodgers left the AA and joined the NL. One reason for abandoning the AA was because the newly formed Players League (PL) failed to break the reserve clause in baseball. As the PL gradually weakened the AA and NL, the latter league decided to expand. Thus, the AA's Dodgers and Red Stockings—renamed Reds—accepted an invitation to become members of the more established and financially stronger NL.

Team Performances

As a member of the NL and specifically the league's CD from 1994 to 2015, the Reds—also named Red Stockings (1876–1880) and Redlegs (1954–1959)—played 19,741 games and had victories in approximately 50 percent of them. During their 131 seasons they won eleven division titles, nine pennants, five World Series, and appeared in fifteen playoffs. Among fourteen other NL teams as of 2015, Cincinnati ranked fifth in winning division titles, tied for third with the Dodgers in number of pennants, and tied for second with the Pirates and Dodgers in World Series titles. With respect to only those in the league's CD, the Reds won fewer championships than the Cardinals but not the Cubs, Brewers, or Pirates (Table A7).

In comparison to all MLB clubs as of their 2015 season, Cincinnati ranked seventh in number of division titles, tied for sixth in pennants, and tied for fourth in World Series titles. Based on these results, the Reds have been a competitive team for more than a century and also successful at winning championships especially in their division and league.

Besides appearing in four World Series and winning two of them before 1969, the Reds qualified for consecutive playoffs during 1972–1973, 1975–1976, and 2012–2013. Their teams included such outstanding players as Frank Robinson, Joe Morgan, Johnny Bench, Pete Rose, George Foster, Barry Larkin, and Joey Votto. Because of various problems with its managers and players, the club failed to win enough games to compete in back-to-back playoffs, for example, in 1980–1989, 1991–1994, and 1996–2009.

The franchise's best team was in 1975 when it finished the regular season 108–54 and outscored opponents 840 to 586 in runs scored. That ball club ranked first in the NL in runs and third in earned run average (ERA), and also defeated the Pirates in three games in the league championship series and then the AL Red Sox in seven games to win the World Series. The starting lineup featured four Hall of Famers along with very talented players like shortstop Dave Concepcion and slugger George Foster.[9]

For the franchise's worst team ever, the Reds were 52–99 in 1934. They were last in runs scored and their pitching staff allowed the most runs and hits in the NL. The offense also ranked last in hits, doubles, batting average, on-base percentage, slugging percentage, and total bases while defensively three players each had at least twenty-five errors.

Franchise Owner

Born in Cincinnati, Ohio, Robert Castellini earned an economics degree from Georgetown University in 1963 and four years later, an MBA from the Wharton School. After graduating from Wharton, he became executive vice-president at the Castellini Group of Companies, and then in 1970, served as president of it until 1992. Involved in baseball for more than thirty years, Robert was once a part of the St. Louis Cardinals' ownership group, had previously invested in the AL's Texas Rangers and Baltimore Orioles, and held a minor ownership stake in the Reds until 1984.[10]

After MLB's 2005 season, Cincinnati endured five consecutive losing seasons—the team's longest such streak in fifty years—while under the ownership of Carl Lindner. As a result, Castellini led a group that purchased the Reds from Lindner for $270 million, and in January 2006, Castellini was named the chief executive officer (CEO) of the franchise. One of his first decisions was replace general manager Dan O'Brien with Wayne Krivsky and then select and introduce new uniforms for the team.

Among other current owners of NL teams as of 2015, Castellini's Reds tied for fifth with two division titles, tied for seventh with zero pennants, and tied for fifth in World Series victories. With respect to teams' performances of all MLB owners, Cincinnati respectively tied for twelfth, fourteenth, and ninth. Except for three playoffs, his clubs have been mediocre since 2006 (Table A8).

After losing ninety-eight games in 2015 and trading prominent players such as pitchers Johnny Cueto, Mike Leake, and Aroldis Chapman, and infielder Todd Frazier, the Reds face a bleak 2016 and likely future. Not even the financial commitment of the ownership group headed by owner Castellini can rescue the franchise from its small-market abyss. Because the team finished last in its division in 2015, they learned the big-market lesson that money does not always buy championships or even winning seasons.

Great American Ball Park

Before 2003, the Reds played their home games at League Park (1890–1901), Palace of the Fans (1902–1911), Redland Field (1912–1933), Crosley Field (1934–1969), and Riverfront Stadium (1970–1995)—renamed Cinergy Field (1996–2002). During this 113-year period, attendances at home ranged from 1,800 per game in 1890 to 31,600 in 1994.[11]

After the Reds and NFL Bengals shared Riverfront Stadium for almost three decades, Hamilton County voters approved a bond in 1996 to increase the county sales tax and fund a facility for each pro team. Then two years later, voters agreed to build the ballpark along the city's riverfront. Following Reds owner Marge Schott's threat but failure to move her team from Cincinnati to Northern Kentucky because of a dispute about a lease agreement, the new 42,271-seat ballpark was built and named Great American Ball Park after Great American Insurance bought naming rights to it for $75 million over thirty years.

Adjacent to the Reds' Hall of Fame Museum, team store, and a garden remembering Pete Rose, the ballpark consists of three levels with the lower grandstand extending from the left field foul pole to home plate and around to the right field foul pole. The second deck has club seats, luxury suites, and a press box while the upper deck includes two large seating sections for fans.

The ballpark has several amenities. For example, there is a brewpub with a bar that includes memorabilia from the "Big Red Machine" era; dining options at the Fox Sports Ohio Championship Club, Handlebar at Riverfront Club, and Diamond Club; a two-story Riverboat Deck to be used as a party area; an LED video board above the Sun/Moon Deck seats; and statues of former ballplayers throughout the landscape.

Compared to the ballparks of fourteen other NL teams as of 2015, thirteen-year-old Great American Ball Park tied for ninth in age and also ranked ninth in construction cost and value. Among those of all MLB clubs, the Reds' home venue was tied for twenty-second in age and fourteenth in both cost and value. These results indicate, in part, that the Reds play in a modern ballpark with enough amenities to generate an average amount of gate receipts and revenue from their home games (Table A9).

In the 2011–2015 MLB seasons, the FCIs for a family to attend a regular-season Reds home game ranged from $162 in 2011 to $168 in 2014. To reveal specific costs for families during a recent year, Cincinnati ballpark's FCI in 2015 was $166 or 1 percent less than in 2014. Listed from most to least in amount by item for one person, the team's nonpremium (premium) tickets averaged between $22 and $23 ($66 and $67), parking one vehicle and a baseball cap each $20, beer between $5 and $6, and a hot dog and a soft drink each $1. Thus, families paid $45 or 21 percent less at Cincinnati's home games than baseball's average FCI of $211 in 2015.

Among other clubs in the league's CD, they had rankings and FCIs from most to least as follows in the 2015 MLB season: Cubs third at $300; Cardinals sixth at $236; Brewers twenty-second at $182; and Pirates twenty-third at $175. These differences in FCIs occurred, in part, because of these teams' popularity and competitiveness, population and population growth of their metropolitan area, and disposable income and wealth of sports fans in the local market.

In a recent study by CSN Mid-Atlantic, Great American Ball Park ranked nineteenth in MLB. According to an online report in *USA Today*, the author said:

> Change the seats from red to blue, and you might think you were at Nationals Park. There are some real similarities. The shame of the Reds' stadium is that while it faces the Ohio River, the water is too far away for anybody with a bat to reach it. And the view on the other side of the river is Northern Kentucky, hardly awe-inspiring. Downtown Cincinnati, meanwhile, is directly behind home plate, so you don't get a view of that unless you're seated in the outfield. Oh, the dimensions are too small, as well, turning this place into a home run haven.[12]

Financial Data

According to data and other financial information published in *Forbes* for franchises in the NL as of their 2015 season, Cincinnati ranked eleventh in market value at $885 million, tenth in revenue at $227 million, twelfth in operating income at $2.2 million, ninth in gate receipts at $64 million, and tied for twelfth with the Brewers in their debt-to-value ratio at 6 percent. Among only the league's CD teams, the Reds had a higher market value than the Brewers but were fourth in both revenue and gate receipts and also fifth in operating income (Table A11).[13]

In comparison to twenty-nine other MLB teams as of 2015, Cincinnati's market value was twentieth while tied for eighteenth with the AL White Sox in revenue, ranked twenty-fifth in operating income, sixteenth in gate receipts, and tied for twenty-first in its debt percent. According to these results, the Reds exist in a relatively small sports market and struggle to earn enough money to consistently spend on high-priced free agents and veteran players and also be a successful business enterprise from a financial perspective.

Besides market size, salary inflation, and other factors, an MLB team's annual payroll partly reflects its commitment to players and their current and potential contribution individually and as a group to winning games in regular seasons and postseasons. From 2011 to 2015, for example, the Reds payroll among NL teams ranked from sixth in 2013 ($106 million) to eleventh in 2012 ($75 million). With respect to other CD clubs, however, Cincinnati had the third lowest payroll in both 2011 and 2012 but second-highest during 2013–2015 (Table A12).

In comparison to payrolls of all MLB teams as of 2015, the Reds' ranged in rank from eleventh in 2013 to twenty-first in 2012. For various reasons including owner Castellini's motivation to win games while containing costs, the team's payroll significantly increased from 2012 to 2013 and then again from 2014 to 2015. These fluctuations in payroll amounts, in some way, contributed to the club's playoff appearance in 2013 and perhaps its losing seasons in 2011, 2014, and 2015.

The Reds have a new television contract to evaluate during MLB's 2016 season. If negotiated smartly, it could provide them an increase of $25–$30 million per year in revenue above their previous deal. As usual, the team has been consistent as one of the most-watched competitors in their local market of any in the league. With a resurgence of all-star Joey Votto—the player in whom it has made its most significant investment—2015 was an above-average year for the franchise from a bottom-line perspective.

Business Relations

Besides regular-season and postseason games, MLB franchises are involved in—and affected by—their former and current front-office policies, community events, and local commercial activities, investments, and projects. In no specific order, the following are a few of them for Cincinnati's NL team as of 2015.[14]

First, despite the Reds' rebuilding efforts and dismal outlook for their 2016 season, sponsors are still jumping on board. According to the Reds' vice-president of corporate partnerships Bill Reinberger, the team's sponsorship sales are actually up 3 percent from where they were in 2015. That is especially significant after the franchise hosted the All Star game, which caused some companies to sign up as sponsors to catch the publicity wave from the game and surrounding events.

In addition, the Reds added at least six new sponsors. One, for example, provides fans with something beyond strikeouts to root for during games.

Scene75—a family entertainment center featuring arcade games, go-kart racing, laser tags, and inflatables—will give fans a free go-kart or laser tag ticket if the Reds steal two or more bases during a home game. Fans can redeem a ticket stub for these things at Scene75's locations in nearby cities. Scene75 is also installing some carnival games such as Pop-A-Shot in the Machine Room down the left field line at Great American Ball Park.

Second, the Reds created a new social gathering space in the left field corner of its ballpark before the 2016 season. Named the Cincinnati Bell Fioptics District Rooftop, it is a rooftop patio situated behind the left field stands in the upper deck. The patio contains tables and chairs, drink rails, and televisions to accommodate about four hundred fans. Single-game tickets cost $15 and include general admission to sit in seats among three sections of outfield seats with a limited view to the field from the patio. One free drink comes with the ticket, whether a beer, soda, or bottled water.

The new space was designed to cater to twenty-one to thirty-five-year-old fans as an area for them to hang out and meet other singles at the game. For the millennial generation, the game is not so much the focus of their interest as much as hanging with a group of friends and communicating on their mobile devices. In MLB, the Reds are the latest team to develop social gathering spaces that may not have a good view to the game but eventually could become popular destinations among fans of all ages.

Third, the University of Cincinnati's Goering Center for Family and Private Business sponsored the Red's Family Business Day at Great American Ball Park during July 2014. At the event friends, families, and coworkers recognized family-owned businesses and their tremendous impact on the local economy. The school's Goering Center, which is the nation's largest family business center, joined with the team to bring small business-owners and their families and employees together for a special afternoon.

Cincinnati family businesses were encouraged to celebrate and watch the Reds play the Pirates. There was a special pregame parade for all family businesses and employees, who stood out by wearing shirts displaying their company's pride and products. People could choose discounted single tickets from eleven different levels in the ballpark or make it a group outing by purchasing a block of tickets through group sales. For an additional cost, a 'meal-deal' from Kroger supermarkets could be added to each ticket.

Fourth, Reds' chief operating officer Phil Castellini manages the business of the organization. While decisions about players are handled on the baseball side of the front office, he oversees everything else. That is from information technology, human resources, and ticket sales to marketing and ballpark operations.

He has been with the Reds since 2006, when his father—Reds CEO Bob Castellini—led a group of investors to buy the team. As they took over the franchise, the Castellinis realized their profiles were about to become more visible to the public. Reporters, for example, would be asking them questions, something that did not happen in their prior experience in the food industry. To prepare for these events, they did interview simulations with a local marketing firm.

At game nights, Phil is somewhere at the ballpark. For pregame festivities, he is on the field greeting guests, and in the first few innings, visits sponsors and large groups and also thanks them for their support. After the meeting and greeting ends, Castellini settles into a suite to finish paperwork and watch innings of the game. While his job concentrates on the team's business operations, he is also an enthusiastic fan, and like any of them, he cares about what happens on the diamond.

Fifth, Cincinnati's African-American Chamber of Commerce and the Reds, Major League Baseball, and DeFuze It partnered for a Black History Month community forum in February 2016 at the city's National Underground Railroad Freedom Center. The "Black Businesses Matter: Pathway to Prosperity" forum included an historical look at black-owned businesses and a panel discussion on the economic gaps facing African Americans as well as growth and success strategies for diverse businesses. Besides community leaders, event hosts and speakers included Reds' chief operating officer Phil Castelllini and Wendy Lewis, Major League Baseball's senior vice president of Diversity, Inclusion & Strategic Alliances. The event was a continuation of the "All Lives Matter: A Social Justice Dialogue of Faith, Community and Baseball Diversity Summit" held at the Freedom Center during All-Star game festivities in July 2015.

MILWAUKEE BREWERS

An AL expansion franchise in MLB's 1969 season, the Seattle Pilots had a 64–98 record and finished thirty-three games behind the Minnesota Twins and sixth in the league's West Division. Due to dismal performance, low attendance at home games, and an outdated ballpark, the club was almost broke at the end of its first year in operation.[15]

As a result, team owner Dewey Soriano agreed to sell the Pilots for $10–$13 million to Wisconsin automobile dealer Bud Selig who planned to move the team to Milwaukee and rename it the Brewers. However, MLB owners rejected Soriano's deal because of political pressure from Washington state senators Warren Magnuson and Henry Jackson and also attorney general Slade Gorton. After MLB asked Soriano and co-owner William Daley to find a local buyer, baseball's franchise owners dismissed the idea since it would devalue their clubs' value.

After a winter and spring of court action, the Pilots reported for spring training unsure of where they would play in MLB's 1970 season. When the state of Washington filed an injunction to stop the club's sale to a syndicate from Milwaukee, Soriano filed for bankruptcy in order to forestall any post-sale legal action. At the bankruptcy hearing a week later, a team official testified that not enough money existed in the bank to pay the Pilots' coaches, players, and office staff.

Based on these circumstances, a federal bankruptcy referee declared the Pilots bankrupt as of April 1970, which in turn, cleared the way for them to relocate from Seattle to southeast Wisconsin. Therefore an investor group led by Selig purchased the franchise for approximately $11 million and moved it to Milwaukee. The team's new full name became Milwaukee Brewers.

For MLB's 1998 regular season, the expansion Tampa Bay Devil Rays joined the AL's ED and Arizona Diamondbacks the NL's WD. This resulted in fourteen AL teams and sixteen in the NL. In addition to these changes, baseball officials shifted the Detroit Tigers from the AL's ED to the CD and another club from the AL's CD to the NL's CD.

This realignment, in part, was considered a great financial benefit to the clubs involved in these movements. To avoid a conflict of interest, MLB Commissioner Bud Selig decided another team should have the first opportunity to switch leagues. The choice was offered to the Kansas City Royals, who preferred to remain in the AL's CD. The next was the Brewers, who in late 1997, agreed to move to the NL's CD. Consequently, the Brewers' performances and other information about the franchise refer primarily to their 1998 to 2015 seasons.

Team Performances

While a member of the AL's WD (1970–1971), ED (1972–1993), and then the league's CD (1994–1997), the Brewers played 4,490 games and had victories in approximately 47 percent of them. During baseball's 1981 season, they won their division but lost in the divisional playoffs in five games to the Yankees. One year later, the Brewers won their division and an AL pennant but then were defeated by the NL Cardinals in the World Series. Except for a few seasons, the club usually finished between third and seventh in its division.

As a team in the NL's CD from 1998 to 2015, the Brewers played 2,820 games and won 1,369 or approximately 48 percent of them. During the eighteen-year period, they appeared in two playoffs while winning a division title in 2011 but zero pennants and World Series. Among fourteen other clubs in the league as of their 2015 season, Milwaukee ranked thirteenth in number of division titles, tied for fourteenth with the Nationals in winning pennants, and tied for twelfth with the Nationals, Rockies, and Padres in World Series titles. With respect to only CD teams, the Brewers had the fewest total championships partly because of their relatively brief time in the NL and also such factors as inferior managers and players, and relatively small payrolls (Table A7).

In comparison to results of all MLB clubs as of 2015, Milwaukee was twenty-seventh in winning division titles, tied for twenty-seventh in pennants, and tied for twenty-third in World Series titles. Based on this data and other information from the literature, Brewers' teams have underperformed since 1998 for various reasons including their lack of talented players at key positions on the field, bad decisions by managers during games, and ownership problems.

For appearing in playoffs, Milwaukee had successful seasons in 2008 and 2011. To win games, its most prominent players included pitchers C. C. Sabathia, Ben Sheets, and Yovani Gallardo, and power hitters Prince Fielder, Ryan Braun, and Corey Hart. Alternatively, the club failed to appear in playoffs consecutively during the 1998–2007, 2009–2010, and 2012–2015 seasons.

While the 2011 Brewers team was their best—winning ninety-six games and competing for a pennant—the franchise's least successful team was in 2002. Besides a 56–106 record and finishing sixth in the CD, it had the worst run-differential in history. Although Richie Sexson swatted twenty-nine home runs and pitcher Ben Sheets won eleven games, the club's pitchers' ERA was the highest in MLB at 4.73.

Since taking control of the Brewers' baseball operations after the 2015 season, thirty-year-old general manager David Stearns made several trades as of March 2016. A total of nine Milwaukee players (plus cash) were traded to acquire sixteen others, with most of them being young minor leaguers. Including these deals, twenty players have come off the Brewers' forty-man roster, which was an extraordinary number even for an organization in the early stages of a massive rebuilding program.[16]

Regarding his strategy for the future, Stearns has two objectives: first, to sign potentially talented but inexperienced players who will spend the next few years as minor leaguers on teams in places such as Brevard County, Florida, and Biloxi, Mississippi; and second, to try and field a reasonably competitive MLB team especially in games against rivals in the league's CD. Interestingly, Stearns was energized by his first real contact with Brewers fans when more than twelve thousand of them attended a recent event. An important part of his job is to communicate the team's goals to all fans as the rebuilding process unfolds.

Franchise Owner

Born in the Bronx, New York, Mark Attanasio lived and attended high school in Tenafly, New Jersey. He spent much of his childhood memorizing trivia from the Baseball Encyclopedia and playing whiffle ball with his brother in a church parking lot. While making his fortune in junk bonds, Attanasio relaxed with rotisserie baseball and spent hours carefully picking players and strategies for his fantasy team.

Mark graduated with a Bachelor of Arts from Brown University in 1979 and three years later, received his Doctor of Law Degree (J.D.) at Columbia Law School. In 1991, he founded Dallas investment firm Crescent Capital Partners, which was bought by Trust Company of the West in 1995. Six years later, Attanasio joined the board of directors at telecommunications company Global Crossing, which filed for bankruptcy in early 2002. Shortly thereafter, he resigned his position on the company's board.

To the relief of Milwaukee fans unhappy with the team's lackluster performances and poor management by MLB Commissioner Bud Selig's daughter Wendy Selig-Prieb, Bud announced that his ownership group was selling the Brewers effective January 2004. Several months later, the Brewers made a verbal agreement with Attanasio who bid to purchase the team for approximately $223 million. In January 2005, the deal was completed at MLB's quarterly owners meeting.

Since becoming the franchise owner, Attanasio has tried to build bridges with Milwaukee baseball fans. These efforts included, for example, providing fans with free tickets to every seat to a final home game in 2005 and bringing back the classic "ball and glove" logo of the club's glory days on "Retro Friday" home games.

Compared to the performances of other NL teams with their current owners as of 2015, Attanasio's Brewers tied for ninth in winning division titles, tied for seventh in pennants, and tied for fifth in World Series titles. Among all MLB clubs and their three types of championships, Milwaukee respectively tied for twenty-first, tied for fourteenth, and tied for ninth. Thus, Attanasio has not been a superior or inferior owner, or very successful, since purchasing the franchise in 2005 (Table A8).

Miller Park

While a member of the NL's CD for three years, the Brewers played their home games at Milwaukee's County Stadium. During this period the club's home attendances declined from 22,300 per game in 1998 to 21,200 in 1999 and then one year later, to 19,400. Built for the Milwaukee Braves in 1953, the 28,100-seat ballpark—later expanded to 53,200 seats—was obsolete and needed replacement by the mid- to late 1990s.

After the Brewers unveiled plans for a retractable roof ballpark in late 1995 and then getting financial approval for its construction, fans at their games could watch it being built beyond County Stadium's outfield bleachers. Despite a tragic crane accident killing three workers and destroying part of the ballpark's first base side, it was completed in 2001.

Named after the Miller Brewing Company—which has naming rights for $2.1 million per year through 2020—41,900-seat Miller Park is a structure with a façade that consists of red brick, arched windows, and a clock tower at the home plate entrance. Directly outside of it are statues of such Milwaukee icons as Hank Aaron and Robin Yount. The 12,000-ton, seven-panel retractable roof has a unique fan-shape design and opens or closes in ten minutes. While fans can buy their favorite Brewers merchandise at the team's new store, there is also upscale dining for them at the Johnson Controls Stadium Club on the club level down the left field foul line.

Although not available at the former County Stadium, some of the ballpark's unique amenities, for example, are the Hall of Fame; children's area and brewpub; open air patios and walkways; a T.G.I. Friday's Front Row Sports Grill located in the left field area known as the Front Row; and the Miller Park Kids Zone—an 8,000-square-foot interactive play area that includes a replica of Bernie the Brewer's slide.

Compared to the ballparks of fourteen other NL teams as of 2015, fifteen-year-old Miller Park tied for seventh in age with Pittsburgh's PNC Park and also ranked eighth in construction cost and tenth in value. Among those of all MLB clubs, the Brewers' home site was tied for twentieth in age and finished twelfth in cost and sixteenth in value. These results indicate, in part, that Milwaukee plays in a modern ballpark with enough amenities to generate an average amount of gate receipts from attendances at their home games (Table A9).

In the 2011–2015 MLB seasons, the FCIs for a family to attend a regular-season Brewers' home game ranged from $160 in 2011 to $182 in 2015. To reveal specific costs for families during 2015, listed from most to least in amount by item for one person, the team's nonpremium (premium) tickets averaged between $22 and $23 ($66 and $67), a baseball cap and parking one vehicle each $20, beer between $5 and $6, and a hot dog and soft drink each $1. Thus, families paid $45 or 26 percent less, on average, to attend a game at Miller Park than those at other NL ballparks (Table A10).

Among other clubs in the league's CD, they had rankings and FCIs from most to least as follows in the 2015 MLB season: Cubs third at $300; Cardinals sixth at $236; Pirates twenty-third at $175; and Reds twenty-fifth at

$166. These differences in FCIs occurred, in part, because of these teams' popularity and competitiveness, population and population growth of their metropolitan area, number of jobs, and the income per capita and wealth of sports fans in the local market.

In a recent study by CSN Mid-Atlantic, Miller Park ranked twenty-first in MLB. According to an online report in *USA Today*, the author said:

> It needs to be said that Brewers fans are among the best in baseball, and they help create a fun, party-like atmosphere inside (and especially outside) Miller Park. But this isn't a ranking of fans, it's a ranking of ballparks. And Miller Park simply doesn't stack up to most of the rest of the league. The fan-like retractable roof is oddly shaped, coming to a point behind home plate. And even when the roof and outfield panels are open, there's not much of anything to see. Downtown Milwaukee is several miles away, and not in that direction. It just feels like they missed the boat a little bit on this one.[17]

Financial Data

According to data and other financial information published in *Forbes* for franchises in the NL as of their 2015 season, Milwaukee ranked twelfth in market value at $875 million, eleventh in both revenue at $226 million and operating income at $11.3 million, eight in gate receipts at $65 million, and tied for twelfth with the Reds in their debt-to-value ratio at 6 percent. Among only the league's CD teams, the Brewers had the lowest value and revenue, but also the third-highest gate receipts and fourth-most operating income which, in turn, reflects their small-market status from a financial perspective (Table A11).

In comparison to twenty-nine other MLB teams as of 2015, Milwaukee's market value and revenue were each twenty-first, operating income twentieth, gate receipts fifteenth, and debt ratio tied for twenty-first. Although the Brewers are less valuable than the majority of big-league clubs, they earn sufficient gate receipts from their home games and enough total revenue as a franchise to continue operating at Miller Park in baseball's regular seasons.

Beside market size, wage inflation, and other factors, an MLB team's annual payroll partly reflects its commitment to players and their current and potential contribution individually and as a group to winning games in regular seasons and postseasons. From 2011 to 2015, for example, the Brewers payroll among NL teams ranged in rank from sixth in 2012 ($97 million) to tenth in 2015 ($98 million). With respect to other CD clubs, however, Milwaukee had the third or fourth lowest payroll in most seasons which, in part, was a factor in the team's failure to qualify for the playoffs during 2012–2015 (Table A12).

Regarding the payrolls of all MLB teams as of 2015, the Brewers ranked from eleventh in 2012 to twenty-first in 2015. For various reasons including efforts to compete against the Cardinals and other rivals in the league's CD, the team's payroll rose from 2011 to 2012 and then again in 2015. To win another division title, however, Milwaukee's payroll for players on its roster must increase soon by at least $15 million.

Business Relations

Besides regular-season and postseason games, MLB franchises are involved in—and affected by—their former and current front-office policies, community events, and local commercial activities, investments, and projects. In no specific order, the following are a few of them for Milwaukee's NL team as of 2015.[18]

First, the minor-league Colorado Springs Sky Sox—in their twenty-eighth year of operation—agreed during late 2014 to a two-year player development contract with the Brewers through their 2016 season. The Brewers become the third affiliate in the history of the Sky Sox organization following the Cleveland Indians (1988–1992) and Colorado Rockies (1993–2014). This is also the second time a Milwaukee team affiliated with a club in Colorado. Indeed the NL Milwaukee Braves were affiliates with the Denver Bears in 1963–1964. Recent minor-league affiliates that have won titles while associated with the Brewers include the Nashville Sounds (AAA-Pacific Coast League in 2005); Huntsville Stars (AA-Southern League in 2001); Wisconsin Timber Rattlers (A-Midwest League in 2012); and Helena Brewers (Rookie-Pioneer League in 1995, 1996, and 2010).

Second, before he purchased the NBA Cleveland Cavaliers in 2004, billionaire businessman Dan Gilbert submitted a bid to acquire the Brewers franchise. Instead, Milwaukee automobile dealer and MLB Commissioner Bud Selig sold his team to Crescent Capital Partners' founder Mark Attanasio. Regarding the team's sale, Gilbert stated: "I am deeply disappointed that the Brewers have chosen another direction in the sale of the club. After nearly eight long months of negotiations, I believed we were on the verge of announcing a deal when I was informed of the Brewers' decision to sell the team to another party."[19]

Third, for all Brewers fans attending their home games, a local hotel and convention center package includes spacious suites, complimentary breakfast, and a tailgate party with food and beverages before the game. There is no parking fee for these fans with a game-day shuttle providing transportation to and from Miller Park.

Fourth, Kenny Chesney's "Spread the Love" tour performed at Miller Park in mid-June 2016. In addition to Chesney and female country singer Miranda Lambert, the concert included vocal group of the year Little Big Town and emerging star Old Dominion. Because of these singers' talent, this event was a success.

Fifth, cofounder of the private equity fund Ares Management and a minority owner of the Brewers, Anthony Ressler, assembled a syndicate to purchase the NBA Atlanta Hawks in 2015 for $850 million. Besides Ressler, the investment group consisted of former NBA star Grant Hill and Spanx founder Sara Blakely and her husband, entrepreneur Jesse Itzler. In a statement to the media, Ressler said: "We are honored and thrilled to have been chosen to become the new stewards of the Hawks. We respect the NBA's approval process and can say no more other than we are incredibly excited by the Hawks' success and wish them luck in the playoffs." The deal, which also included operating rights to Philips Arena, was not a problem. In fact, the basketball league's officials were familiar with Ressler after he attempted to buy the NBA Los Angeles Clippers in a prior year.[20]

PITTSBURGH PIRATES

As a professional sport, baseball has existed in the Pittsburgh, Pennsylvania, area since the early to mid-1870s. The teams there actually played as 'independents while barnstorming throughout the region and unaffiliated with any organized league. Moreover, they operated as business organizations and paid salaries to their coaches and players.[21]

During October 1881, the strongest team in the area joined the American Association (AA) as a founding member of the association's 1882 season. Its home fields were in Allegheny City, which was across the Allegheny River from Pittsburgh. While listed as simply "Allegheny" in the baseball standings, the team was sometimes named "Alleghenys" in the same generic way that others from Boston, New York, and Chicago were sometimes referred to, respectively, as "Bostons," "New Yorks," and "Chicagos" in the sports writing style of the period.

While playing in the AA, the Alleghenys won 236 or 44 percent of their games and finished second, third, fourth, seventh, and eleventh in five seasons. The club became the first AA team to switch to the NL, and in 1887, it replaced the Kansas City Cowboys who were seventh in 1886. After joining the NL, the Pittsburgh Alleghenys played their home games at 17,000-seat Recreation Park. Subsequently, co-owner and manager Horace Phillips sold the club to Dennis McKnight but nevertheless continued as its manager.

Team Performances

As a member of the NL from 1887 to 1968 and specifically the league's ED (1969–1993) and then CD (1994–2015), Pittsburgh played 19,772 games and had victories in approximately 51 percent of them. During its 129 MLB seasons, the club won eight division titles, seven pennants, five World Series, and appeared in seventeen playoffs. Among fourteen other teams in the league as of 2015, the Pirates ranked seventh in winning division titles, tied for fifth with the Phillies in number of pennants, and tied for second with the Reds and Dodgers in World Series titles. Compared to the league's CD teams as of 2015, Pittsburgh had fewer total championships than the Cardinals and Reds but not the Cubs or Brewers (Table A7).

With respect to twenty-nine MLB teams as of their 2015 season, the Pirates tied for thirteenth with the AL Royals in winning division titles, tied for eighth in pennants, and tied for fourth in World Series victories. Based on these results and other information in the literature, this has been a very competitive club in its division and league despite existing in a relatively small baseball market and having fewer resources and financial assets than many of its rivals.

Besides appearing in five World Series between 1887 and 1969 and winning three of them, the Pirates most successful back-to-back seasons included 1970–1972, 1974–1975, 1990–1992, and 2013–2015. During one or more of these periods, a few of the club's prominent players were sluggers Roberto Clemente, Dave Parker, Willie Stargell, Barry Bonds, and Andrew McCutchen, and pitchers Dock Ellis, Jerry Reuss, Steve Blass, John Smiley, and Gerrit Cole. However, because of poor performances of their players, the Pirates failed to qualify for postseasons in such consecutive seasons as 1887–1902, 1910–1924, 1928–1959, and 1993–2012.

Since 1887, the Pirates' best team was in 1902. The club won 74 percent of its games, outscored its opponents by 335 runs, and led the NL in runs, hits, doubles, triples, batting average, on-base percentage, slugging percentage and total bases, and also finished second in homers, steals, and walks. In contrast to that team, the 1952 Pirates were 42–112, finished 54.5 games out of first place and also last in the league in runs, hits, doubles, triples, home runs, batting average, on-base percentage, slugging and total bases, and in pitchers' ERA, strikeouts, home runs allowed, walks, errors, and fielding percentage.

Based on such criteria as number of playoffs, winning pennants and World Series, Hall of Fame players, and the quality of its farm system, Pittsburgh ranks in the top ten among MLB's all-time greatest franchises. Although many Pirates teams failed to win a majority of their games in regular seasons especially before 1969, the franchise has been popular and successful despite being located in a small market with limited resources and financial support compared to clubs with ballparks in large and more prosperous metropolitan areas.

Franchise Owner

Born in Wheeling, West Virginia, in 1962, Robert "Bob" Nutting earned a bachelor of arts degree in history from Williams College in Williamstown, Massachusetts. In 1990, he became CEO of Ogden Newspapers, a West Virginia-based chain of many dailies, weeklies/shoppers, magazines, and independent telephone directories located in several U.S. states.

Kevin McClatchy, who was the Pirates' principal owner from 1996 to 2007, decided to cut ties with the franchise. His minority share—less than 5 percent—was purchased by the current controlling owner, Bob Nutting, who added to his majority stake of more than 60 percent. McClatchy remains CEO but dropped the title of managing general partner. He reports to Nutting and oversees all daily operations while general manager Dave Littlefield reports directly to him. McClatchy also has served on MLB's executive council and labor and international committees.

Since becoming a board member of the team's front office in 2002 and five years later the franchise's majority owner, Nutting rarely schedules interviews or makes local appearances. His behavior, in turn, has been criticized by the team's fan base and media, and caused a perception that he cares more about profits than winning games and championships.

Compared to owners of other NL teams, Nutting's Pirates have won zero division titles, pennants, and World Series although they finished second in their division in 2013, 2014, and 2015. Based on his team's performances in its division and league since he became majority owner in 2007, Nutting has been an inferior leader for not winning any championships. These results also apply to such NL owners as the Cubs' Tom Ricketts and Padres' Ron Fowler (Table A8).

As of 2012, Nutting ranked twenty-seventh best among thirty MLB owners. Although he built the Pirates a training academy in the Dominican Republic, added a single-A affiliate in Florida, renovated the team's spring training complex and increased players' payroll, the Pirates had six consecutive losing seasons. However, because of Pittsburgh's playoff appearances following their 2013–2015 regular seasons, Nutting's results improved and perhaps placed him among baseball's top fifteen owners.

PNC Park

Before 2001, the NL Pirates played their home games at Recreation Park (1887–1890), Exposition Park (1891–1908), Forbes Field (1909–1969), and then Three Rivers Stadium (1970–2000). During this period, the team's attendances ranged from a low of 1,800 per game in 1914 to 25,300 in 1990.

Several years after Pittsburgh Mayor Sophie Masloff proposed a new ballpark near Three Rivers Stadium, the Pirates were offered for sale with moving them being an option. But when McClatchy purchased the franchise in 1996, he and the city established plans for a new ballpark. After financing was approved, construction began on the facility in 1999. Completed and named PNC Park after PNC Financial Services purchased naming rights, the 38,600-seat venue opened in April 2001.

Being one of baseball's smallest venues, PNC Park features two main seating decks. These extend from the right field foul pole to home plate and down to the left field pole with club seats in the lower section of the upper deck and a press box at the top, and luxury suites between decks. Fans may walk around the main concourse without losing sight of the field and sit in the left or right field bleachers to catch a home run while overlooking the bullpens. A scoreboard is part of the right field fence and a video scoreboard exists behind bleachers in left field.

The ballpark's amenities include a restaurant above the left field bleachers; two elaborate food courts—a smorgasbord and Pop's Plaza, named after former player Willie Stargell; such accessible shops along General Robinson Street as Diamond Pizza and Artia's Restaurant; an outer promenade known as River Walk that gives fans views of the city, river, and field; and in the right field corner, the Budweiser Bowie Bar where fans mingle, eat at Manny's BBQ, and enjoy an adult beverage while watching a game. In short, PNC Park has a quaint setting and provides excellent views of the downtown Pittsburgh skyline.

Compared to ballparks of fourteen other NL teams as of 2015, fifteen-year-old PNC Park tied for seventh in age with the Brewers' Miller Park and also ranked eleventh in construction cost and thirteenth in value. Among those of all MLB clubs, the Pirates' home venue was tied for twentieth in age and placed eighteenth in cost and twenty-third in value. These results indicate, in part, that Pittsburgh plays in a very charming and unique but modern ballpark with enough amenities to generate an average amount of gate receipts from their home games (Table A9).

In the 2011–2015 MLB seasons, the FCIs for a family to attend a regular-season Pirates' home game ranged from $127 in 2011 to $175 in 2015. To reveal specific costs for families during a recent year, Pittsburgh ballpark's FCI in 2015 was $5 or 3 percent more than in 2014. Listed from most to least in amount by item for one person, the team's nonpremium (premium) tickets were between $19 and $20 ($61 and $62), a baseball cap $22, parking one vehicle $15, single beer between $5 and $6, and a hot dog and soft drink each between $3 and $4. Thus, families paid less to be at games in PNC Park than at those at twenty-two other ballparks in MLB.

Among other clubs in the league's CD, they had rankings and FCIs from most to least as follows in the 2015 MLB season: Cubs third at $300; Cardinals sixth at $236; Brewers twenty-second at $182; and Reds twenty-fifth at $166. These differences in FCIs occurred, in part, because of these teams' popularity and competitiveness, population and population growth of their host cities and metropolitan areas, and disposable income and wealth of sports fans in the local market.

In a recent study by CSN Mid-Atlantic, PNC Park ranked first in MLB. According to an online report in *USA Today*, the author said:

> To me, this is the perfect ballpark. And I know I'm not alone in thinking that. It has everything: An unmatched vista of downtown Pittsburgh beyond the Allegheny River, the Roberto Clemente Bridge ushering fans back and forth, an intimate seating bowl with only two decks (the first ballpark built with fewer than three decks since Milwaukee's County Stadium in the 1950s) and just enough quirks to make games there distinct without threatening the quality of play. And after two decades of awful baseball, it's been great to see Pirates games become a real event inside the best ballpark in America.[22]

Financial Data

According to data and other financial information published in *Forbes* for franchises in the NL as of their 2015 season, Pittsburgh ranked ninth in market value at $900 million, revenue at $229 million, and its debt-to-value ratio at 10 percent; fourth in operating income at $43.6 million, and twelfth in gate receipts at $54 million. Among the league's CD teams, the Pirates had the smallest gate receipts and only third or fourth highest market value and other amounts (Table A11).

In comparison to twenty-nine other MLB teams as of 2015, Pittsburgh's market value and revenue were each seventeenth, operating income fifth, gate receipts twenty-first, and debt percent fifteenth. Despite being a small-market team, the Pirates are a valuable and profitable business enterprise whose financial results, except for their operating income, rank average to below average compared to their rivals.

Besides market size, salary inflation, and other factors, an MLB team's annual payroll partly reflects its commitment to players and their current and potential contribution individually and as a group to winning games in regular seasons and postseasons. From 2011 to 2015, for example, the Pirates payroll among NL teams ranged in rank from ninth in 2014 ($77 million) to sixteenth in 2011 ($45 million). With respect to other CD clubs, Pittsburgh had the smallest payroll in three of five seasons which, in turn, did not negatively affect the team's performances in qualifying for the playoffs during 2013–2015 (Table A12).

With respect to the payrolls of all MLB teams as of 2015, the Pirates ranged in rank from nineteenth in 2013 to twenty-eighth in 2011. For various reasons including efforts to compete against the Cardinals and other rivals in the CD, the team's payroll was higher in 2012 ($63 million), 2013 ($77 million), and 2015 ($85 million). To win another division title, however, Pittsburgh's annual payroll for players on its roster must increase by at least $20 million.

Although the Pirates committed about $93 million to their payroll including arbitration projections in 2016, they were only responsible for $90 million because the Dodgers provided some cash in the Michael Morse trade. Among other teams' payrolls in the NL's CD, the Cubs led the way with a $133 million; Cardinals behind them at $132.6 million; Reds at $118 million; and the Brewers just ahead of the Pirates at $98 million. The Dodgers, meanwhile, had baseball's highest payroll at $291 million followed by the Yankees' $223 million, and Red Sox's $185 million. Interestingly the World Series champion Royals ranked thirteenth at $128 million, while the Marlins recorded an MLB-low of $63 million.[23]

Business Relations

Besides regular-season and postseason games, MLB franchises are involved in—and affected by—their former and current front-office policies, community events, and local commercial activities, investments, and projects. In no specific order, the following are a few of them for Pittsburgh's NL team as of 2015.[24]

First, the Pirates and MLB congratulated Oscars Limited (LTD) and Cronmiller Marketing who each won a Jackie Robinson Most Valuable Diverse Business Partner (MVDBP) award. In recognition of Robinson's extraordinary contribution in breaking the color barrier in MLB, these MVDBPs reflect the character and commitment to excellence of Jackie.

Incorporated in 1983, the African-American-owned Oscars LTD sells corporate gifts, advertising specialties, and custom products. Renowned for the high quality of its products and customer service, extensive product range and attention to details, the company addresses the diverse marketing needs of some of Pittsburgh's largest law firms and Fortune 500 companies, and has served as a vendor of the Pirates for more than two decades. By providing customers with creative solutions, dependable service, and quality products for over sixty years, Cronmiller Marketing builds solutions for customers and tailored to meet their needs.

Second, as the executive vice president and chief sales and marketing officer of the Pirates, Drew Cloud is responsible for leading all sales and marketing operations of the franchise and PNC Park. These duties include ticketing, membership, premium experience, corporate partnerships, and marketing programs. He joined the Pirates after spending years in various leadership roles within the NBA by working, for example, with the league's Phoenix Suns and also the Women's National Basketball Association (WNBA) Mercury as vice president of ticket sales and guest experience. While in these positions, Drew was responsible for record business growth as well as development of some of the top sports executives in the industry.

Third, Bryan Stroh guides the legal department of the Pirates as senior vice president of business affairs and general counsel. While his title sounds straightforward, his duties intertwine legal and business operations with America's favorite pastime. The trifecta enables him to weigh in on the organization's latest venture: real estate development in North Shore—the area that surrounds the Pirates' home ballpark based in Pittsburgh, Pennsylvania. Passionate about law, baseball, and business, Stroh joined the club in 2011, meaning he suffered through only two years of the Pirates' twenty-season playoff drought before postseasons in 2013–2015.

Fourth, during late 2015, some Pirates' media, marketing, and sales executives led a symposium about internships, networking, and careers with sports, arts, and entertainment management students in the business center at PNC Park, which is located walking distance from their downtown campus.

Panelists from the Pirates front office included such people as graphic designer Dan Bogacz; play-by-play announcer Greg Brown; senior director of corporate sponsorships Aaron Cohn; director of media relations Dan Hart; new business development director Nick McNeill; manager of business communications and social media Terry Rodgers; and special events and game presentation director Christine Serkoch. During the symposium, the panelists offered words of advice for students on how to make the most out of their college experience and future career.

Fifth, University of Pittsburgh's Katz School of Business management professor Ray Jones studied the business side of the Pirates both as an academic and working with the Academy of Sports Marketing—a program which provides undergraduate business students with marketing internships in the University's Department of Athletics. The Pirates' struggles to become competitive, both on-the-field and with respect to ticket sales and personnel management, were a focal point of discussion and debate in his classes.[25]

The club's 2013 playoff run, for example, generated a high level of interest for students. Jones was pleased that even though it had not been in the playoffs since 1992, the team became strategic by pursuing opportunities through its postseason ticket offerings. First, the Pirates' playoff tickets were tied to deposits for 2014 season tickets. This was a great example of how to design effective promotions by linking an organization's sales promotions with its long-range objectives. Second, the Pirates gave priority for playoff tickets to fans that purchased season ticket plans during the 2013 season. In other words, the organization designed a promotion in a manner that linked a sales offer to a strategic objective—in this case encouraging future consumption from customers who have shown a willingness to commit to season-ticket plans.

According to Jones, it would not surprise him if these fans decided to return in 2014 and even commit to larger season ticket plans, particularly if the Pirates team had an impressive run in the previous playoffs. While the Pirates organization should be commended for strategic vision in its design of sales promotions for playoff tickets, it must address the fact that the club's brand is largely associated with two consecutive decades of losing baseball. The challenge, therefore, is to repair its reputation among two distinct groups of the fan base—any fans over thirty-years-old and also those under the age of thirty.

In sum, the Pirates won ninety-eight games in 2015. This was second most in baseball although NL Cy Young award winner and Cubs pitcher Jake Arrieta silenced them in the wild-card game by allowing just four hits in nine dominant innings. Still, Pittsburgh's recent turnaround on the diamond—three consecutive playoff appearances after twenty straight losing seasons—enabled the team to increase its average nonpremium ticket prices by more than 2 percent and average attendance at PNC Park since 2012 to 30,846. In addition the Pirates' twenty-nine-year-old star centerfielder Andrew McCutchen, who is under contract for at least two more seasons at the bargain rate of $41.5 million, has finished in the top five of the league in MVP voting for four straight years including the award in 2013.

ST. LOUIS CARDINALS

In 1875, the St. Louis Brown Stockings entered the National Association (NA) and finished their season in fourth among fourteen teams. After the NA folded, one year later the St. Louis club joined the NL as a charter member. Because of two fewer victories than the Hartford Dark Blues in 1876, the Brown Stockings placed third at 45–19 and six games behind the champion Chicago White Stockings. Due to a game-fixing scandal and bankruptcy, however, St. Louis was expelled from the NL after its 1877 season. Without a league, they continued to play as a semiprofessional barnstorming team through 1881.[26]

Before pro baseball's 1882 season, German-American businessman Chris von der Ahe purchased and reorganized the Brown Stockings franchise and made it a founding member of the American Association (AA). From 1882 to 1891, the Brown Stockings—renamed simply Browns in 1893—became the dominant team in the AA as manager Charlie Comiskey guided it to four consecutive pennants. Besides these championships, the team also finished second three times, third once, fourth in 1884, and fifth in 1882.

Following three of its AA pennants, the Browns played the NL winner in a predecessor of the World Series. In these games, they tied the Chicago White Stockings 3–3–1 in 1885; defeated the Chicago White Stockings 4–2 in 1986; lost to the Detroit Tigers 10–5 in 1887; and lost to the New York Giants 6–4 in 1888.

During the Brown Stockings' one and Browns' nine seasons playing in the AA, they compiled an all-time league-high 781 wins and a .643 winning percentage. However, they lost 432 games but also tied in twenty-two others. When the AA went bankrupt after its 1891 season, the Browns transferred to the NL and joined to compete with eleven other members including the champion Boston Beaneaters. In 1900, the team's nickname changed from Browns to Cardinals—aka Redbirds.

Team Performances

While playing as the Browns (1892–1898), Perfectos (1899), and Cardinals (1900–2015), the team had victories in 9,790 games or approximately 51 percent of their games. During this period they won thirteen division titles, nineteen pennants, eleven World Series, and appeared in twenty-eight playoffs. Among fourteen other NL clubs as of their 2015 season, St. Louis ranked third in winning division titles and first in both number of pennants and World Series titles. With forty total championships since 1892, the franchise has more of them than any team in the league including the Dodgers, Reds, and Braves (Table A7).

In comparison to all MLB clubs as of 2015, St. Louis was fifth in division titles and finished second to the AL Yankees in both number of pennants and World Series championships. Based on these results, the Cardinals have been a competitive, elite, and winning team in their division since 1994 and the league for more than a century.

Besides playing in fifteen World Series and winning nine of them before the late 1990s, the club's most successful periods with consecutive postseasons include 2000–2002, 2004–2006, and 2011–2015. Led primarily by managers Tony La Russa and Mike Matheny, such prominent players as sluggers Albert Pujols, Jim Edmonds, and Yadier Molina, and pitchers Matt

Morris, Chris Carpenter, and Adam Wainwright became stars in the sport. For various reasons, however, the Cardinals failed to qualify for postseasons in some back-to-back years. These were, for example, 1900–1925 and also 1947–1963, 1969–1981, and 1988–1995.

Regarding the franchise's best and worst teams, respectively, the 1942 Cardinals not only won 106 games and posted the highest winning percentage in franchise history, they led the league in runs scored and fewest runs allowed but also fended off a collapse while competing for a pennant; then in five games, they defeated the AL Yankees in the World Series. The St. Louis lineup featured a pair of Hall of Famers in Stan Musial and Enos Slaughter with shortstop Marty Marion and center fielder Terry Moore providing stellar defense. While on the pitching mound, Mort Cooper twirled his way to the NL MVP award. Interestingly, the 1943 and 1944 Cardinals squads each won 105 games.

For its least successful team, St. Louis finished 49–105 in 1908 and last in the league. Being outscored by their opponents by 254 runs, they were lucky their record was not worse after ending fifty games behind the first-place Cubs. In the lineup, 50 percent of the team's regulars batted below .215, and in a related matter, they were shut out thirty-three times on the year. Ace pitcher Bugs Raymond managed to lose twenty-five games despite an ERA of 2.03.

With respect to the all–time best MLB franchises, the Redbirds have the second-most appearances in World Series and runners-up with five championships in the expansion era. During this period of seasons, Hall of Famers Bob Gibson, Lou Brock, and Ozzie Smith called St. Louis home as did managers Whitey Herzog and Tony La Russa and future Hall of Famer Albert Pujols. Besides their winning years, the Cardinals went without a World Series championship in such periods as the early 1890s to 1920s, late 1940s to early 1960s, and late 1960s to early 1980s.

As of 2015, the question was not which team had set baseball's gold standard for five consecutive seasons, but whether any were close to the Cardinals to merit the silver. During 2011–2015, St. Louis won and lost a World Series, advanced to the NL championship series four times, and lost in the league's divisional series. They are the third team in the wild-card era to attain such consistent excellence, joining the 1995–1999 Braves and 1998–2001 Yankees. Arguably, the Cardinals are the first or second preeminent franchise in baseball today.

Franchise Owner

The son of longtime MLB executive Bill DeWitt and his wife Margaret, William DeWitt Jr. was born in St. Louis, Missouri. He was involved with baseball constantly as a child, inasmuch as his father once owned the St. Louis Browns and Cincinnati Reds. After attending St. Louis Country Day School, DeWitt Jr. earned a bachelor's degree in economics from Yale University in 1963 and two years later, an MBA from Harvard University.

Dewitt Jr. joined Cincinnati investment firm Gradison & Company in 1974. Five years later, he and Mercer Reynolds founded the investment firm Reynolds, DeWitt & Company. The firm, which owns several Arby franchises estimated at more than $50 million, is an investor in Cincinnati-based U.S. Playing Card Company—worth an estimated $120 million. It also holds a multimillion-dollar stake in Kentucky-based Newport Aquarium. DeWitt Jr. is also involved with private equity's the DeWitt Capital Group.

When businessman Eddie Chiles intended to sell MLB's Texas Rangers franchise in 1989, DeWitt Jr. and former U.S. president George W. Bush brought a group of investors together to purchase the Rangers. Six years later, DeWitt Jr. and Stephen and Frederick Brauer purchased the Cardinals from Anheuser-Busch for $150 million. As chairman and CEO, DeWitt Jr. oversees all league, financial, operational, and baseball affairs for the club while his son William DeWitt III serves as its president.

Compared to the performances of other NL teams under their current owners as of 2015, DeWitt Jr.'s Cardinals had ranked first in winning division titles, tied for first with Giants' owner Charlie Johnson in number of pennants, and placed second in World Series victories following the Giants. Among all owners of MLB clubs in championships, St. Louis ranked respectively first, tied for first, and third. Thus, DeWitt Jr. has been an outstanding leader based on the performances of his Cardinals teams since 1995 (Table A8).

In 2013, *Sports Illustrated* ranked DeWitt Jr. as MLB's third best owner, in part, because of the Cardinals' .535 winning percentage and two World Series championships in eleven playoffs. He did things to keep one of baseball's most historic franchises near the top. After buying the team, DeWitt Jr. hired Tony La Russa, built the club a new $365 million ballpark, and awarded superstar Albert Pujols with a nine-figure contract. Moreover, the team handled the deaths of pitchers Darryl Kile and Josh Hancock, and longtime announcer Jack Buck, with respect and dignity.

Busch Stadium

Before 2006, the NL Browns played their home games at Sportsman Park (1892) and then Robison Field (1893–1898), Perfectos at Robison Field (1899), and Cardinals at Robison Field (1900–1919), Sportsman's Park (1920–1952), Busch Stadium I (1953–1965), and Busch Stadium II (1966–2005). During this period, the club's attendances ranged from a low of 2,200 per game in 1897 to 43,600 in 2005.

In June 2001, the Cardinals and state of Missouri signed a contract to construct a new ballpark in downtown St. Louis and adjacent to Busch Stadium II. Owned by the Cardinals, Busch Stadium III was privately financed using a combination of private bonds—obligating the team—and also bank loans, cash from the franchise's owners, and a long-term loan from St. Louis County. In 2004, the team and Anheuser-Busch signed a twenty-year naming rights deal to the ballpark.

As fans approach the 46,700-seat ballpark, they see a façade consisting of brick and steel with arched openings at the main entrances. There are main, loge, and terrace concourses and also bleachers in both left and right field providing spectators with a different view of action on the field. Beyond the outfield is the skyline of downtown St. Louis in addition to the Gateway Arch.

Busch Stadium III has several amenities. For example, there is the U.S. Cellular Family Pavilion where fans enjoy interactive games and activities; Coca-Cola Rooftop Deck and Backstop Bar; Ballpark Village, which includes a three-story building containing a Hall of Fame Museum and Cardinals Nation Restaurant & Bar; and Budweiser Brew House, which showcases Anheuser-Busch's connection to the franchise featuring a beer garden and an estimated one hundred different beers.

Compared to the ballparks of fourteen other NL teams as of 2015, ten-year-old Busch Stadium III ranked twelfth in age and also fourth in both construction cost and value. Among those of all MLB clubs, the Cardinals' home venue was twenty-fifth in age and placed eighth in cost and sixth in value. These results indicate, in part, that St. Louis's NL team plays in a modern ballpark with enough amenities to generate an above-average amount of gate receipts from its home games (Table A9).

In the 2011–2015 MLB seasons, the FCIs for a family to attend a regular-season Cardinals home game ranged from a low of $223 in 2011 to $236 in 2015. Among fourteen other NL ballparks, Busch Stadium's FCI ranked between fourth in both 2014 ($233) and 2015 ($236) to fifth in 2011 ($223), 2012 ($225), and 2013 ($230). For only the league's CD teams, Cardinals home games cost less than did Cubs games at Wrigley Field but not for those at the ballparks of the Brewers, Pirates, or Reds.

To reveal specific costs for families during a recent year, St. Louis's ballpark's FCI in 2015 was $3 or 1 percent more for them than in 2014. Listed from most to least in amount by item for one person, the team's non-premium (premium) tickets were between $34 and $35 ($83 and $84), parking one vehicle $20, a baseball cap $16, soft drink between $5 and $6, a single beer $5, and a hot dog between $4 and $5. Based on these amounts, it was relatively expensive for a family to buy nonpremium or premium tickets for their seats and spend for things at games in Busch Stadium.

Among other clubs in the league's CD, their games had rankings and FCIs from most to least as follows in the 2015 MLB season: Cubs third at $300; Brewers twenty-second at $182; Pirates twenty-third at $175; and Reds twenty-fifth at $166. These differences in FCIs occurred, in part, because of these teams' popularity and competitiveness, population and population growth of their host cities, and disposable income and wealth of sports fans in the local market.

In a recent study by CSN Mid-Atlantic, Busch Stadium ranked fifteenth in MLB. According to an online report in *USA Today*, the author said:

> There is the Gateway Arch looming in the background, and that is a cool thing to see as you gaze out beyond the sea of red seats. But that's about the only thing that distinguishes the third Busch Stadium from the other parks that occupy the middle section of this list. You would think the Cardinals, so rich with tradition and with such a passionate fan base, would have come up with something a little more interesting than this. But they didn't. The dimensions are symmetrical. The seating areas look just like the seating areas in other stadiums. There's nothing particularly wrong with the place. There's just nothing particularly exciting about it, either.[27]

Financial Data

According to data and other financial information published in *Forbes* for franchises in the NL as of their 2015 season, St. Louis ranked fourth in both market value at $1.4 billion and revenue at $294 million, and also first in operating income at $73.6 million, second in gate receipts at $133 million, and sixth in its debt-to-value ratio at 21 percent. Among only the league's CD teams, the Cardinals had the highest market value, operating income and gate receipts, but less revenue and a smaller debt percent than the Cubs (Table A11).

In comparison to twenty-nine other MLB teams as of 2015, St. Louis's market value was sixth, revenue seventh, operating income first, gate receipts fourth, and debt percent ninth. Consequently, the Cardinals are a valuable and profitable business enterprise whose financial results rank above average with respect to their rivals. In other words this is an organized, popular, and well-respected franchise because of its avid fan base and also ballpark, owner, and history of winning championships.

Besides market size, salary inflation, and other factors, an MLB team's annual payroll partly reflects its commitment to players and their current and potential contribution individually and as a group to winning games in regular seasons and postseasons. From 2011 to 2015, for example, the Cardinals payroll among NL teams ranged in rank from fourth in 2013 ($112 million) to sixth in 2015 ($120 million). With respect to other CD clubs, St. Louis had the highest payroll each season which, in turn, reflected the team's performances in qualifying for five consecutive playoffs during 2011–2015 (Table A12).

With respect to the payrolls of all MLB teams as of 2015, the Cardinals ranged in rank from ninth in 2013 to twelfth in 2015. To remain competitive and win more division titles, pennants, and World Series, principal owner William DeWitt Jr. will continue to sign free agents and veteran players to lucrative long-term contracts with incentives to reward them for their outstanding performances.

Business Relations

Besides regular-season and postseason games, MLB franchises are involved in—and affected by—their former and current front-office policies, community events, and local commercial activities, investments, and projects. In no specific order, the following are a few of them for St. Louis's NL team as of 2015.[28]

First, to generate additional revenue from selling more season tickets, the Cardinals introduced dynamic ticket pricing in October 2012. The team was relatively conservative in its dynamic pricing execution by altering prices at most once a day and often once every other day. But like such clubs as the AL Athletics and NL Giants, St. Louis sought to use dynamic pricing as a means to seek out a more realistic view of the marketplace. "What we're trying to do is get the pricing right," said Cardinals vice president of ticket sales Joe Strohm. "There's less vagaries in the system for the playoffs just given there's far less runway before each game in terms of time. But conceptually, it's the same as the regular season in that we're trying to optimize the pricing."[29]

Second, Cardinals president William DeWitt III delivered the keynote address at the *Business Journal*'s Top 150 Privately Held Companies dinner during May 2016 at Busch Stadium. The Top 150 Privately Held Companies section—which is published in the *Journal's* March 25 issue—will feature stories about the highest-revenue-producing private companies in the region. Such companies as Enterprise Holdings, World Wide Technology, Delmar Gardens, and the Cardinals organization perennially appear in this exclusive section which recaps their business performance during the previous year.

Third, the former director of baseball development for the Cardinals pleaded guilty during early 2016 to charges of unauthorized access to the Houston Astros' computers, according to the U.S. Department of Justice. Christopher Correa, who was named the Cardinals' director of baseball development in 2013, pleaded guilty to five counts of unauthorized access of a protected computer. Among his violations, Correa accessed scout rankings of every player eligible for the draft through the Astros' computers, and he admitted to illicitly hacking into the Astros' private online database and/or the email accounts of others in order to get proprietary information. Each conviction of unauthorized access to a protected computer carries a maximum possible sentence of five years in federal prison and possibly a $250,000 fine.

Fourth, in a recent post on the Internet, the Zimmer Radio and Marketing Group listed seven things to learn about marketing from the Cardinals. In other words, they are social; get involved in the community; offer a variety of contents; share a story; use seasonal marketing; use videos; and have an integrated marketing strategy. In Zimmer's view, the Cardinals win in marketing because they go out of their way to contact and build a connection with their fans. This social and emotional investment leads to the kind of brand loyalty that otherwise cannot be built.[30]

Fifth, Equifax Workforce Solutions (EWS) announced a partnership with the Cardinals organization during March 2015. As part of this multiyear agreement, EWS will have a noted presence at Busch Stadium including highly visible signage in right field on the famous wagon-gate doors that welcome attendees from across the nation. The company will also celebrate its community spirit and the St. Louis roots of its workforce solutions business by hosting an employee game night and sponsoring a give-away night for fans during the season. "We are proud to partner with Equifax," said Thane van Breusegen, vice president of corporate sales and marketing and stadium entertainment for the team. "Both organizations have a longstanding presence in St. Louis and a shared goal of supporting our community."[31]

NOTES

1. Two books about the history of big-league teams are Frank P. Jozsa Jr., *National League Franchises: Team Performances and Business Success* (New York: Springer, 2015), and James Quirk and Rodney D. Fort, *Pay Dirt: The Business of Professional Team Sports* (Princeton, NJ: Princeton University Press, 1992).
2. For details about the performances of MLB clubs including those in this chapter, see such websites as http://www.baseball-reference.com, http://www.mlb.com, and http://www.baseball-almanac.com.
3. Besides a profile of them on their team's website, another source is "List of Major League Baseball Principal Owners," http://www.baseball-reference.com, cited January 22, 2016.
4. The primary reference for historical facts and other information about Wrigley Field and other venues is the website http://www.ballparksofbaseball.com.

5. See “Fan Cost Index,” http://www.teammarketingreport.com, cited January 25, 2016.

6. This quote appeared in “Ranking All 30 MLB Ballparks,” http://www.csnmidatlantic.com, cited January 26, 2016.

7. The Cubs’ business relations were in various sources, including magazines and newspapers, and also specific editions of *Business Week*, *Forbes*, *Fortune*, and the *SportsBusiness Journal* and *Wall Street Journal*. Examples are Don Muret, “For Cubs, Dynamic Pricing’s a One-Way Street,” *SportsBusiness Journal* (March 18, 2013): 7; Ira Boudway, “Holy Cow! The Chicago Cubs Finally Have a Winning Business Plan,” http://www.bloomberg.com, cited May 18, 2016; Lewis Lazare, “Chicago Cubs Proudly Show Off How to Do a Clubhouse Right,” http://www.bizjournals.com, cited April 13, 2016; “Nuveen Pleased to Show Support of Chicago Cubs,” http://www.businesswire.com, cited April 26, 2016.

8. The Official Major League Baseball Fact Book 2005 Edition (St. Louis, MO: Sporting News, 2005) is an important media guide to review for the records of teams and their players and managers.

9. Matt Snyder, “Franchise Best/Worsts,” http://www.cbssports.com, cited March 13, 2016.

10. For Robert Castellini’s profile and success, see “List of Major League Baseball Principal Owners” and Rick Weiner, “Power Ranking Every MLB Owner from Worst to First,” http://www.bleacherreport.com, cited March 3, 2016.

11. “Cincinnati Reds Attendance, Stadiums, and Park Factors,” http://www.baseball-reference.com, cited March 15, 2016.

12. See note 6 in this chapter for an evaluation of the Reds’ Great American Ball Park and others of teams in the NL’s CD.

13. Kurt Badenhausen, Michael Ozanian, and Christina Settimi, “MLB Worth $36B As Team Values Hit Record $1.2B Average,” http://www.forbes.com, cited January 18, 2016.

14. The Reds’ business relations topics include “Cincinnati Reds Keep Their IT on the Ball,” http://www.news.microsoft.com, cited September 25, 2012; Steve Watkins, “Reds TV Ratings Defy Dire Predictions,” http://www.bizjournals.com, cited April 7, 2016; “Reds COO Castellini Talks Business in Q&A,” http://www.cincinnati.suntimes.com, cited February 12, 2016; “Black Business Matters: Pathway to Prosperity,” http://www.thecincinnatiherald.com, cited March 16, 2016; Alexander Coolidge, “Reds Get 7-Year Extension on Sponsorship,” http://www.cincinnati.com, cited April 15, 2016.

15. For the Seattle Pilots’ history, see Frank P. Jozsa Jr., *Major League Baseball Expansions and Team Relocations: A History, 1876–2008* (Jefferson, NC McFarland, 2010).

16. For his short- and long-term strategies as general manager, read Tom Haudricourt, “Brewers GM Refuses to Equate Rebuilding to ‘Tanking,’” http://www.jsonline.com, cited March 15, 2016.

17. Besides “Ranking All 30 MLB Ballparks,” another interesting source is “Ranking MLB’s Ballparks,” http://www.athlonsports.com, cited January 26, 2016.

18. For a few Brewers' business topics, see "Sky Hawks Officially Sign with Milwaukee," http://www.csbj.com, cited October 13, 2014; "Some Advertisers Cut Spending on Milwaukee Brewers Radio Broadcasts This Season," http://www.milwaukee.suntimes.com, cited May 6, 2016; "Associated Bank Expands Partnership with Milwaukee Brewers," http://www.prnewswire.com, cited March 31, 2016.

19. Bill Shea, "Dan Gilbert Almost Bought Milwaukee Brewers instead of Cleveland Cavaliers," http://www.crainsdetroit.com, cited March 17, 2016.

20. Augustino Fontevecchia, "Billionaires Tony Ressler and Sara Blakely Snatch Atlanta Hawks for $730 Million," cited http://www.forbes.com, March 20, 2016.

21. For the Pirates and its performances, franchise owner, PNC Park, financial data and business highlights, see previous notes in this chapter similar to the Cubs, Reds, and Brewers.

22. "Ranking All 30 MLB Ballparks" and "Ranking MLB's Ballparks" contain information about the construction and specifications of Pittsburgh's PNC Park.

23. "Major League Baseball Team Payrolls," http://www.usatoday.com, cited January 23, 2016.

24. Some Pirates' business relations are reported in Abraham Madkour, "By Design: High Standards Set by Pittsburgh Facilities," http://www.sportsbusinessdaily.com, cited June 23, 2014; "Pirates' Business Model," http://www.bucsdugout.com, cited May 18, 2016; Kurt Badenhausen, "The Pittsburgh Pirates Are Baseball's Best and Business Is Thriving," http:www.forbes.com, cited May 18, 2016; Paul Gough, "Pirates Reach Partnership Deals with Six Companies," http://www.bizjournals.com, cited May 16, 2016.

25. Ray Jones, "Business Lessons from the 2013 Pittsburgh Pirates—Strategy and Opportunity," http://www.katz.pitt.edu, cited March 25, 2016.

26. The Cardinals' performances, franchise owner, Busch Stadium, financial data, and business highlights are contained in previous Notes regarding the other four CD franchises.

27. CSN Mid-Atlantic, "Ranking All 30 MLB Ballparks" and "Ranking MLB's Ballparks."

28. Judy Greenwald, "Former St. Louis Cardinals Exec Pleads Guilty to Hacking Astros' Computers," http://www.businessinsurance.com, cited January 11, 2016; and Vince Brennan, "Cardinals' DeWitt III to Headline *Business Journal* Top 150 Event at Busch," http://www.bizjournals.com, cited February 11, 2016 are two business relations topics.

29. See Eric Fisher, "Dynamic Pricing Comes to MLB Postseason," *SportsBusiness Journal* (October 22, 2012): 3; and Bill King, "Ticket Challenge: Getting the Price Right," *SportsBusiness Journal* (March 19, 2012): 1.

30. For more details, see "7 Things We Can Learn about Marketing from the St. Louis Cardinals," http://www.zimmercommunications.com, cited March 26, 2016.

31. The article to access and read is "Equifax Announces Partnership with the St. Louis Cardinals," http://www.equifax.com, cited March 30, 2016.

Chapter Six

West Division

As stated in the previous chapter, prior to 1969 there were no individual or geographic divisions within the American League (AL) or National League (NL) of Major League Baseball (MLB). However, because of expansion between 1969 and 1993, the AL and NL consisted of either six or seven teams each in the East Division (ED) and West Division (WD). Then in 1994 the two leagues realigned again and besides their ED and WD, they added a Central Division (CD). As a result, the AL's and NL's ED and CD each had five teams while their WD included four. After 1997 other differences occurred in divisions until 2013 when five each played in the ED, CD, and WD.[1]

Given these changes in the structure of big-league baseball, this chapter discusses the historical development—and highlights financial data and business relations—of NL teams based in Phoenix, Arizona; Denver, Colorado; Los Angeles, California; San Diego, California; and San Francisco, California, as of MLB's 2015 season. Which of them, for example, won the most division titles but fewest pennants? What were their estimated values and actual gate receipts and operating income in 2015? Among the five franchises' owners, which of them had teams that qualified for the least number of playoffs but won at least one World Series? How did teams' current ballparks compare to others with respect to their ages and attendances, and also to costs for families at home games? The answers to these and other questions are elements covered in the chapter.

ARIZONA DIAMONDBACKS

During late 1993/early 1994, the National Basketball Association (NBA) Phoenix Suns owner Jerry Colangelo formed an ownership group to apply for an MLB expansion team. Confident of being awarded a franchise, the group held a name-the-team contest for it and published a full-page advertistement in a February 1995 edition of the Arizona Republic. The winning choice, Diamondbacks, refers to a rattlesnake in the region that injects a large amount of venom when striking its victims.[2]

Colangelo's bid for an expansion team received strong support from his friend, Chicago White Sox and Bulls owner Jerry Reinsdorf and also from Bud Selig, the acting Commissioner of Baseball and Milwaukee Brewers founder. Furthermore, there were plans for a new retractable-roof ballpark to be built in an industrial/warehouse district on the southeast edge of downtown Phoenix. As a result of these facts, Colangelo's group was awarded a franchise in early March 1995 to begin play in the 1998 season, and his syndicate paid MLB a fee of $130 million for it.

After the Diamondbacks were assigned to join the AL, five of the league's teams threatened to block it because of concerns of playing additional games out of their time zone. This, in turn, would cause early starts and perhaps decrease their revenue and television ratings. Eventually, the Arizona Diamondbacks were officially voted into the NL, while their expansion counterparts in Tampa Bay entered the AL.

Team Performances

As a member of the NL's WD from 1998 to 2015, Arizona played 2,916 games and had victories in approximately 49 percent of them. During the period, the club won five division titles and one each pennant and World Series in five playoffs. With respect to other NL teams, the Diamondbacks tied for ninth with the Chicago Cubs and San Diego Padres in winning division titles, tied for twelfth with the Colorado Rockies in number of pennants, and tied for tenth with the Atlanta Braves in World Series titles. Among only those in the WD, Arizona won fewer championships than the Los Angeles Dodgers, San Diego Padres, and San Francisco Giants, but not the Rockies (Table A7).

Compared to all MLB clubs as of 2015, the Diamondbacks tied for twenty-first in winning division titles, tied for twenty-third in pennants, and tied for twentieth in World Series victories. Despite existing only eighteen years, the team has been competitive in its division and league and won more pennants plus World Series than the NL's Washington Nationals, Milwaukee Brewers, and Colorado Rockies, and AL's Tampa Bay Rays and Seattle Mariners.

Through 2015, Arizona's most successful seasons were 1999, 2001, 2002, 2007, and 2011. The club was in playoffs because of such players as pitchers Randy Johnson, Curt Shilling, and Brandon Webb, and sluggers Luis Gonzalez, Matt Williams, and Justin Upton. From 1999 to 2004, for example, Johnson won four consecutive Cy Young awards while Shilling was a two-time all-star and also twenty-game winner. But partly because of managers like A. J. Hinch and Al Pedrique and their lack of talented players, the Diamondbacks had losing seasons in nine years.

Although the 2001 team won a World Series, the 1999 squad was the best in franchise history because it had a .632 winning percentage and also 100 wins. Moreover, the club improved its win total by thirty-five games from the 1998 season. The offense clouted 216 homers—second most in the league—and Matt Williams drove in 142 runs while Randy Johnson and Omar Daal excelled as pitchers. In contrast to their 1999 and 2001 seasons, the 2004 Diamondbacks lost 111 games, were outscored 284 runs by opponents, and finished 42 games behind the first-place Dodgers. Except for pitchers Johnson and Webb, the rotation was miserable.

As of baseball's 2015 season, Arizona ranked eighteenth best among thirty MLB franchises. Because of more friendly expansion rules than its predecessors, Arizona won a division title in only its second season and became World Series champion in its fourth. Starting pitchers Johnson and Schilling dominated NL hitters in 2001–2002 and combined for 45 victories each season. But after the Diamondbacks had five straight winning years, which included three division titles, the club sank to an all-time low with just fifty-one victories in 2004 and during eleven seasons later, finished above .500 only four times.

Franchise Owner

Born in Princeton, West Virginia, Ken Kendrick earned a bachelor of science degree in business administration from West Virginia University in 1965. Three years after starting his career with International Business Machine (IBM), he founded Datatel Inc., which became the worldwide leader in the development of computer software for the management of infrastructure technology at colleges, universities, and foundations.[3]

As Datatel continued to grow and prosper, Kendrick stepped down from daily oversight of it to explore new business opportunities. He served, for example, as president of a Texas-based financial services technology company for four years in the 1980s and then in 1989, became the principal investor in Woodforest National Bank in Woodlands, Texas. It developed into one of the nation's largest employee-owned banks. A $4.5 billion entity with five thousand employees, the bank is a subsidiary of Woodforest Financial Group, which was founded by Kendrick and also includes Merchants Choice Credit Card Services and Par Real Estate.

A charter member of the ownership group that brought baseball to the Phoenix area during the late 1990s, Ken's involvement in the team's general partnership took on added significance in 2004 when he assumed the role of managing general partner. Besides participating in the club's day-to-day operations, he is the organization's designated representative when MLB owners convene and schedule meetings during the year.

In comparison to the performances of NL teams and their owners as of 2015, Kendrick's Diamondbacks tied for fifth in winning two division titles and zero World Series each, and also tied for seventh in number of pennants. Among twenty-nine other franchises in MLB, Arizona respectively tied for twelfth in titles, tied for ninth in World Series, and tied for fourteenth in pennants. Thus Ken's teams have won two championships, which are the same number in the NL as owner of the Miami Marlins, Jeffrey Loria; Washington Nationals, Ted Lerner; and Cincinnati Reds, Robert Castellini (Table A8).

As of 2012, Kendrick ranked as MLB's eleventh worst owner. He is a hands-on guy who doesn't hesitate to speak his mind to the press—not always the best idea. For example, frustrated with the team's performance after raising players' payroll, he publicly blamed a former shortstop and right fielder by questioning the shortstop's motivation for not returning sooner from an injury and whether or not the fielder would be a long-term contributor in Arizona. Earlier, he criticized the team's top pitching prospect and possibly damaged the player's trade value should the team look to move him in a deal. Perhaps allowing his baseball people to deal with how the club operated would lead to more success for this 2001 World Series champion.[4]

Chase Field

When MLB awarded an expansion franchise to Phoenix, construction began on the stadium in November 1995. Shaped like a massive airport hangar and originally named Bank One Ballpark, it was the first stadium built with a retractable roof because of extreme summer temperatures and with a natural grass field to allow outdoor games late in the baseball season. After the merger between Bank One and JP Morgan Chase in 2005, the $354 million ballpark was renamed Chase Field.[5]

The Diamondbacks made their debut before a packed house at Bank One Ballpark on March 31, 1998. More than 3.6 million fans filled the 48,500-seat facility to see the team during its first year in the league. Regarding the ballpark's structure, a four-tier grandstand extends from the left field foul pole to home plate and around to the right field foul pole. Thousands of bleacher seats are behind both the left and right field fences and a twenty-five-foot center field wall serves as the hitters' backdrop with the main video scoreboard above it. The ballpark's most unusual feature is a swimming pool—located behind part of the right field fence.

Other than the pool, Chase Field has several other amenities. Overlooking left field and third base is Friday's Front Row Sports Grill, which offers food and provides entertainment. Although the Diamondbacks are one of the youngest franchises in MLB, the team has had some success in its young history, winning four of seven games at Bank One Ballpark and the 2001 World Series against the AL Yankees. The newest addition to the ballpark is the $12 million, 136-feet wide by 46-feet high HD video scoreboard, installed in 2008.

With respect to other NL ballparks as of 2015, Chase Field was fifth oldest at eighteen-years-old, sixth most expensive to build at $354 million, and fourteenth in estimated value at $135 million. Among all MLB teams' ballparks, Arizona's is tied for fifteenth in age, tenth in construction cost, and twenty-fifth in value. Based on this data and other information in the literature, the Diamondbacks play in a relatively new and modern stadium but because of their low attendances and other factors, the club generates an insufficient amount of gate receipts and revenue from its home games (Table A9).

In the 2011–2015 MLB seasons, the Fan Cost Index (FCI) for a family to attend a regular-season Diamondbacks game at Chase Field ranged from $120 in 2011 to $151 in 2013. During this five-year period among ballparks of fourteen other NL clubs, Arizona's FCI ranged in rank from a low of fifteenth in 2011 ($151) to high of sixteenth in 2012 ($145)—which included Houston's Astro Minute Maid Park. Among big-league teams' ballparks, games at Chase Field were the lowest in cost for families each season (Table A10).

To reveal specific costs for families during a recent year in MLB, the Diamondbacks' ballpark's FCI in 2015—ranked thirtieth at $126—was the same as in 2014. Listed from most to least in amount by item for one person, the team's non-premium (premium) tickets averaged between $17 and $18 ($52 and $53), parking one vehicle and a baseball cap each $10, single beer $4, a hot dog approximately $3, and a soft drink between $1 and $2. Thus, families paid $85 or 40 percent less to attend any of Arizona's games at Chase Field in 2015 than those at the typical team's ballpark in MLB.

Among other clubs in the WD, they had rankings and FCIs from most to least as follows in the 2015 MLB season: Giants fifth at $241; Dodgers twelfth at $218; Rockies eighteenth at $196; and Padres twenty-ninth at $153. These differences in FCIs occurred because of these teams' popularity and competitiveness, the availability of amateur and other outdoor sports in their respective metropolitan area and region, and the disposable income and wealth of local households in the marketplace.

In a recent study by CSN Mid-Atlantic, Chase Field ranked twenty-second in MLB. According to an online report in *USA Today*, the author said:

> Similar in look to Miller Park, Chase Field has a retractable roof that splits open in the middle, plus panels beyond the outfield wall. This stadium, though, is massive, and can be seen from miles away, resembling a huge airplane hangar more than a ballpark. There are plenty of distractions, from restaurants and bars to the famous swimming pool behind the right-field fence. Like Coors Field, it was built too big, back when ticket demand was sky-high. Now, the Diamondbacks have trouble coming close to sellouts even for big games against prime opponents. The shame is that if you can block out all the extra stuff and focus simply on the playing field and the lower seating bowl, it's quite a nice place. It's just really hard to block out everything else.[6]

Financial Data

According to data and other financial information published in *Forbes* for franchises in the NL as of their 2015 season, Arizona ranked fourteenth in market value at $840 million, revenue at $211 million and gate receipts at $42 million, thirteenth in operating income at –$2.2 million, and tied for seventh with the Dodgers in their debt-to-value ratio at 17 percent. Among only the league's WD teams, the Diamondbacks had the lowest market value, revenue and gate receipts, but a less negative operating income than the Dodgers (Table A11).

In comparison to twenty-nine other MLB teams as of 2015, Arizona's market value was twenty-fourth, revenue twenty-fifth, operating income twenty-sixth, gate receipts tied for twenty-sixth, and debt percent tied for tenth. According to these rankings, the Diamondbacks are a relatively low-valued and unprofitable team, and not a successful business operation or enterprise from a financial perspective.

Besides market size, wage inflation, and other factors, an MLB team's annual payroll partly reflects its commitment to players and their current and potential contribution individually and as a group to winning games in regular seasons and postseasons. From 2011 to 2015, for example, the Diamondbacks payroll compared to those of fourteen other NL teams' ranged in rank from sixth in 2014 ($111 million) to fifteenth in 2015 ($65 million). During the five-year period, Arizona's payroll among the league's WD teams was only the third or fourth highest except in 2015. These changes, in part, reflect the team's below-average performances and owner Ken Kendrick's decision to minimize costs and reduce losses (Table A12).

With respect to payrolls of all MLB teams as of 2015, the Diamondbacks' ranged in rank from a low of eleventh in 2014 to a high of thirtieth in 2015.

For various reasons, the team's payroll increased from 2011 to 2014 but then decreased by $46 million or more than 50 percent in 2015. These changes in payroll amounts, in some way, contributed to the club's average performances at 81–81 for two seasons and also its losing records during 2014–2015.

Business Relations

Besides regular-season and postseason games, MLB franchises are involved in—and affected by—internal affairs and problems, community events, and business-related activities and projects. In no specific order, the following are a few of them for Arizona's NL team as of 2015.[7]

First, even though they are one of MLB's youngest franchises, the Diamondbacks dramatically transformed themselves in December 2015. The club introduced a radical new set of uniforms that featured eight distinct options and combined the current color mix of Sedona red and black with gray and the club's original teal, which was used from 1998 to 2006. Also introduced in the new look was a snakeskin diamond pattern on the shoulders of players' jerseys and calves of their pants.

The uniform set—at once larger and more aggressive in design than anything else used in MLB—is aimed in large part to appeal to young people who have increasingly become a focal point of league activity. Interestingly, players were involved in redoing the team's uniforms and also were focus groups of all ages, key partners, and such licensees as New Era, Majestic, and Nike. This project was coordinated through the franchise's in-house creative services personnel as opposed to an outside group.

Second, to break the mold of traditional team-run sponsor summits, the Diamondbacks held the club's first Most Valuable Partner Awards in early 2012. This was a black-tie gala complete with song-and-dance numbers, a red carpet, and celebrity award presenters. The event, patterned after the Oscars, had the team's president and chief executive officer (CEO) Derrick Hall in the role of Billy Crystal. In addition to serving as emcee, he prepared an opening musical segment highlighting sponsor activities during the 2011 season when the team made a tremendous effort to win the NL's WD title and then a pennant and World Series.

Awards were presented to sponsors in several categories. These included marketing activation, brand integration, top new partner, and community involvement. The event's equivalent to a best picture award—Most Valuable Partner of the Year—was divided into silver slugger and gold glove divisions to account for differences in company size and sponsorship spending.

Third, after serving as Arizona State University's baseball operations director, Graham Rossini became the Diamondbacks' vice president of special projects and fan experience during late 2015. He has several responsibilities on the business operations of the team. These include such tasks as being the point-person in coordinating events like MLB's All-Star game or World Baseball Classic, negotiating with Chase Field vendors and restaurants, and overseeing community outreach programs such as the club's baseball academy.

Fourth, since their inception, the Diamondbacks have made countless trips to the state of Sonora to play exhibition games, build relationships, and promote the sport of baseball in Mexico. In recent years, however, these trips have become increasingly more regular. When the team's delegation boarded a flight back from Hermosillo, Mexico, to Phoenix in early 2016, that visit to Phoenix's sister city was different from a business perspective. In fact, the Diamondbacks introduced their newest employees including former first baseman and native son Erubiel Durazo and also Latin America coordinator Francisco Cartaya and Mexico-based scout Rodrigo Aguirre.

Equally important, the club signed a partnership with the Hermosillo Naranjeros team and established plans to redouble its efforts to scout for talent south of the border. The partnership includes baseball clinics hosted by Durazo—who joined the team as a special advisor to Diamondbacks' president/CEO Derrick Hall—and others managed by former great player and special assistant Luis Gonzalez. Perhaps this MLB team will create an academy in Mexico where young talent is developed—similar to those in other Latin American countries.

Fifth, after chief human resources and diversity officer Marian Rhodes joined the club in June 2007, she implemented new training and development strategies and also created new employee programs with the executive management team. Diamondbacks University, Employee of the Month program, and President's Council are ways to invest in the employees throughout the organization.

Rhodes' determination and the organization's investment in its employees resulted in the club being named one of the "Best Places to Work" in Phoenix by the Phoenix Business Journal and *BestCompaniesAZ* each year from 2007 to 2014, and to become the first sports organization to win such an honor. In 2014, Rhodes headed a program to further the education of the team's Latin American players and staff. This ensures that participants are able to complete their high school education, develop English skills, and successfully integrate in the culture of North America while building a foundation to have career alternatives.

COLORADO ROCKIES

For decades Denver, Colorado, had been a hotbed for baseball teams including the minor league AAA Denver Zephyrs. Being competitive and popular, they played their home games at Mile High Stadium and, while a member of the American Association (AA) from 1984 to 1992, won two championships.[8]

During the mid- to late 1980s, the Colorado Baseball Commission, led by banking executive Larry Varnell, was successful in getting Denver voters to approve a 0.1 percent sales tax to finance the construction of a new baseball stadium. Then in 1990, an advisory committee was formed by Colorado Governor Roy Romer to recruit an ownership group for an MLB baseball team. Shortly thereafter, the committee selected a group led by Ohio beverage distributor John Antonucci and also Michael Monus, head of the Phar-Mor drugstore chain. Beside them, such local and regional companies as Erie Lake, Hensel Phelps Construction, KOA Radio, and the Rocky Mountain News were also members of the group.

During July 1991, baseball's NL approved Denver and South Florida as sites for an expansion team to begin play in 1993. However, after Antonucci and Monus were forced to drop out of the ownership group in 1992 primarily because of Monus's connection to and potential involvement in an accounting scandal, trucking magnate Jerry McMorris stepped in and decided to save Denver's franchise. As a result, he and meatpacking heirs Charlie and Dick Monfort joined to acquire a controlling interest in the new team. Named the Colorado Rockies, they played their home games for two years at 76,100-seat Mile High Stadium until the construction of Coors Field in 1995.

Team Performances

While a member of the NL's WD from 1993 to 2015, the Rockies played 3,664 games and had victories in approximately 46 percent of them. During the period, they won zero division titles, one pennant, and zero World Series in three playoff appearances. Among other clubs in the league as of their 2015 season, Colorado tied for fourteenth with the Marlins in winning division titles, tied for twelfth with the Diamondbacks in number of pennants, and tied for twelfth with the Nationals, Brewers, and Padres in World Series titles. Within their division, the Rockies had fewer championships than did rivals (Table A7).[9]

In comparison to all MLB team as of 2015, Colorado tied for twenty-eighth in division titles, tied for twenty-third in winning pennants, and tied for twenty-third in World Series victories. Based on these results, this has been a relatively low-performing team that failed to win enough games in a majority of its regular seasons to consistently compete for titles and championships in the NL.

Besides finishing above .500 in 1996–1997, 2000, and 2010, the club's most successful years were qualifying for playoffs in seasons 1995, 2007, and 2009. In one or more of these seasons, its prominent players included sluggers Larry Walker, Todd Helton, and Troy Tulowitzki and also pitchers Kevin Ritz, Jeff Francis, and Ubaldo Jimenez. However, because of their managers' bad decisions, lack of talented players at key positions, intra-division competition from the Dodgers and Giants, and other reasons, the Rockies had sixteen losing seasons as of 2015.

The Rockies' all-time best team was in 2007. Despite an 18–27 record in May and still more than four games out of a wild-card spot with nine left in the regular season, they played in the World Series by winning twenty-one of twenty-two overall including an epic tiebreaker against the division's San Diego Padres. What made the club playoff-worthy was its pitching staff, which had four above-average adjusted Earned Run Averages (ERAs) in the rotation and an excellent bullpen. In contrast to that team, Colorado lost a franchise-record ninety-eight games in 2012 and finished thirty behind the WD champion Giants.

Several years ago, a senior sports writer ranked the Rockies franchise as the sixth worst in MLB history. Despite scoring 13,689 runs in 90,308 at-bats, 25,147 hits, 3,000 home runs, and a .278 batting average through 2009, Colorado pitchers allowed 14,318 runs with an ERA of 5.15. The club's best manager, Don Baylor, had a 440–469 record or .484 winning percentage while the worst leader was Jim Leyland, who won seventy-two games or 44 percent of them.[10]

Franchise Owner

After graduating from the University of Utah in 1982 with a bachelor's degree in marketing and business management, Charlie Monfort worked for the family business in Colorado as its president of International Sales until 1996. He then became president of ConAgra Foods International but left there in 1998 to focus on his commitment to the Rockies. His brother Richard, who graduated from the University of Northern Colorado in 1976 with a bachelor's degree in business management, joined Monfort of Colorado in 1974 as a cattle buyer. After serving as vice president of federal cattle procurement, group vice president of cattle products and executive vice president, Dick eventually became president and CEO of ConAgra Red Meats in 1991 and then retired four years later.[11]

During September 1992, multimillionaire Jerry McMorris welcomed Charlie Monfort and Oren Benton to join him in buying a controlling interest in the Rockies. Dick Monfort replaced Benton in the ownership group and became vice chairman in 1997. Six years later, Charlie was named CEO of the Rockies, and in 2005, he and Dick purchased McMorris's financial interest in the team and became its principal owners. Currently, Charlie's a general partner while Dick is chairman and CEO of the franchise.

In comparison to fourteen other NL team owners as of 2015, the Monforts' teams tied for eleventh in winning division titles, fourth in number of pennants, and fifth in World Series victories. Among all MLB owners, respectively, the Rockies tied for twenty-fifth, eighth, and ninth. Because of these rankings and other reasons, Charlie and Dick have been inferior as leaders of their franchise and especially for winning only one pennant. Until some semblance of normalcy returns to the club—both with an experienced major league manager and the addition of a pitching staff that the team desperately needs—the Monforts are in the lower tier among MLB owners (Table A8).

Coors Field

During the late 1980s, the state of Colorado formed the Denver Metropolitan MLB Stadium to plan and build a new ballpark for the Rockies. Before the city was awarded an expansion franchise in 1991, voters in a six-county area approved a one percent sales tax to fund the ballpark. After MLB's decision to expand in Denver, construction began on the stadium in October 1992. When the team's attendance exceeded three million at Mile High Stadium in 1993 and 1994, the new ballpark's capacity was increased from 43,000 to 50,000.

Named Coors Field, it has an old-fashioned brick façade and on 20th and Blake Street, a large clock exists for fans to meet at prior to a game. The three-tiered grandstand extends from the left field foul pole to home plate and then down to the right field pole and around to center field. Marking one mile above sea level is a row of purple seats that extend around the entire upper deck a 2,300-seat bleacher section called the "Rockpile" is located behind the center field backdrop. The main HD video scoreboard is beyond the left field bleachers and another one makes up part of the right field wall.

Coors Field has several amenities. These include 4,400 club seats; the Roundeus at the Sandlot Brewery; a microbrewery located at the right field entrance; the Diamond Dry Good gift shop; a merchandise store; and the Mountain Ranch Club that features upscale dining on six tiers located down the right field line. Completed in 2014, an extensive renovation project removed the majority of upper-deck seats in right field and replaced them with a two-level rooftop deck. This area contains the 5280 Craft Bar, CHUBurger Restaurant, and the VIP Cabana Terrace.

In comparison to other NL teams' ballparks as of 2015, twenty-one-year-old Coors Field is the third oldest following Wrigley Field and Dodger Stadium and also ranks thirteenth in construction cost and twelfth in value. Among all MLB ballparks, the Rockies' home venue is older than seventeen others and twentieth in cost and twenty-first in value. According to these results, Colorado plays in a relatively middle-aged ballpark with enough amenities and attendances to generate sufficient but not abundant gate receipts and revenue from the team's home games (Table A9).

In the 2011–2015 MLB seasons, the FCIs for a family to attend a regular-season Rockies home game ranged from a low of $161 in 2011 to $201 in 2014. Among fourteen other NL clubs' ballparks, Coors Field's FCI ranked between ninth in 2013 ($196), 2014 ($201), and 2015 ($196) to eleventh ($161) in 2011. For only the league's WD teams, Rockies home games cost less than did the Dodgers' at Dodger Stadium and Giants' at A&T Park but not for those at the ballparks of the Diamondbacks and Padres (Table A10).[12]

To reveal specific costs for families during a recent year, Colorado's ballpark's FCI in 2015 was $5 or 2 percent less for them than in 2014. Listed from most to least in amount by item for one person, the team's nonpremium (premium) tickets were between $23 and $24 ($47 and $48), a baseball cap $22, parking one vehicle $13, single beer $6, and a hot dog and soft drink each between $3 and $5. At $196 each, Rockies home games for families were $15 below MLB's average FCI.

Among other clubs in the league's WD, they had rankings and FCIs from most to least as follows in the 2015 MLB season: Giants fifth at $241; Dodgers twelfth at $218; Padres twenty-ninth at $153; and Diamondbacks thirtieth at $126. These differences in FCIs occurred, in part, because of these teams' popularity and competitiveness, population and population growth of their host cities, and income per capita and wealth of sports fans in the local market.

In a recent study by CSN Mid-Atlantic, Coors Field ranked eleventh in MLB. According to an online report in *USA Today*, the author said:

> The Nationals spent the last three days in Colorado, and though the pitching staff may not have loved the best hitter's ballpark in the country, you better believe the lineup did. Home runs aside, this is a really nice ballpark. It's a true retro park, brick and steel, and it fits right in with the old buildings in downtown Denver. The Rockies did build the park too big, a reaction to the ridiculous crowds they drew in their first two seasons of existence at Mile High Stadium, and so they tore down the third deck in right field and converted it to a party zone. Don't worry, though, you'll still find the vast majority of the purple row of seats in the upper deck, so designated to mark 5,280 feet above sea level.[13]

Financial Data

According to data and other financial information published in *Forbes* for franchises in the NL as of their 2015 season, Colorado ranked thirteenth in both market value at $855 million and revenue at $214, and also tenth in operating income at $12.6 million, tied for tenth with the Braves in gate receipts at $58 million, and eleventh in its debt-to-value ratio at 7 percent. Among the league's WD teams, the Rockies had the second lowest market value, revenue, and debt percent, but third most operating income and gate receipts (Table A11).

In comparison to twenty-nine other MLB teams as of 2015, Colorado's market value was twenty-third, revenue twenty-fourth, operating income nineteenth, gate receipts tied for eighteenth, and debt ratio twentieth. According to these rankings, the Rockies are a relatively low-valued but profitable team and also average to below average from a financial perspective.

Besides market size, wage inflation, and other factors, an MLB team's annual payroll partly reflects its commitment to players and their current and potential contribution individually and as a group to winning games in regular seasons and postseasons. From 2011 to 2015, for example, the Rockies' payroll compared to those of fourteen other NL teams' ranged in rank from seventh in 2011 ($88 million) to thirteenth in both 2013 ($64 million) and 2014 ($64 million). During the five-year period, its payroll among the league's WD teams was the third or fourth highest of the group. These results, in part, reflect franchise owners Charlie and Dick Monfort's efforts to minimize costs and increase profits (Table A12).[14]

With respect to payrolls of all MLB teams as of 2015, the Rockies' ranked from a low of fourteenth in 2011 to a high of twenty-sixth in 2014. For various reasons, the team's relatively low payroll was the same at $88 million during 2011 and 2012, reduced to $64 million in both 2013 and 2014, and increased by $34 million or more than 50 percent from 2014 to 2015. These changes in payroll amounts, in some way, had contributed to the club's performances in finishing fourth twice and fifth three times in its division during 2011–2015.

Business Relations

Besides regular-season and postseason games, MLB franchises are involved in—and affected by—internal affairs and problems, community events, and business-related activities and projects. In no specific order, the following are a few of them for Colorado's NL team as of 2015.[15]

First, the new upper-deck attraction at Coors Field, named the Rooftop, has paid off financially for the Rockies. Through thirty-seven home games in 2014, for example, the team sold 60,000 general admission tickets for the right field space which matched the total number of tickets sold for all of 2013 for 3,400 old reserved seats in that space. In addition, food and beverage revenue at the Rooftop tripled year-to-year. The redeveloped 38,000-square-foot space, a multimillion dollar project, spans two levels at the ballpark's highest point.

The Rooftop serves as the stadium's only general admission space. The seating setup is mostly tables and chairs on a first come/first serve schedule, but the destination is accessible to all fans regardless of seat location. It opens two hours before the first pitch of a game or thirty minutes earlier than the rest of the ballpark. The club sells "power tickets" for the Rooftop, a marketing slogan tied to loaded tickets. The price is approximately $14 to $15 depending on the day of the week and the team's opponent. Six dollars of credit is embedded into every ticket, and fans can use the credit to buy food and drinks, including beer.

Second, Molson Coors announced selling its 15 percent stake in the Rockies to Arizona developer Jay Stein in late 2013, which ended the equity ownership it held in the franchise since the team's inception in 1991. The sale, however, did not affect the company's long-standing naming-rights deal of Coors Field. The move occurred when the *Denver Post* took its 7.3 percent share of the team off the market, in part, because Coors was not getting full-value for its stake. Although sources don't know what Stein paid for the Coors ownership in the team, a finance expert suggested it is difficult to get full-value for such a large limited-partnership piece of it.

Colorado-based Coors played an integral role in the Rockies development and has been linked to the club since the early 1990s. After Coors and Molson agreed to merge in 2005, the new company—renamed Molson Coors—created a joint venture with SABMiller in 2007 called MillerCoors. As a result of that deal, the corporate headquarters for the combined organization moved to Chicago, Illinois.

Third, although Rockies' real estate was never at the top in general valuation models, properties around Coors Field had values 33 percent higher than other parts of the metropolitan area. Prior to opening day of MLB's 2016 season, real estate company Truila released a report listing which stadiums in the nation were surrounded by the most costly real estate relative to their metropolitan areas. Properties within a one-mile radius were considered "near" the stadium.

In Denver, properties surrounding Coors Field had an average value of $439,351, according to Trulia's estimates, while the rest of the metropolitan areas carried an average value of $329,568. The 33 percent premium on properties within a mile of Coors Field was the seventh-highest of all areas surveyed by Trulia. Similarly, prices near Coors Field were greater than the median rent within a mile of the area. According to Tulia, it brought in $2,350 while the median rent in other parts of metropolitan Denver was $2,000, or a 17.5 percent differential.

Fourth, a group of fifty-five business scholars traveled to Scottsdale, Arizona, to attend a Rockies spring training game in March 2013 and met

Rockies owner and David Eccles School of Business alumnus, Charlie Monfort. During weeks before their visit, the students worked with accounting Professor Mike Lewis to solve a case study of sports management and read *Moneyball*.[16]

After a tour of Salt River Fields including the Rockies' practice fields, weight rooms, and locker rooms, the students met with Charlie and asked him questions about the business of baseball. He operates his organization like a family and treats all employees with respect. Monfort also advised the students to consider international opportunities such as studying abroad and to keep themselves available for opportunities in the global market.

Fifth, Rockies Fest was held at Coors Field during late January 2016. The annual event featured appearances by the team's players, coaches, and alumni. All ticket proceeds benefitted the team's Foundation, which makes charitable grants to several organizations in the Denver area that support underprivileged and at-risk youth through programs for youth baseball, education, and health.

While at the Fest, fans had opportunities to participate in question-and-answer sessions with Rockies players and coaches, take self-guided tours of the Rockies clubhouse and other exclusive areas, play in hitting and pitching clinics in the team's batting cages, and engage in contests and games including the always-popular Rockies Family Feud. There were also dedicated areas and activities for children of all ages. Returning for the Fest was the Rock Social Studio, where Rockies players participated on social media sites to answer questions from fans and also connect live with them via Skype and FaceTime.

LOS ANGELES DODGERS

When he bought the shares of team co-owners Branch Rickey and the estate of the late John L. Smith in 1950, real estate businessman Walter O'Malley acquired majority ownership of the Dodgers franchise. He then purchased land in Brooklyn for a new, more accessible, and better structured ballpark than Ebbets Field. Unfortunately, Ebbets was old, not well served by fan infrastructure, and to the point where the Dodgers could not "sell out" the ballpark even during a pennant race—despite largely dominating the NL from 1946 to 1957.[17]

New York City construction coordinator Robert Moses tried to force O'Malley into using a site for baseball games in Flushing Meadows, Queens. This involved a city-built and -owned ballpark, which was at odds with O'Malley's real-estate savvy. When O'Malley realized of not being allowed to buy a suitable parcel of land in Brooklyn, he began to think about transferring the Dodgers to another city.

Although O'Malley was free to purchase real estate of his own choosing, he asked Moses to condemn land along the Atlantic Railroad Yards in downtown Brooklyn under Title I authority rather than pay market value for the property. With Title I, the city could sell the land to O'Malley at a below-market price. Nevertheless, Moses refused to honor O'Malley's request regarding the property.

Meanwhile, since nonstop transcontinental airline travel had become routine after World War II, MLB teams were no longer bound by much slower railroad timetables. Because of civil aviation advances, it became possible to locate teams farther apart—even as far west as California—while maintaining the same schedule of games and busy seasons.

At the same time, O'Malley looked for a contingency in case Moses and other New York politicians rejected his plan to build a new stadium for the Dodgers in Brooklyn. Thus, he contacted Los Angeles, California, officials who offered him what New York would not: an opportunity to buy land suitable for building and owning a ballpark, and giving him complete control of all revenue streams.

Besides O'Malley, New York Giants owner Horace Stoneham was also having difficulty finding a replacement for his team's antiquated home stadium, the Polo Grounds. Rather than shift the Giants to Minneapolis, Stoneham was persuaded instead to move them to San Francisco—ensuring the Dodgers a rival closer than St. Louis, Missouri. Consequently, the Dodgers and Giants moved from the New York area to the nation's West Coast after their 1957 season.

Team Performances

While a member of the NL from 1958 to 1968 and specifically the league's WD during 1969–2015, the Dodgers played 9,239 games and had victories in approximately 54 percent of them. During the period, they won fifteen division titles, nine pennants, five World Series, and appeared in twenty playoffs. Among teams in the league as of their 2015 season, Los Angeles ranked second in winning division titles, tied for third with the Reds in number of pennants, and tied for second with the Reds and Pirates in World Series titles. With respect to only those in the WD, the club had the most total championships followed by the Giants, Padres and Diamondbacks, and Rockies (Table A7).

In comparison to all MLB teams as of their 2015 season, the Dodgers ranked fourth in division titles, tied for sixth in pennants, and tied for fourth in World Series victories. Based on these results, they have been a superior performing team within their division and league but with fewer championships than the AL Yankees' eighty-six.

Besides winning World Series in 1959, 1963, and 1965, the Dodgers' most successful periods consecutively include 1977–1978, 1995–1996, 2008–2009, and 2013–2015. Among their most prominent players were sluggers, Ron Cey, Mike Piazza and Pedro Guerrero, and pitchers Sandy Koufax, Don Drysdale, and Clayton Kershaw. For various reasons involving problems with its managers and players, the club failed to qualify for the NL playoffs in such consecutive seasons as 1967–1973, 1989–1994, and 1997–2003.

For the franchise's best team, the 1963 Dodgers won 99 games and finished atop an NL group in which seven of ten posted winning seasons. In the lineup, shortstop Maury Wills batted .302 and swiped forty bases; corner outfielders Tommy Davis and Frank Howard had on-base plus slugging percentages (OPS+) respectively of 142 and 150; pitcher Sandy Koufax had a 25–5 record with an 1.88 ERA in 311 innings; Don Drysdale an adjusted ERA of 114—average equals 100—over 315 innings; and relief ace Ron Perranoski an unadjusted ERA of 1.67 in a now-unthinkable 129 innings. In the World Series, the Dodgers swept the 104-win Yankees. Conversely, the Dodgers' 1992 squad lost 99 games and managed to score just 548 runs although significantly limited in experience and talent because of injuries to its key players.

Following the Yankees and Cardinals in rank, the Dodgers are baseball's third greatest franchise. They played in various postseasons from the 1960s to 2000s and since 1961, led their league in attendances twenty-six times and became the first team to reach three million in a season; had four consecutive rookies-of-the-year from 1979 to 1982 and another five from 1992 to 1996; and established the second-highest winning percentage of teams in MLB history.[18]

Franchise Owner

Born in Cedar Rapids, Iowa, in 1960, Mark Walter graduated from Cedar Rapids Jefferson High School and then earned a bachelor of science degree from Creighton University and later a J.D. from Northwestern University. Four years after he cofounded Liberty Hampshire as a Limited Liability Company (LLC), Walter helped others to start Guggenheim Partners LLC. Currently, he is the CEO of Guggenheim Partners, which is a global, diversified financial services organization with more than $170 billion in assets, at least 2,200 employees, and twenty-five or more offices in several countries.

After a number of personal problems and also business failures, including bankruptcy of the Dodgers in 2011, owner Frank McCourt sold the franchise and Dodger Stadium to Guggenheim Baseball Management (GBM) during mid-2012 for approximately $2.15 billion. In addition, GBM paid $150 million for a 50 percent interest in the property surrounding Chavez Ravine and the stadium's parking lots in a joint venture with McCourt.

As a result of the deal, Walter became chairman and controlling partner of the team, longtime sports executive Stan Kasten its president and CEO, and former Lakers great-turned-businessman Magic Johnson a co-owner and partner with a public role. The ownership group also included Mandalay Entertainment chairman Peter Guber, Guggenheim Partners president Todd Boehly, and Texas energy investor Bobby Patton.

In comparison to other owners of NL teams as of 2015, GBM's Dodgers ranked fourth in winning division titles, tied for seventh with several clubs in number of pennants, and tied for fifth with zero World Series titles. Among all MLB owners and the performances of their teams, GBM tied for seventh in division titles, for fourteenth in winning pennants, and for ninth in World Series victories. Based on this data and other information in the literature, GBM has been a successful owner of the Dodgers for its appearances in playoffs from 2012 to 2015 (Table A8).

According to a fans' opinion poll conducted by Fangraphs in early 2016, GBM ranked fourth among current owners of MLB teams. While 82 percent of respondents rated the Dodgers' ownership group very to pretty good, 8 percent had GBM as average and another 10 percent from very to pretty bad. Because of their three recent World Series, playing in a privately funded but beautiful ballpark, providing an excellent game-day experience for fans, and doubling of players' payroll during the last six or seven years, the San Francisco Giants' owners were first in the poll and Miami Marlins' Jeffrey Loria thirtieth.

Dodger Stadium

During their first four seasons on the West Coast, the Dodgers played their home games temporarily in the 93,600-seat Los Angeles Memorial Coliseum. Before moving there in 1958, however, the city agreed to exchange 352 acres of land at Chavez Ravine for the team to build a privately funded, 50,000-seat ballpark. Three years after its construction started in 1959, the $23 million Dodger Stadium opened to host MLB games.

Located a few miles from downtown Los Angeles, Dodger Stadium was constructed on a hillside with parking areas surrounding the facility. The ballpark has five seating levels extending from the left field foul pole to home plate and then down to the right field foul pole, except for the top deck. Bleachers are in both left and right field and feature a wavy top roof, and behind them are two jumbo hexagonal HD video scoreboards. After several renovations during the 2000s, including an expanded dugout section, two new Baseline Box Clubs, a team store, and other improvements, Dodger Stadium is an attractive, clean, and well-landscaped facility.

With respect to other NL ballparks as of 2015, Dodger Stadium was second oldest and ranked fourteenth in construction cost and second in value. Compared to those of all MLB teams in age, cost, and value, respectively, it was third, twenty-eighth, and third. Thus the Dodgers play in a relatively old and inexpensively built but valuable ballpark within a large and prosperous sports market.

In the 2011–2015 MLB seasons, the FCIs for a family to attend a regular-season Dodgers home game ranged from a low of $204 in 2013 to $226 in 2011. Among fourteen other NL clubs' facilities, Dodger Stadium's FCI ranked between fourth in 2011 ($226) to eighth in 2012 ($213), 2013 ($204), 2014 ($217), and 2015 ($218). For only the league's WD teams, Los Angeles's games cost more than other teams' did in 2011 but also less than the Giants games at A&T Park from 2012 to 2015 (Table A10).

To reveal specific costs for families during a recent year, Dodgers Stadium's FCI in 2015 was about the same as in 2014. Listed from most to least in amount by item for one person, the team's nonpremium (premium) tickets were between $28 and $29 ($222 and $223), a cap $18, parking one vehicle $10, single beer between $6 and $7, a soft drink $6, and a hot dog between $5 and $6. With an FCI ranked twelfth at approximately $218, games at Dodger Stadium were each $7 more expensive for families than those of the average team.

Among other clubs in the league's WD, they had rankings and FCIs from most to least as follows in the 2015 MLB season: Giants fifth at $241; Rockies eighteenth at $196; Padres twenty-ninth at $153; and Diamondbacks thirtieth at $126. These differences in FCIs occurred, in part, because of these teams' popularity and competitiveness, population and population growth of their host cities, and disposable income and wealth of sports fans in the local market.

In a recent study by CSN Mid-Atlantic, Dodger Stadium ranked eighth in MLB. According to an online report in *USA Today*, the author said:

> Though it's clearly showing its age, Dodger Stadium remains a national treasure. There's just nothing like stepping out from the fourth deck high above home plate and looking out at the magnificent vista, with Chavez Ravine in the immediate background and the San Gabriel Mountains off in the distance. There's also something about the grass there. It just looks greener than any ballpark you've ever seen. Yeah, the clubhouses are cramped and the PA system will blow your ears out, but there are few things in life that top eating a Dodger Dog while listening to Vin Scully announcing a game on-site.[19]

Financial Data

According to data and other financial information published in *Forbes* for franchises in the NL as of their 2015 season, Los Angeles ranked first in both market value at $2.4 billion and revenue at $403, fourteenth in operating income at –$12.2 million, third in gate receipts at $123 million, and tied for seventh with the Diamondbacks in their debt-to-value ratio at 7 percent. Among only the league's WD teams, the Dodgers had the highest market value and revenue, worst operating income, lower gate receipts than the Giants, and second highest debt percent following the Padres (Table A11).

In comparison to twenty-nine other MLB teams as of 2015, the Dodgers' market value and revenue were each second, operating income twenty-seventh, gate receipts fifth, and debt-to-value ratio tied for tenth. According to these rankings, this Los Angeles team is a relatively high-valued MLB franchise with enough revenue from gate receipts and other sources to be an above-average business enterprise from a financial perspective.

Besides market size, wage inflation and other factors, an MLB team's annual payroll partly reflects its commitment to players and their current and potential contribution individually and as a group to winning games in regular seasons and postseasons. From 2011 to 2015, for example, the Dodgers payroll compared to those of fourteen other NL teams ranged in rank from first in 2013 ($178 million), 2014 ($241 million), and 2015 ($230 million) to sixth in 2011 ($104 million). During the five-year period, its payroll among the league's WD teams was second highest in 2011 to highest from 2012 to 2015. These results, in part, reflect franchise owner GBM's efforts to win games and division titles, pennants, and World Series while increasing the team's attendance and revenue from its home games (Table A12).

With respect to payrolls of all MLB teams as of 2015, the Dodgers ranked from first in 2014 and 2015 to twelfth in 2011. For various reasons, the team's payroll significantly increased in 2012, 2013, and 2014, but also declined by $11 million or almost 5 percent in 2015. These changes in payroll amounts, in some way, had contributed to the club's performances in finishing third, second, and then first three times in its division during 2011–2015.

Business Relations

Besides regular-season and postseason games, MLB franchises are involved in—and affected by—internal affairs and problems, community events, and business-related activities and projects. In no specific order, the following are a few of them for Los Angeles's NL team as of 2015.[20]

First, during late 2015, the Dodgers' sports tech Accelerator program was ready to be launched to determine whether it and others were good enough to be successfully applied in big-time business. It took the team and its Accelerator partner—global digital agency R/GA—a month to select ten firms from among 570 applicants in thirty-one countries. Applications were accepted by the program from mid-April through June, and the companies were notified in July after being reviewed by a secret panel.

Although the club's Accelerator management team wants to earn a healthy return on its investment, Dodgers chief financial officer Tucker Kain believes the program also builds brand equity. The ten Accelerator firms range from near-startups with good ideas needing help executing and raising cash to profitable companies that look to increase their market share. Accelerator officials say none of these firms compete with each other but some could be complementary. The businesses include such services as fan experience apps, a college recruiting social network, and advanced fantasy analytics. The program finishes on Demo Day at Dodger Stadium, where each company's representative stands at home plate with five minutes to pitch their product to three hundred investors and sports business and media executives seated in the stands.

Second, at the end of the 2014 regular season, the Dodgers' 0.79 rating on SportsNet LA was on pace to be not only one of the lowest local television ratings in the league, but also the lowest local number in the history of the franchise. The main reason their ratings were dismal came down to distribution. Only a fraction of the pay television subscribers in Los Angeles had access to SportsNet LA. Furthermore, the regional sports network did not have a deal with satellite providers DirecTV and Dish Network or with telecommunications companies like AT&T and Verizon. Dodgers games on SportsNet LA averaged forty-two thousand homes—paltry numbers for a division-winning team playing in the country's second-biggest media market. Perhaps helped by SportNet LA's troubles, the crosstown rival Los Angeles Angels' audience was more than twice as large by averaging ninety-five thousand homes.

Third, the Dodgers are committed to providing the maximum practical opportunity to diverse businesses as potential providers of goods and services. Indeed, the team's Supplier Registration Portal facilitates the sourcing for potential diverse suppliers by providing buyers with online access to detailed supplier capability profiles. However, MLB does not guarantee or warrant the reliability or accuracy of the information obtained on the Diverse Business Partners SupplierGATEWAY website. This site and linked sites are intended to give only general information and guidelines. They do not create any expressed or implied promises or contracts for business or employment for any benefit, or for specific treatment in any specific situation.

Fourth, the Dodgers and John Hancock Financial Services Inc. announced in mid-2009 a new four–year partnership that promoted the Massachusetts-based company in the Los Angeles marketplace. As part of the agreement,

John Hancock received two permanent Pavilion signs located above Dodger Stadium's outfield wall in left center and right center field. The multiyear partner kicked off their sponsorship with the Dodgers in a pregame reception on the Loge Terrace prior to a home game where John Hancock hosted thirty youngsters from the Boys and Girls Club of Venice, California.

Besides the signage and branding displayed prominently at Dodger Stadium at two permanent locations above the outfield wall, the financial services company received home plate rotational signage for half an inning every game. The partnership had several hospitality elements including the Loge Terrace reception, which was one of two planned in the 2015 season, and also access to Dodger Stadium's luxury suites, private batting practice events at both it and Camelback Ranch-Glendale starting in 2016, and other unique experiential events.

Fifth, according to the Associated Press, the Dodgers had to pay a record luxury tax of nearly $43.6 million for a payroll that fell just shy of $300 million during the 2015 season. Based on calculations by MLB and Yahoo Sports, the Los Angeles-based team had a record payroll of $297.6 million—benefits included—which far exceeded the $189 million threshold. Any way you slice it, that is a lot of money to have tied up in a baseball team, and a good chunk of it turned out to be dead money. As noted following the Dodgers activity at the trade deadline, the team owed $87.5 million just to players no longer with the franchise. In addition, another good chunk was tied up in players who were injured and could not play in games.

An aside, a record twenty-two MLB teams had payrolls of $100 million or more in 2015, up from seventeen in 2014, while the average payroll was just under $130 million. Total spending on forty-man major league payrolls totaled nearly $3.9 billion, according to MLB's calculation. The average salaries of players on big league rosters and disabled lists on August 31, 2015, were $3.95 million—a 3.5-percent increase from 2014. But MLB, which used a slightly different methodology to calculate payrolls, had the average at $3.84 million, up 3.9 percent.

SAN DIEGO PADRES

From 1936 to 1968, the San Diego Padres were a minor-league baseball team in the Pacific Coast League (PCL). Affiliated with the Boston Red Sox (1936), Cleveland Indians (1949–1951, 1957–1959), Chicago White Sox (1961), Cincinnati Reds (1962–1965), and Philadelphia Phillies (1966–1968), the team's nickname refers to the Spanish Franciscan friars who founded San Diego in 1769. During its thirty-three-year history while located in the city, the club won PCL championships in 1962, 1964, and 1967, and also in 1937 when led by eighteen-year-old Ted Williams, a current Hall of Famer and native of San Diego.

In 1969, the Padres joined MLB as one of four new expansion teams. Besides the Padres, these were the NL Montreal Expos (now Washington Nationals), AL Kansas City Royals, and Seattle Pilots (now NL Milwaukee Brewers). The Padres' original owner, C. Arnholt Smith, was a prominent San Diego businessman—and former owner of the PCL team—whose interests included banking, hotels, real estate, and an airline. He headed a syndicate, including former Brooklyn and Los Angeles Dodgers executive Emil J. "Buzzie" Bavasi, which paid MLB a $12.5 million fee for their franchise.

To acquire an expansion franchise, Smith and Bavasi had to convince existing team owners that San Diego's population and economy would support a new NL club. They also spoke about the area's ideal weather conditions and wonderful climate, a local ballpark with enough capacity to host a big-league team, and the city's experience with the minor league's Padres.

Team Performances

While a member of the league's WD from 1969 to 2015, the Padres played 7,488 games and had victories in 3,472 or approximately 46 percent of them. During its forty-seven seasons, the club won five division titles, two pennants, and zero World Series in five playoff appearances. Among NL teams as of their 2015 season, San Diego tied for ninth with the Cubs and Diamondbacks in winning division titles, tied for tenth with the Marlins in number of pennants, and tied for twelfth with the Nationals, Brewers, and Rockies in World Series titles. With respect to only WD clubs, the Padres had won more championships than the Rockies but not the Dodgers or Giants (Table A7).

In comparison to all MLB teams as of 2015, San Diego tied for twenty-first in winning division titles, tied for nineteenth in number of pennants, and tied for twenty-third in World Series victories. Based on these results, the Padres have been mediocre and performed below average in their division, league, and across MLB.

The most successful Padres teams played their games in 1984, 1996, 1998, and 2005–2006. For one or more seasons, among their prominent players were such sluggers as Tony Gwynn, Ken Caminiti, and Mike Cameron, and pitchers Rich Gossage, Kevin Brown, and Jake Peavy. Because of its managers' bad decisions, the lack of talented players, and competition primarily from the Dodgers and Giants, San Diego's teams did not appear in postseasons consecutively during 1969–1983, 1985–1995, 1998–2004, and 2007–2015.

The Padres' all-time best and worst clubs played, respectively, in 1998 and 1969. The former won ninety-eight games in a path to the World Series. That club boasted two franchise icons in Tony Gwynn and Trevor Hoffman and also a top-three Cy Young finisher in Kevin Brown and 50-homer guy in Greg Vaughn, and recent MVP Ken Caminiti. The ball club was good enough to bring home a World Series title, but its timing was bad. While competing against the 114–48 Yankees, they were swept in four games. In 1969, however, the Padres finished 41 games behind the Braves and last in the NL in runs, hits, doubles, walks, batting average and on-base and slugging percentages, while their pitchers ranked eleventh of twelve in ERA.

Through 2015, the Padres rank among the worst in MLB. They boast the lowest all-time regular-season winning percentage of any current team. To be fair, they advanced to the World Series twice since joining the league in 1969. These two seasons were the only ones in which they won a playoff series.

Franchise Owner

Born in 1943 and a graduate of the University of St. Thomas in Minneapolis-St. Paul, Minnesota, the CEO of San Diego beer distributorship Liquid Investments Inc. Ron Fowler was a member of a minority group that owned approximately 49 percent of the Padres. Headed by then-Padres chief executive Jeff Moorad, the group had attempted to buy the Padres from controlling owner John Moores for $530 million, but the deal failed in April 2012. Fowler then replaced Moorad as the minority group's general partner and served on the Padres executive committee.

To purchase the Padres, Ron joined a new group that included four heirs to the O'Malley family who had owned the Dodgers franchise for five decades. These heirs were Kevin and Brian O'Malley—sons of former Dodgers owner Peter O'Malley and grandsons of Walter O'Malley—and Peter and Tom Seidler, nephews of Peter O'Malley.

In August 2012, MLB approved the sale of the franchise to the group for $800 million. As much as $200 million of the sales price included the team's 20 percent stake in Fox Sports San Diego—a cable channel that pays the Padres annual fees as part of a $1.2 billion, twenty-year agreement. Because of his leadership, Fowler was named the ownership group's executive chairman and designated to represent the Padres in all league meetings. Consequently, he became the first locally-based control person of the team since founding owner C. Arnholdt Smith.

Compared to owners of other NL teams as of their 2015 season, Fowler's Padres tied for eleventh in winning zero division titles and also tied for seventh in number of pennants and fifth in World Series titles. Among all

MLB clubs' performances with respect to their current owners, the Padres respectively tied for twenty-fifth, fourteenth, and ninth. Based on these rankings, Fowler has not been a successful owner for failing to win any titles or championships since 2012 (Table A8).

According to a recent study in the literature, Ron Fowler was the seventeenth most likable MLB owner. Although he spends money on payroll and truly ambitious to win games, the Padres were an unmitigated disaster in 2015 after their big offseason strategies blew up in their faces. Because Fowler and the Padres made different but risky adjustments in early 2016, the team seems far, far away from contention in a top heavy division. While the desire is there, it's questionable whether he knows the right thing to do and will make good decisions for the club.

Petco Park

Before 2004, the Padres played their home games at 67,500-seat, multipurpose San Diego Stadium from 1969 to 1980—renamed Jack Murphy Stadium in 1981 and then Qualcomm Stadium from 1997 to 2003. During this thirty-five-year period, their home attendances ranged from a low of 6,300 per game in 1969 to a high of 31,500 in 1998.

While playing in an aging Jack Murphy Stadium and sharing it with the NFL Chargers, the Padres announced plans in 1996 to replace it. After the club appeared in but lost the 1998 World Series, local voters approved the construction of a new ballpark for it in downtown San Diego. Originally scheduled to open in 2002, funds for it were not allocated for more than a year. In November 2001, the city approved a $166 million bond to resume its construction. Two years later, Petco Animal Supplies Inc. purchased naming rights to the stadium for $60 million over twenty-two years. As a result, Petco Park opened in 2004.

With its white steel and sandstone façade and palm/jacaranda trees along the perimeter, Petco Park has a southern California appearance. At the entrance, fans pass by a palm court and waterfalls and the ballpark's blue seats are close to the field and angled toward the pitcher's mound. The three-tier grandstand extends from the right field foul pole to home plate and down to the left field foul pole where a San Diego landmark, the Western Metal Supply Building, is part of the left field wall. While the Building contains the team's store on the first floor, party/luxury suites exist on the second and third floors and a restaurant on the fourth.

Petco Park has several amenities. These include such things as an elevated but manicured grass park outside the stadium with lawn seats at $5 each; a Padres Hall of Fame, 250-seat auditorium, kids entertainment zone, and a theatre; a new HD video board; and two levels of social space for fans in right center field modeled after beach piers and featuring pilings and decking constructed from recycled composite wood.

With respect to other NL ballparks as of 2015, Petco Park was eleventh oldest and ranked tenth in construction cost and eleventh in value. Compared to those of all MLB teams in age, cost, and value, respectively, it was twenty-fourth, fifteenth, and eighteenth. As a result, the Padres play in a relatively new but expensive and valuable ballpark within a midsized but expanding sports market (Table A9).

In the 2011–2015 MLB seasons, the FCIs for a family to attend a regular-season home game at Petco Park ranged from a low of $125 in 2011 to $153 in both 2014 and 2015. Among fourteen other NL teams' ballparks, San Diego's FCI ranked from fourteenth during 2011 and 2013–2015 to fifteenth in 2012. Compared to those of all big-league clubs, games at Petco Park for families were twenty-eighth in cost in 2011 and twenty-ninth in the other four years (Table A10).

To reveal specific costs for families at games during a recent year, Petco Park's FCI in 2015 was the same as in 2014. Listed from most to least in amount by item for one person, the team's nonpremium (premium) tickets were between $16 and $17 ($41 and $42), a baseball cap $19, parking one vehicle $8, single beer $5, and a soft drink and hot dog each $4. With an FCI ranked twenty-ninth in MLB at $153, Padres games at Petco Park were each $58 less expensive than the league average in 2015.

Among other clubs in the league's WD, they had rankings and FCIs from most to least as follows in the 2015 MLB season: Giants fifth at $241; Dodgers twelfth at $218; Rockies eighteenth at $196; and Diamondbacks thirtieth at $126. These differences in FCIs occurred, in part, because of these teams' popularity and competitiveness, population and population growth of their host cities, and income per capita and wealth of sports fans in the local market.

In a recent study by CSN Mid-Atlantic, Petco Park ranked fifth in MLB. According to an online report in *USA Today*, the author said:

> For starters, you're in San Diego, so it's hard to go wrong, no matter what the place looks like. But the Padres did a fantastic job designing and building Petco Park, which combines modern niceties with some old-fashioned flair. For example, the Western Metal Supply Co. building, one corner of which serves as the left-field foul pole. Genius! There's also the beach area behind the center-field fence. And the neighboring Gaslamp District has been completely revitalized, a bustling corner of downtown San Diego that offers no shortage of places to go before and after Padres games.[21]

Financial Data

According to data and other financial information published in *Forbes* for franchises in the NL as of their 2015 season, San Diego ranked tenth in market value at $890 million, twelfth in revenue at $224, sixth in operating income at $35 million, thirteenth in gate receipts at $43 million, and fifth in its debt-to-value ratio at 22 percent. Among only the league's WD teams, the Padres had the third highest market value and revenue, second most operating income, fourth highest gate receipts, and the top debt percent (Table A11).[22]

In comparison to twenty-nine other MLB teams as of 2015, San Diego's market value was nineteenth, revenue twenty-second, operating income seventh, gate receipts tied for twenty-fourth with the AL White Sox, and debt-to-value ratio tied for seventh with the AL Rays. According to these statistics, the Padres are a relatively low-valued but profitable MLB franchise whose gate receipts and revenue rank it below average from a financial perspective.

Besides market size, wage inflation, and other factors, an MLB team's annual payroll partly reflects its commitment to players and their current and potential contribution individually and as a group to winning games in regular seasons and postseasons. From 2011 to 2015, for example, the Padres payroll compared to those of other NL teams ranged in rank from fifth in 2015 ($126 million) to sixteenth—included Houston Astros—in 2012 ($50 million). During the five-year period, San Diego's payroll among only the league's WD teams was the lowest from 2011 ($46 million) to 2014 ($53 million) but then third highest in 2015 ($126 million). These results, in part, reflect franchise owner Ron Fowler's efforts to minimize costs and increase profits (Table A12).

With respect to payrolls of all MLB teams as of 2015, the Padres ranked from tenth in 2015 to thirtieth in 2012. For various reasons, however, the team's payroll marginally increased in 2012 and 2013, and significantly in 2015, but remained constant in 2014. These changes in payroll amounts, in some way, contributed to the club's two each third- and fourth-place finishes and also a fifth in the league's WD during 2011–2015.

Business Relations

Besides regular-season and postseason games, MLB franchises are involved in—and affected by—internal affairs and problems, community events, and business-related activities and projects. In no specific order, the following are a few of them for San Diego's NL team as of 2015.[23]

First, the Padres introduced a radio frequency identification (RFID) system in 2014 that combined ticketing, concessions, its fan loyalty program, and in-game entertainment. Like the NL Nationals and AL Rays, San Diego aligned with London-based customer management group Fortress GB to connect all fan touch-points into one system. But the Padres took a significant step by also folding the program into MLB Advanced Media's "At The Ballpark" mobile application. This RFID system is recognized in the app, and fans have a smart card embedded with the RFID chip. Thus, they can manage their tickets, buy food and merchandise, and enhance their in-game experience through the app.

Along with MLB Advanced Media, the team developed several mobile games and social elements and aligned itself with San Diego-based startup technology firm Goodsnitch to allow fans at Petco Park to provide feedback on their in-game experience. The system also manages the Padres' fan loyalty program—The Faithful—which rewards them for virtually any behavior associated with the team. That includes from buying tickets and merchandise to reading articles online and retweeting tweets.

Second, the Padres launched a new Membership Miles Program during 2012. The first phase of it focused on season-ticket holders whose purchase of a ticket plan qualified them as a member. The Program's second phase focused on general ticket sales prior to the 2013 season. For these prospective new members, signing up to become a member was free. They were able to move into blue-, gold-, and platinum-level memberships that included respectively twenty-one-game, forty-one-game, and full-season plans.

Blue, gold, and platinum members select which type of membership best fits them such as fanatic, social, business, or family. As members' status increases, so do their benefits. It is not a loyalty program based upon points, but rather a membership program designed to give fans a greater sense of belonging with the team, and also benefits and opportunities reflecting their interests and type of relationship with the organization.

Third, the Padres' season-ticket sales staff—a group that has grown in numbers and training since 2009—scored the highest performance rating among a field of MLB clubs in a 2011 mystery shopper survey conducted exclusively for the *SportsBusiness Journal* by research firm IntelliShop. It graded teams' sales agents' proficiency by having two dozen professional mystery shoppers call each club to inquire about buying new season tickets. The shoppers evaluated how well agents performed through the various steps of the sales process including touting the benefits of season-ticket ownership, assessing the needs of prospective buyers, closing sales, and overall ability to emotionally engage a prospect.

In San Diego, the staff consistently outscored their MLB counterparts in the survey categories. The club's agents, for example, made a concerted effort to have callers visit the stadium to sit in available seats during 96 percent of the calls. Also, the staff built rapport by engaging callers in conversation not directly related to the sale during 69 percent of the calls.

Fourth, as of 2015, the Padres had re-signed their second-round pick from the 1993 draft even though he had not played in nearly twenty years. After former pitcher Matt LaChappa had a heart attack in the bullpen at a game in 1996, he sustained brain damage that cut his career short and confined him to a wheelchair. Priscilla Oppenheimer, who was the club's director of minor league operations when LaChappa had a heart attack, said that he had a virus around his heart that went undetected during a physical. To help him keep his health insurance and maintain a steady income, the Padres re-signed him to a minor league contract each season. Although these contracts are not lucrative—about $3,000 to $7,500 for a five-month season—they include benefits.

Fifth, one of the largest private lenders of small business loans, National Funding, announced in April 2016 that it formed a partnership with the hometown Padres. This is the first financial technology or Fintech Company to be a sponsor of an MLB team. The partnership includes designation as the "Proud Small Business Lending Partner of the San Diego Padres" and also branding opportunities such as an iconic billboard above upper right field at Petco Park, television-visible and in-park exposure, and invitations to various events throughout the season. "We are proud to welcome another long-standing San Diego business into the Padres family," said vice president of corporate partnerships Sergio Del Prado. "National Funding is a well-known FinTech company in San Diego and an organization that shares our commitment to supporting the community. We look forward to working together in 2016 and growing our relationship."[24]

SAN FRANCISCO GIANTS

From 1883 to 1884, the NL's New York Gothams had victories in 108 games or approximately 52 percent of them. Nevertheless, they finished sixth and then fifth in the league. After changing their nickname to Giants in 1885, the New York team performed another seventy-three seasons and won seven World Series but also lost nine. During this seventy-five-year period, they played their home games at the Polo Grounds in Upper Manhattan of New York City but shared the stadium with various American football teams.[25]

With the Polo Grounds slated to be demolished and then replaced by housing projects in the mid-1950s, Giants owner Horace Stoneham began looking for a another site to relocate his team. After winning a World Series in 1954, the Giants attendance fell from 15,000 per game to 8,100 in 1957. Meanwhile, San Francisco mayor George Christopher had plans to lure an existing MLB team to his city. In fact, he heard about Stoneham's unhappiness and Dodgers owner Walter O'Malley's threats to move from New York.

Through conversations with O'Malley and Los Angeles Mayor Norris Paulson, Christopher discovered that the Dodgers were transferring to the West Coast. As a result, O'Malley and Christopher convinced Stoneham that the two clubs should move together. During August 1957, Stoneham announced the Giants would relocate to the Bay Area before their 1958 season. In their final year in New York, the Giants finished sixth with a dismal 69–85 record and 26 games behind the champion Milwaukee Braves. After the Dodgers and Giants left their hometown, the AL Yankees were the only MLB team in New York until the expansion Mets joined the NL in 1962.

Team Performances

As a member of the NL from 1958 to 1968 and specifically the league's WD during 1969–2015, the Giants played 9,239 games and had victories in approximately 52 percent of them. During the period, they won nine division titles, six pennants, and three World Series in eleven playoffs. With respect to fourteen other NL teams as of 2015, San Francisco ranked sixth in winning division titles, seventh in pennants, and fifth in number of World Series titles. Among only WD clubs, the Giants had fewer total championships than the Dodgers but more than the Diamondbacks, Rockies, and Padres (Table A7).

In comparison to all MLB teams as of their 2015 season, San Francisco tied for ninth with the AL Blue Jays in division titles, tied for tenth with the AL Orioles and Athletics in pennants, and tied for ninth with the AL Orioles and White Sox in World Series victories. Based on these results, the forty-seven-year-old Giants have been very competitive because they frequently outperformed the majority of teams in their division and league to win several titles and championships.

While in its division, the club's most successful seasons included one each in the 1960s, 1970s, and 1990s, two in the 1980s, and six from 2000 to 2015. During one or more of these years, its prominent players included such sluggers as Willie Mays, Barry Bonds, Will Clark, and Buster Posey, and pitchers as Jack Sanford, Juan Marichal, Gaylord Perry, and Madison Bumgarner. Because of problems with various managers and players, however, the Giants failed to qualify for playoffs during different consecutive seasons like in 1958–1961, 1972–1986, 1990–1996, and 2004–2009.

Based in San Francisco, the franchise's best team played in 1962. Despite stiff competition from the league's Dodgers, Reds, and Pirates—who each won more than ninety-two games—the Giants finished first that year because of great performances by the Alou brothers and Mays, Marichal, and Willie McCovey. But in the World Series, the club lost a taut seven-game set to the Yankees that stands as one of the greatest fall MLB classics. But twenty-three years later, the Giants' worst team was outscored by 118 runs and finished thirty-three games behind the Dodgers in the league's WD. On offense, for example, one player led the team with sixty-two runs batted in (RBIs).

Since the 1960s, San Francisco ranks as baseball's seventh greatest franchise. Such players as Mays, McCovey, and Marichal made for a fun first decade in San Francisco although their presence led to just one World Series appearance. Interestingly, the Giants have been eliminated in Game 7 three times—once in an NL championship series and twice in the World Series. But there were three World Series wins during 2010–2014. In addition, the team has a way of being in contention for a title during regular seasons. From 1997 to 2003, for example, it played just eleven games that had no bearing on the postseason. During the period, the Giants won three division titles and a wild card game.

Franchise Owner

Born in New Jersey in 1933, Charles Johnson graduated from Yale University. He served two years in the U.S. Army and then took control of his father's ten-year-old firm, Franklin Templeton Investments, in 1957. Thirty-five years later, Johnson joined an investment group and became a minority owner of the San Francisco Giants. He gradually increased his share of the ball club and in 2011 became its majority owner.

Among the team's multimember ownership group—named San Francisco Baseball Associated LP—Johnson reportedly owns about 25 percent of the franchise. He relies on CEO and minority owner Larry Baer and also senior vice president and general manager Brian Sabean to oversee day-to-day operations including decisions on payroll and other financial matters. Besides Johnson, other important investors in the team include venture capitalist Arthur Rock, who financed the infancy of major Silicon Valley businesses, former Yahoo Inc. president Jeff Mallett, who also co-owns British professional soccer team Derby County; and Rochester sports entrepreneur Andy Appleby.

In comparison to owners of different NL teams and their performances as of 2015, Johnson's Giants rank third in winning division titles, tied for first with the Phillies and Cardinals in number of pennants, and first in World Series championships. Among all current owners of MLB teams, his tied for third in division titles but also for first in pennants and World Series. Thus Johnson's Giants won thirteen total championship through 2015, which is the same number as Phillies' owner Dave Montgomery but one less than the Cardinals' owner William DeWitt Jr. (Table A8).

Based on likability as of 2016, Johnson ranks first among all MLB owners. His Giants teams have won three World Series championships since 2009, play in a privately financed jewel of a ballpark, and sell out every home game. He and his ownership group have a reputation for caring about their players financially and not being afraid to spend money on them when warranted, as evidenced by the almost quarter billion dollars they shelled out on free agents since November 2015. Although Johnson is hands off as an owner, he built an organization that operates like a well-oiled machine.

AT&T Park

After leaving New York for San Francisco in late 1957, the Giants played their home games at Seals Stadium (1958–1959) and then Candlestick Park (1960–1995)—renamed 3Com Park during 1996–1999. Within this forty-two–year period, their attendances ranged from a low of 6,400 per game in 1974 to a high of 32,100 in 1993. Notorious for its windy conditions and also home of the NFL 49ers, Candlestick Park/3Com Park became an inferior stadium and not a profitable investment.

After residents in San Francisco and also in neighboring Santa Clara and San Jose rejected referendums for the construction of a new ballpark during the late 1980s, the Giants announced plans in 1995 to build a new stadium in downtown San Francisco within the China Basin district. Privately financed by the team, construction began in late 1997 and was completed in April 2000. Originally known as Pacific Bell Park—when the telecommunication company purchased naming rights for $50 million over twenty-four years—it was renamed SBC Park in 2004 and then two years later, AT&T Park.

As fans approach the 41,900-seat ballpark, they see a steel and brick structure that features two clock towers with pyramid-shaped roofs topped by flagpoles. Once inside the ticket gates, expansive concourses allow fans to easily find their seats. The main three-tier grandstand consists of green seats that extend from behind home plate down to both foul poles. While bleachers are located behind the left field fence, a walkway is above the right field fence because of the China Basin, aka McCovey Cove. A sidewalk between the water and right field commemorates historical moments in Giants history. People without tickets can see games through a screened section of the right field fence.

Besides a video scoreboard behind the right field fence, spectators have other entertainment options. For example, the Coca Cola Fan Lot is an interactive play area for children and adults to enjoy a slide into home plate from one of the four slides inside the Coca Cola contour bottle. In addition, fans can stroll up to the world's largest baseball glove or view the Bay Area from the ballfield's outfield area. After a Giants player hits a home run, strobe lights flash inside the bottle, bubbles appear to float from the bottle's mouth, and green and white lights flash up and down the neon tubes running along its ribs.

With respect to other NL ballparks as of 2015, AT&T Park was tied for seventh in age and ranked fifth in construction cost and first in value. Compared to those of all MLB teams in time, cost, and value, respectively, it was tied for nineteenth, ninth, and second. As a result, the Giants play in a relatively new and valuable ballpark within a large sports market (Table A9).

In the 2011–2015 MLB seasons, the FCIs for a family to attend a regular-season home game at AT&T Park ranged from a low of $208 in 2011 to $241 in 2015. Among fourteen other NL teams' ballparks, the Giants home facility ranked third most costly in 2013–2015 and seventh in 2011 and 2012. With respect to FCIs of all MLB ballparks, San Francisco's was between fifth and twelfth (Table A10).

To reveal specific costs for families during a recent year, AT&T's FCI in 2015 was about $2 or 1 percent more than in 2014. Listed from most to least in amount by item for one person, the team's nonpremium (premium) tickets were between $33 and $34 ($95 and $96), parking one vehicle $21, a baseball cap $15, single beer $7, and a soft drink and hot dog each between $4 and $6. Thus, it cost fans $30 more at Giants home games than those at other MLB teams' ballparks.

Among other clubs in the league's WD, they had rankings and FCIs from most to least as follows in the 2015 MLB season: Dodgers twelfth at $218; Rockies eighteenth at $196; Padres twenty-ninth at $153; and Diamondbacks thirtieth at $126. These differences in FCIs occurred, in part, because of these teams' popularity and competitiveness, population and population growth of their host cities, and income per capita and wealth of sports fans in the local market.

In a recent study by CSN Mid-Atlantic, AT&T Park ranked second in MLB. According to an online report in *USA Today*, the author said:

> There's certainly a valid argument for the Giants' home park to rank No. 1 on the list, and I wouldn't question anyone who picked it. The view of San Francisco Bay is breathtaking. The see-through brick wall in right field is a great touch for pedestrians walking outside the park to be able to see in. The best view of the place, though, actually is from the last seat in the last row of the upper deck down the first-base line. From there, you see not only the field and the bay, but the Bay Bridge and downtown San Francisco behind the third-base line. It's just phenomenal.[26]

Financial Data

According to data and other financial information published in *Forbes* for franchises in the NL as of their 2015 season, San Francisco ranked second in both market value at $2 billion and revenue at $387 million, and also third in operating income at $68.4 million, first in gate receipts at $165 million, and fourteenth in its debt-to-value ratio at 4 percent. Among only the league's WD teams, the Giants had the highest operating income and gate receipts but a smaller market value and less revenue than the Dodgers (Table A11).

In comparison to twenty-nine other MLB teams as of 2015, San Francisco's market value ranked fourth and its revenue, operating income, and gate receipts each third, and debt percent twenty-fourth. From a financial perspective, the Giants are a very valuable and lucrative business enterprise because of their ballpark and its location, large fan base, historical success in regular seasons and postseasons, and popularity in the Bay Area.

Besides market size, wage inflation, and other factors, an MLB team's annual payroll partly reflects its commitment to players and their current and potential contribution individually and as a group to winning games in regular seasons and postseasons. From 2011 to 2015, for example, the Giants payroll compared to those of other NL teams' ranked third each season. During the five-year period, their payroll among the league's WD teams was the highest in 2011 but second to the Dodgers during 2012–2015. These results, in part, reflect franchise owner Charles Johnson's commitment to win games and championships (Table A12).

With respect to payrolls of all MLB teams as of 2015, the Giants were seventh in 2011–2012 and sixth during 2013–2015. For various reasons, however, the team's payroll significantly increased for the 2013 and 2015 seasons. These changes in amounts, in some way, contributed to the club's two World Series victories between 2011 and 2015.

Business Relations

Besides regular-season and postseason games, MLB franchises are involved in—and affected by—internal affairs and problems, community events, and business-related activities and projects. In no specific order, the following are a few of them for San Francisco's NL team as of 2015.[27]

First, the Giants strengthened their aggressive entry into dynamic pricing in 2012 after a scorching resale market for World Series tickets set records. For the past several seasons, the club, with the aid of Texas-based analytics company Qcue, readjusted prices for single-game tickets based on supply and demand. The league expanded the program to both its division series and championship series for the first time, and also allowed teams to run a limited dynamic pricing test for the World Series.

As a result, dynamic pricing has generated incremental boosts to the Giants total ticket revenue of 7–8 percent a year. The club's season-ticket base soared to nearly thirty thousand full-season equivalents, up by nearly half in just two years, but capped leaving a quarter of the ballpark's seats at most subject to price changes. But the overall ticket revenue growth figure could still move into double-digit percentages as the club's pricing model becomes more detailed and dynamic ticketing is truly accepted by fans.

Second, since AT&T Park in 2004 became the first professional stadium to offer free Wi-Fi, it has also been a key barometer of fan demand for in-venue bandwidth. For much of the past decade, Giants officials have been in a constant chase to boost capacity and are continually adding more access points and other hardware to expand their Wi-Fi network. Upgrades involved placing additional antennas underneath seats and attached to some handrails.

The 2014 World Series illuminated a tipping point when traffic data from the three games at AT&T Park was predictably historic. A record 1.57 terabytes of data transmitted for Game 3 was nearly five times the 370 gigabytes of data transmitted during the team's first home game of the 2012 World Series. The Giants then topped that number again the following night with 1.62 terabytes of transmitted data. For each of the club's three home games in the Series, roughly half of the forty-three thousand people at AT&T Park accessed the network—up from 38 percent two years ago and 18 percent during the 2010 World Series.

Third, a recent lawsuit alleges that Giants owner Charles Johnson played a hand, perhaps unsuspectingly, in depriving one of his early investors of stock now worth in excess of $150 million when counting dividend payments. The lawsuit, filed in a San Francisco court during early 2015 by Anthony P. Miele III, claims that Johnson and Franklin Resources did not transfer shares of the company's stock left to him in 1974 by his deceased father, Anthony P. Miele Jr.

The elder Miele, according to the lawsuit, made a $100,000 loan to Franklin Resources that in 1973 also included a four thousand-share grant in a deal to help the company absorb brokerage firm Winfield & Company. Miele III contends that after his father's death, the principal on the loan was never repaid and the stock never delivered to him. Due to stock splits and appreciation in value, those four thousand shares have paid approximately $20 million in dividends. Franklin Resources and Johnson are named codefendants in the lawsuit, which is seeking compensation for the present value of the shares left to Miele III.

Fourth, the "Giants Ferry," which was nixed in March 2016, was officially reinstated in time for the baseball team's home opener. Originally, the Golden Gate Transportation District announced that service from the Larkspur Ferry Terminal to AT&T Park on opening day was cancelled because of no ship to transport fans.

At the time of cancellation, three out of the fleet's seven vessels were in maintenance and the service could not both continue its regular commute schedule and also dedicate a ship to carry fans to the ballpark. But the ferry service became lucky when one of its vessels, The Marin, returned from maintenance early. Round trip, Golden Gate Giants ferry tickets cost just $12.50; however, riders must purchase theirs' in advance online or over the phone.

Fifth, the Giants won during early 2015 because San Francisco voters approved Proposition D, which waived building height restrictions in the area surrounding AT&T Park. An area where the Giants lease land, this allowed them to continue a real estate development proposal called "Mission Rock," which allows for more than twenty high-rises, offices, and shopping on land currently used as a parking lot. This business project will make the Giants more money. In fact, there is an extreme housing crunch going on in the city caused by an expanding population, skyrocketing real estate costs, and building and zoning laws that, for years, have made it difficult to increase the number of housing units in the city.[28]

NOTES

1. Two books about the history of MLB teams are Frank P. Jozsa Jr., *National League Franchises: Team Performances and Business Success* (New York: Springer, 2015); and James Quirk and Rodney D. Fort, *Pay Dirt: The Business of Professional Team Sports* (Princeton, NJ: Princeton University Press, 1992).

2. Besides such websites as http://www.mlb.com, http://www.baseball-almanac.com, http://www.sportecyclopedia.com, and http://www.baseball-reference.com, there is historical information concerning big-league franchises in Frank P. Jozsa Jr., *Major League Baseball Expansions and Team Relocations: A History, 1876–2008* (Jefferson, NC: McFarland, 2010).

3. Various online articles from journals, magazines, and newspapers contain profiles of MLB's franchise owners including their role in controlling and financing a team.

4. One reference is Rick Weiner, "Power Ranking Every MLB Owner from Worst to First," http://www.bleacherreport.com, cited March 3, 2016.

5. To learn about MLB ballparks and their amenities, see http://www.ballparksofbaseball.com.

6. "Ranking All 30 MLB Ballparks," http://www.csnmidatlantic.com, cited January 26, 2016, is the primary source to read regarding a recent evaluation of these facilities.

7. For Diamondbacks' business relations topics, see Eric Fisher, "Diamondbacks Bring Experimentation to Uniforms," *SportsBusiness Journal* (December 14, 2015): 12; Stefan Modrich, "Arizona Diamondbacks Exec Works to Create New Fans," http://www.bizjournals.com, cited October 18, 2015; Steven Totten, "Arizona Diamondbacks Make International MLB History," http://www.bizjournals.com, cited

January 28, 2016; "Front Office Biographies: Marian Rhodes," http://www.arizona.diamondbacks.mlb.com, cited May 1, 2016.

8. Regarding the Rockies and other new MLB teams, see for example, *Major League Baseball Expansions and Team Relocations: A History, 1876–2008* in note 2 above.

9. Team performances are also in the *Official Major League Baseball Fact Book* 2005 Edition (St. Louis, MO: Sporting News, 2005).

10. Matt Snyder, "Franchise Best/Worst," http://www.cbssports.com, cited March 13, 2016.

11. Specific information and other facts and data about the Colorado Rockies' franchise owner, Coors Field, financial data, and business relations are contained in notes 1–6 of this chapter.

12. "Fan Cost Index," http://www.teammarketingreport.com, cited January 25, 2016.

13. Besides "Ranking All 30 MLB Ballparks," another interesting but important and current reference is "Ranking MLB's Ballparks," http://www.athlonsports.com, cited January 26, 2016.

14. "Major League Baseball Team Payrolls," http://www.usatoday.com, cited January 23, 2016.

15. To read more about Rockies' business relations topics, see Don Muret, "Rockies' Room Popular with Fans," *SportsBusiness Journal* (June 30, 2014): 4; Daniel Kaplan, "Molson Coors to Sell Its Stake in Rockies," http://www.businesssportsdaily.com, cited November 25, 2013: 1; Molly Armbrister, "Colorado Rockies Real Estate Is No Steal," http://www.bizjournals.com, cited March 29, 2015; "2016 Rockies Fest," http://www.colorado.rockies.mlb.com, cited January 23, 2016.

16. Michael Lewis, *Moneyball: The Art of Winning an Unfair Game* (New York: W. W. Norton & Company, 2004).

17. Similar but not same sources were used to research the Dodgers' history, team performances, franchise owner, Dodger Stadium, financial data, and business highlights as for the Diamondbacks and Rockies.

18. The primary reading is Charles Miller, "Ranking All 30 MLB Franchises over the Past 50 Years," http://www.athlonsports.com, cited March 7, 2016.

19. See articles in note 13 for this quote and other information in the literature about how Dodger Stadium ranks in comparison to NL and AL ballparks.

20. Read Dodgers' business relations topics in Robert Gray, "Dodgers Give Tech Firms a Swing at Investors," http://www.sportsbusinessdaily.com, cited October 12, 2015; John Ourand and David Broughton, "Ratings for Dodgers, Astros Show the Challenges of Starting RSN," http://www.sportsbusinessdaily.com, cited September 29, 2014; Meg James, "Dodgers' TV Channel Ratings Off to Bumpy Start," http://www.latimes.com, cited April 10, 2015; "Supplier Data Management System," https://www.appsuppliergateway.com, cited May 19, 2016; "John Hancock Enters into Partnership with the Los Angeles Dodgers," http://www.losangeles.dodgers.mlb.com, cited May 19, 2016.

21. "Ranking All 30 MLB Ballparks" and also "Ranking MLB's Ballparks" describe the primary amenities at Petco Park.

22. Kurt Badenhausen, Michael Ozanian, and Christina Settimi, "MLB Worth $36B As Team Values Hit Record $1.2B Average," http://www.forbes.com, cited January 18, 2016.

23. The Padres' business relations are discussed in Eric Fisher, "Padres' RFID System to Combine Ticketing, Concessions, Other Fan Touch Points," http://www.sportsbusinessdaily.com, cited January 20, 2014; Bill Button, "How One Franchise Is Making Membership More Meaningful," *SportsBusiness Journal* (October 8, 2012): 11; David Broughton, "Padres Rank Highest in Mystery Shopper Survey," http://www.sportsbusinessdaily.com, cited May 19, 2016; Scott Davis, "The San Diego Padres Resign a 39-Year-Old Ex-Player Every Season So He Can Keep His Health Insurance," http://www.businessinsider.com, cited May 19, 2016.

24. Several reports are available including Tracy Rubin, "National Funding Partners with San Diego Padres," http://www.prnewswire.com, cited April 8, 2016.

25. Similar sources were used for information about the San Francisco Giants' history as for the Diamondbacks, Rockies, Dodgers, and Padres. There are also business facts and additional details in Frank P. Jozsa Jr., *Baseball, Inc.: The National Pastime as Big Business* (Jefferson, NC: McFarland, 2006).

26. This quote about AT&T appears in "Ranking All 30 MLB Ballparks."

27. For a few Giants' business relations topics, see "Sales Boost Confidence in Dynamic Pricing," *SportsBusiness Journal* (October 29, 2012): 3; Eric Fisher, "Growing Demand for Bandwidth No Problem for AT&T Park's Expanded Wi-Fi Network," http://www.sportsbusinessdaily.com, cited May 19, 2016; William Cohan, "Mutual Fund Billionaire Accused of Fraud in Suit," http://www.dealbook.nytimes.com, cited May 19, 2016; Joe Fitzgerald Rodriguez, "Ferry Service to AT&T Park Not Available Opening Day," http://www.sfexaminer.com, cited March 30, 2016.

28. Ron Leuty, "Giants' Massive Mission Rock Development Jumps First Hurdle with S.F. Voter Okay," http://www.bizjournals.com, cited April 8, 2016.

Conclusion

Chapters 1–3 and 4–6 of *Major League Baseball Organizations* reveal how teams in, respectively, the American League (AL) and National League (NL) each performed in regular seasons and postseasons of Major League Baseball (MLB). To report and highlight their historical progress and success as franchises from a financial perspective, the chapters also contain data and other business-related information and topics from the literature about them while located within their sports market.

TEAM PERFORMANCES

To compare and analyze the performances of five teams each within three divisions of the AL and also NL as of MLB's 2015 season, Table 1.1 contains some interesting results. First, the AL's East Division (ED) clubs won the most division titles of the six groups primarily because of the New York Yankees' and Boston Red Sox's performances, while the NL's West Division (WD) had the fewest of them, in part, due to the Colorado Rockies' zero titles and only five each by the Arizona Diamondbacks and San Diego Padres.

Second, besides the Yankees winning the largest majority (33 percent) of pennants in MLB history, such NL CD clubs as the Chicago Cubs and St. Louis Cardinals combined have won twenty-nine (16 percent) of them as of 2015. Alternatively, the NL's WD Diamondbacks, Padres, and Rockies performed poorly in divisional and/or championship series especially against such rivals in the league's ED as the Atlanta Braves and Philadelphia Phillies, CD's Cubs and Cardinals, and WD's Los Angeles Dodgers and San Francisco Giants.

Table 1.1. Team Performances, Leagues by Division, Selected Years

American League	*Division Titles*	*Pennants*	*World Series*	*Total*
East Division	46	61	40	147
Central Division	38	28	13	79
West Division	35	9	5	49
National League				
East Division	37	19	7	63
Central Division	38	45	23	103
West Division	34	19	9	62

Note: Because of (a) historical differences in number of teams in each league and their divisions and seasons, (b) ties for division titles between two or more teams, (c) one each split and strike season, and/or (d) teams switching between divisions and from one league to another, there is variation in the data. Performances include American League and National League teams' division titles (1969–2015); American League (1901–1993, 1995–2015) and National League (1876–1993, 1995–2015) pennants; and World Series (1903, 1905–1993, 1995–2015). (*Source*: Teams' number of division titles, pennants, and World Series are available online at http://www.baseball-reference.com and also at http://www.sportsecyclopedia.com).

Third, the Yankees and Boston Red Sox have won a total of thirty-five World Series or 60 percent of those in the AL and approximately 36 percent of all in MLB. In contrast to these two clubs' victories, four others in each league either did not appear in a World Series or not win one. Among the first group are the AL's Houston Astros and Seattle Mariners and NL's Washington Nationals and Milwaukee Brewers—who each failed to win a pennant—and in the second group, the AL's Tampa Bay Rays and Texas Rangers and NL's Colorado Rockies and San Diego Padres—who lost a majority of games in their World Series.

Fourth, AL teams have won approximately 55 percent of total championships—division titles plus pennants and World Series—and forty-seven more than those in the 140-year-old NL. In the former league, the Yankees and then Red Sox and Athletics have the largest share of them while the NL's Cardinals won forty-three, Dodgers twenty-nine, and Reds twenty-five.

Fifth, the data denotes that for various reasons including demographic, monetary, socioeconomic, and team-specific factors, some significant differences exist in performances between the two leagues and their respective divisions, and clubs within these divisions, as of MLB's 2015 season.

FINANCIAL RESULTS

In contrast to the performances of MLB teams in three divisions of each league, Table 2.1 depicts them from a financial perspective—in other words, as franchises whose objective is to earn maximum profits while playing in

Table 2.1. Average Financial Results, Leagues by Division, 2015 MLB Season

American League	*Value*	*Revenue*	*OI*	*Gate Receipts*	*D/V%*
East Division	1,559	307	15.6	116	7.4
Central Division	904	228	13.6	59	12.4
West Division	1,045	239	17.8	62	11.0
National League					
East Division	1,136	254	15.2	69	19.0
Central Division	1,172	255	40.8	85	13.4
West Division	1,397	287	20.3	84	13.4

Note: Value is based on the current stadium deal (unless new stadium is pending) without deduction for debt (other than annual stadium debt). Revenue amount is net of stadium revenues used for debt payments. Operating Income (OI) is earnings before intetest, taxes, depreciation, and amortization. Gate receipts include income from club seats. Debt/Value (D/V) includes ballpark debts. The amounts are each in millions of U.S. dollars. The symbol % is percent. (*Source*: Kurt Badenhausen, Michael Ozanian, and Christina Settimi, "MLB Worth $36B As Team Values Hit Record $1.2B Average," http://www.forbes.com, cited January 8, 2016).

regular-season games at ballparks, and if successful, then a few more in postseasons. Given information in the table as of 2015, the group of NL teams had the highest average market value, revenue, operating income, and gate receipts, and also the largest average debt-to-value percent.

Based on the data, following are highlights of each financial category. First, NL teams' average market value (column two) was roughly $3.7 billion or $200 million more than those in the AL. Despite the Yankees at $3.2 billion and Red Sox at $2.1 billion, eight NL clubs had amounts greater than $1.1 billion including the Dodgers at $2.4 billion and Giants at $2 billion. Moreover, they are less valuable, for example, than fourteen others in the NL.

Second, there was a relatively small difference between each league's average revenue (column three). Because they play home games in large, populated, and wealthy sports markets before many fans at their ballparks, the Yankees at $508 million, Dodgers at $403 million, and Giants at $387 million generated the most revenue among the group. The Astros, meanwhile, had the least amount at $175 million followed by the Tampa Bay Rays and Miami Marlins each at $188 million. For various reasons, the AL's CD and WD, and also NL's ED and CD each had similar amounts.

Third, the AL's average operating income (column four) was approximately $30 million or 61 percent below the NL's. While the ED Red Sox's $49 million was the largest amount among AL teams, the NL CD's Cardinals and Cubs and the WD's Giants each exceeded $68 million. Interestingly, such midsized-to big-market teams as the AL Blue Jays and Tigers and NL Phillies and Dodgers had negative operating income because they were inefficient or simply negligent with respect to managing their operations.

Fourth, the leagues' average gate receipts (column five) were approximately equal at $237–$238 million in MLB's 2015 season. Although the AL's Yankees at $269 million and Red Sox at $172 million had the largest amounts of thirty teams, gate receipts of the NL's Cubs, Cardinals, Dodgers, and Giants were each greater than $112 million. Due to differences in their home attendances, premium and nonpremium ticket prices, radio and television deals, and performances in regular season, there was greater deviation in amounts among AL than NL teams.

Fifth, the AL's and NL's average debt-to-value percent (column six) totaled respectively to about 31 percent and 46 percent. While the Red Sox and four other AL teams had zero debt ratios, eight NL clubs each exceeded 16 percent. Such franchises in the former league as the Astros, Twins, and Rays, and also the NL Marlins, Nationals, and Mets were each responsible for proportionately high annual debt payments, in part, to pay off construction costs and/or renovations of their ballparks.

Appendix

Table A1. AL Team Performances, by Division, Selected Seasons

		Champion		
Team	*Seasons*	*Division*	*Pennants*	*World Series*
East Division				
Baltimore Orioles	62	9	6	3
Boston Red Sox	115	7	12	8
New York Yankees	113	19	40	27
Tampa Bay Rays	18	2	1	0
Toronto Blue Jays	39	9	2	2
Central Division				
Chicago White Sox	115	6	5	3
Cleveland Indians	115	7	5	2
Detroit Tigers	115	7	11	4
Kansas City Royals	47	8	4	2
Minnesota Twins	55	10	3	2
West Division				
Houston Astros	3	0	0	0
Los Angeles Angels of Anaheim	55	9	1	1
Oakland Athletics	48	16	6	4
Seattle Mariners	39	3	0	0
Texas Rangers	44	7	2	0

Note: AL is American League as of 2015. Performances include seasons of teams with name changes. These were the Boston Americans (1901–1907); New York Highlanders (1903–1912); Tampa Bay Devil Rays (1998–2007); Cleveland Blues (1901), Cleveland Broncos (1902), and Cleveland Naps (1903–1914); Los Angeles Angels (1961–1964), California Angels (1965–1996), and Anaheim Angels (1997–2004). Data in table includes performances of the Houston Astros only while in the AL (2013–2015) but excludes those of franchises at their previous sites such as the Seattle Pilots (1969). (*Source*: "MLB Links," http://www.sportsecyclopedia.com, cited January 19, 2016; and "Complete Baseball Team and Baseball Team Encyclopedias," http://www.baseball-reference.com, cited January 19, 2016).

Table A2. AL Teams, History—Principal Owners

	Principal Owners			*Team Champion*		
Team	*Name*	*Year*	*Price*	*Division*	*Pennants*	*WS*
East Division						
Baltimore Orioles	Peter Angelos	1993	173	2	0	0
Boston Red Sox	John Henry	2002	380	2	3	3
New York Yankees	Hal Steinbrenner	2009	NA	3	1	1
Tampa Bay Rays	Stuart Sternberg	2004	200	2	1	0
Toronto Blue Jays	Edward Rogers	2008	NA	1	0	0
Central Division						
Chicago White Sox	Jerry Reinsdorf	1981	20	5	1	1
Cleveland Indians	Larry Dolan	2000	323	2	0	0
Detroit Tigers	Mike Illitch	1992	82	4	2	0
Kansas City Royals	David Glass	2000	96	1	2	1
Minnesota Twins	Jim Pohlad	2009	NA	2	0	0
West Division						
Houston Astros	Jim Crane	2011	610	0	0	0
Los Angeles Angels	Arturo Moreno	2003	184	6	0	0
Oakland Athletics	Lewis Wolff	2005	180	3	0	0
Seattle Mariners	Nintendo	1992	125	3	0	0
Texas Rangers	Ray Davis	2010	593	3	2	0

Note: AL is American League as of 2015. Year is date of purchase by the designated principal owners. Price is amount paid for the team in millions by the principal owners or their syndicates.WS is World Series. NA is not applicable because Hal Steinbrenner inherited the Yankees franchise from his father George who purchased it for $10 million in 1973. Edward Rogers inherited the Toronto Blue Jays in 2008. His father Ted purchased it in 2000 for $137 million. Jim Pohlad inherited the Twins in 2009. Its sale price was $44 million in 1984. (*Source*: "List of Major League Baseball Principal Owners," http://www.baseball-reference.com, cited January 22, 2016, and "MLB Links," http://www.sportsecyclopedia.com, cited January 19, 2016).

Table A3. AL Ballparks, by Team and Division, 2015

		Owner			
Ballpark (Team)	*Age*	*Private*	*Public*	*Cost*	*Value*
East Division					
Fenway Park (Red Sox)	105	X		<1	403
Oriole Park at Camden Yards (Orioles)	25		X	107	158
Rogers Centre (Blue Jays)	28	X		370	162
Tropicana Field (Rays)	27		X	203	98
Yankee Stadium (Yankees)	8	X		1,100	593
Central Division					
Comerica Park (Tigers)	17		X	300	247
Kauffman Stadium (Royals)	44		X	272	134
Progressive Field (Indians)	23	X		175	107
Target Field (Twins)	6		X	435	183
U.S. Cellular Field (White Sox)	26		X	137	152
West Division					
Angel Stadium of Anaheim (Angels)	51		X	117	237
Globe Life Park (Rangers)	23		X	191	279
Minute Maid Park (Astros)	17	X	X	252	165
O.co Coliseum (Athletics)	48		X	200	122
Safeco Field (Mariners)	18		X	517	186

Note: AL is American League. Ballparks are listed in alphabetical order by division. Age is number of years from when these ballparks opened to 2015. Cost is the initial construction cost in millions including renovations. Minute Maid Park is owned jointly by the Astros and Harris County. The symbol < means less than the amount. Value is the portion of each franchise's estimated market value in millions attributable to the team's ballpark. (*Source*: Kurt Badenhausen, Michael Ozanian, and Christina Settimi, "MLB Worth \$36B As Team Values Hit Record \$1.2B Average," http://www.forbes.com, cited January 18, 2016).

Table A4. AL Teams, Fan Cost Indexes, 2011–2015

Team	*2011*	*2012*	*2013*	*2014*	*2015*
East Division					
Baltimore Orioles	174	176	169	173	163
Boston Red Sox	339	336	336	350	350
New York Yankees	338	324	324	337	337
Tampa Bay Rays	139	153	155	170	157
Toronto Blue Jays	212	216	254	217	209
Central Division					
Chicago White Sox	258	222	231	210	208
Cleveland Indians	171	173	157	162	166
Detroit Tigers	207	233	207	219	214
Kansas City Royals	160	185	172	191	213
Minnesota Twins	213	225	221	215	229
West Division					
Houston Astros	NA	NA	224	216	220
Los Angeles Angels of Anaheim	129	159	197	195	190
Oakland Athletics	178	186	180	200	195
Seattle Mariners	183	195	203	207	212
Texas Rangers	159	183	196	203	191

Note: AL is American League. Amounts are in hundreds of dollars. NA is not applicable. The Houston Astros played in the National League in the 2011 and 2012 seasons. A fan cost index comprises the prices of four adult average-price tickets, two small draft beers, four small soft drinks, four regular-size hot dogs, parking for one car, two game programs, and two least expensive, adult-sized adjustable caps for a typical four-person family to attend a team's regular-season home game. (*Source*: "Fan Cost Index," http://www.teammarketingreport.com, cited January 25, 2016).

Table A5. AL Teams, Financial Data by Division, 2015

Teams	*Value*	*Revenue*	*OI*	*Gate Receipts*	*D/V*
East Division					
Baltimore Orioles	1,000	245	31.4	60	15
Boston Red Sox	2,100	370	49.2	172	0
New York Yankees	3,200	508	8.1	269	0
Tampa Bay Rays	625	188	7.9	33	22
Toronto Blue Jays	870	227	–17.9	48	0
Central Division					
Chicago White Sox	975	227	31.9	43	5
Cleveland Indians	825	207	8.9	30	9
Detroit Tigers	1,125	254	–20.7		15
Kansas City Royals	700	231	26.6	69	8
Minnesota Twins	895	223	21.3	71	25
West Division					
Houston Astros	800	175	21.6	48	34
Los Angeles Angels of Anaheim	1,380	304	16.7	93	0
Oakland Athletics	725	202	20.8	42	8
Seattle Mariners	1,100	250	26.4	56	0
Texas Rangers	1,220	266	3.5	74	13

Note: AL is American League. Value is based on the current stadium deal (unless new stadium s pending) without deduction for debt (other than annual stadium debt). Revenue amount is net of stadium revenues used for debt payments. Operating Income (OI) is earnings before intetest, taxes, depreciation, and amortization. Gate receipts include income from club seats. Debt/Value (D/V) is percent and includes ballpark debts. Value, Revenue, OI, and Gate Receipts are each in millions of U.S. dollars. (*Source*: Kurt Badenhausen, Michael Ozanian, and Christina Settimi, "MLB Worth $36B As Team Values Hit Record $1.2B Average," http://www.forbes.com, cited January 18, 2016).

Table A6. AL Teams, Payrolls Rank, 2011–2015 Seasons

	Payrolls				
Teams	*2011(Rank)*	*2012(Rank)*	*2013(Rank)*	*2014(Rank)*	*2015 (Rank)*
East Division					
Baltimore Orioles	85 (9th)	81 (9th)	80 (7th)	105 (6th)	118 (7th)
Boston Red Sox	161 (2nd)	161 (2nd)	149 (2nd)	149 (3rd)	168 (3rd)
New York Yankees	202 (1st)	197 (1st)	211 (1st)	208 (1st)	213 (1st)
Tampa Bay Rays	41 (13th)	64 (11th)	50 (13th)	82 (10th)	74 (14th)
Toronto Blue Jays	62 (11th)	62 (12th)	79 (8th)	116 (5th)	116 (8th)
Central Division					
Chicago White Sox	127 (4th)	96 (6th)	116 (5th)	89 (9th)	110 (10th)
Cleveland Indians	49 (12th)	78 (10th)	76 (10th)	76 (12th)	87 (12th)
Detroit Tigers	105 (6th)	138 (4th)	146 (3rd)	163 (2nd)	172 (2nd)
Kansas City Royals	36 (14th)	60 (13th)	78 (9th)	78 (11th)	112 (9th)
Minnesota Twins	112 (5th)	112 (5th)	72 (11th)	72 (13th)	108 (11th)
West Division					
Houston Astros	NA	NA	18 (15th)	44 (15th)	69 (15th)
Los Angeles Angels	138 (3rd)	153 (3rd)	127 (4th)	128 (4th)	146 (4th)
Oakland Athletics	66 (10th)	55 (14th)	47 (14th)	47 (14th)	80 (13th)
Seattle Mariners	86 (8th)	82 (8th)	60 (12th)	89 (8th)	123 (6th)
Texas Rangers	92 (7th)	92 (7th)	101 (6th)	101 (7th)	144 (5th)

Note: Teams' payrolls are for opening day of the 2011–2015 American League (AL) seasons. Since payrolls are in millions of U.S. dollars, teams actually had different amounts and ranked from first to fourteenth in 2011 and 2012 and to fifteenth in 2013–2015. Thus, there were no ties in rank each season. NA is not applicable. The Houston Astros played in the National League in the 2011 and 2012 seasons. (*Source*: "Major League Baseball Team Payrolls," http://www.usatoday.com, cited January 23, 2016).

Table A7. NL Team Performances, by Division, Selected Seasons

Team	*Seasons*	*Champion*		
		Division	*Pennants*	*World Series*
East Division				
Atlanta Braves	50	17	5	1
Miami Marlins	23	0	2	2
New York Mets	54	6	5	2
Philadelphia Phillies	133	12	7	2
Washington Nationals	11	2	0	0
Central Division				
Chicago Cubs	140	5	10	2
Cincinnati Reds	131	11	9	5
Milwaukee Brewers	18	1	0	0
Pittsburgh Pirates	129	8	7	5
St. Louis Cardinals	124	13	19	11
West Division				
Arizona Diamondbacks	18	5	1	1
Colorado Rockies	23	0	1	0
Los Angeles Dodgers	58	15	9	5
San Diego Padres	47	5	2	0
San Francisco Giants	58	9	6	3

Note: NL is National League as of 2015. Performances include seasons of teams with name changes. These were the Florida Marlins (1993–2011); Philadelphia Quakers (1883–1889); Chicago White Stockings (1876–1889), Chicago Colts (1890–1897), and Chicago Orphans (1898–1902); Cincinnati Red Stocking (1876–1880) and Cincinnati Redlegs (1954–1959); Pittsburgh Alleghenys (1882–1890); St. Louis Brown Stockings (1892–1898) and St. Louis Perfectos (1899). Data excludes performances of franchises at their previous sites such as the Montreal Expos (1969–2004) and Milwaukee Brewers while in the AL (1970–1997). (*Source*: "MLB Links," http://www.sportsecyclopedia.com, cited January 19, 2016, and "Complete Baseball Team and Baseball Team Encyclopedias," http://www.baseball-reference.com, cited January 19, 2016).

Table A8. NL Teams, History—Principal Owners

	Principal Owners			*Team Champion*		
Team	*Name*	*Year*	*Price*	*Division*	*Pennants*	*WS*
East Division						
Atlanta Braves	Liberty Media	2007	450	1	0	0
Miami Marlins	Jeffrey Loria	2002	158	0	1	1
New York Mets	Fred Wilpon	2002	391	2	1	0
Philadelphia Phillies	Dave Montgomery	1981	30	8	4	1
Washington Nationals	Ted Lerner	2006	450	2	0	0
Central Division						
Chicago Cubs	Tom Ricketts	2009	845	0	0	0
Cincinnati Reds	Robert Castellini	2006	270	2	0	0
Milwaukee Brewers	Mark Attanasio	2005	223	1	0	0
Pittsburgh Pirates	Robert Nutting	2007	92	0	0	0
St. Louis Cardinals	William DeWitt Jr.	1995	150	10	4	2
West Division						
Arizona Diamondbacks	Ken Kendrick	2004	238	2	0	0
Colorado Rockies	Charles/Richard Monfort	1992	95	0	1	0
Los Angeles Dodgers	Mark Walter	2012	2,150	3	0	0
San Diego Padres	Ron Fowler	2012	800	0	0	0
San Francisco Giants	Charles Johnson	1992	100	6	4	3

Note: NL is National League as of 2015. Year is date of purchase by the designated principal owners. Price is amount paid for the team in millions by the principal owners or their syndicates. WS is World Series. The purchase price of the Atlanta Braves included trading cash, stocks, and assets with AOL Time Warner. In a winning bid selected through a bankruptcy process, the purchase of the Los Angeles Dodgers included $150 million for land surrounding Dodger Stadium. (*Source*: "List of Major League Baseball Principal Owners," http://www.baseball-reference.com, cited January 22, 2016, and "MLB Links," http://www.sportsecyclopedia.com, cited January 19, 2016).

Table A9. NL Ballparks, by Team and Division, 2015

Ballpark (Team)	*Age*	*Owner*		*Cost*	*Value*
		Private	*Public*		
East Division					
Citi Field (Mets)	8		X	688	237
Citizens Bank Park (Phillies)	13		X	346	237
Marlins Park (Marlins)	5		X	515	89
Nationals Park (Nationals)	9		X	611	282
Turner Field (Braves)	19		X	235	211
Central Division					
Busch Stadium III (Cardinals)	10	X		365	338
Great American Ball Park (Reds)	13		X	291	198
Miller Park (Brewers)	16		X	310	185
PNC Park (Pirates)	16		X	237	153
Wrigley Field (Cubs)	100	X		<1	355
West Division					
AT&T Park (Giants)	16	X		357	494
Chase Field (Diamondbacks)	18	X	X	354	135
Coors Field (Rockies)	21		X	215	159
Dodger Stadium (Dodgers)	54	X		23	452
Petco Park (Padres)	12	X	X	285	168

Note: NL is National League. Age is number of years from when these ballparks opened to 2015. Cost is the initial construction cost in millions including renovations. Petco Park is owned jointly by the Padres and City of San Diego. The symbol < means less than the amount. Value is the portion of each franchise's estimated market value in millions attributable to the team's ballpark. (*Source*: Kurt Badenhausen, Michael Ozanian, and Christina Settimi, "MLB Worth $36B As Team Values Hit Record $1.2B Average," http://www.forbes.com, cited January 18, 2016).

Table A10. NL Teams, Fan Cost Indexes, 2011–2015

Team	*2011*	*2012*	*2013*	*2014*	*2015*
East Division					
Atlanta Braves	169	172	170	171	174
Florida/Miami Marlins	170	242	229	221	224
New York Mets	241	230	223	229	219
Philadelphia Phillies	240	257	257	258	252
Washington Nationals	196	198	236	227	232
Central Division					
Chicago Cubs	305	300	298	304	300
Cincinnati Reds	162	165	165	168	166
Houston Astros	221	224	NA	NA	NA
Milwaukee Brewers	160	171	176	176	182
Pittsburgh Pirates	127	152	164	169	175
St. Louis Cardinals	223	225	230	233	236
West Division					
Arizona Diamondbacks	120	145	151	126	126
Colorado Rockies	161	184	196	201	196
Los Angeles Dodgers	226	213	204	217	218
San Diego Padres	125	150	152	153	153
San Francisco Giants	208	223	237	239	241

Note: NL is National League. Amounts are in hundreds of dollars. NA is not applicable. The Houston Astros transferred from the NL to American League in 2013. The Miami Marlins were named Florida Marlins in the 2011 season. A fan cost index comprises the prices of four adult average-price tickets, two small draft beers, four small soft drinks, four regular-size hot dogs, parking for one car, two game programs, and two least-expensive, adult-sized adjustable caps for a typical four-person family to attend a team's regular-season home game. (*Source*: "Fan Cost Index," http://www.teammarketingreport.com, cited January 25, 2016).

Table A11. NL Teams, Financial Data by Division, 2015

Teams	*Value*	*Revenue*	*OI*	*Gate Receipts*	*D/V*
East Division					
Atlanta Braves	1,150	267	33.2	58	0
Miami Marlins	650	188	15.4	32	34
New York Mets	1,350	263	25.0	74	26
Philadelphia Phillies	1,250	265	–39.0	89	8
Washington Nationals	1,280	287	41.4	92	27
Central Division					
Chicago Cubs	1,800	302	73.3	113	24
Cincinnati Reds	885	227	2.2	64	6
Milwaukee Brewers	875	226	11.3	65	6
Pittsburgh Pirates	900	229	43.6	54	10
St. Louis Cardinals	1,400	294	73.6	133	21
West Division					
Arizona Diamondbacks	840	211	-2.2	42	17
Colorado Rockies	855	214	12.6	58	7
Los Angeles Dodgers	2,400	403	-12.2	123	17
San Diego Padres	890	224	35.0	43	22
San Francisco Giants	2,000	387	68.4	165	4

Note: NL is National League. Value is based on the current stadium deal (unless new stadium is pending) without deduction for debt (other than annual stadium debt). Revenue amount is net of stadium revenues used for debt payments. Operating Income (OI) is earnings before intetest, taxes, depreciation, and amortization. Gate receipts include income from club seats. Debt/Value (D/V), a percent, includes ballpark debts. Value, Revenue, OI, and Gate Receipts are each in millions of U.S. dollars. (*Source*: Kurt Badenhausen, Michael Ozanian, and Christina Settimi, "MLB Worth $36B As Team Values Hit Record $1.2B Average," http://www.forbes.com, cited January 18, 2016).

Table A12. NL Teams, Payrolls Rank, 2011–2015 Seasons

	Payrolls				
Teams	*2011(Rank)*	*2012 (Rank)*	*2013 (Rank)*	*2014 (Rank)*	*2015 (Rank)*
East Division					
Atlanta Braves	87 (8th)	83 (9th)	73 (11th)	76 (14th)	89 (12th)
Miami Marlins	56 (13th)	56 (15th)	28 (15th)	28 (15th)	84 (14th)
New York Mets	118 (4th)	118 (4th)	71 (12th)	71 (12th)	100 (9th)
Philadelphia Phillies	172 (1st)	174 (1st)	164 (2nd)	179 (2nd)	133 (4th)
Washington Nationals	63 (12th)	81 (10th)	111 (5th)	129 (4th)	174 (2nd)
Central Division					
Chicago Cubs	125 (2nd)	89 (7th)	93 (7th)	73 (11th)	117 (8th)
Cincinnati Reds	75 (10th)	75 (11th)	106 (6th)	106 (7th)	118 (7th)
Houston Astros	70 (11th)	60 (14th)	NA	NA	NA
Milwaukee Brewers	85 (9th)	97 (6th)	78 (9th)	78 (8th)	98 (10th)
Pittsburgh Pirates	45 (16th)	63 (13th)	77 (10th)	77 (9th)	85 (13th)
St. Louis Cardinals	105 (5th)	105 (5th)	112 (4th)	112 (5th)	120 (6th)
West Division					
Arizona Diamondbacks	53 (14th)	74 (12th)	87 (8th)	111 (6th)	65 (15th)
Colorado Rockies	88 (7th)	88 (8th)	64 (13th)	64 (13th)	98 (11th)
Los Angeles Dodgers	104 (6th)	137 (2nd)	178 (1st)	241 (1st)	230 (1st)
San Diego Padres	46 (15th)	50 (16th)	53 (14th)	53 (14th)	126 (5th)
San Francisco Giants	119 (3rd)	119 (3rd)	134 (3rd)	144 (3rd)	166 (3rd)

Note: NL is National League. Teams' payrolls are for opening day of NL seasons. Since payrolls are in millions of U.S. dollars, teams actually had different amounts and ranked from first to sixteenth in 2011 and 2012 and to fifteenth in 2013–2015. Thus, there were no ties in rank each season. NA is not applicable. The Houston Astros transferred from the NL to American League in 2013. (*Source*: "Major League Baseball Team Payrolls," http://www.usatoday.com, cited January 23, 2016).

Bibliography

Armbrister, Molly. "Colorado Rockies Real Estate Is No Steal." http://www.bizjournals.com, cited 29 March 2015.

"Associated Bank Expands Partnership with Milwaukee Brewers." http://www.prnewswire.com, cited 31 March 2016.

"Astros Diversity Program." http://www.houston.astros.mlb.com, cited 1 May 2016.

Badenhausen, Kurt. "The Pittsburgh Pirates Are Baseball's Best and Business Is Thriving." http:www.forbes.com, cited 18 May 2016.

Badenhausen, Kurt, Michael Ozanian, and Christina Settimi. "MLB Worth $36B As Team Values Hit Record $1.2B Average." http://www.forbes.com, cited 18 January 2016.

"Baltimore Orioles Score Homerun with Office 365." http://www.microsoft.com, cited 1 March 2016.

Barker, Jeff. "Orioles Begin to Look at Updating Camden Yards." http://www.baltimoresun.com, cited 24 August 2015.

"Baseball to Business." http://www.miami.marlins.mlb.com, cited 15 May 2016.

Belson, Ken. "Yankees Resale Market Will Compete with StubHub." http://www.bats.blogs.nytimes.com, cited 5 March 2016.

"Black Business Matters: Pathway to Prosperity." http://www.thecincinnatiherald.com, cited 16 March 2016.

Bloom, Barry M. "Astros Sale to Crane, Move to AL Approved." http://www.m.mlb.com, cited 1 March 2016.

———. "Braves Sale Is Approved." http://www.m.mlb.com, cited 1 April 2016.

Boland, Robert. "Wilpons' Financial Morass Offers Lessons for Franchise Owners." http://www.sportsbusinessdaily.com, cited 18 May 2016.

"Boston Red Sox: Like It or Not, Timing Is Right for John Henry to Sell Team." http://www.bleacherreport.com, cited 5 February 2016.

Botta, Christopher. "Detroit's Delivery Man." http://www.sportsbusinessdaily.com, cited 19 February 2016.

Boudway, Ira. "Holy Cow! The Chicago Cubs Finally Have a Winning Business Plan." http://www.bloomberg.com, cited 18 May 2016.

Boudway, Ira, Evan Applegate, and Ritchie S. King. "Smartest Spenders in Sports 2014." http://www.bloomberg.com, cited 1 February 2016.

"Braves Digital 'Bash' Draws More Than 20K." http://www.sportsbusinessdaily.com, cited 18 May 2016.

"Braves, Marlins to Play at Fort Bragg Military Base July 3." http://www.si.com, cited 18 May 2016.

"Braves Say AAA Team Will Remain in Gwinnett Co." http://www.entertainment-managementonline.com, cited 18 May 2016.

Brennan, Vince. "Cardinals' DeWitt III to Headline Business Journal Top 150 Event at Busch." http://www.bizjournals.com, cited 11 February 2016.

"Brian Auld." http://www.tampabay.rays.mlb.com, cited 15 March 2016.

Broughton, David. "Padres Rank Highest in Mystery Shopper Survey." http://www.sportsbusinessdaily.com, cited 19 May 2016.

———. "Yankee Stadium Secures Safety Act." *SportsBusiness Journal* (25 June 2012): 16.

Brown, Maury. "The Mariners New TV Deal Gives Added Flexibility, But Will They Use It?" http://www.lookoutstanding.com, cited 19 April 2016.

"Business of Professional Sports: An Evening with the Owners of the Lightning, Rays and Buccaneers." http://www.poynter.org, cited 5 February 2016.

Butler, Scott. "Phillies Must Develop an Organizational Business Model." http://www.philsbaseball.com, cited 18 May 2016.

Button, Bill. "How One Franchise Is Making Membership More Meaningful." *SportsBusiness Journal* (8 October 2012): 11.

Carlisle, Candace. "Texas Rangers to Upgrade Part of Globe Life Park in Arlington." http://www.bizjournals.com, cited 8 January 2016.

Cassano, Erick. "How Dennis Kuhl Develops Repeat Customers for the Los Angeles Angels of Anaheim." http://www.sbnonline.com, cited 5 July 2011.

"Cincinnati Reds Attendance, Stadiums, and Park Factors." http://www.baseball-reference.com, cited 15 March 2016.

"Cincinnati Reds Keep Their IT on the Ball." http://www.news.microsoft.com, cited 25 September 2012.

"Cleveland in the Cloud: Overhauling the Indians' Infrastructure." http://www.vmware.com, cited 17 February 2016.

Cohan, William. "Mutual Fund Billionaire Accused of Fraud in Suit." http://www.dealbook.nytimes.com, cited 19 May 2016.

"Complete Baseball Team and Baseball Team Encyclopedias." http://www.baseball-reference.com, cited 19 January 2016.

Coolidge, Alexander. "Reds Get 7-Year Extension on Sponsorship." http://www.cincinnati.com, cited 15 April 2016.

Davidi, Shi. "Blue Jays to Part Ways with Stephen Brooks, Hire Indians' Andrew Miller." http://www.sportsnet.ca, cited 12 April 2016.

Davis, Scott. "The San Diego Padres Resign a 39-Year-Old Ex-Player Every Season So He Can Keep His Health Insurance." http://www.businessinsider.com, cited 19 May 2016.

Divish, Ryan. "Ken Griffey Jr. Elected to Baseball Hall of Fame, Sets Voting Record." http://www.seattletimes.com, cited 4 March 2016.

———. "Mariners Announce Title Changes, Additions to Baseball Operations Staff." http://www.seattletimes.com, cited 29 October 2015.

Durrett, Richard. "Rangers Fan Dies after 20-Foot Fall." http://www.espn.go.com, cited 15 May 2016.

Dutton, Bob. "Seattle Mariners Promote Tom Allison to Oversee All Baseball Scouting Operations." http://www.thenewstribune.com, cited 21 October 2015.

Ecker, Danny. "Cubs, Sox TV Ratings Are a Tale of Two Cities." http://www.chicagobusiness.com, cited 15 March 2016.

Eidelson, Josh. "Oakland A's Will Pay Back Wages to Interns and Clubhouse Workers." *BusinessWeek* (1 September 2014): 1.

"Equifax Announces Partnership with the St. Louis Cardinals." http://www.equifax.com, cited 30 March 2016.

"Fan Cost Index." http://www.teammarketingreport.com, cited 25 January 2016.

"Fenway Sports Management Announces Liverpool Club North America Summer Tour." http://www.reuters.com, cited 2 February 2016.

Fink, James. "Buffalo Bisons, Toronto Blue Jays Extend Affiliation Pact through 2018." http://www.bizjournals.com, cited 13 April 2016.

Fisher, Eric. "A's, Giants Take Public Their Longtime Territorial Dispute over San Jose." http://www.sportsbusinessdaily.com, cited 12 March 2016.

———. "Astros Enlist MLBAM to Create Online Fan Research Forum to Gain Feedback on Team Initiatives." *SportsBusiness Journal* (30 April 2012): 7.

———. "Astros Eye $40M for Civic-Sponsored Program." http://www.sportsbusinessdaily.com, cited 25 June 2012.

———. "Braves, Sun Trust Move Quickly, Quietly on Ballpark." *SportsBusiness Journal* (22 September 2014): 8.

———. "Diamondbacks Bring Experimentation to Uniforms." *SportsBusiness Journal* (14 December 2015): 12.

———. "Dynamic Pricing Comes to MLB Postseason." *SportsBusiness Journal* (22 October 2012): 3.

———. "Growing Demand for Bandwidth No Problem for AT&T Park's Expanded Wi-Fi Network." http://www.sportsbusinessdaily.com, cited 19 May 2016.

———. "Laura Day, Minnesota Twins." *SportsBusiness Journal* (14 September 2015): 12A.

———. "Nationals Re-Create Successful Club 24 with K Street Boxes." *Sports Business Journal* (2 March 2015): 6.

———. "Padres' RFID System to Combine Ticketing, Concessions, Other Fan Touch Points." http://www.sportsbusinessdaily.com, cited 20 January 2014.

———. "Snow Go? Indians to Evaluate Winter Carnival After It Doesn't Spin Profit for Second Year." http://www.sportsbusinessdaily.com, cited 23 January 2016.

———. "Weather Cost Twins 'Deep into Seven Figures.'" *SportsBusiness Journal* (29 April 2013): 35.

———. "White Sox Sponsor Links Deal to Charities." http://www.sportsbusinessdaily.com, cited 28 January 2016.

———. "World Series: Outer Markets Will Drive Royals' 2015 Ticket Growth." http://www.bizjournals.com, cited 31 October 2014.

Fontevecchia, Augustino. "Billionaires Tony Ressler and Sara Blakely Snatch Atlanta Hawks for $730 Million." http://www.forbes.com, cited 20 March 2016.

Ford, Bob. "Phillies Changing the Way They Do Business." http://www.articles.philly.com, cited 18 May 2016.

"Front Office Biographies: Marian Rhodes." http://www.arizona.dimondbacks.mlb.com, cited 1 May 2016.

George, John. "Phillies CEO Breaks Down TV Deal." http://www.sportsbusinessdaily.com, cited 18 May 2016.

Gough, Paul. "Pirates Reach Partnership Deals with Six Companies." http://www.bizjournals.com, cited 16 May 2016.

Grathoff, Pete. "The Royals Are Up for Sports Illustrated's Sportsman of the Year Award." http://www.kansascity.com, cited 22 February 2016.

Gray, Robert. "Dodgers Give Tech Firms a Swing at Investors." http://www.sportsbusinessdaily.com, cited 12 October 2015.

Greenberg, Jon. "Sox Pulling Out Stops to Bump Attendance." http://www.espn.go.com, cited 15 April 2016.

Greenwald, Judy. "Former St. Louis Cardinals Exec Pleads Guilty to Hacking Astros' Computers." http://www.businessinsurance.com, cited 11 January 2016.

Halter, Nick. "Fans Will Finally be Able to Stream Minnesota Twins Games in Minnesota." http://www.bizjournals.com, cited 19 November 2015.

Haudricourt, Tom. "Brewers GM Refuses to Equate Rebuilding to 'Tanking.'" http://www.jsonline.com, cited 15 March 2016.

"Helios Education Foundation and Rays Baseball Foundation Announce 2015 Scholars." http://www.helios.org, cited 15 April 2016.

Heyman, John. "Inside Baseball: Rival Executives Upset by Marlins' Tiny Revenue." http://www.cbssports.com, cited 18 May 2016.

Hiltzik, Michael. "The Rich L.A. Angels Try to Nickle-and-Dime Their Stadium Workers—Again." http://www.latimes.com, cited 9 February 2015.

Hopkins, Jared S., and Melissa Harris. "Reinsdorf Recommends Selling Sox after He Dies." http://articles.chicagotribune.com, cited 9 February 2016.

"Houston Astros Set to Install Musco's LED Lighting System." http://www.musco.com, cited 25 February 2015.

Hoynes, Paul. "Cleveland Indians Reorganize Latin American Baseball Operations." http://www.cleveland.com, cited 15 February 2016.

———. "Paul Dolan Has No Interest in Selling Majority Share of Cleveland Indians." http://www.cleveland.com, cited 12 February 2016.

"Interest in Selling Majority Share of Cleveland Indians." http://www.cleveland.com, cited 12 February 2016.

"Is It Time for Arte Moreno to Sell the Angels?" http://www.halosheaven.com, cited 2 March 2016.

James, Meg. "Dodgers' TV Channel Ratings Off to Bumpy Start." http://www.latimes.com, cited 10 April 2015.

"John Hancock Enters into Partnership with the Los Angeles Dodgers." http://www.losangeles.dodgers.mlb.com, cited 19 May 2016.

Jones, Ray. "Business Lessons from the 2013 Pittsburgh Pirates—Strategy and Opportunity." http://www.katz.pitt.edu, cited 25 March 2016.

Jozsa, Frank P. Jr. *American League Franchises: Team Performances and Business Success.* New York: Springer, 2015.

———. "An Economic Analysis of Franchise Relocation and League Expansion in Professional Team Sports, 1950–1975." Ph.D. diss., Georgia State University, 1977.

———. *Baseball Beyond Borders: From Distant Lands to the Major Leagues.* Lanham, MD: Scarecrow Press, 2013.

———. *Baseball in Crisis: Spiraling Costs, Bad Behavior, Uncertain Future.* Jefferson, NC: McFarland, 2008.

———. *Baseball, Inc.: The National Pastime as Big Business* Jefferson, NC: McFarland, 2006.

———. *Major League Baseball Expansions and Team Relocations: A History, 1876–2008.* Jefferson, NC: McFarland, 2010.

———. *National League Franchises: Team Performances and Business Success.* New York: Springer, 2015.

Kaminski, Matthew. "Cross Country: The Money Feud Spicing up the Nationals-Orioles Rivalry." *Wall Street Journal* (4 October 2014): A11.

Kaplan, Daniel. "Molson Coors to Sell Its Stake in Rockies." http://www.businesss-portsdaily.com, cited 25 November 2013.

———. "Tigers Refinancing $130M a Good Sign." http://www.sportsBusinessdaily.com, cited 13 September 2010.

———. "Yankees Group Carries Nearly $2 Billion in Debt." *SportsBusiness Journal* (20 September 2010): 1.

Kelps, Kevin. "Losing Proposition? Shapiro Says Dolans Haven't Turned a Profit during 'a Few' Indians Seasons." http://www.crainscleveland.com, cited 1 September 2015.

King, Bill. "Angels Seek Messaging That Will Play across Both the Hispanic and General Markets." http://www.sportsbusinessdaily.com, cited 24 June 2013.

———. "Ticket Challenge: Getting the Price Right." *SportsBusiness Journal* (19 March 2012): 1.

King, Bill, and John Ourand. "The RSN Conundrum." *SportsBusiness Journal* (17 March 2014): 1.

Koo, Andrew. "A Decade after *Moneyball*, Have the A's Found a New Market Inefficiency?" http://www.regressing.deadspin.com, cited 1 March 2016.

Laurilta, David. "Ruben Amaro on Analytics (and Evaluation)." http://www.fangraphs.com, cited 11 March 2016.

Lazare, Lewis. "Chicago Cubs Proudly Show Off How to Do a Clubhouse Right." http://www.bizjournals.com, cited 13 April 2016.

Lefton, Terry. "Bank of America Renews Its Big Sponsorship with the Yankees." *SportsBusiness Journal* (10 November 2014): 11.

———. "DePaoli, Mets Working for the Weekend." http://www.sportsbusinessdaily.com, cited 18 May 2016.
———. "Loria's Eye for Art Key to Logo." http://www.sportsbusinessnews.com, cited 13 March 2016.
———. "Yankees Sign Eight-Year Marketing Agreement with New Era." *SportsBusiness Journal* (15 July 2013): 4.
Leuty, Ron. "Giants' Massive Mission Rock Development Jumps First Hurdle with S.F. Voter Okay." http://www.bizjournals.com, cited 8 April 2016.
Lewis, Michael. *Moneyball: The Art of Winning an Unfair Game*. (New York: W. W. Norton & Company, 2004).
"List of Major League Baseball Principal Owners." http://www.baseball-reference.com, cited 22 January 2016.
Madkour, Abraham. "By Design: High Standards Set by Pittsburgh Facilities." http://www.sportsbusinessdaily.com, cited 23 June 2014.
"Major League Baseball Team Payrolls." http://www.usatoday.com, cited 23 January 2016.
Marcin, Tim. "How New York Mets' LGBT Pride Night Can Increase Fans and Profit for MLB Franchises." http://www.ibtimes.com, cited 23 February 2016.
McIntyre, Mike. "Cleveland Indians Cancel Snow Days at Progressive Field Because Crowds Were Too Small." http://www.cleveland.com, cited 1 June 2012.
"Miami Marlins Official Barber Hugo 'Juice' Tandron Becomes Cult Hero." http://www.miamiherald.com, cited 17 May 2016.
Miller, Charles. "Ranking All 30 MLB Franchises Over the Past 50 Years." http://www. athlonsports.com, cited 7 March 2016.
"MLB Links." http://www.sportsecyclopedia.com, cited 19 January 2016.
Modrich, Stefan. "Arizona Diamondbacks Exec Works to Create New Fans." http://www.bizjournals.com, cited 18 October 2015.
Muret, Don. "For Cubs, Dynamic Pricing's a One-Way Street." *SportsBusiness Journal* (18 March 2013): 7.
———. "JetBlue Park: Fenway Takes Flight in Florida." http://www.sportsbusinessdaily.com, cited 3 February 2016.
———. "Original Retractable Roof in Toronto Getting $9M Modernization." http://www.sportsbusinessdaily.com, cited 12 April 2016.
———. "Red Sox Sign Jeweler Alex and Ani as Presenting Sponsor for Redesigned Banquet Space." http://www.sportsbusinessdaily.com, cited 1 February 2016.
———. "Rockies' Room Popular with Fans." *SportsBusiness Journal* (30 June 2014): 4.
"Nuveen Pleased to Show Support of Chicago Cubs." http://www.businesswire.com, cited 26 April 2016.
"Oakland A's Scoping Out Sites for New Stadium." http://www.mercurynews.com, cited 6 March 2016.
Official Major League Baseball Fact Book 2005 Edition. St. Louis, MO: Sporting News, 2005.
"122 Pro Sports Franchises—Ranked!" http://www.espn.go.com, cited 4 March 2016.

Ourand, John, and David Broughton. "Multiple Story Lines Help Lift Tigers to Top of Local TV Ratings List," http://www.sportsbusinessdaily.com, cited 21 February 2016.

———. "Ratings for Dodgers, Astros Show Challenge of Starting RSN." http://www.sportsbusinessdaily.com, cited 29 September 2014.

Padilla, Doug. "White Sox GM Denies Conflict with Boss Kenny Williams." http://www.espn.go.com, cited 1 April 2016.

Payne, Marissa. "Woman Suing Red Sox Owner After Being Hit by Foul Ball in Stadium." http://www.washingtonpost.com, cited 9 February 2016.

"Pirates' Business Model." http://www.bucsdugout.com, cited 18 May 2016.

"Play Ball: Nats Deploy Software, Social Media to Boost Game Experience." http://www.bizjournals.com, cited 18 May 2016.

Powtak, Ken. "Hall of Famer Rod Carew Touched by Twins' Tribute on 1st." http://www.businessinsider.com, cited 27 February 2016.

Quirk, James, and Rodney D. Fort. *Pay Dirt: The Business of Professional Team Sports* (Princeton, NJ: Princeton University Press, 1992).

Ramstad, Evan, "Twins See Lots of On-Field and Off-Field Possibilities with New Player from South Korea," http://www.startribune.com, cited 5 December 2015.

"Ranking All 30 MLB Ballparks." http://www.csnatlantic.com, cited 26 January 2016.

"Ranking MLB's Ballparks." http://www.athlonsports.com, cited 26 January 2016.

"Rays' Group among Those Seeking South Florida Ticket Sales Job." *SportsBusiness Journal* (2 May 2011): 12.

"Red Sox Introduce Variable Pricing for 2014 Season." http//www.m.mlb.com, cited 1 February 2016.

"Reds COO Castellini Talks Business in Q&A." http://www.cincinnati.suntimes.com, cited 12 February 2016.

"Ricoh and Miami Marlins Partner for Baseball and Business." http://www.ricoh-usa.com, cited 16 May 2016.

Rieper, Max. "Alex Gordon Signs 4-Year Deal with Royals." http://www.royalsreview.com, cited 6 January 2016.

Roberts, Tim. "New Video Board and Foul Poles Coming to Globe Life Park." http://www.cw33.com, cited 1 March 2016.

Rodriguez, Joe Fitzgerald. "Ferry Service to AT&T Park Not Available Opening Day." http://www.sfexaminer.com, cited 30 March 2016.

Rosenberg, Michael. "For Impatient Tigers Owner Illitch, Firing Dombrowki Was a Personal Move." http://www.si.com, cited 1 September 2015.

"Royals Continue 'Forever Royal' into the 2016 Season." http://www.ksn.com, cited 1 February 2016.

Rubin, Tracy. "National Funding Partners with San Diego Padres." http://www.prnewswire.com, cited 8 April 2016.

Rymer, Zachary. "Boston Red Sox: Like It or Not, Timing Is Right for John Henry to Sell Team." http://www.bleacherreport.com, cited 5 February 2016.

"SAIC Continues Sponsorship of the Washington Nationals Patriotic Series." http://www.businesswire.com, cited 4 April 2016.

"Sales Boost Confidence in Dynamic Pricing." *SportsBusiness Journal* (29 October 2012): 3.

Schmidt, Michael S. "Co-Owner of the Mets Is Said to Be Interested in Selling," http://www.nytimes.com, cited 10 March 2016.

Segui, Alcides. "St. Pete City Council Approves Rays Stadium Deal." http://www.fox13news.com, cited 1 April 2016.

"7 Things We Can Learn about Marketing from the St. Louis Cardinals." http://www.zimmercommunications.com, cited 26 March 2016.

Shaikin, Bill. "Angels Acquire Andrelton Simmons from Braves for Erick Aybar, Prospects." http://www.latimes.com, cited 12 November 2015.

———. "Tustin Wants Angels, But Who Pays for the Ballpark?" http://www.latimes.com, cited 3 March 2016.

Sharrow, Ryan. "Orioles' TV Ratings on MASN among the Highest in MLB." http://www.bizjournals.com, cited 5 October 2015.

Shea, Bill. "Dan Gilbert Almost Bought Milwaukee Brewers instead of Cleveland Cavaliers." http://www.crainsdetroit.com, cited 17 March 2016.

———. "Pure Michigan Extends Relationship with Tigers, MIS." http://www.crainsdetroit.com, cited 16 December 2015.

"Sky Hawks Officially Sign with Milwaukee." http://www.csbj.com, cited 13 October 2014.

Sleezer, John. "Royals Extend Contracts of Manager Ned Yost, GM Dayton Moore." http://www.kansascity.com, cited 18 February 2016.

Snyder, Matt. "Franchise Best/Worsts." http://www.cbssports.com, cited 13 March 2016.

———. "Franchise Best/Worsts: Philadelphia Phillies." http://www.cbssports.com, cited 13 March 2016.

"Some Advertisers Cut Spending on Milwaukee Brewers Radio Broadcasts This Season." http://www.milwaukee.suntimes.com, cited 6 May 2016.

Sullivan, T.R. "Ryan Announces Retirement from Rangers' CEO Post." http://www.m.mlb.com, cited 16 May 2016.

"Supplier Data Management System." https://www.appsuppliergateway.com, cited 19 May 2016.

Theil, Art. "Death of Nintendo CEO Won't Affect Mariners." http://www.sportspressnw.com, cited 5 March 2016.

"Thinking Back with Howard Starkman." *SportsBusiness Journal* (30 June 2014): 38.

Totten, Steven. "Arizona Diamondbacks Make International MLB History." http://www.bizjournals.com, cited 28 January 2016.

Tucker, Tim. "Liberty Media, Pitching Braves Stock Plan, Discloses Finances." http://www.ajc.com, cited 1 March 2016.

"TU School of Business Partnering with Cleveland Indians for Real World Experience." http://www.tiffin.edu, cited 1 February 2016.

"2016 Rockies Fest." http://www.colorado.rockies.mlb.com, cited 23 January 2016.

Van Romburgh, Marlize. "Why Oakland A's Owner Is Not a Fan of Proposed Oakland Coliseum Buyout." http://www.bizjournals.com, cited 3 August 2015.
Watkins, Steve. "Reds TV Ratings Defy Dire Predictions." http://www.bizjournals.com, cited 7 April 2016.
Weiner, Rick. "Power Ranking Every MLB Owner from Worst to First." http://www.bleacherreport.com, cited 3 March 2016.
Wolbrum, Eliott, and Barry Smith. "Major Energy Inks Deal with New York Yankees on New Multi-Year Marketing Relationship." http://www.majorenergy.com, cited 1 February 2016.
Wolf, Elizabeth. "Delta Extends Deals with Mets, Yankees." http://www.news.delta.com, cited 15 May 2016.
Wyatt, Edward, and Megan Specia. "The Cost of Closing the Baltimore Orioles Game during the Riots: $7.5 Million." http://www.mashable.com, cited 5 May 2015.
"Yankees Owner Steinbrenner Defends Trade for Aroldis Chapman." http://www.foxsports.com, cited 9 February 2016.
"Yankee Stadium." http://www.ballparksofbaseball.com, cited 1 February 2016.
Yousefi, Ryan. "The Dodgers Are Now Paying 25 Percent of the Marlins' Payroll." http://www.miaminewtimes.com, cited 11 March 2016.

Index

American Association (AA), 134, 165, 178, 186, 203

American League Franchises, 38n3, 76n10, 114n1.n*See also* Jozsa, Frank P., Jr.

Angelos, Peter, 4–5, 12

Arizona Diamondbacks: Team Performances, 196–97; Franchise Owner, 197–98; Chase Field, 198–200; Financial Data, 200–201; Business Relations, 201–2

Atlanta Braves: Team Performances, 120–21; Franchise Owner, 121–22; Turner Field, 122–24; Financial Data, 124–25; Business Relations, 125–26

Attanasio, Mark, 174

Autry, Gene, 87, 89

Baltimore Orioles: Team Performances, 4; Franchise Owner, 4–5; Oriole Park at Camden Yards, 6–7; Financial Data, 7–8

Business Relations, 8–10

Bank of America (BOA), 22

Baseball, Inc., 38n1. *See also* Jozsa, Frank P., Jr.

Boston Red Sox: Team Performances, 10–11; Franchise Owner, 11–12; Fenway Park, 12–14; Financial Data, 14–15; Business Relations, 15–17

Boston Red Stockings, 158, 165

Busch, August A., Jr., 3

Bush, George H.W., 134, 188

Castellini, Phil, 170–71, 193n14

Castellini, Robert, 166–67, 169–71, 198

Chicago Cubs: Team Performances, 158–59; Franchise Owner, 159–60; Wrigley Field, 160–62; Financial Data, 162–63; Business Relations, 163–64

Chicago White Sox: Team Performances, 42; Franchise Owner, 43–44; U.S. Cellular Field, 44–45; Financial Data, 46; Business Relations, 47–48

Chicago White Stockings, 157–58

Cincinnati Reds: Team Performances, 165–66; Franchise Owner, 166–67; Great American Ball Park, 167–68; Financial Data, 168–69; Business Relations, 169–71

Cleveland Indians: Team Performances, 49; Franchise Owner, 49–50; Progressive Field, 50–52; Financial Data, 52–53; Business Relations, 53–55

Collective Bargaining Agreement (CBA), 81, 126, 132, 148
Colangelo, Jerry, 195–96
Colorado Rockies: Team Performances, 203–4; Franchise Owner, 204–5; Coors Field, 205–6; Financial Data, 206–207; Business Relations, 207–9
Continental League (CL), 80, 87, 133–34
Crane, Jim, 81–82, 86, 114nn3–4

Davis, Ray, 18, 103, 109–110m 113
Detroit Tigers: Team Performances, 56; Franchise Owner, 56–57; Comerica Park, 57–59; Financial Data, 59–60; Business Relations, 60–62
DeWitt, William Jr., 187–88, 191, 194n28
Dolan, Larry, 49–50, 53
Dynamic Ticket Pricing, 191

Earned Run Average (ERA), 109, 166, 179, 187, 204, 211
Entertainment Sports Programming Network (ESPN), 26, 48, 95, 126

Fan Cost Index (FCI): Baltimore Orioles, 6–7; Boston Red Sox, 13–14; New York Yankees, 20; Tampa Bay Rays, 27; Toronto Blue Jays, 34; Chicago White Sox, 44–45; Cleveland Indians, 51–52; Detroit Tigers, 58; Kansas City Royals, 65–66; Minnesota Twins, 72; Houston Astros, 83–84; Los Angeles Angels of Anaheim, 90; Oakland Athletics, 96–97; Seattle Mariners, 104; Texas Rangers, 111; Atlanta Braves, 123–24; Miami Marlins, 130–31; New York Mets, 137; Philadelphia Phillies, 144; Washington Nationals, 151; Chicago Cubs, 161–62; Cincinnati Reds, 167–68; Milwaukee Brewers, 175–76; Pittsburgh Pirates, 181–82; St. Louis Cardinals, 189–90; Arizona Diamondbacks, 199; Colorado Rockies, 206; Los Angeles Dodgers, 213; San Diego Padres, 220; San Francisco Giants, 227
Finley, Charlie, 87, 94
Fort, Rodney D., 38n1, 75n1, 114n1, 154n1, 192n1, 230n1. *See also Pay Dirt*
Fowler, Ron, 180, 218–19, 221

Glass, David, 43, 57, 63–64, 67–68
Griffey, Ken Jr., 101, 107, 116n26
Griffith, Calvin, 69–70
Griffith, Clark, 69–70
Guggenheim Baseball Management (GBM), 16–17, 211–12, 214

Henry, John, 11–12, 16, 18, 129, 147
Houston Astros: Team Performances, 80–81; Franchise Owner, 81–82; Minute Maid Park, 82–84; Financial Data, 84–85; Business Relations, 85–86
Houston Colt .45s, 80, 82, 86
Huizenga, H. Wayne, 126
Hulbert, William Ambrose, 158

Illitch, Mike, 56–57, 60–62, 64

Johnson, Ban, 10, 42, 49, 69
Johnson, Charles, 188, 225–26, 229
Jozsa, Frank P., Jr., 38n1, 38n3, 75n1, 76n10, 114n1, 154n1, 155n17, 192n1, 193n15, 230nn1–2, 231n8. *See also American League Franchises Baseball Inc. Major League Baseball Expansions and Team Relocations, 1876–2008 National League Franchises*

Kansas City Royals: Team Performances, 63; Franchise Owner, 63–64; Kauffman Stadium, 64–66; Financial Data, 66–67; Business Relations, 67–69

Kauffman, Ewing, 63
Kaye, Danny, 101–102
Kendrick, Ken, 197–98

Lerner, Ted, 149–50, 152, 198
Liberty Media Corporation (LMC), 121–22, 126, 143, 154n6
Loria, Jeffrey, 128–29, 131–32, 143, 147, 198
Los Angeles Angels of Anaheim: Team Performances, 87–88; Franchise Owner, 88–89; Angel Stadium of Anaheim, 89–91; Financial Data, 91–92; Business Relations, 92–93
Los Angeles Dodgers: Team Performances, 210–11; Franchise Owner, 211–2; Dodger Stadium, 212–3; Financial Data, 214; Business Relations, 214–16
Lucchino, Larry, 11, 16

Mack, Connie, 94
Maddon, Joe, 163
Major League Baseball Expansions and Team Relocations, 1876–2008, 75n1, 155n17, 193n15, 230n2, 231n8. *See also* Jozsa, Frank P., Jr.
Master of Business Administration (MBA), 159
Miami Marlins: Team Performances, 127–28; Franchise Owner, 128–29; Marlins Park, 129–31; Financial Data, 131–32; Business Relations, 132–33
Mid-Atlantic Sports Network (MASN), 9
Milwaukee Braves, 120
Milwaukee Brewers:Team Performances, 172–73;Franchise Owner, 174; Miller Park, 174–76; Financial Data, 176–77; Business Relations, 177–78
Minnesota Twins: Team Performances, 70; Franchise Owner, 70–71; Target Field, 71–73; Financial Data, 73–74; Business Relations, 74–75
MLB Advanced Media, 86, 153, 222
MLB Commissioner: Bud Selig, 18, 88, 171–72, 174, 177, 196
Monfort, Charles, 203–5, 207, 209
Monfort, Richard, 203–5, 207
Montgomery, Dave, 142–43, 145
Moreno, Arte, 88–89, 91, 115n10
Most Valuable Player (MVP), 88, 135, 187, 218

National Association of Base Ball Players (NABBP), 119, 157–58
National Basketball Association (NBA), 24, 51, 69, 73, 95, 99, 122, 178, 195
National Football League (NFL), 73, 89, 96, 163, 226
National Hockey League (NHL), 36–37, 57, 95, 163
National League Franchises, 154n1, 192n1, 230n1. *See also* Jozsa, Frank P., Jr.
New York Mets: Team Performances, 134–35; Franchise Owner, 135–36; Citi Field, 136–38; Financial Data, 138; Business Relations, 138–40
New York Yankees: Team Performances, 17–18; Franchise Owner, 18–19; Yankee Stadium, 19–21; Financial Data, 21–22; Business Relations, 22–24
Nintendo of America (NOA), 18, 102–3, 106
North Carolina, Charlotte, 100, 148
Nutting, Robert, 180

Oakland Athletics: Team Performances, 94–95; Franchise Owner, 95–96 O.co Coliseum, 96–97 Financial Data, 97–98; Business Relations, 98–100
O'Malley, Walter, 86–87, 209–210, 218, 223–24

Pacific Coast League (PCL), 85–87, 100, 216–17

Pay Dirt, 38n1, 75n1, 114n1, 154n1, 192n1, 230n1. *See also* Quirk, James Fort, Rodney D.
Philadelphia Phillies: Team Performances, 141–42; Franchise Owner, 142–43; Citizens Bank Park, 143–44; Financial Data, 144–45; Business Relations, 145–47
Pittsburgh Pirates: Team Performances, 179–80; Franchise Owner, 180 PNC Park, 180–82; Financial Data, 182–83; Business Relations, 183–85
Players League (PL), 48, 165
Pohlad, Jim, 70–71

Quirk, James, 38n1, 75n1, 114n1, 154n1, 192n1, 230n1. *See also Pay Dirt*

Radio Frequency Identification System (RFIS), 153–54, 221
Regional Sports Network (RSN), 146, 163
Reinsdorf, Jerry, 43–44, 47, 64, 76n3, 196
Ricketts, Tom, 159–60, 163, 180
Ripken, Cal, 5
Robinson, Jackie, 183
Rogers, Edward, 12, 33, 36, 64
Ryan, Nolan, 57, 61, 64, 109, 112–13

San Diego Padres: Team Performances, 217–18; Franchise Owner, 218–19; Petco Park, 219–20; Financial Data, 221; Business Relations, 221–23
San Francisco Giants: Team Performances, 224–25; Franchise Owner, 225–26; AT&T Park, 226–27; Financial Data, 227–28; Business Relations, 228–30
Seattle Mariners: Team Performances, 101–2; Franchise Owner, 102–3; Safeco Field, 103–5; Financial Data, 105–6; Business Relations, 106–7
Seattle Pilots, 101, 171–72
Smulyan, Jeff, 102
Sports Fan Loyalty Index (SFLI), 8–9
Sports Illustrated, 68, 188
St. Louis Brown Stockings, 185–86
St. Louis Browns, 3, 120
St. Louis Cardinals: Team Performances, 186–87; Franchise Owner, 187–88; Busch Stadium, 188–90; Financial Data, 190–91; Business Relations, 191–92
Standard Metropolitan Statistical Area (SMSA), 9
Steinbrenner, Hal, 12, 18–19, 39n14, 43, 64, 103
Sternberg, Stuart, 12, 25–26, 30–31, 43
Stoneham, Horace, 210, 223–24
Stubhub, 22, 39n17

Tampa Bay Rays: Team Performances, 25; Franchise Owner, 25–26; Tropicana Field, 26–28; Financial Data, 28–29; Business Relations, 29–31
Team Marketing Report (TMR), 44, 83, 111, 123, 161
Team Payrolls: Baltimore Orioles, 8; Boston Red Sox, 15; New York Yankees, 21–22; Tampa Bay Rays, 28–29; Toronto Blue Jays, 35–36; Chicago White Sox, 46; Cleveland Indians, 53; Detroit Tigers, 59–60; Kansas City Royals, 67; Minnesota Twins, 73–74; Houston Astros, 85; Los Angeles Angels of Anaheim, 92; Oakland Athletics, 98; Seattle Mariners, 105–106; Texas Rangers, 112; Atlanta Braves, 124–25; Miami Marlins, 131–32; New York Mets, 138; Philadelphia Phillies, 145; Washington Nationals, 152; Chicago Cubs, 162–63; Cincinnati Reds, 169; Milwaukee Brewers, 176–77; Pittsburgh Pirates, 182–83; St. Louis Cardinals, 190–91; Arizona Diamondbacks, 200–201; Colorado

Rockies, 207; Los Angeles Dodgers, 214; San Diego Padres, 221; San Francisco Giants, 228
Texas Rangers: Team Performances, 108–9; Franchise Owner, 109–10; Globe Life Park, 110–11; Financial Data, 111–12; Business Relations, 112–14
Toronto Blue Jays: Team Performances, 32; Franchise Owner, 32–33; Rogers Centre, 33–35; Financial Data, 35–36; Business Relations, 36–38
Twin Cities, 75

Union Association, 62

Veeck, Bill, 4, 87

Walter, Mark, 211–12
Washington Nationals: Team Performances, 148–49; Franchise Owner, 149–50; Nationals Park, 150–51; Financial Data, 152; Business Relations, 152–54
Western League (WL), 10, 41–42, 49, 55–56
Wilpon, Fred, 135–136, 138, 140, 143
Wolff, Lewis, 18, 95–96, 98–99, 103

Yankee Global Enterprises (YGE), 18, 23

About the Author

A former college and semiprofessional athlete with an undergraduate degree in accounting, masters' degrees in business administration and economics, and also a doctorate in economics, Frank P. Jozsa Jr. is the author of several books on team sports in professional baseball, basketball, and football, and another on intercollegiate sports programs at American colleges and universities. His memoir, *A Hoosier's Journey: Athlete, Student, Teacher, and Author* were published by Dog Ear Publishing in 2011.

Besides books, Jozsa has written several articles published in journals, magazines, and newspapers. His dissertation, "An Economic Analysis of Franchise Relocation and League Expansion in Professional Team Sports, 1950–1975" was completed in 1977 at Georgia State University in Atlanta, Georgia. After teaching undergraduate and graduate courses in economics, finance, and statistics for more than three decades, Jozsa retired from Pfeiffer University in 2007.

www.ingramcontent.com/pod-product-compliance
Ingram Content Group UK Ltd.
Pitfield, Milton Keynes, MK11 3LW, UK
UKHW041632031026
15587UKWH00001B/245

9 781498 542784